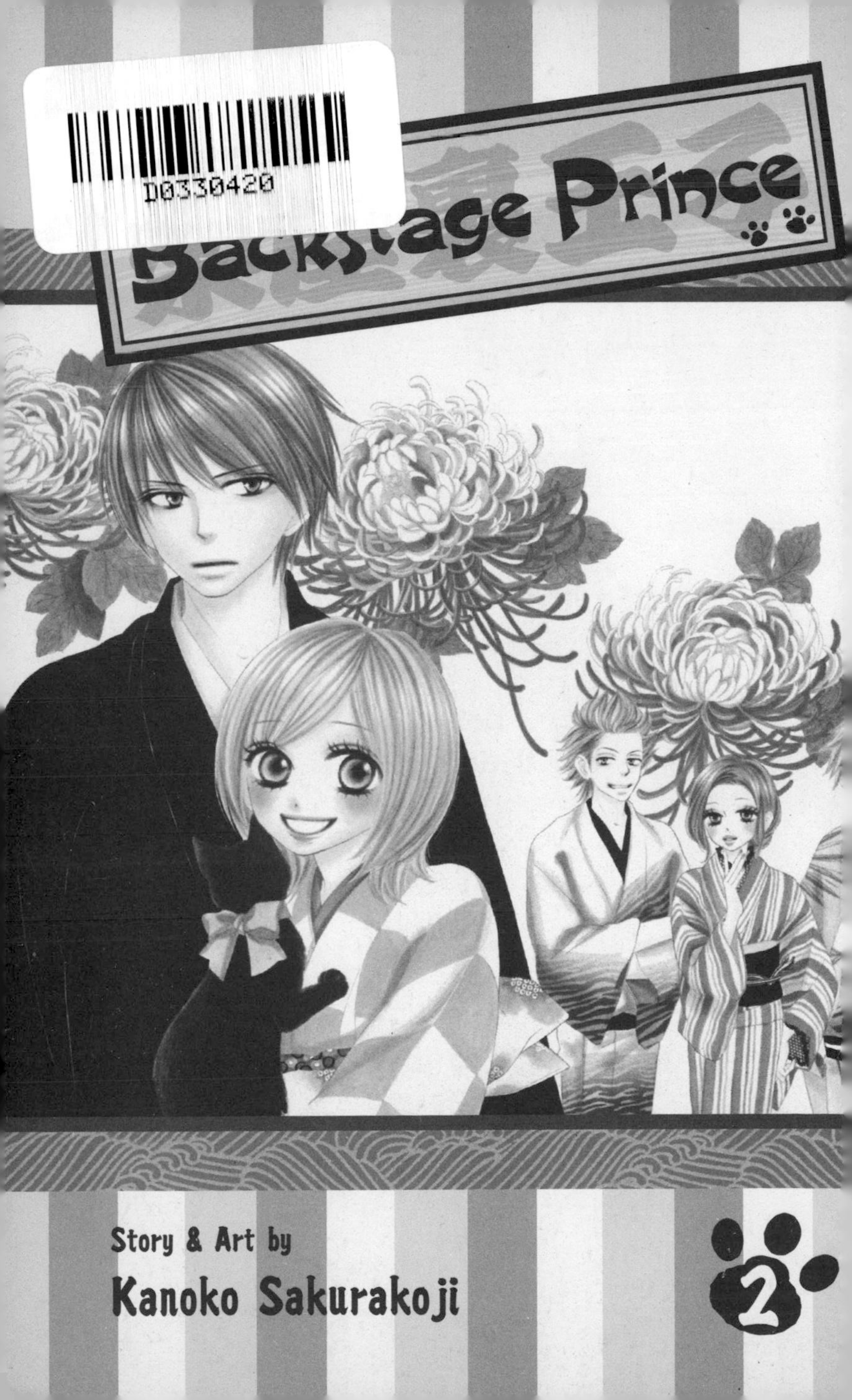
Backstage Prince
Story & Art by
Kanoko Sakurakoji
2

Backstage Prince

Volume 2

-CONTENTS-

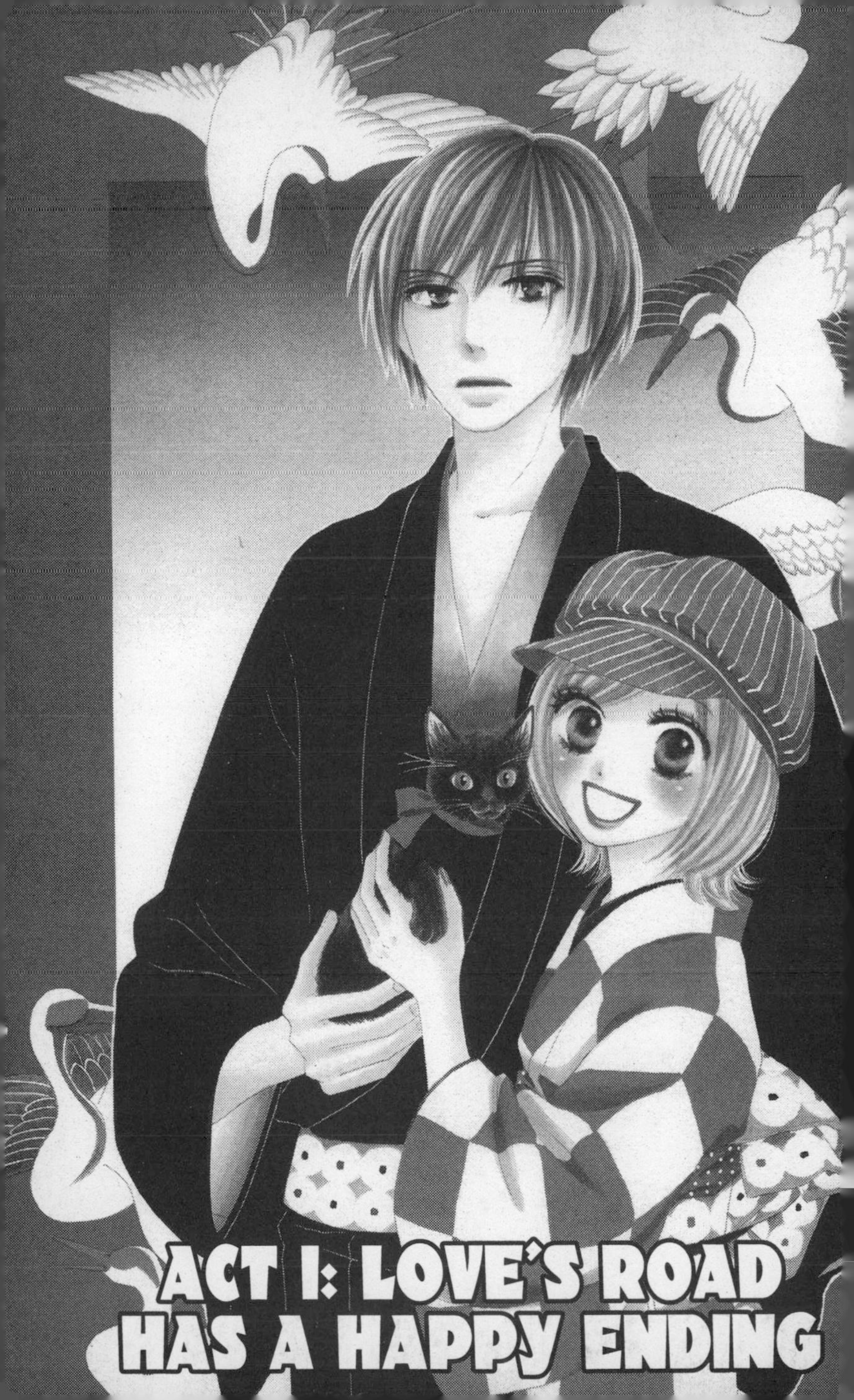
ACT 1: LOVE'S ROAD HAS A HAPPY ENDING

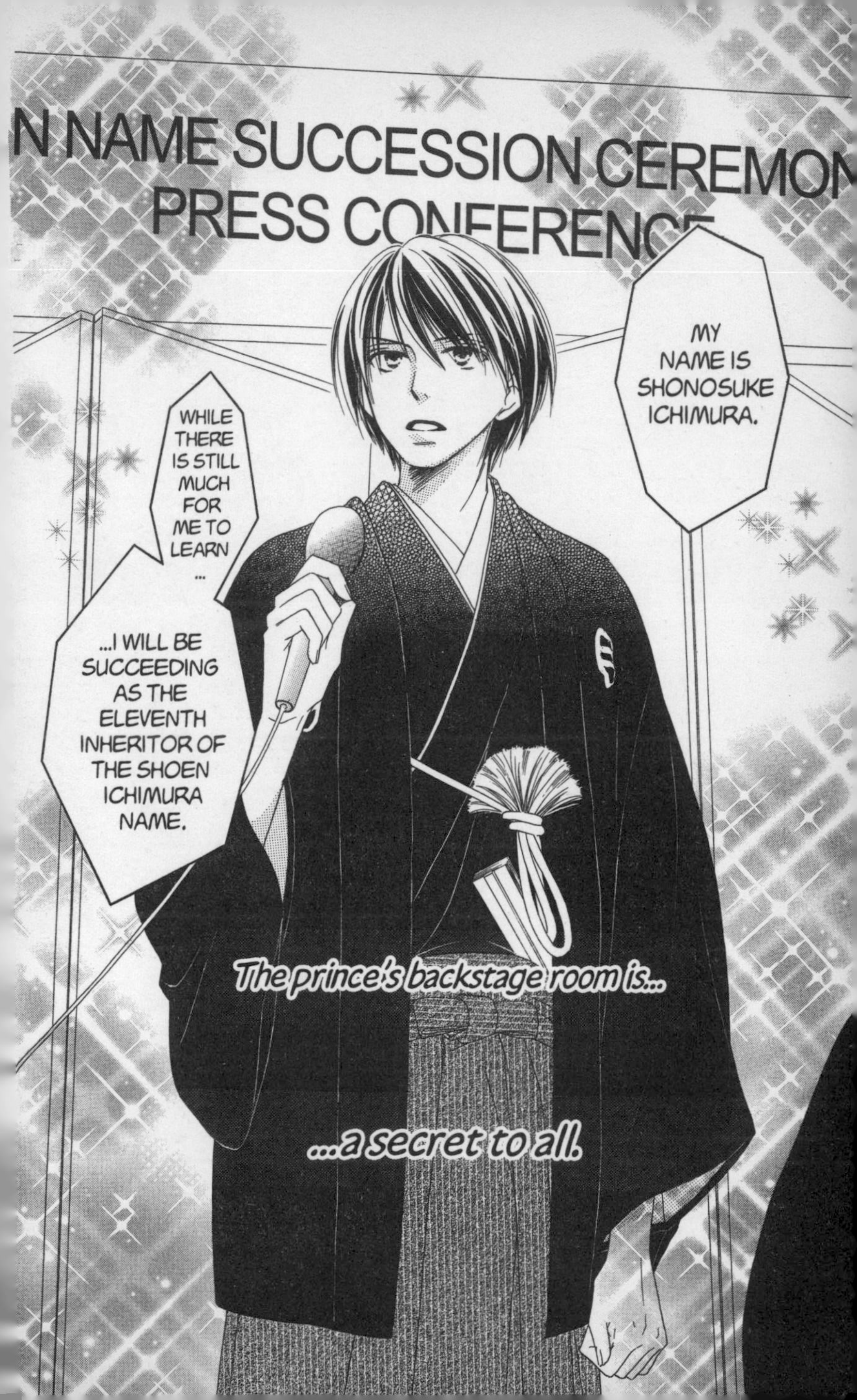
N NAME SUCCESSION CEREMON
PRESS CONFERENC
MY NAME IS SHONOSUKE ICHIMURA.
WHILE THERE IS STILL MUCH FOR ME TO LEARN ...
...I WILL BE SUCCEEDING AS THE ELEVENTH INHERITOR OF THE SHOEN ICHIMURA NAME.
The prince's backstage room is...
...a secret to all.

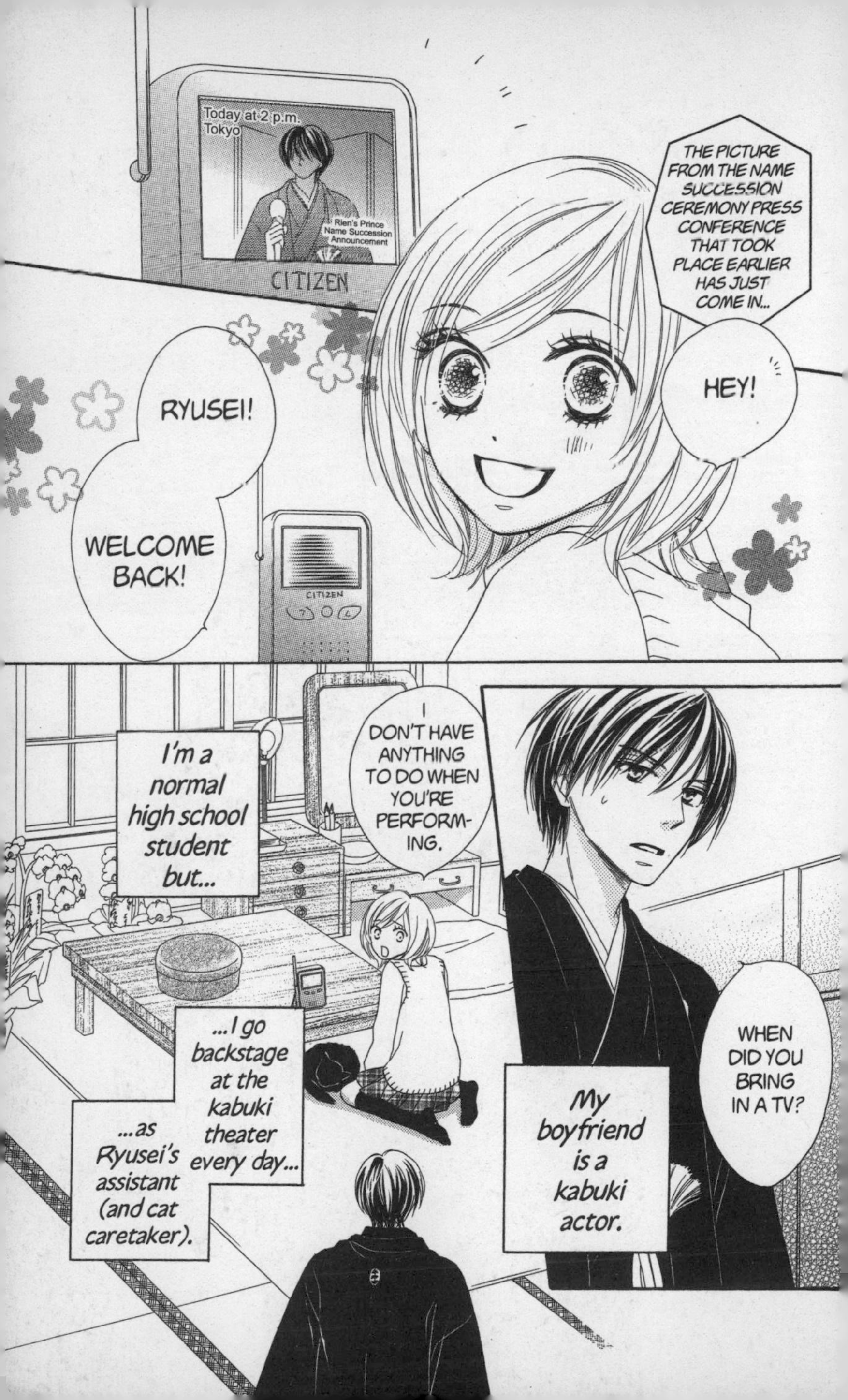
THE PICTURE FROM THE NAME SUCCESSION CEREMONY PRESS CONFERENCE THAT TOOK PLACE EARLIER HAS JUST COME IN...
Today at 2 p.m. Tokyo
Rien's Prince Name Succession Announcement
CITIZEN
HEY!
RYUSEI!
WELCOME BACK!
CITIZEN
WHEN DID YOU BRING IN A TV?
My boyfriend is a kabuki actor.
I DON'T HAVE ANYTHING TO DO WHEN YOU'RE PERFORM-ING.
I'm a normal high school student but...
...I go backstage at the kabuki theater every day...
...as Ryusei's assistant (and cat caretaker).

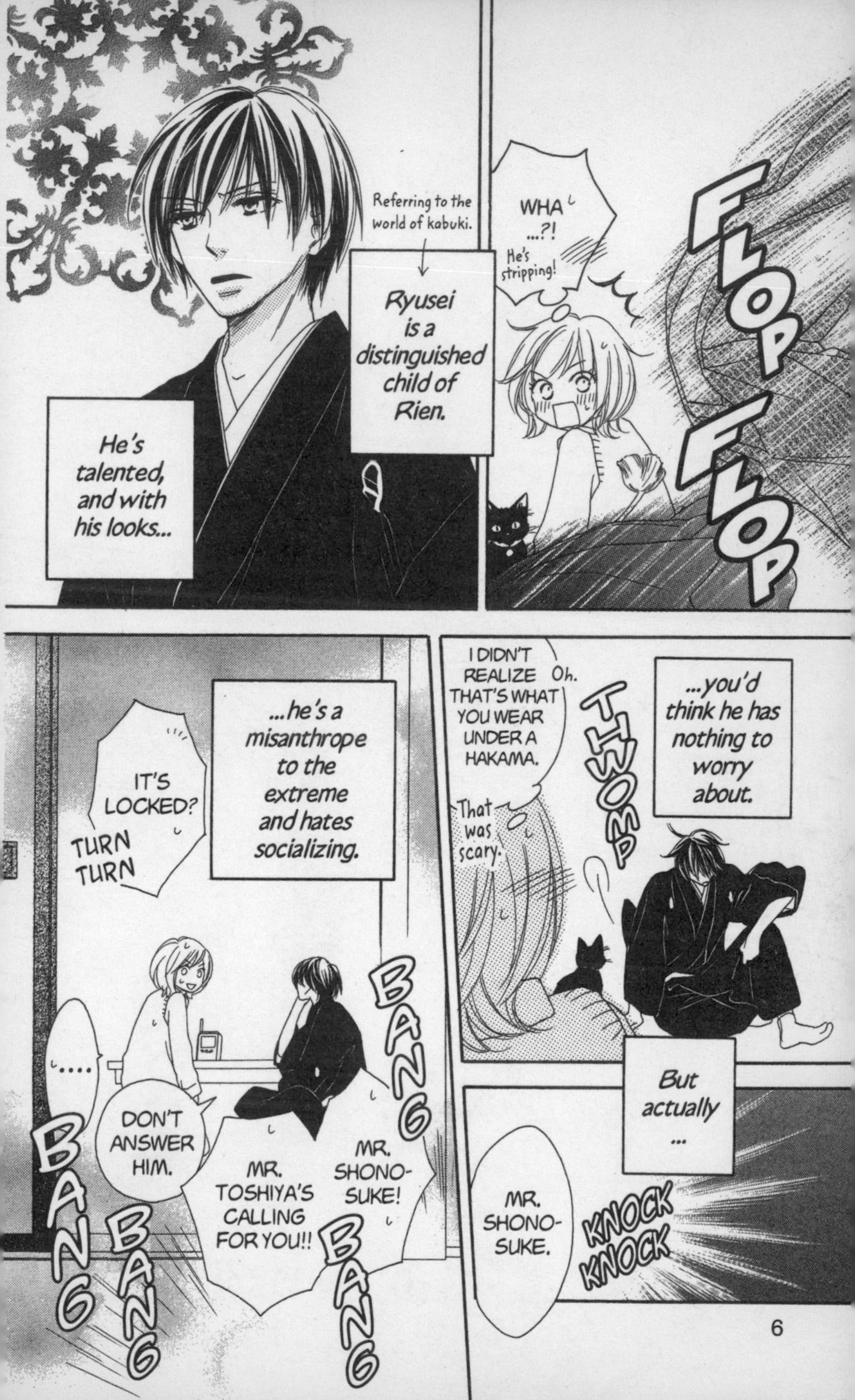
WHA ...?!
He's stripping!
FLOP FLOP FLOP
Referring to the world of kabuki.
Ryusei is a distinguished child of Rien.
He's talented, and with his looks...
...you'd think he has nothing to worry about.
I DIDN'T REALIZE THAT'S WHAT YOU WEAR UNDER A HAKAMA.
Oh.
THWOMP
That was scary.
But actually ...
KNOCK KNOCK
MR. SHONOSUKE.
...he's a misanthrope to the extreme and hates socializing.
IT'S LOCKED?
TURN TURN
BANG BANG
MR. SHONOSUKE!
MR. TOSHIYA'S CALLING FOR YOU!!
BANG
DON'T ANSWER HIM.
.....
BANG BANG BANG

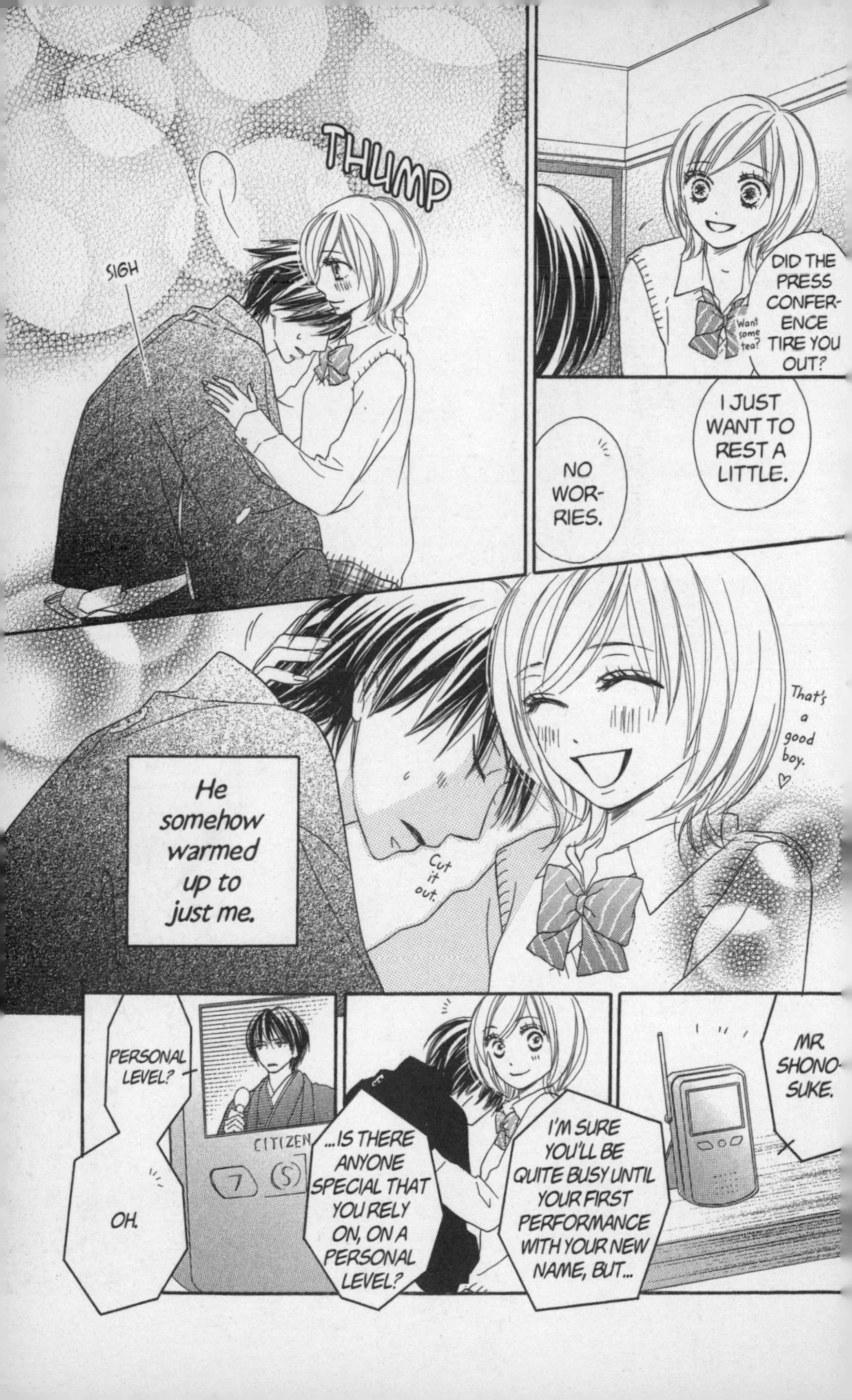
DID THE PRESS CONFERENCE TIRE YOU OUT?
Want some tea?
I JUST WANT TO REST A LITTLE.
NO WORRIES.
THUMP
SIGH
That's a good boy. ♡
Cut it out.
He somehow warmed up to just me.
MR. SHONOSUKE.
I'M SURE YOU'LL BE QUITE BUSY UNTIL YOUR FIRST PERFORMANCE WITH YOUR NEW NAME, BUT...
...IS THERE ANYONE SPECIAL THAT YOU RELY ON, ON A PERSONAL LEVEL?
CITIZEN
PERSONAL LEVEL?
OH.

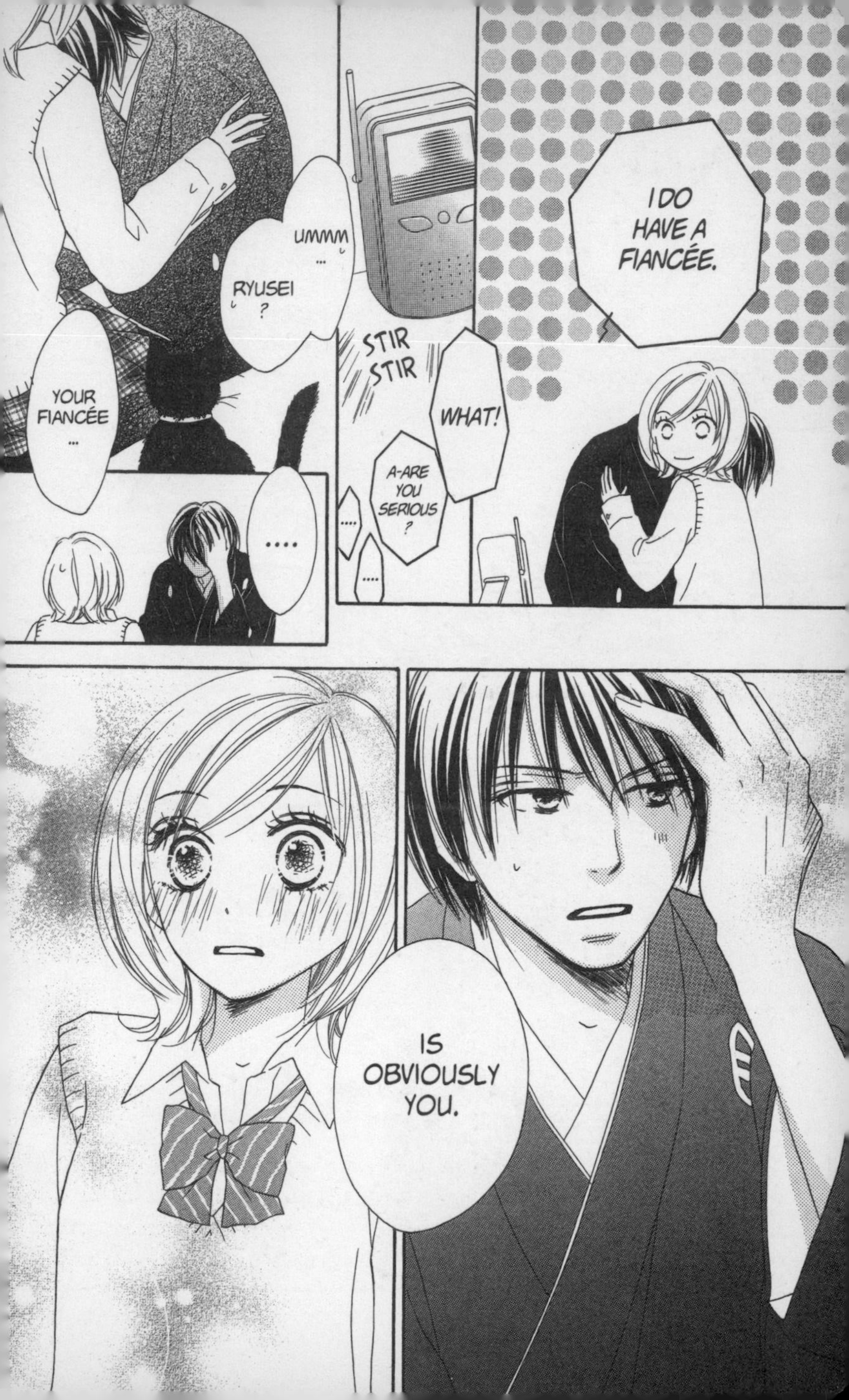

I DO HAVE A FIANCÉE.
STIR STIR
WHAT!
A-ARE YOU SERIOUS?
....
....
UMMM ...
RYUSEI ?
YOUR FIANCÉE ...
....
IS OBVIOUSLY YOU.

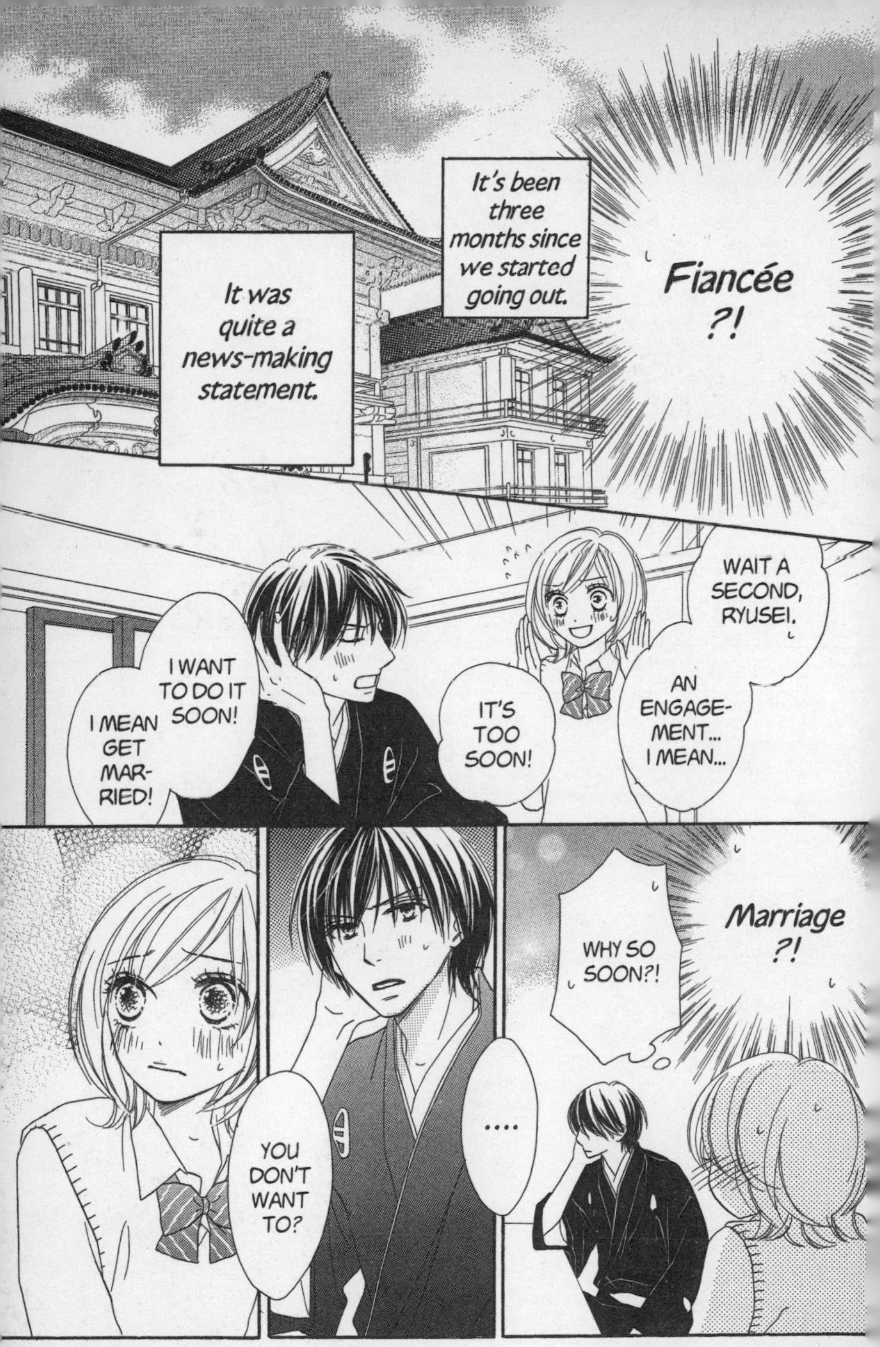
Fiancée ?!
It's been three months since we started going out.
It was quite a news-making statement.
WAIT A SECOND, RYUSEI.
AN ENGAGEMENT... I MEAN...
IT'S TOO SOON!
I WANT TO DO IT SOON!
I MEAN GET MARRIED!
Marriage ?!
WHY SO SOON?!
....
YOU DON'T WANT TO?

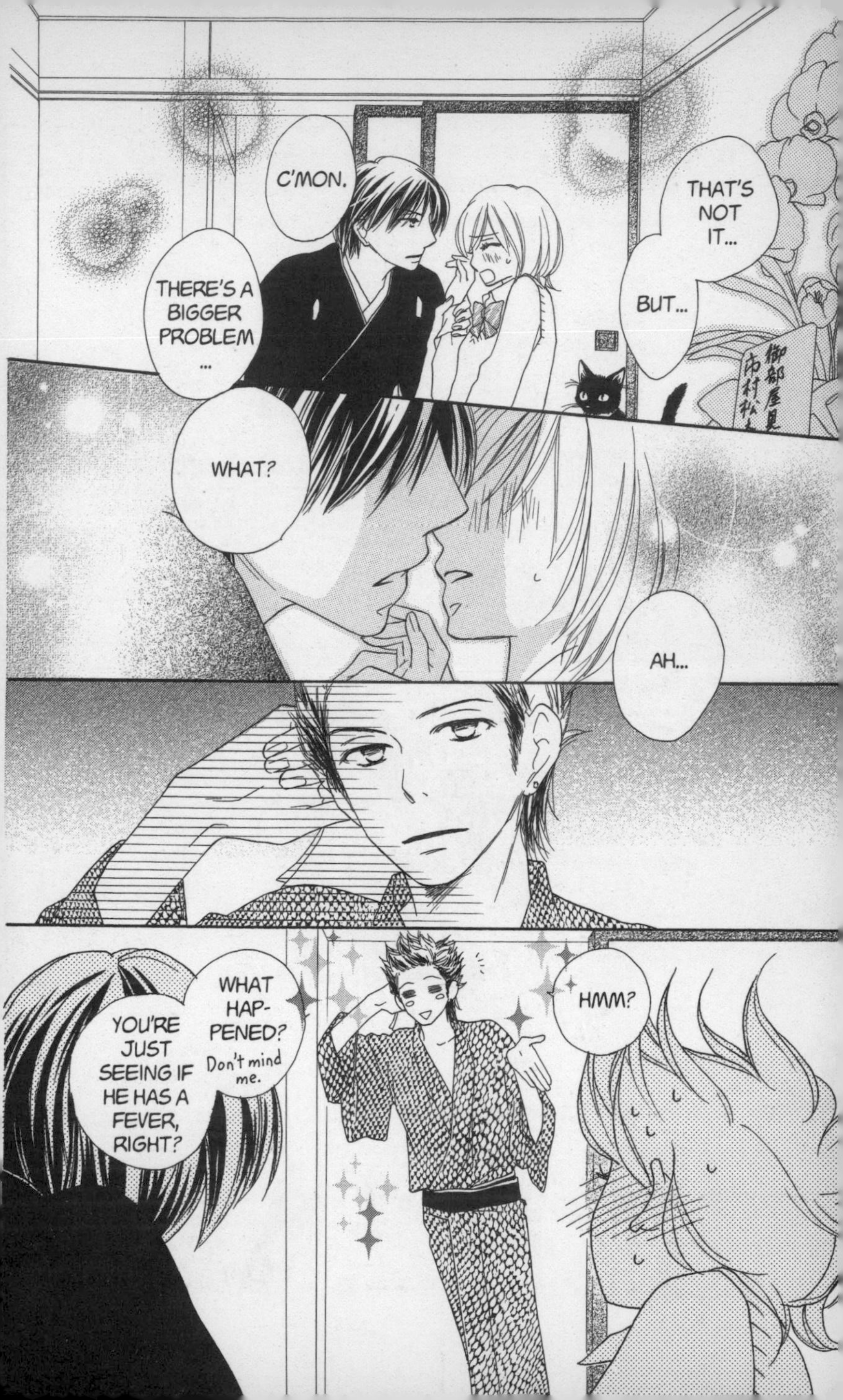
THAT'S NOT IT...
BUT...
C'MON.
THERE'S A BIGGER PROBLEM...
WHAT?
AH...
HMM?
WHAT HAPPENED?
Don't mind me.
YOU'RE JUST SEEING IF HE HAS A FEVER, RIGHT?

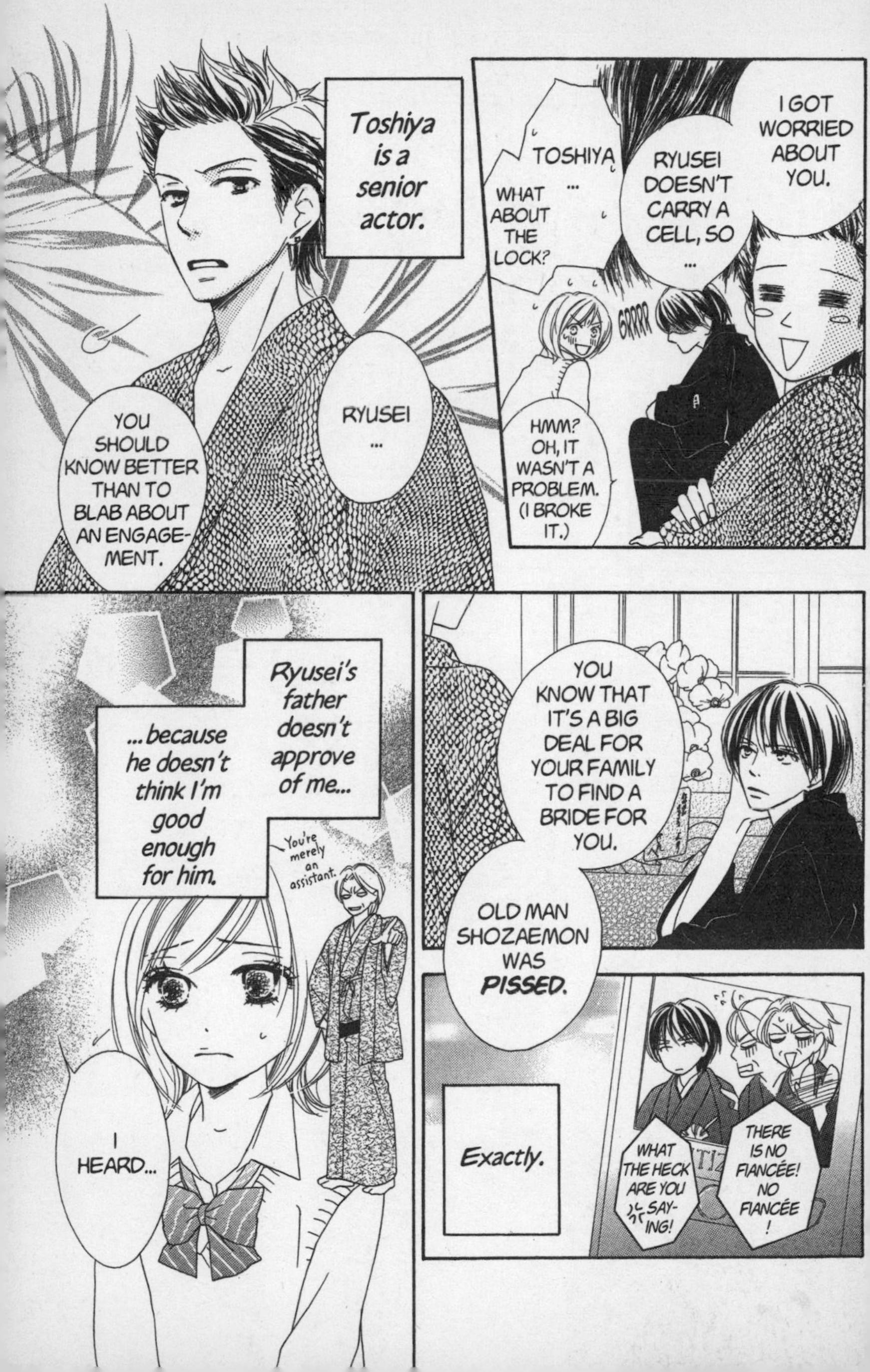

I GOT WORRIED ABOUT YOU.
RYUSEI DOESN'T CARRY A CELL, SO ...
TOSHIYA ...
WHAT ABOUT THE LOCK?
GRRRR
HMM? OH, IT WASN'T A PROBLEM. (I BROKE IT.)
Toshiya is a senior actor.
RYUSEI ...
YOU SHOULD KNOW BETTER THAN TO BLAB ABOUT AN ENGAGE-MENT.
YOU KNOW THAT IT'S A BIG DEAL FOR YOUR FAMILY TO FIND A BRIDE FOR YOU.
OLD MAN SHOZAEMON WAS PISSED.
THERE IS NO FIANCÉE! NO FIANCÉE!
WHAT THE HECK ARE YOU SAY-ING!
Exactly.
Ryusei's father doesn't approve of me...
...because he doesn't think I'm good enough for him.
You're merely an assistant.
I HEARD...

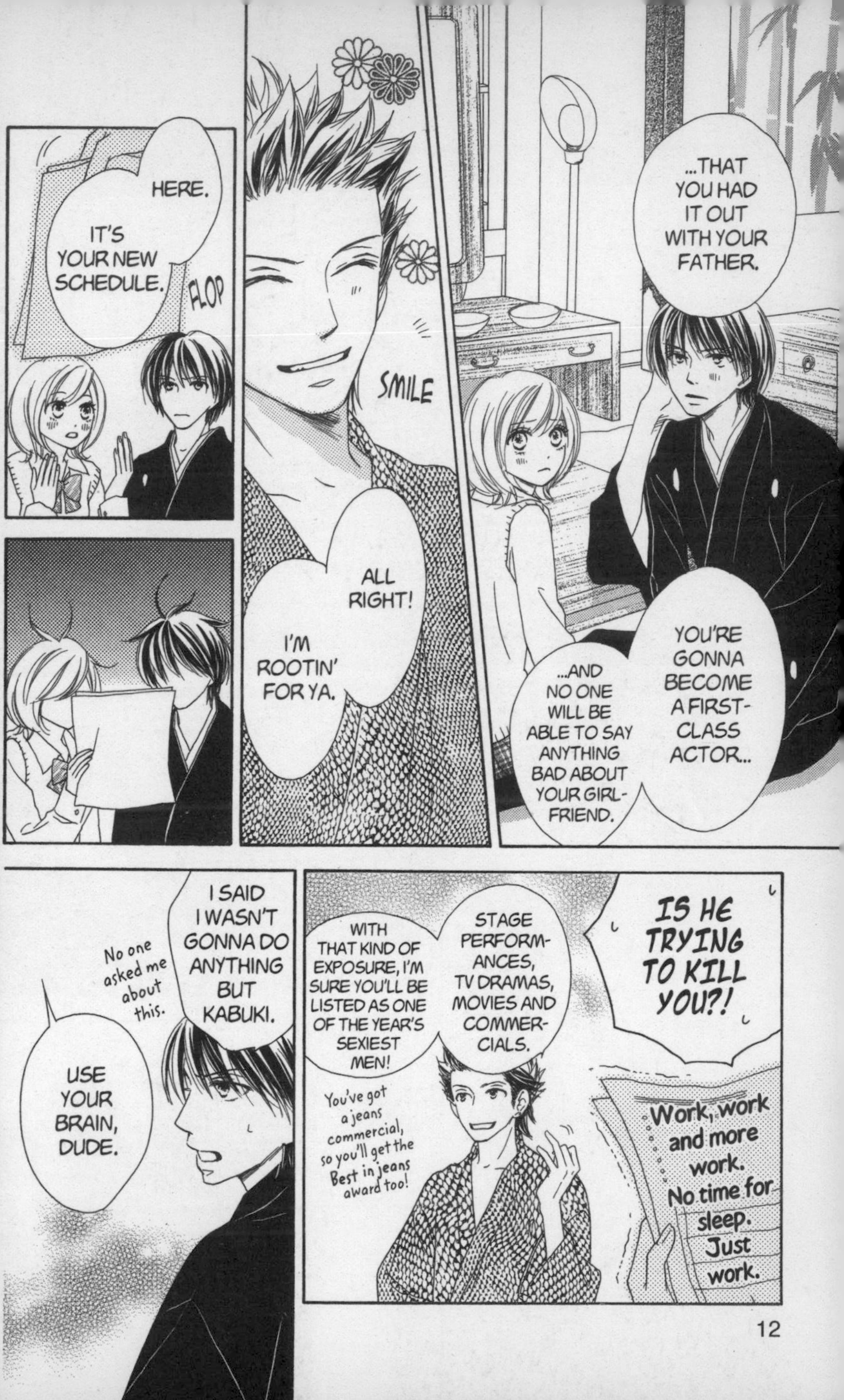
...THAT YOU HAD IT OUT WITH YOUR FATHER.
YOU'RE GONNA BECOME A FIRST-CLASS ACTOR...
...AND NO ONE WILL BE ABLE TO SAY ANYTHING BAD ABOUT YOUR GIRLFRIEND.
SMILE
ALL RIGHT!
I'M ROOTIN' FOR YA.
HERE.
IT'S YOUR NEW SCHEDULE.
FLOP
IS HE TRYING TO KILL YOU?!
Work, work and more work. No time for sleep. Just work.
STAGE PERFORMANCES, TV DRAMAS, MOVIES AND COMMERCIALS.
WITH THAT KIND OF EXPOSURE, I'M SURE YOU'LL BE LISTED AS ONE OF THE YEAR'S SEXIEST MEN!
You've got a jeans commercial, so you'll get the Best in jeans award too!
I SAID I WASN'T GONNA DO ANYTHING BUT KABUKI.
No one asked me about this.
USE YOUR BRAIN, DUDE.

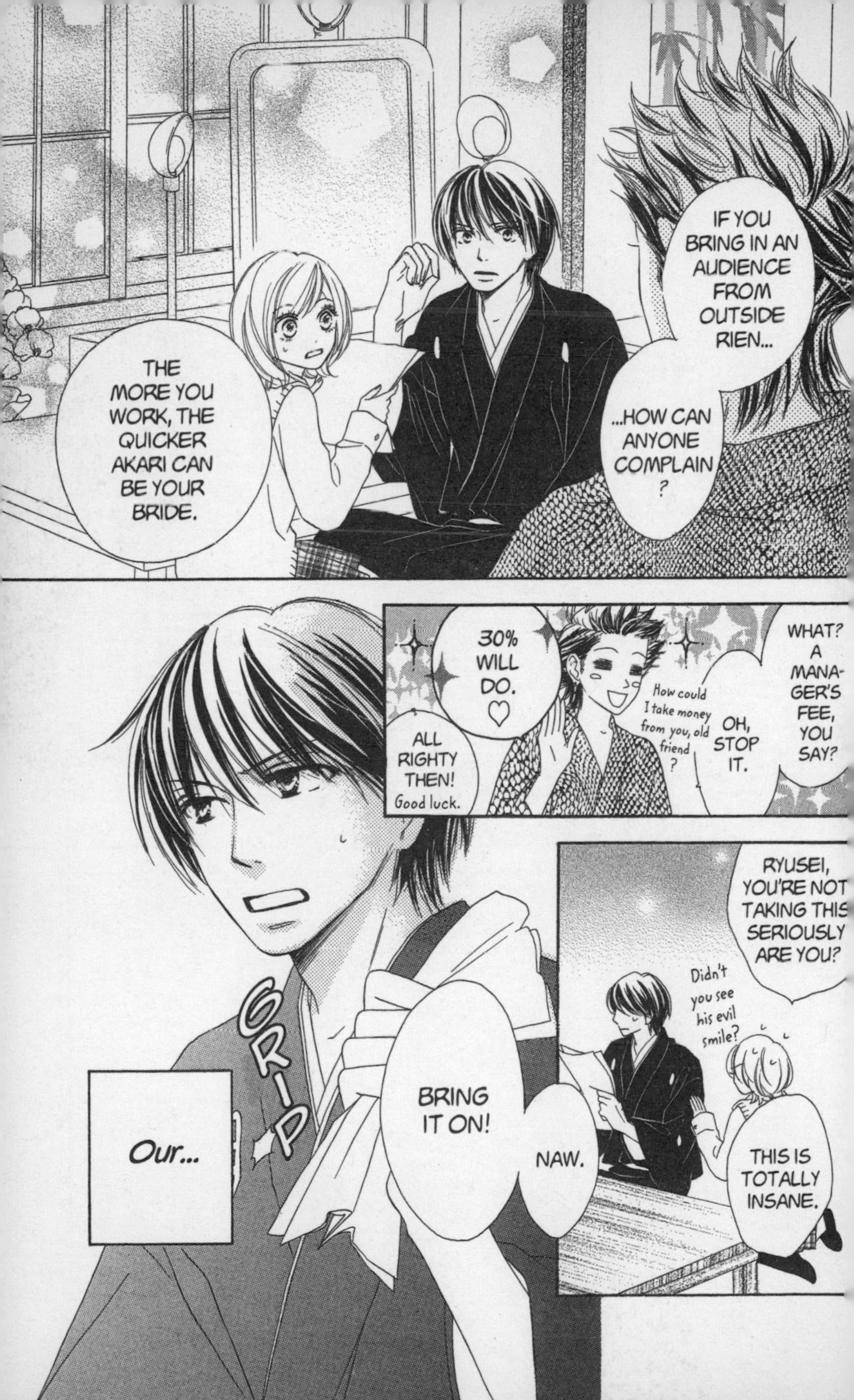
IF YOU BRING IN AN AUDIENCE FROM OUTSIDE RIEN...
...HOW CAN ANYONE COMPLAIN?
THE MORE YOU WORK, THE QUICKER AKARI CAN BE YOUR BRIDE.
WHAT? A MANAGER'S FEE, YOU SAY?
OH, STOP IT.
How could I take money from you, old friend?
30% WILL DO. ♡
ALL RIGHTY THEN! Good luck.
RYUSEI, YOU'RE NOT TAKING THIS SERIOUSLY ARE YOU?
Didn't you see his evil smile?
THIS IS TOTALLY INSANE.
NAW.
BRING IT ON!
GRIP
Our...

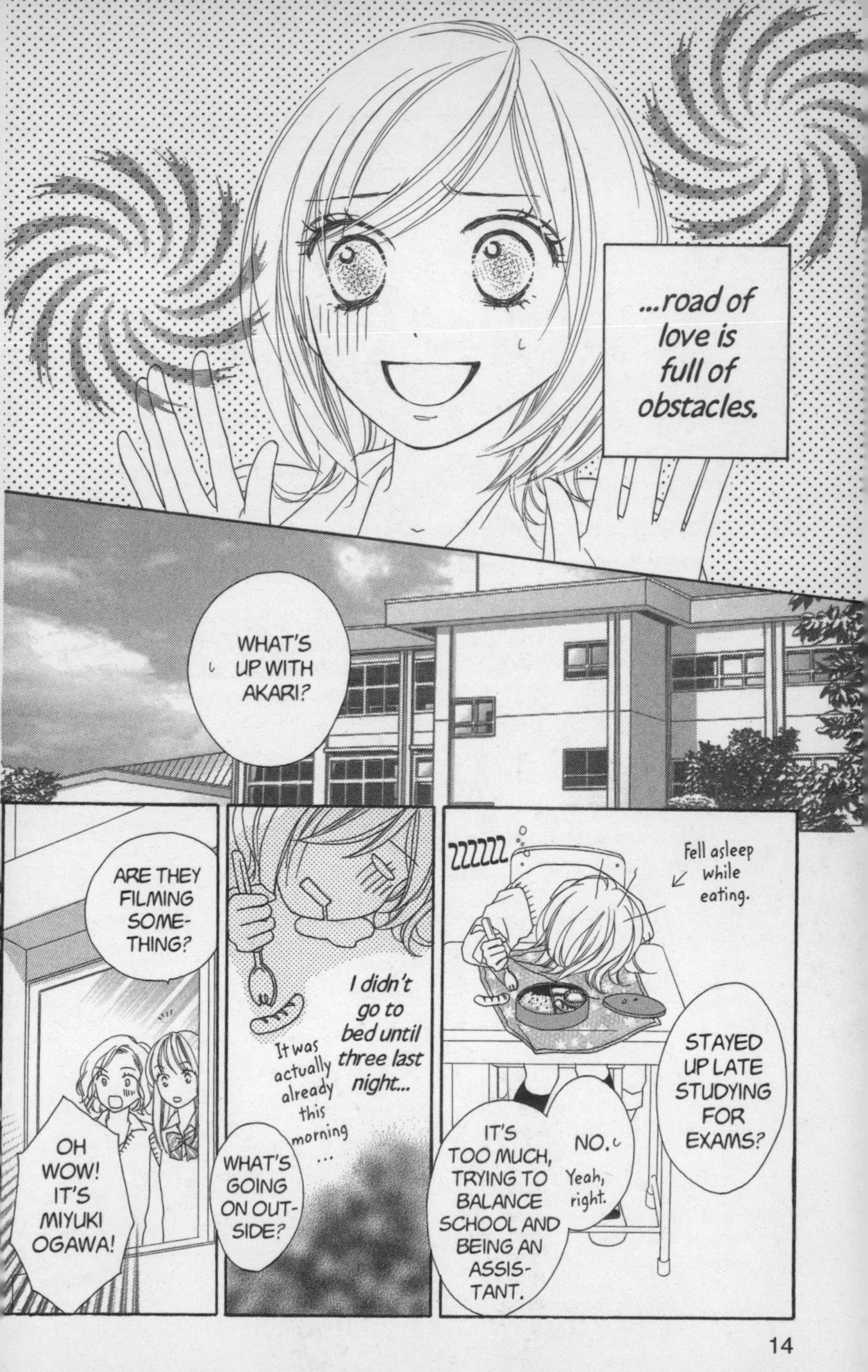
...road of love is full of obstacles.
WHAT'S UP WITH AKARI?
Fell asleep while eating.
ZZZZZZ
STAYED UP LATE STUDYING FOR EXAMS?
NO.
Yeah, right.
IT'S TOO MUCH, TRYING TO BALANCE SCHOOL AND BEING AN ASSISTANT.
I didn't go to bed until three last night...
It was actually already this morning...
WHAT'S GOING ON OUTSIDE?
ARE THEY FILMING SOMETHING?
OH WOW! IT'S MIYUKI OGAWA!

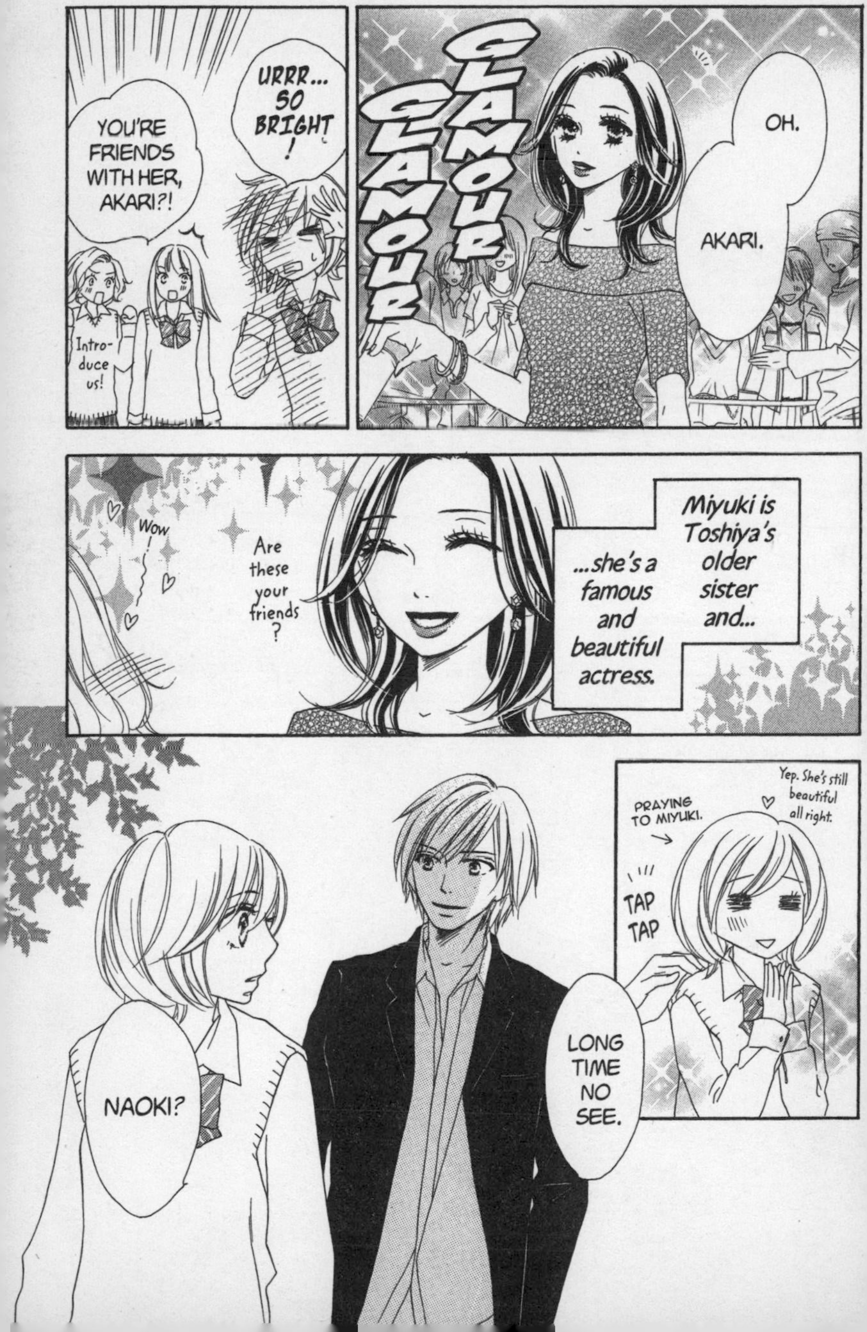

GLAMOUR
GLAMOUR
OH.
AKARI.
URRR... SO BRIGHT!
YOU'RE FRIENDS WITH HER, AKARI?!
Introduce us!
Miyuki is Toshiya's older sister and...
...she's a famous and beautiful actress.
Are these your friends?
Wow!
Yep. She's still beautiful all right.
PRAYING TO MIYUKI.
TAP TAP
LONG TIME NO SEE.
NAOKI?

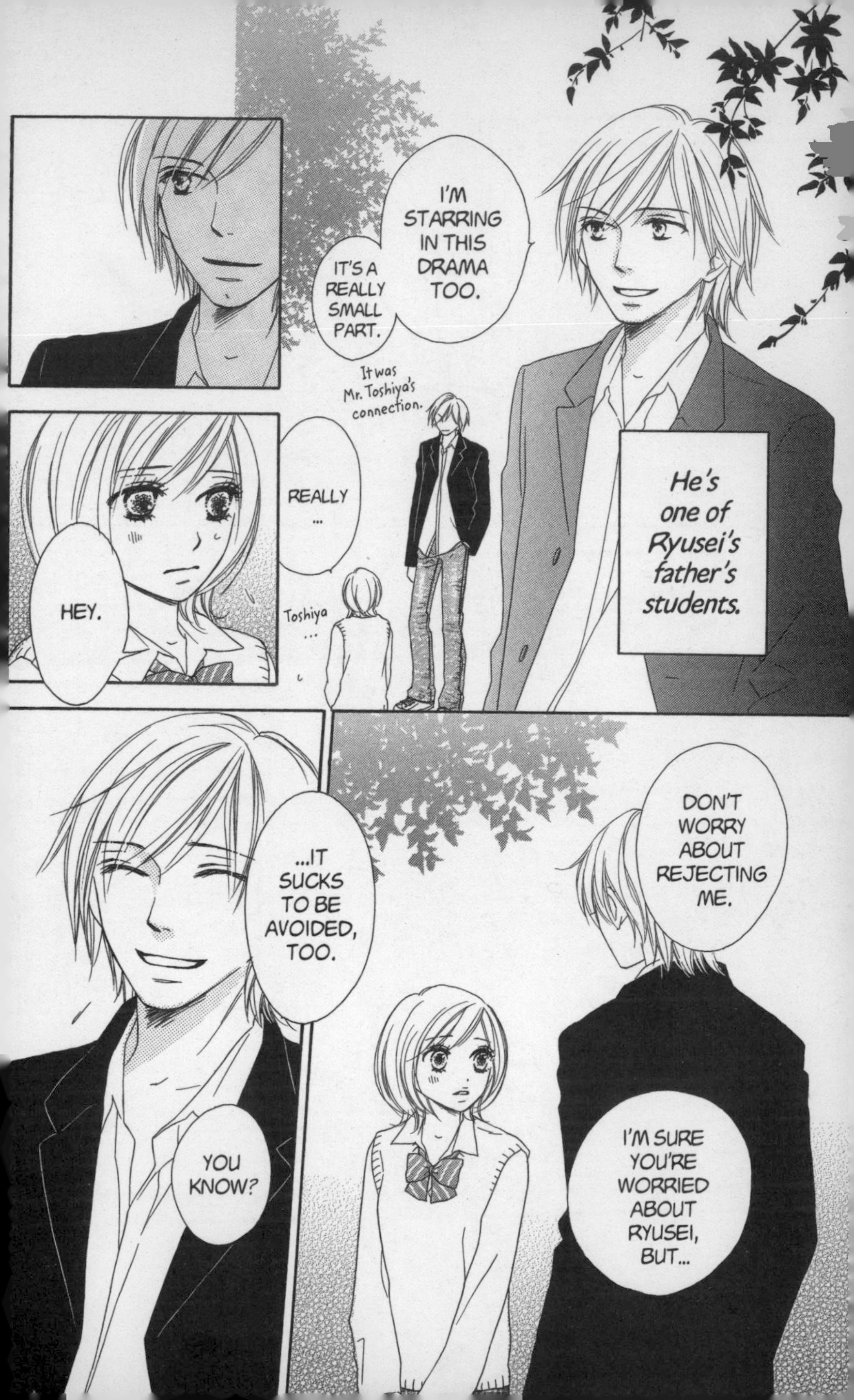

I'M STARRING IN THIS DRAMA TOO.
IT'S A REALLY SMALL PART.
It was Mr. Toshiya's connection.
He's one of Ryusei's father's students.
REALLY ...
Toshiya ...
HEY.
DON'T WORRY ABOUT REJECTING ME.
I'M SURE YOU'RE WORRIED ABOUT RYUSEI, BUT...
...IT SUCKS TO BE AVOIDED, TOO.
YOU KNOW?

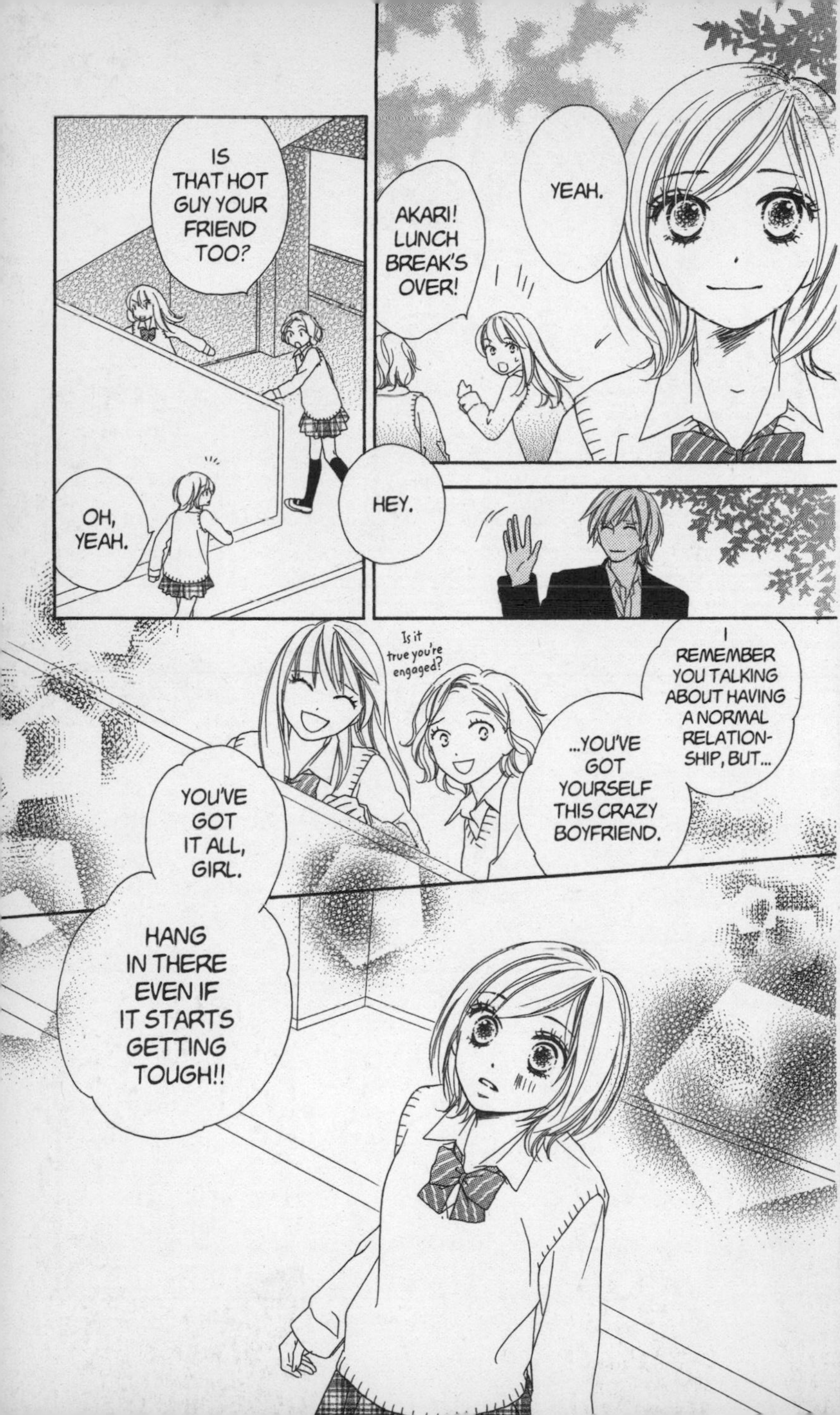
YEAH.
AKARI! LUNCH BREAK'S OVER!
HEY.
IS THAT HOT GUY YOUR FRIEND TOO?
OH, YEAH.
I REMEMBER YOU TALKING ABOUT HAVING A NORMAL RELATION-SHIP, BUT...
...YOU'VE GOT YOURSELF THIS CRAZY BOYFRIEND.
Is it true you're engaged?
YOU'VE GOT IT ALL, GIRL.
HANG IN THERE EVEN IF IT STARTS GETTING TOUGH!!

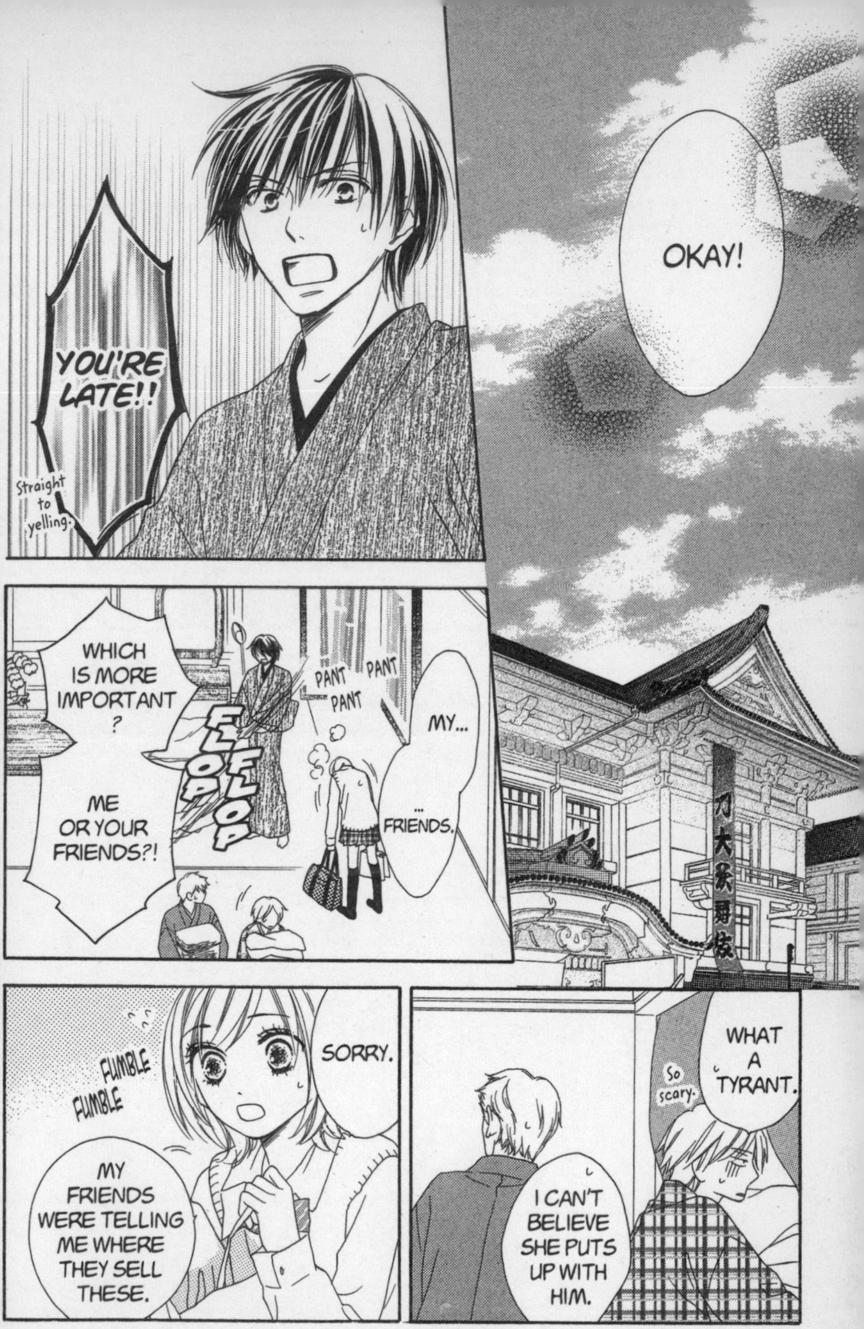
OKAY!
YOU'RE LATE!!
Straight to yelling.
PANT PANT PANT
MY...
...FRIENDS.
FLOP FLOP
WHICH IS MORE IMPORTANT?
ME OR YOUR FRIENDS?!
WHAT A TYRANT.
So scary.
I CAN'T BELIEVE SHE PUTS UP WITH HIM.
SORRY.
FUMBLE FUMBLE
MY FRIENDS WERE TELLING ME WHERE THEY SELL THESE.

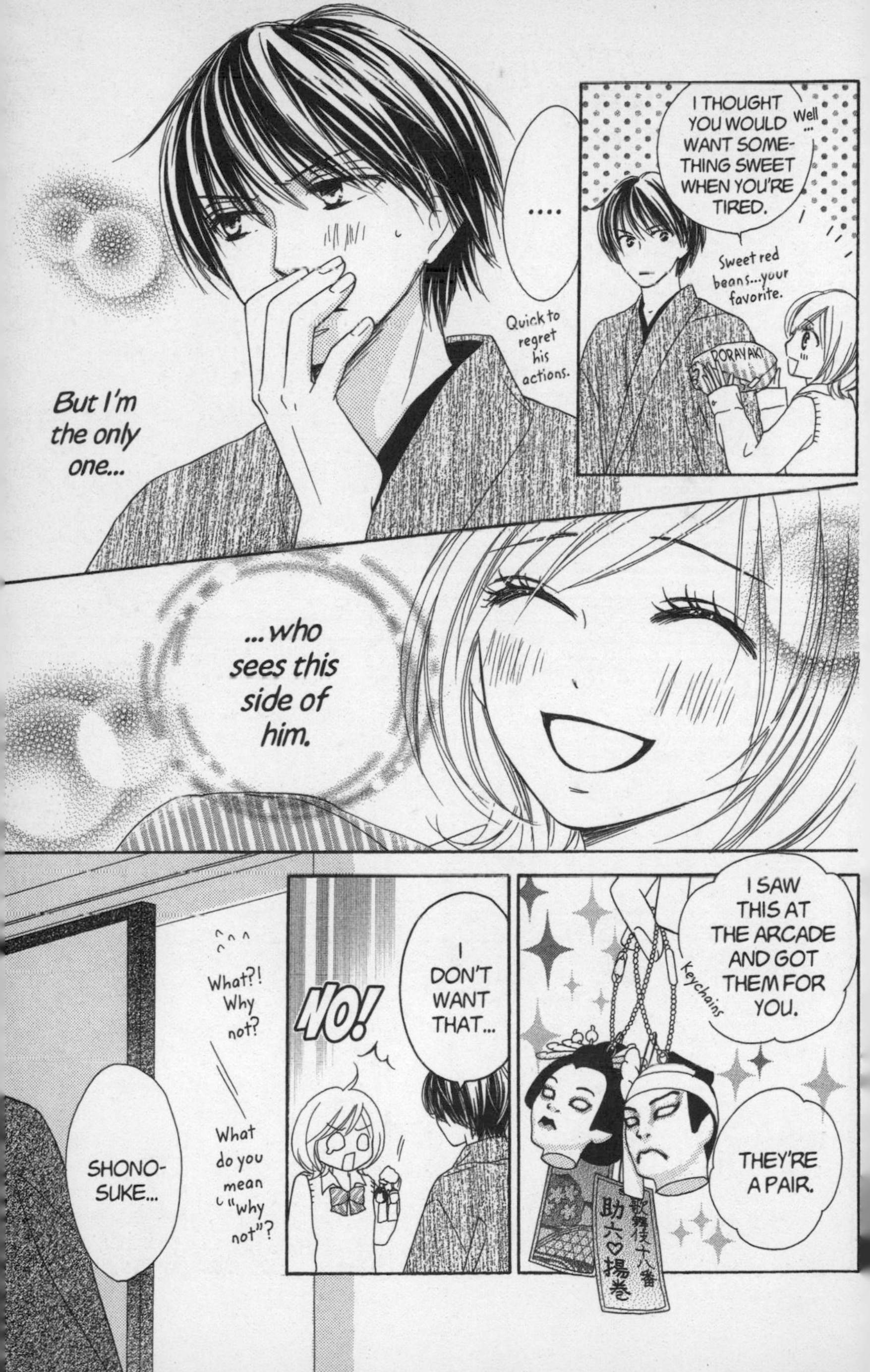
I THOUGHT YOU WOULD WANT SOME-THING SWEET WHEN YOU'RE TIRED.
Well ...
Sweet red beans...your favorite.
DORAYAKI
....
Quick to regret his actions.
But I'm the only one...
...who sees this side of him.
I SAW THIS AT THE ARCADE AND GOT THEM FOR YOU.
Keychains
THEY'RE A PAIR.
歌舞伎十八番
助六♡揚巻
I DON'T WANT THAT...
NO!
What?! Why not?
What do you mean "why not"?
SHONO-SUKE...

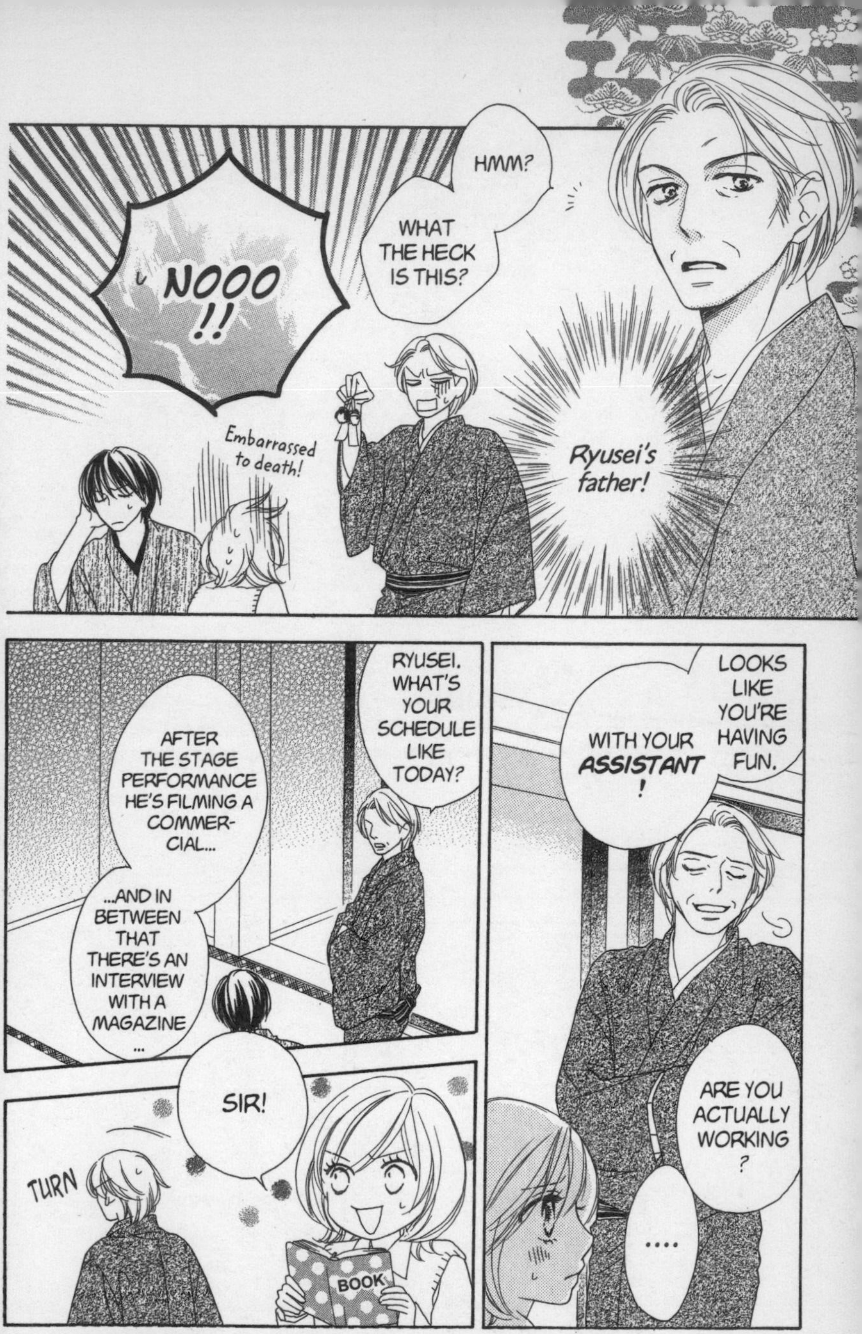
HMM?
WHAT THE HECK IS THIS?
Ryusei's father!
¡NOOO!!
Embarrassed to death!
LOOKS LIKE YOU'RE HAVING FUN.
WITH YOUR ASSISTANT!
ARE YOU ACTUALLY WORKING?
....
RYUSEI. WHAT'S YOUR SCHEDULE LIKE TODAY?
AFTER THE STAGE PERFORMANCE HE'S FILMING A COMMER-CIAL...
...AND IN BETWEEN THAT THERE'S AN INTERVIEW WITH A MAGAZINE...
SIR!
TURN
BOOK

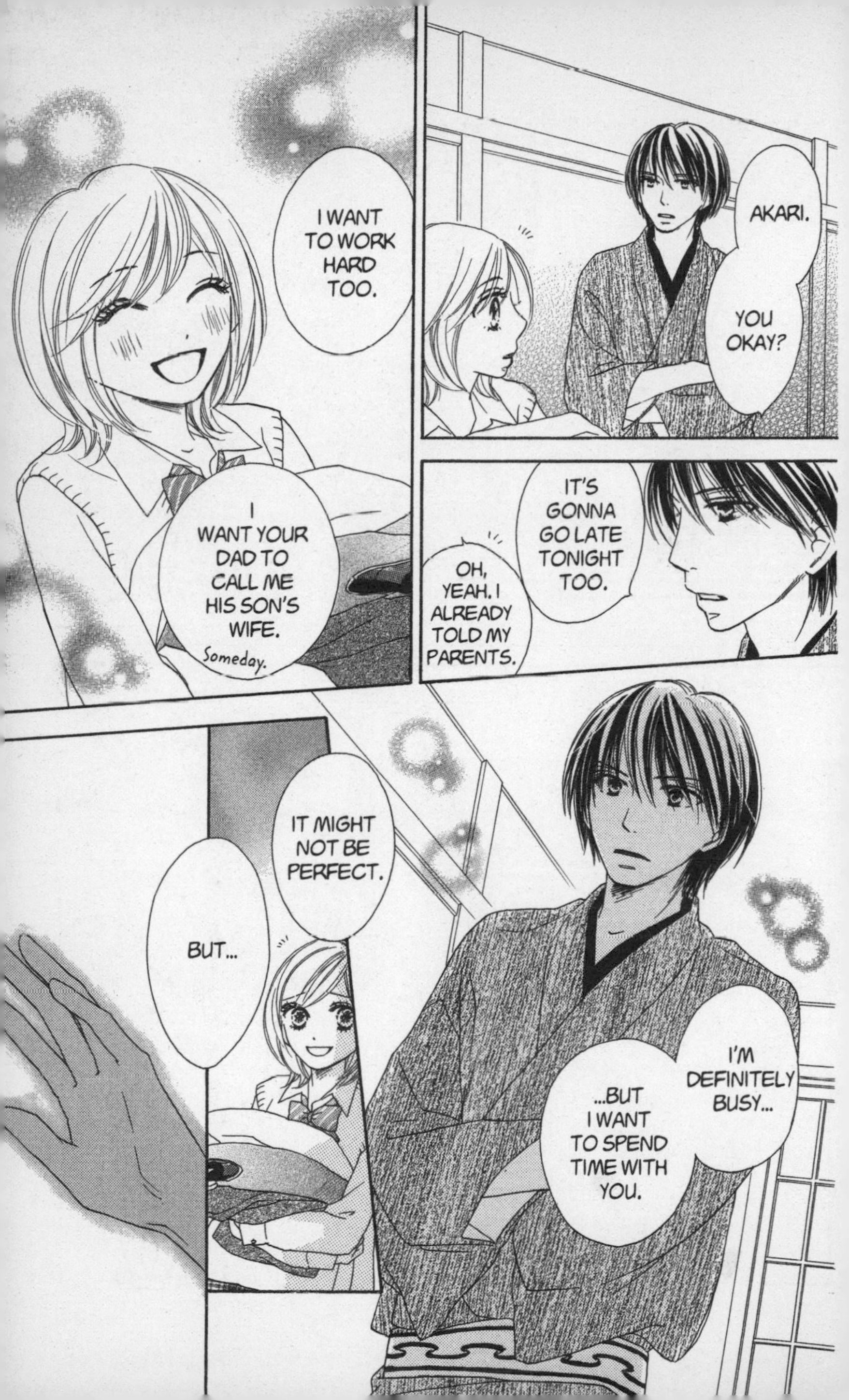
AKARI.
YOU OKAY?
IT'S GONNA GO LATE TONIGHT TOO.
OH, YEAH. I ALREADY TOLD MY PARENTS.
I WANT TO WORK HARD TOO.
I WANT YOUR DAD TO CALL ME HIS SON'S WIFE.
Someday.
I'M DEFINITELY BUSY...
...BUT I WANT TO SPEND TIME WITH YOU.
IT MIGHT NOT BE PERFECT.
BUT...

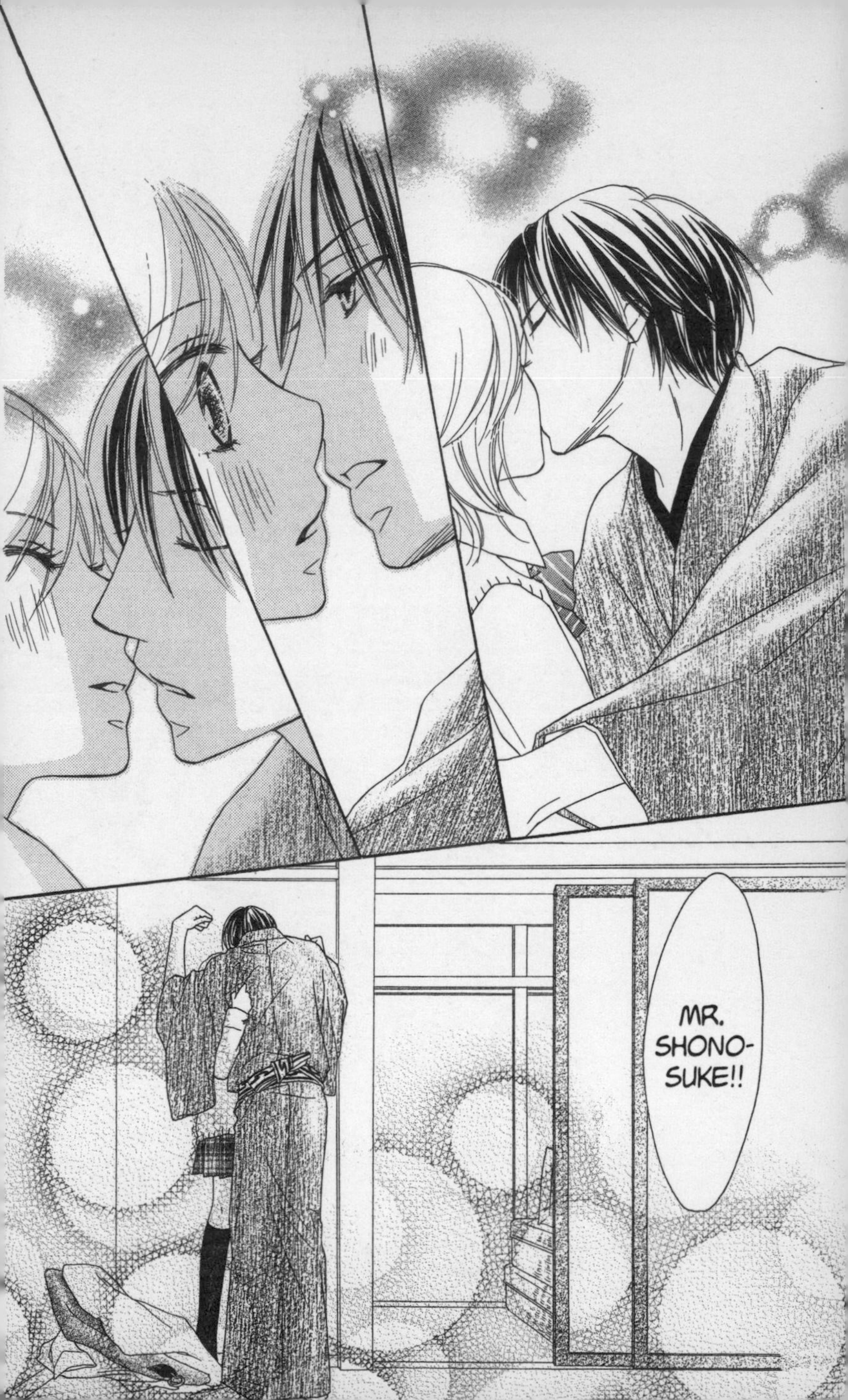
MR. SHONO-SUKE!!

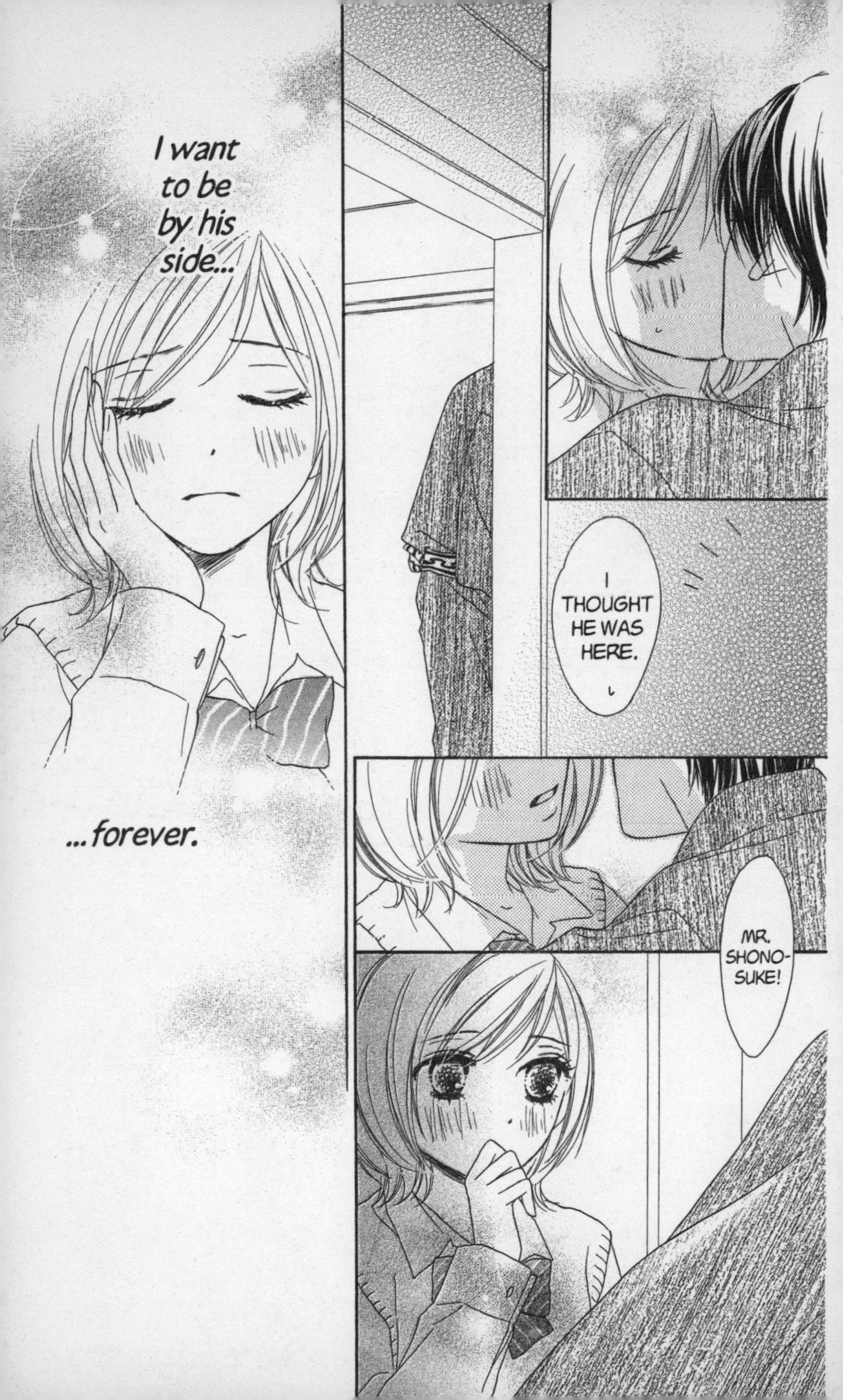

I THOUGHT HE WAS HERE.
MR. SHONO-SUKE!
I want to be by his side...
...forever.

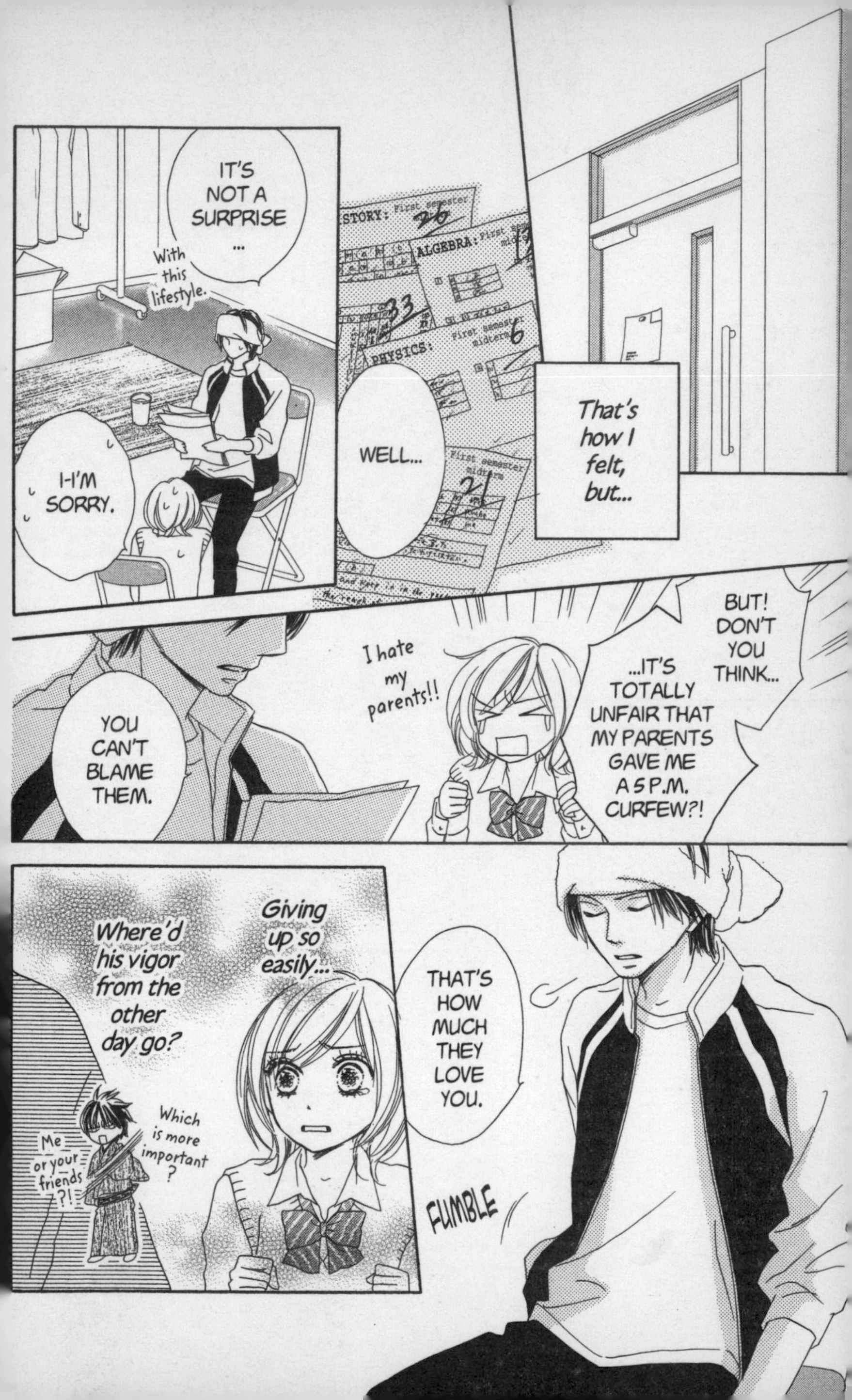
That's how I felt, but...
WELL...
IT'S NOT A SURPRISE ...
With this lifestyle.
I-I'M SORRY.
BUT! DON'T YOU THINK...
...IT'S TOTALLY UNFAIR THAT MY PARENTS GAVE ME A 5 P.M. CURFEW?!
I hate my parents!!
YOU CAN'T BLAME THEM.
THAT'S HOW MUCH THEY LOVE YOU.
FUMBLE
Giving up so easily...
Where'd his vigor from the other day go?
Which is more important?
Me or your friends?!

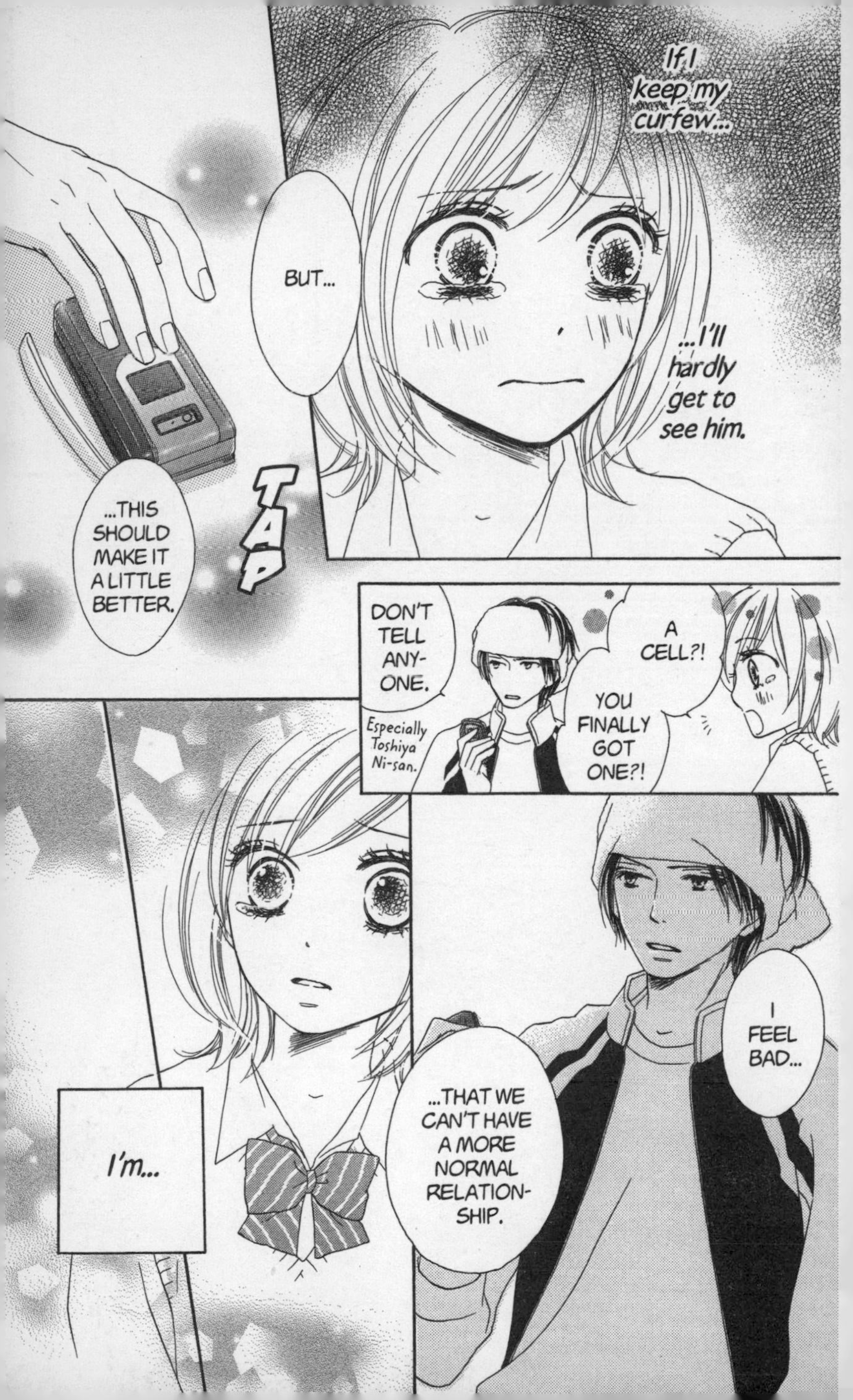
If I keep my curfew...
...I'll hardly get to see him.
BUT...
TAP
...THIS SHOULD MAKE IT A LITTLE BETTER.
A CELL?!
YOU FINALLY GOT ONE?!
DON'T TELL ANY-ONE.
Especially Toshiya Ni-san.
I FEEL BAD...
...THAT WE CAN'T HAVE A MORE NORMAL RELATION-SHIP.
I'm...

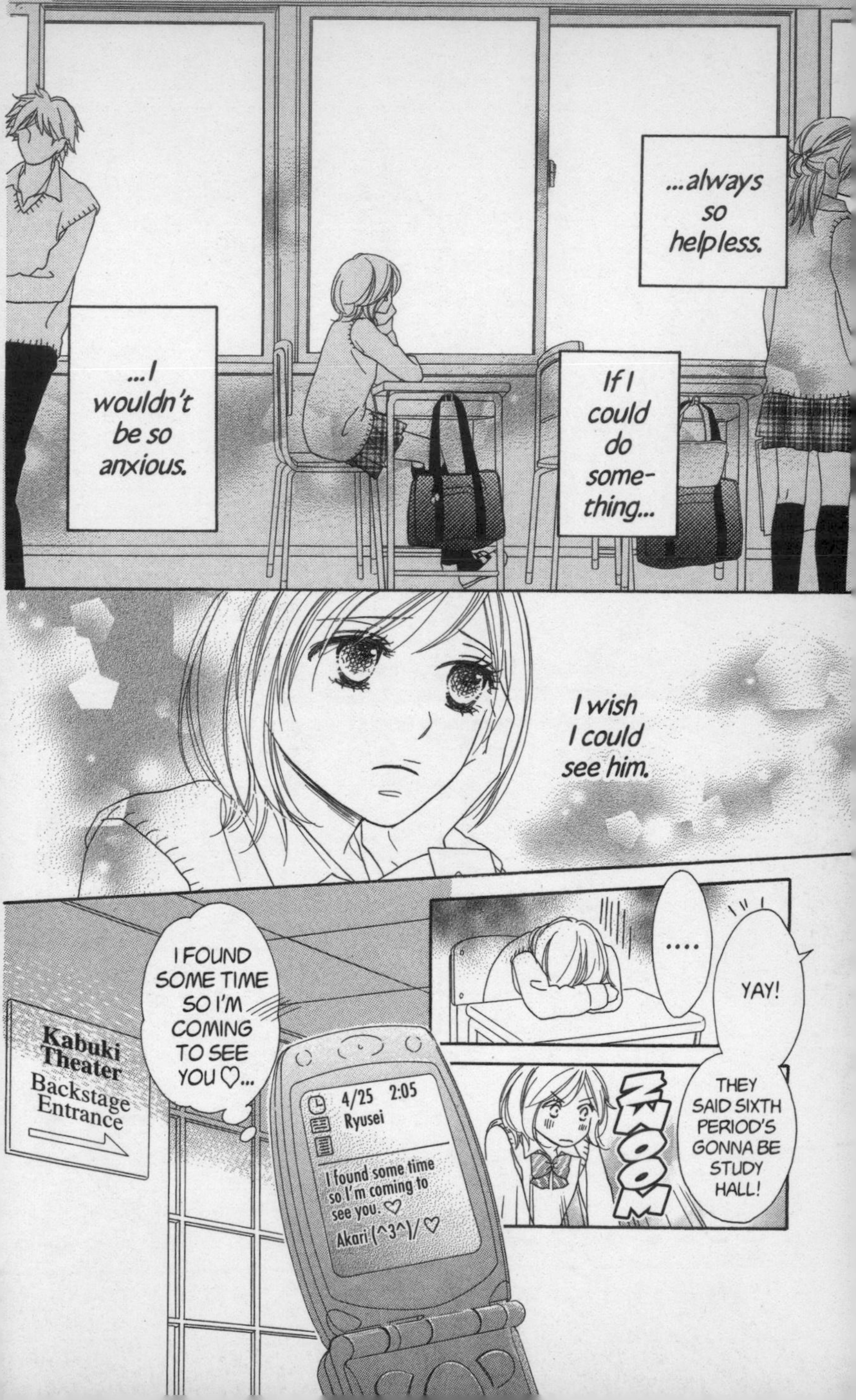
...always so helpless.
If I could do some-thing...
...I wouldn't be so anxious.
I wish I could see him.
YAY!
....
THEY SAID SIXTH PERIOD'S GONNA BE STUDY HALL!
ZOOOM
I FOUND SOME TIME SO I'M COMING TO SEE YOU♡...
Kabuki Theater
Backstage Entrance
4/25 2:05
Ryusei
I found some time so I'm coming to see you. ♡
Akari (^3^)/ ♡

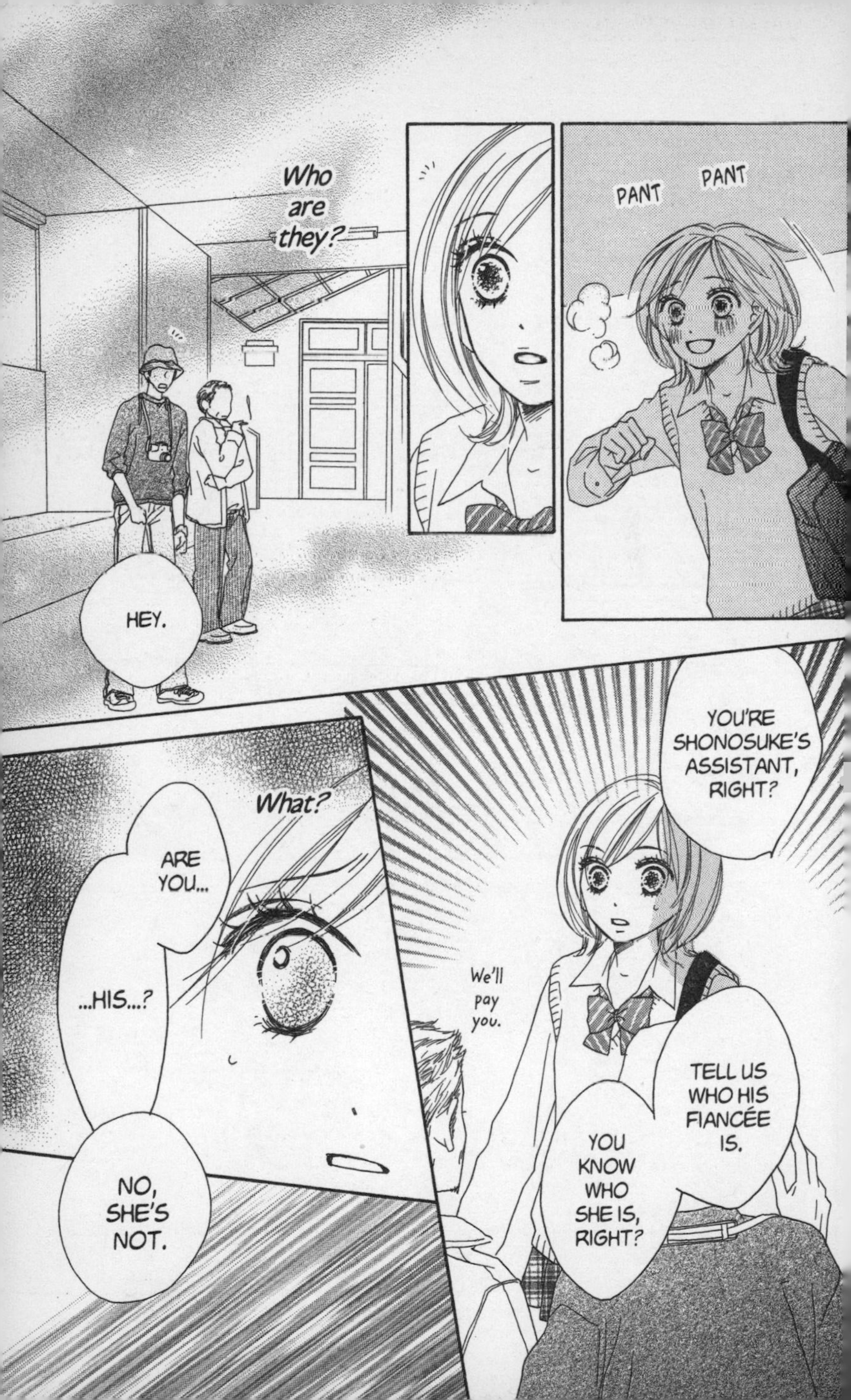
PANT PANT
Who are they?
HEY.
YOU'RE SHONOSUKE'S ASSISTANT, RIGHT?
We'll pay you.
TELL US WHO HIS FIANCÉE IS.
YOU KNOW WHO SHE IS, RIGHT?
What?
ARE YOU...
...HIS...?
NO, SHE'S NOT.

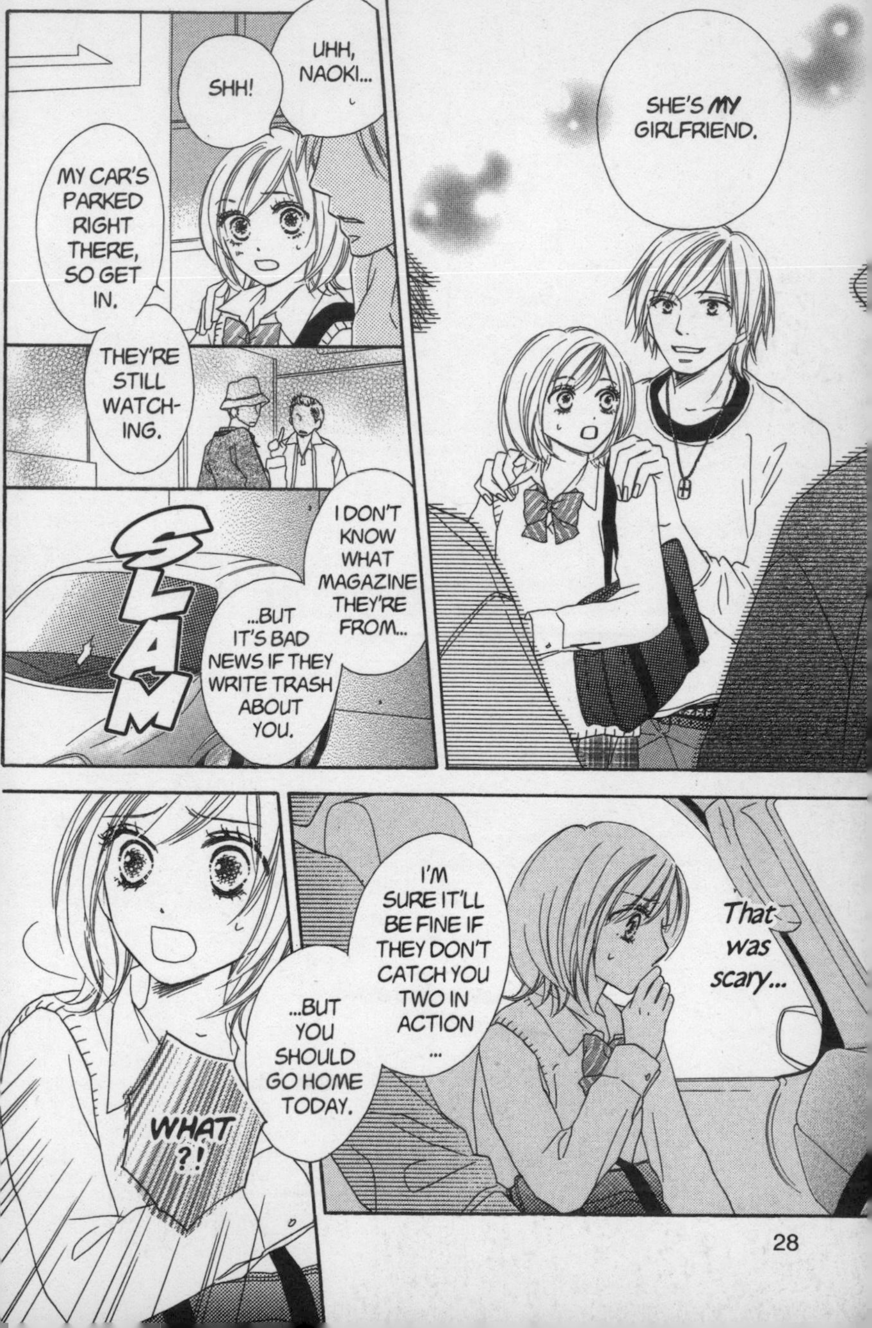
SHE'S MY GIRLFRIEND.
UHH, NAOKI...
SHH!
MY CAR'S PARKED RIGHT THERE, SO GET IN.
THEY'RE STILL WATCH-ING.
I DON'T KNOW WHAT MAGAZINE THEY'RE FROM...
...BUT IT'S BAD NEWS IF THEY WRITE TRASH ABOUT YOU.
SLAM
That was scary...
I'M SURE IT'LL BE FINE IF THEY DON'T CATCH YOU TWO IN ACTION...
...BUT YOU SHOULD GO HOME TODAY.
WHAT?!

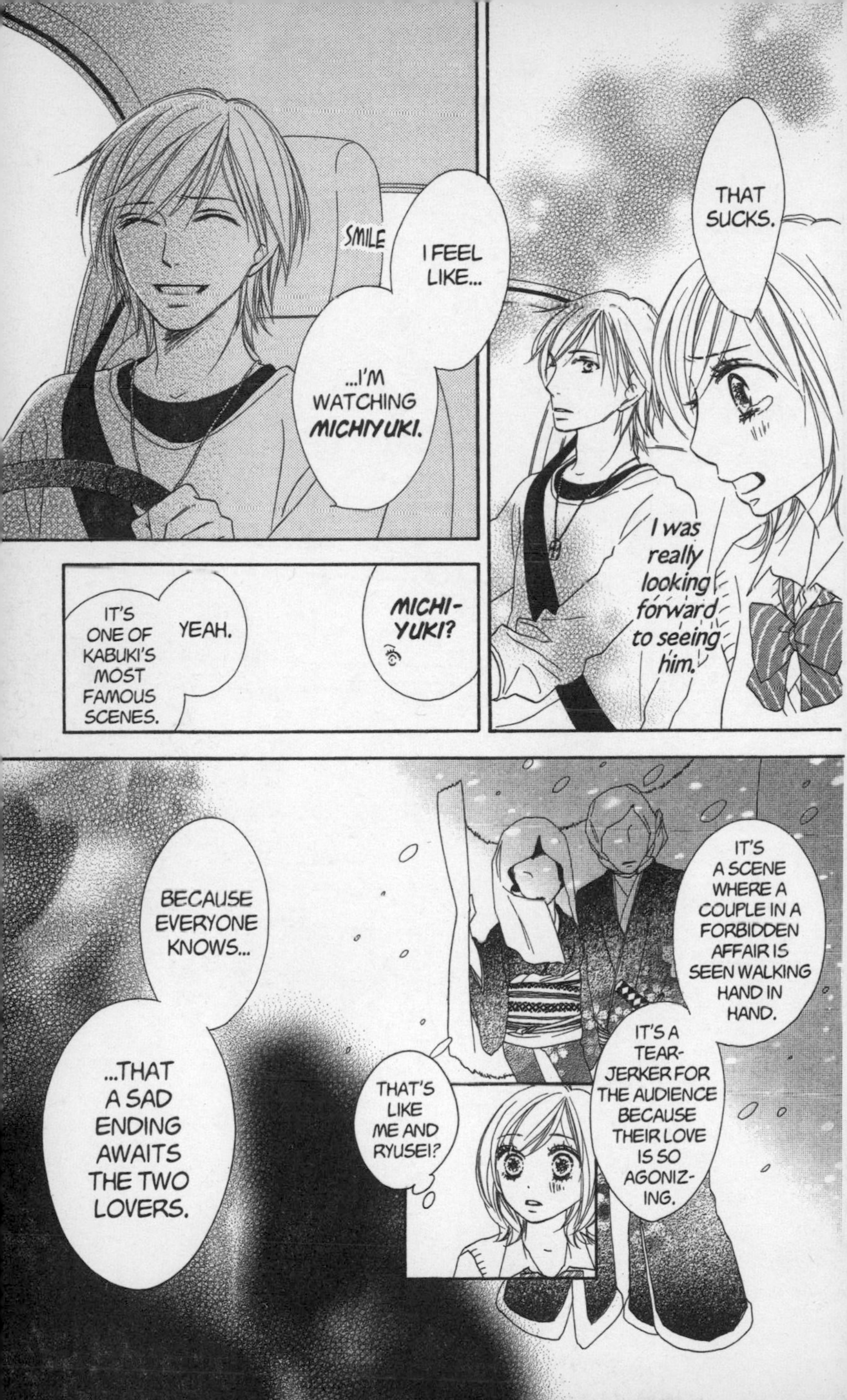
THAT SUCKS.
I was really looking forward to seeing him.
SMILE
I FEEL LIKE...
...I'M WATCHING MICHIYUKI.
MICHI-YUKI?
YEAH.
IT'S ONE OF KABUKI'S MOST FAMOUS SCENES.
IT'S A SCENE WHERE A COUPLE IN A FORBIDDEN AFFAIR IS SEEN WALKING HAND IN HAND.
IT'S A TEAR-JERKER FOR THE AUDIENCE BECAUSE THEIR LOVE IS SO AGONIZ-ING.
THAT'S LIKE ME AND RYUSEI?
BECAUSE EVERYONE KNOWS...
...THAT A SAD ENDING AWAITS THE TWO LOVERS.

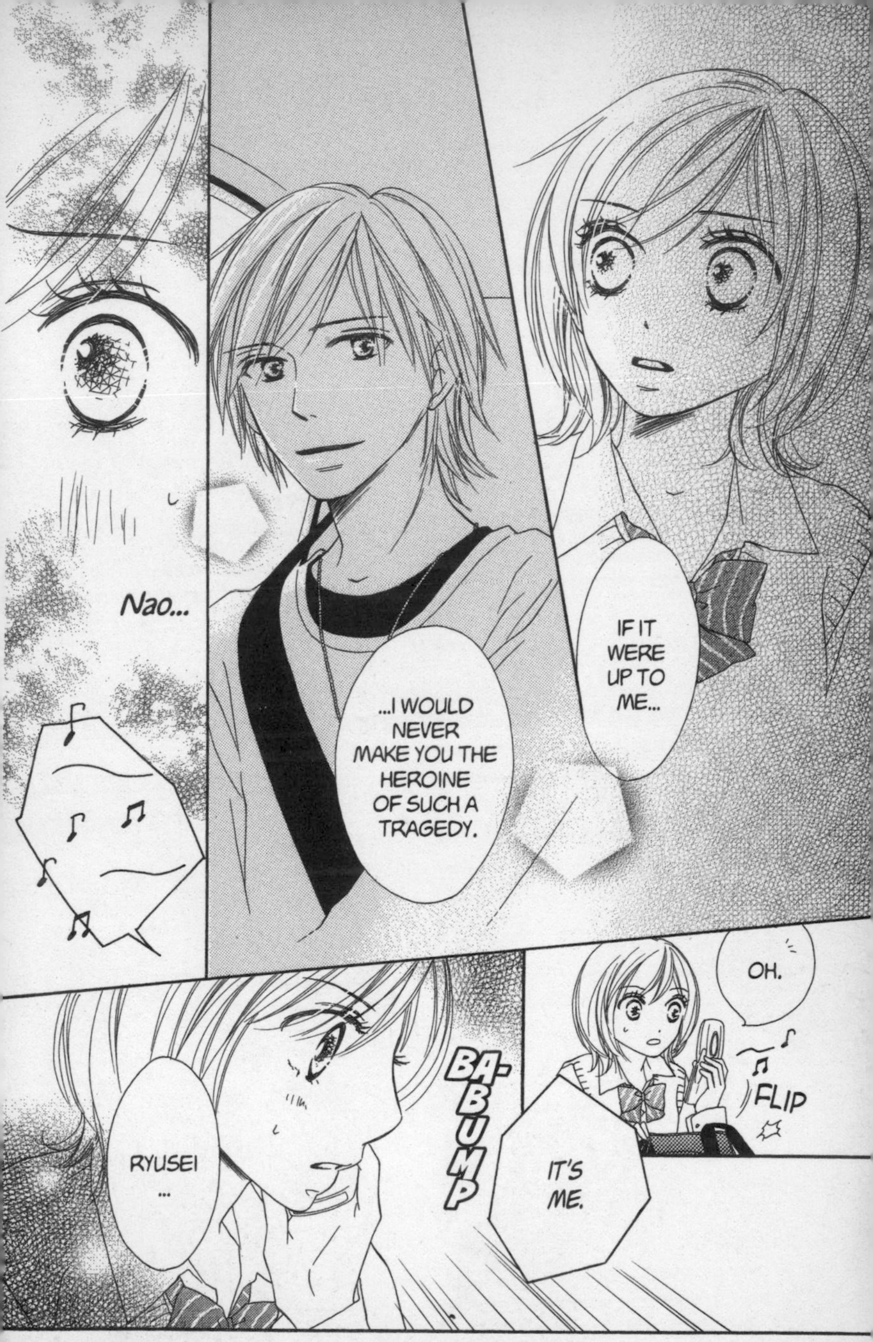
IF IT WERE UP TO ME...
...I WOULD NEVER MAKE YOU THE HEROINE OF SUCH A TRAGEDY.
Nao...
OH.
FLIP
IT'S ME.
BA-BUMP
RYUSEI ...

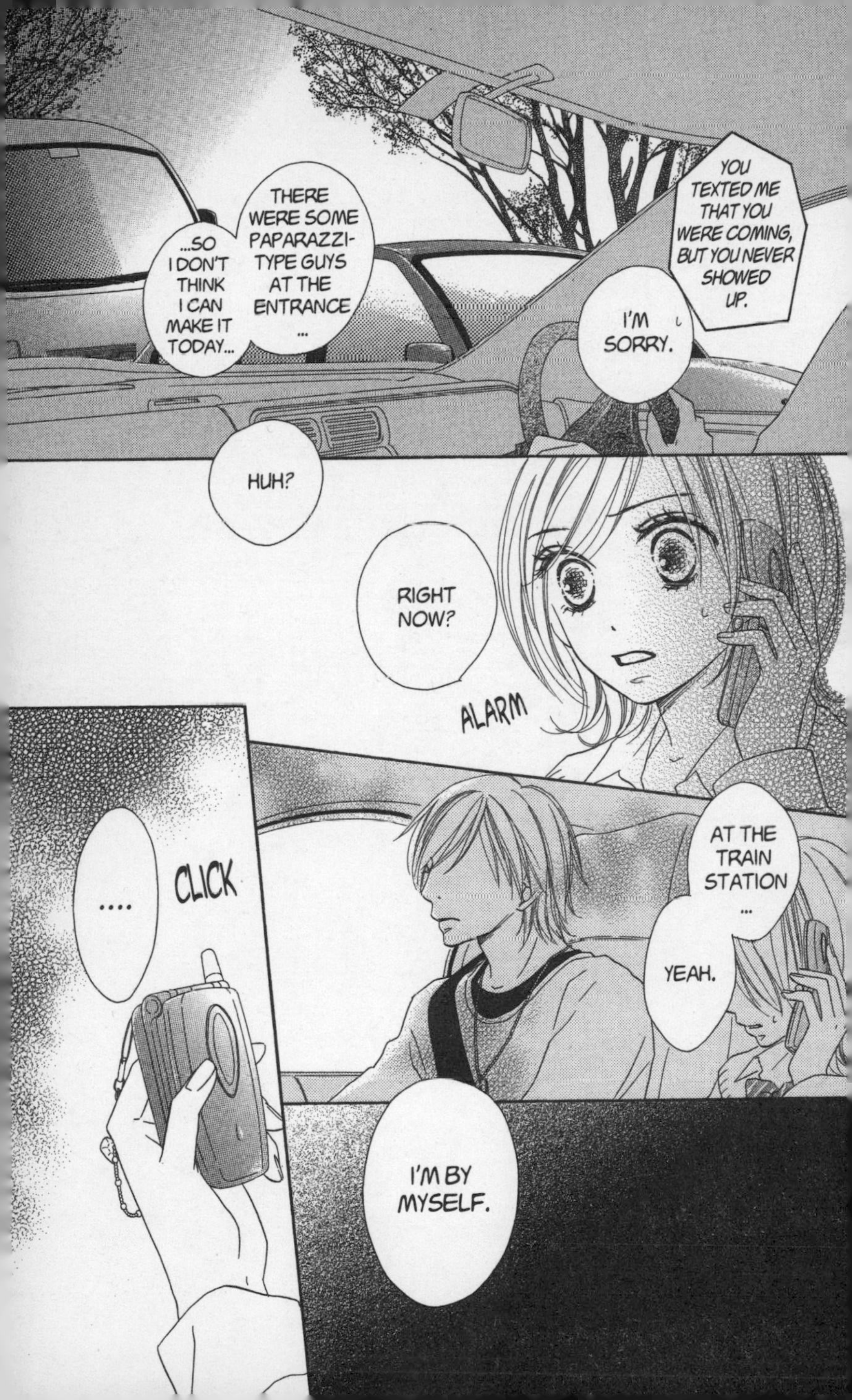
YOU TEXTED ME THAT YOU WERE COMING, BUT YOU NEVER SHOWED UP.
I'M SORRY.
THERE WERE SOME PAPARAZZI-TYPE GUYS AT THE ENTRANCE...
...SO I DON'T THINK I CAN MAKE IT TODAY...
HUH?
RIGHT NOW?
ALARM
AT THE TRAIN STATION...
YEAH.
I'M BY MYSELF.
CLICK
....

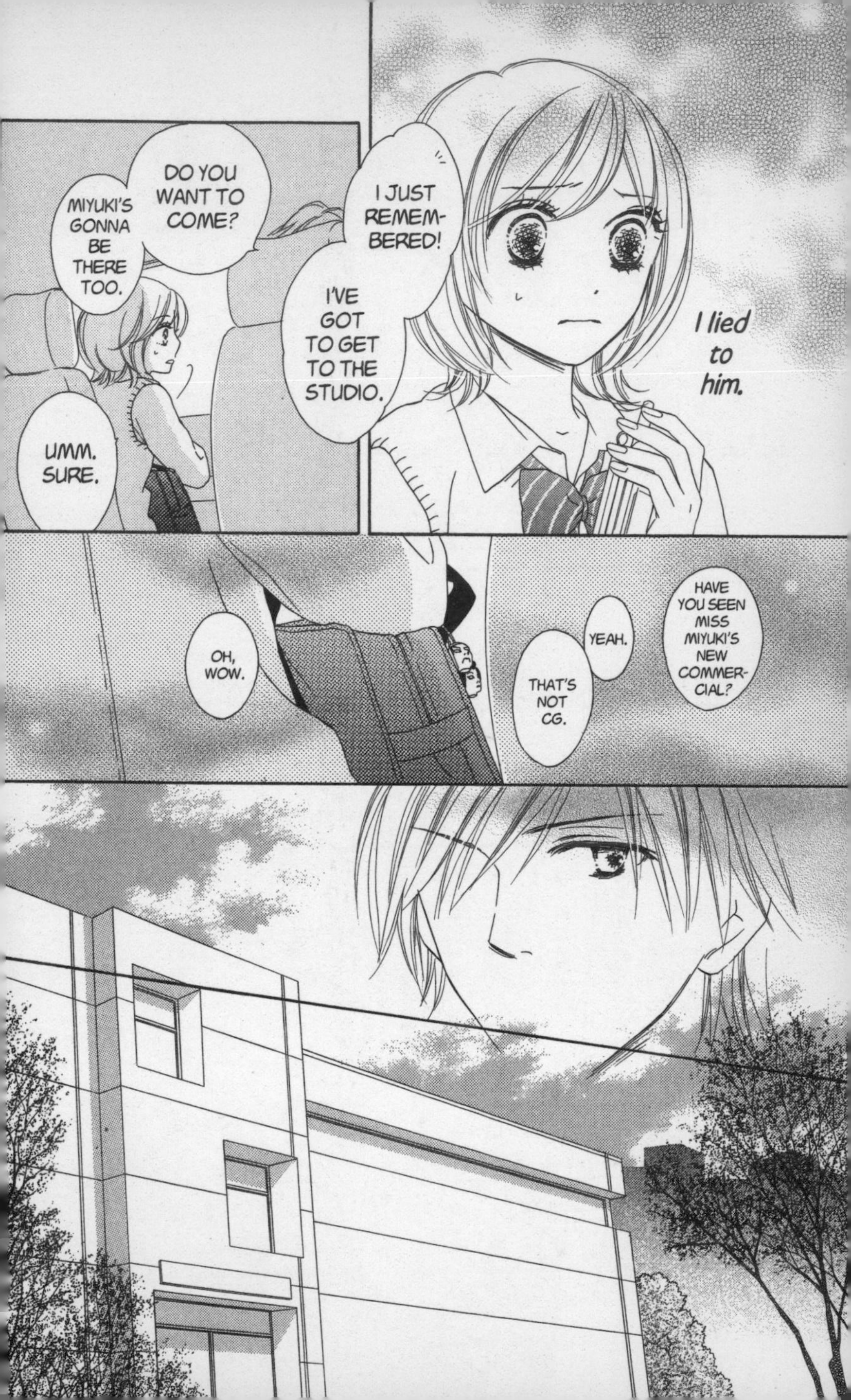
I JUST REMEMBERED!
I'VE GOT TO GET TO THE STUDIO.
I lied to him.
DO YOU WANT TO COME?
MIYUKI'S GONNA BE THERE TOO.
UMM. SURE.
HAVE YOU SEEN MISS MIYUKI'S NEW COMMERCIAL?
YEAH.
THAT'S NOT CG.
OH, WOW.

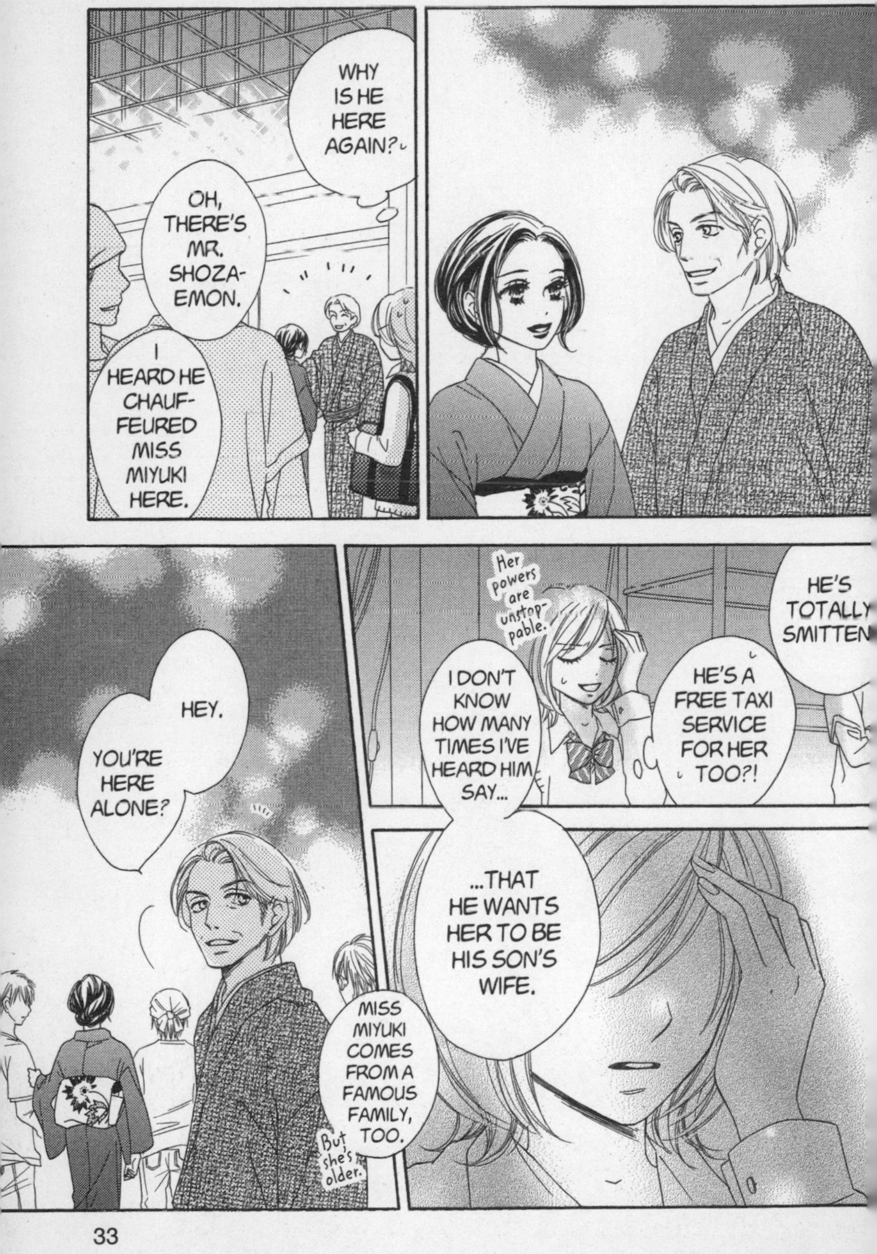
WHY IS HE HERE AGAIN?
OH, THERE'S MR. SHOZA-EMON.
I HEARD HE CHAUF-FEURED MISS MIYUKI HERE.
HE'S TOTALLY SMITTEN
HE'S A FREE TAXI SERVICE FOR HER TOO?!
Her powers are unstop-pable.
I DON'T KNOW HOW MANY TIMES I'VE HEARD HIM SAY...
...THAT HE WANTS HER TO BE HIS SON'S WIFE.
HEY.
YOU'RE HERE ALONE?
MISS MIYUKI COMES FROM A FAMOUS FAMILY, TOO.
But she's older.

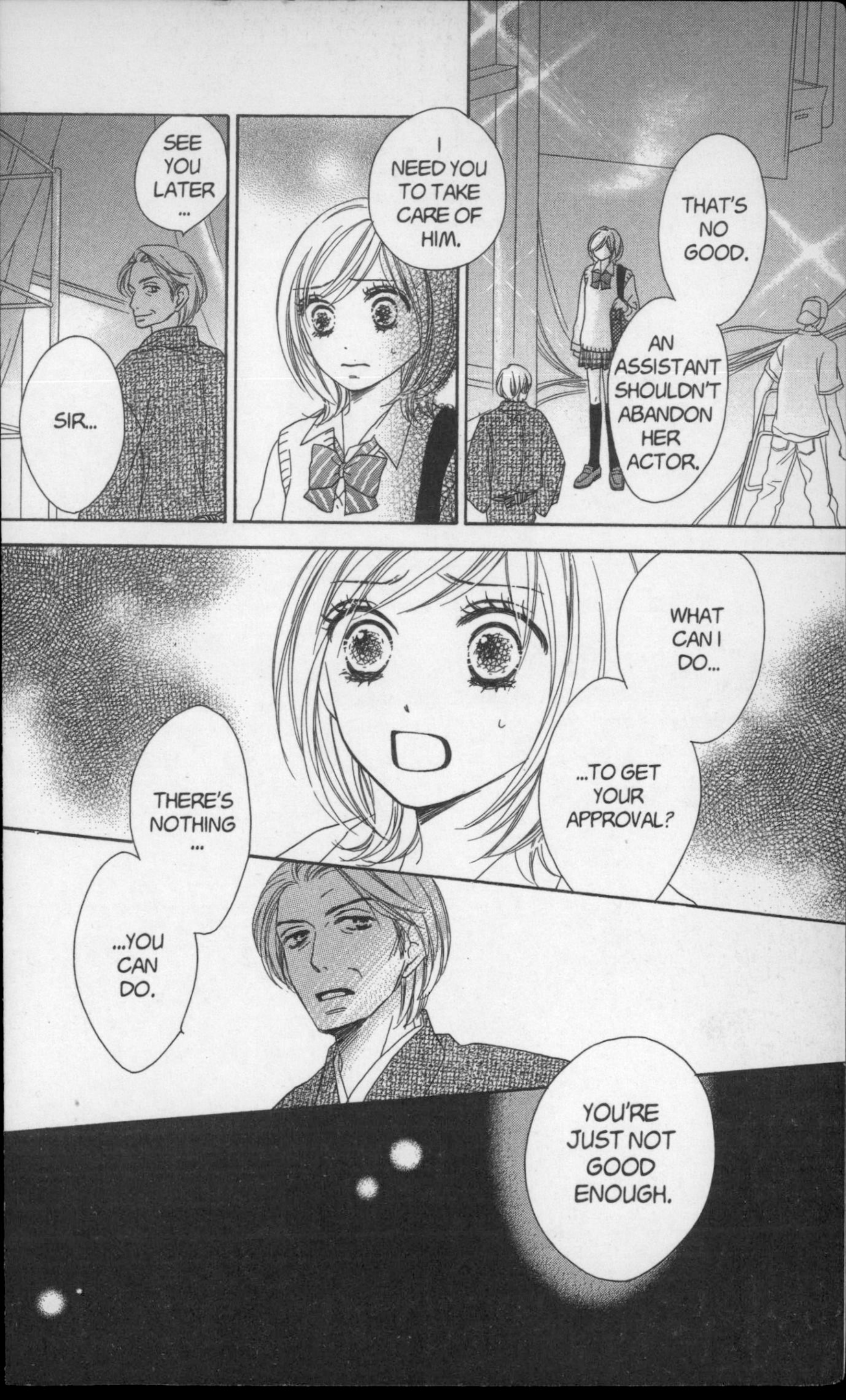
THAT'S NO GOOD.
AN ASSISTANT SHOULDN'T ABANDON HER ACTOR.
I NEED YOU TO TAKE CARE OF HIM.
SEE YOU LATER...
SIR...
WHAT CAN I DO...
...TO GET YOUR APPROVAL?
THERE'S NOTHING...
...YOU CAN DO.
YOU'RE JUST NOT GOOD ENOUGH.

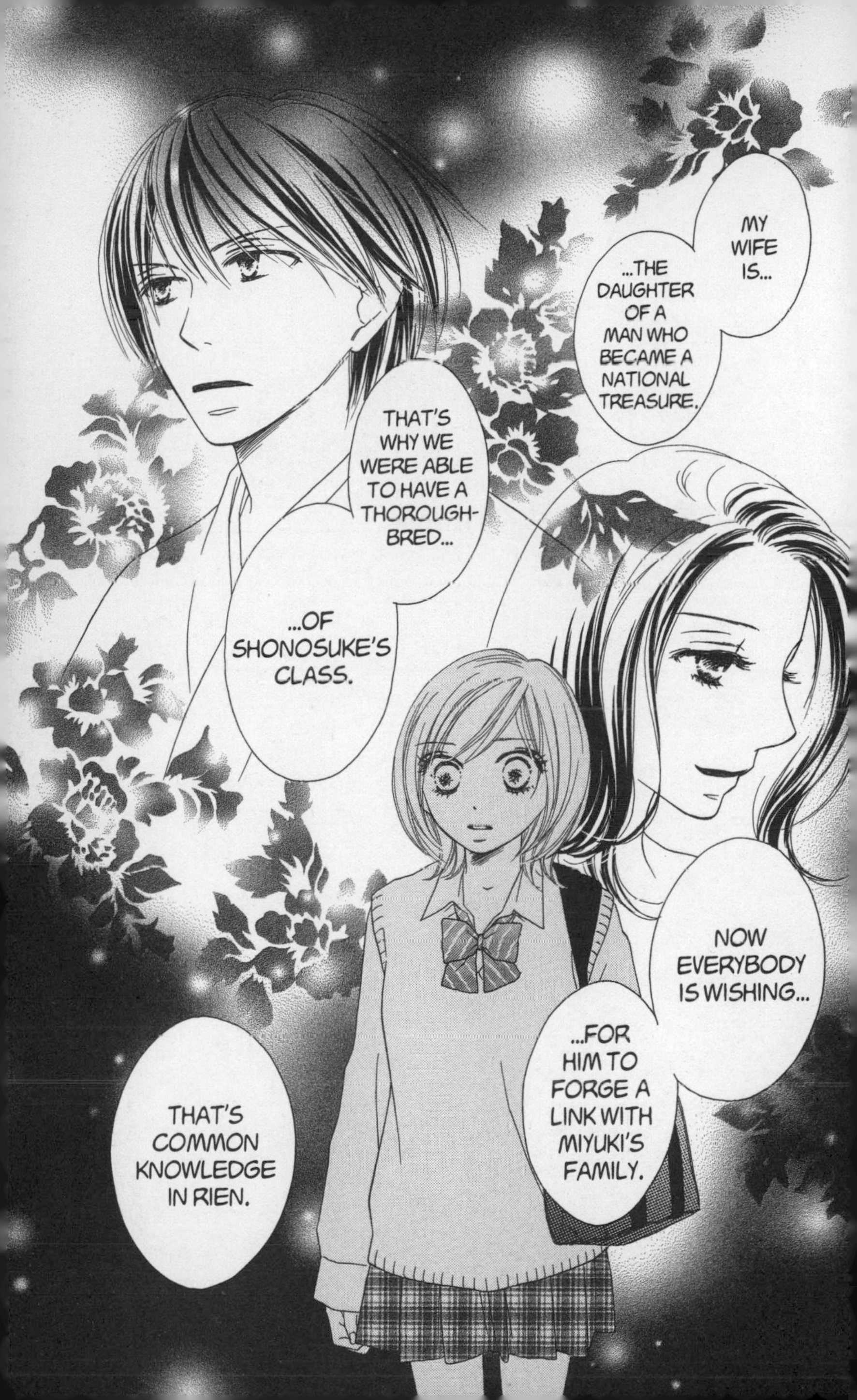
MY WIFE IS...
...THE DAUGHTER OF A MAN WHO BECAME A NATIONAL TREASURE.
THAT'S WHY WE WERE ABLE TO HAVE A THOROUGH-BRED...
...OF SHONOSUKE'S CLASS.
NOW EVERYBODY IS WISHING...
...FOR HIM TO FORGE A LINK WITH MIYUKI'S FAMILY.
THAT'S COMMON KNOWLEDGE IN RIEN.

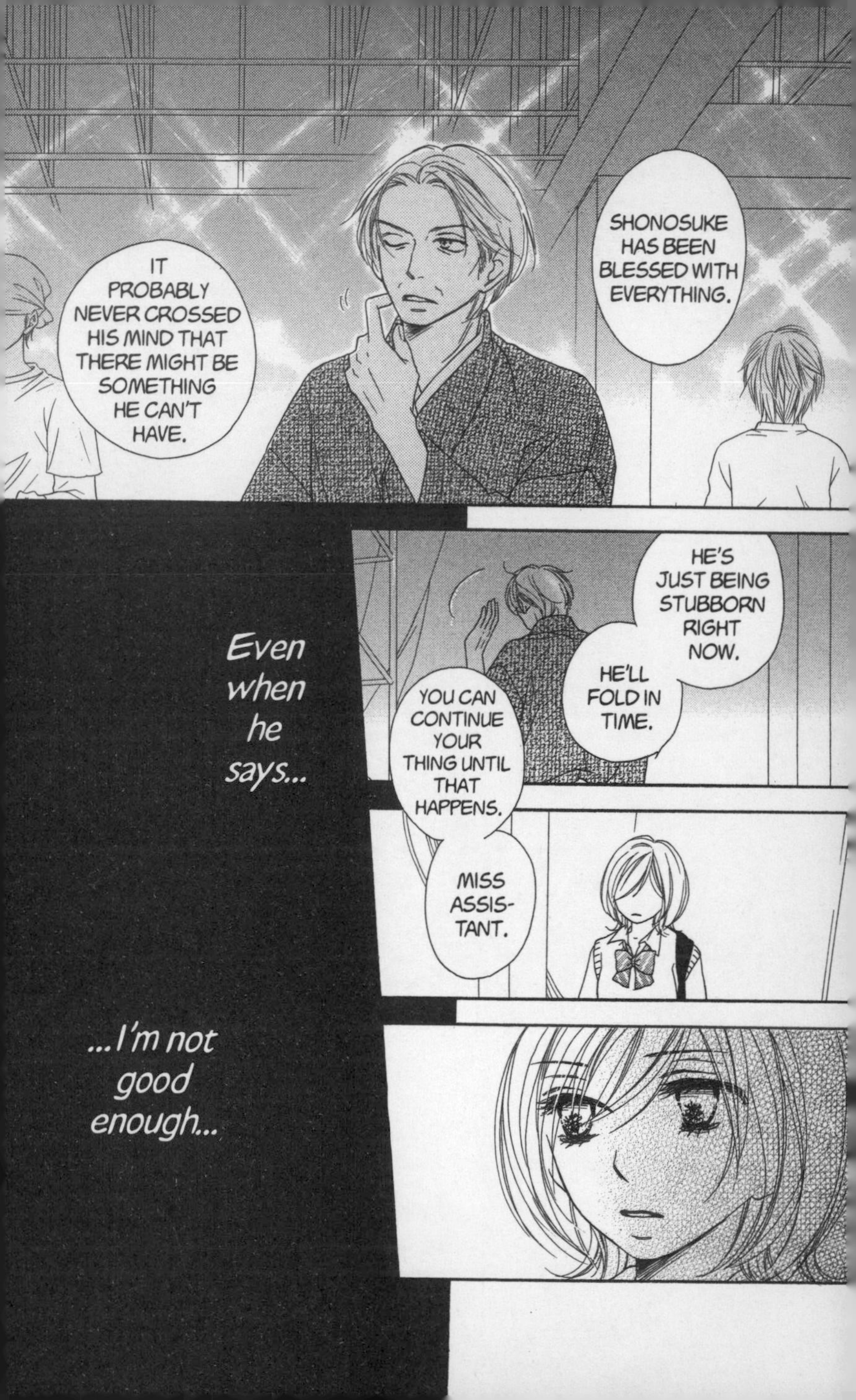
SHONOSUKE HAS BEEN BLESSED WITH EVERYTHING.
IT PROBABLY NEVER CROSSED HIS MIND THAT THERE MIGHT BE SOMETHING HE CAN'T HAVE.
HE'S JUST BEING STUBBORN RIGHT NOW.
HE'LL FOLD IN TIME.
YOU CAN CONTINUE YOUR THING UNTIL THAT HAPPENS.
MISS ASSIS-TANT.
Even when he says...
...I'm not good enough...

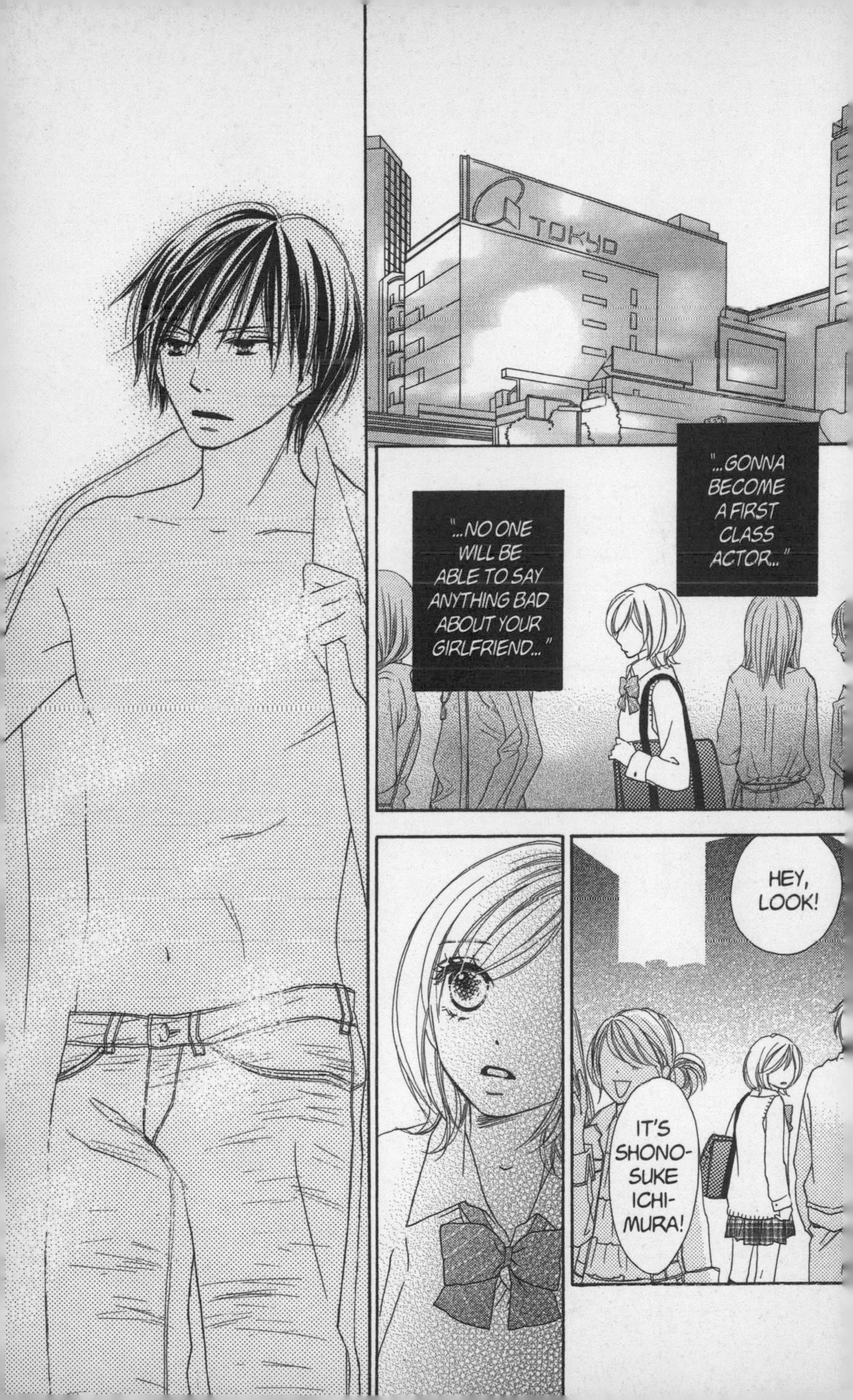
TOKYO
"...GONNA BECOME A FIRST CLASS ACTOR..."
"...NO ONE WILL BE ABLE TO SAY ANYTHING BAD ABOUT YOUR GIRLFRIEND..."
HEY, LOOK!
IT'S SHONO-SUKE ICHI-MURA!

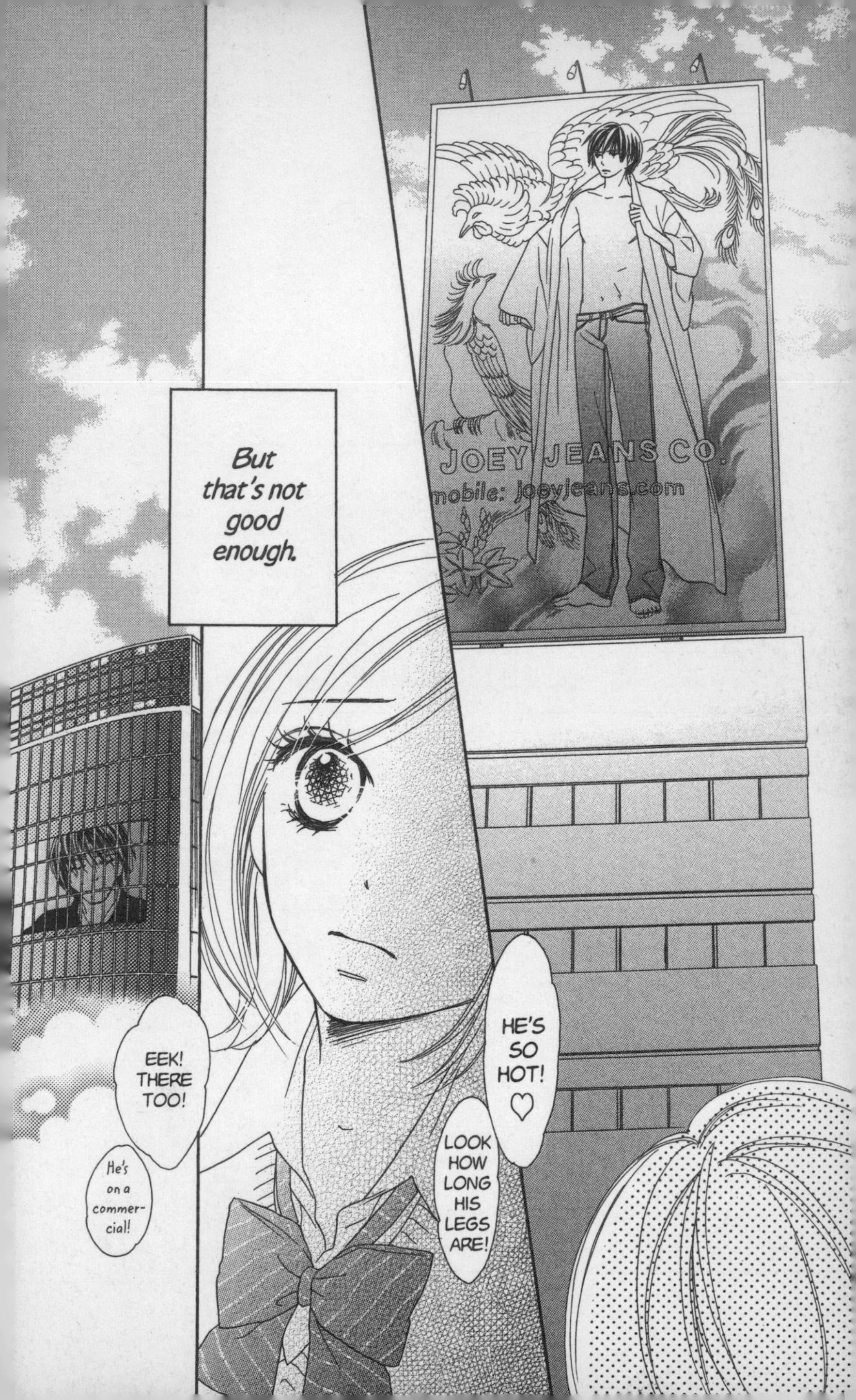

JOEY JEANS CO.
mobile: joeyjeans.com
But that's not good enough.
HE'S SO HOT! ♡
LOOK HOW LONG HIS LEGS ARE!
EEK! THERE TOO!
He's on a commercial!

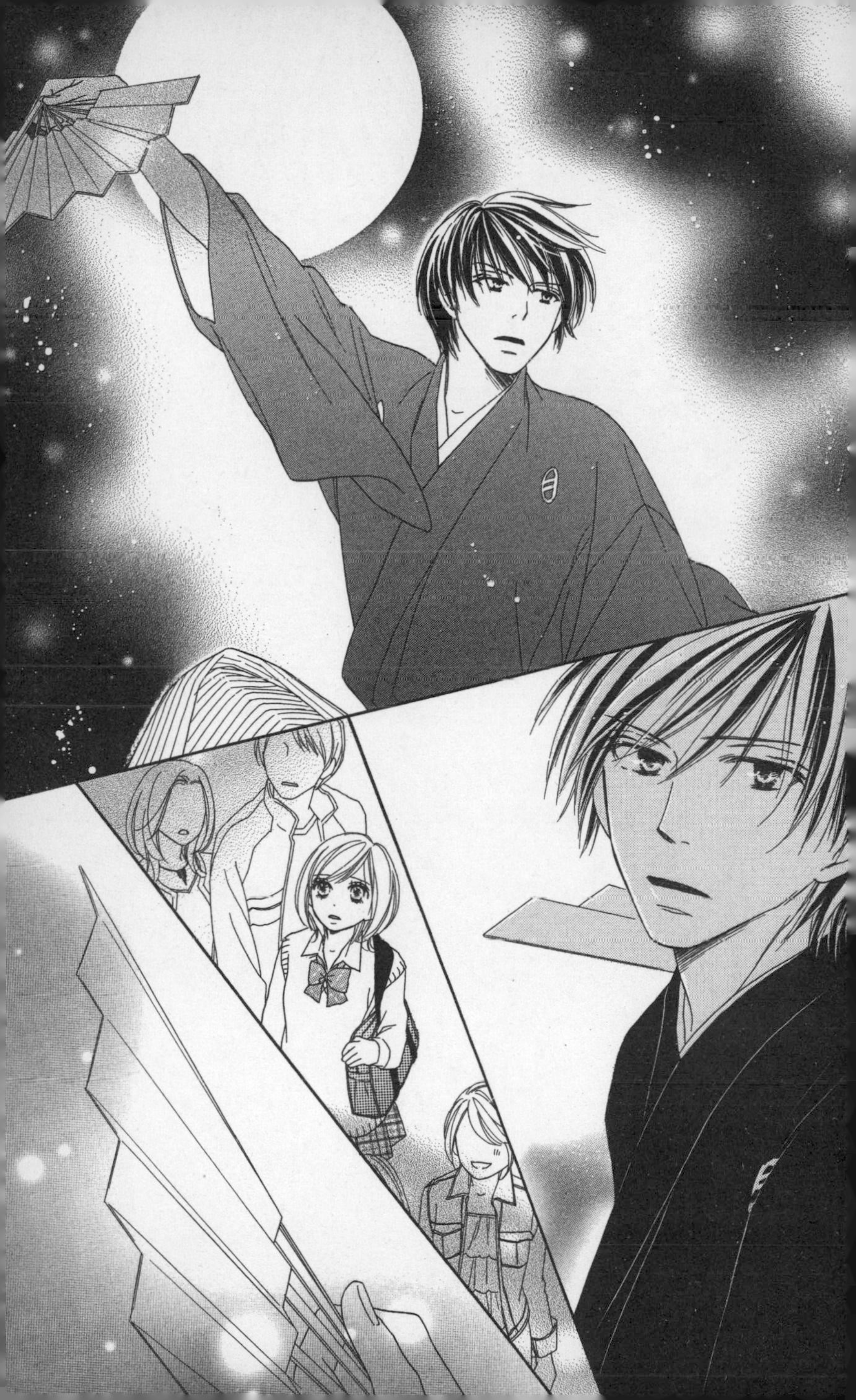

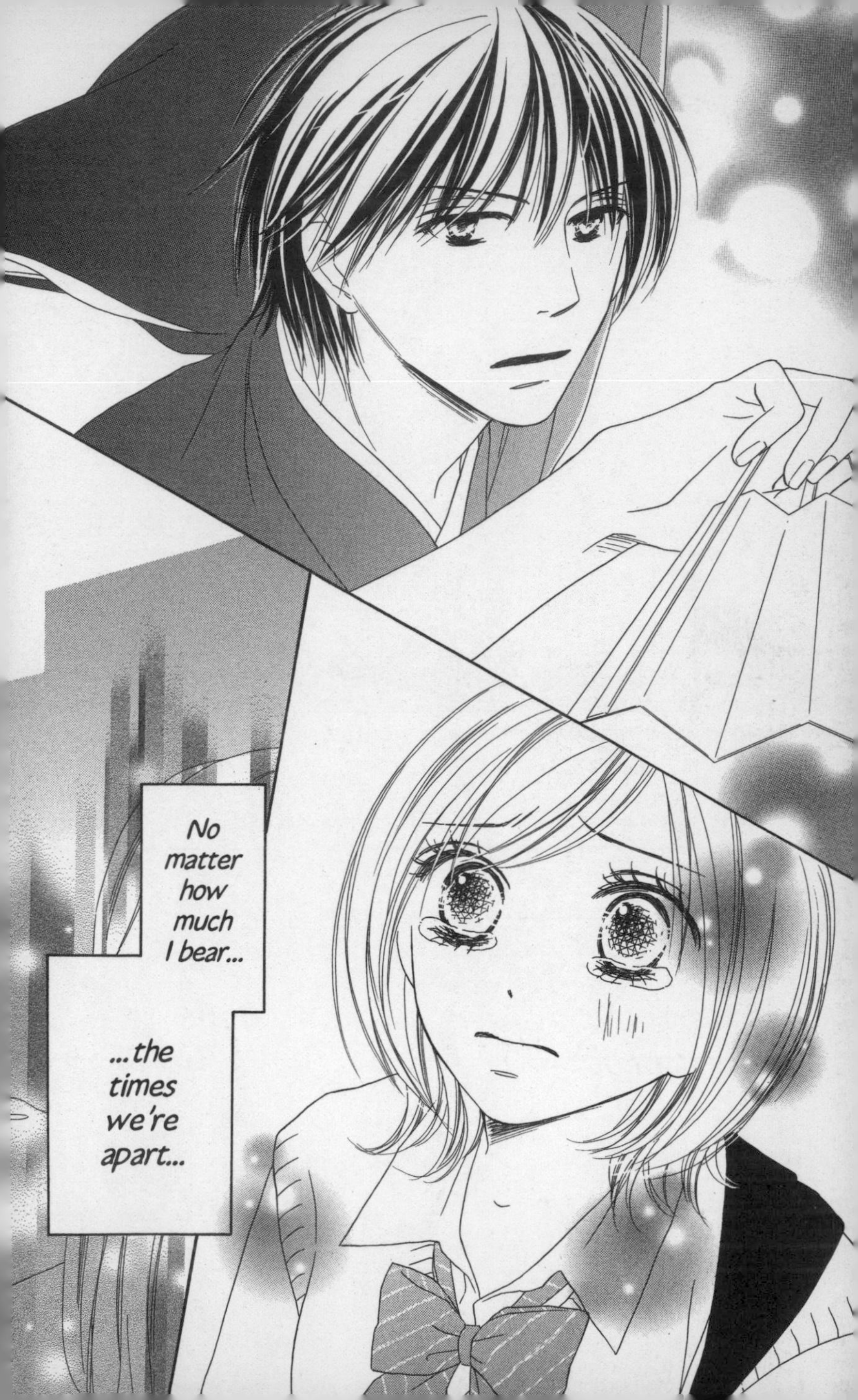
No matter how much I bear...
...the times we're apart...

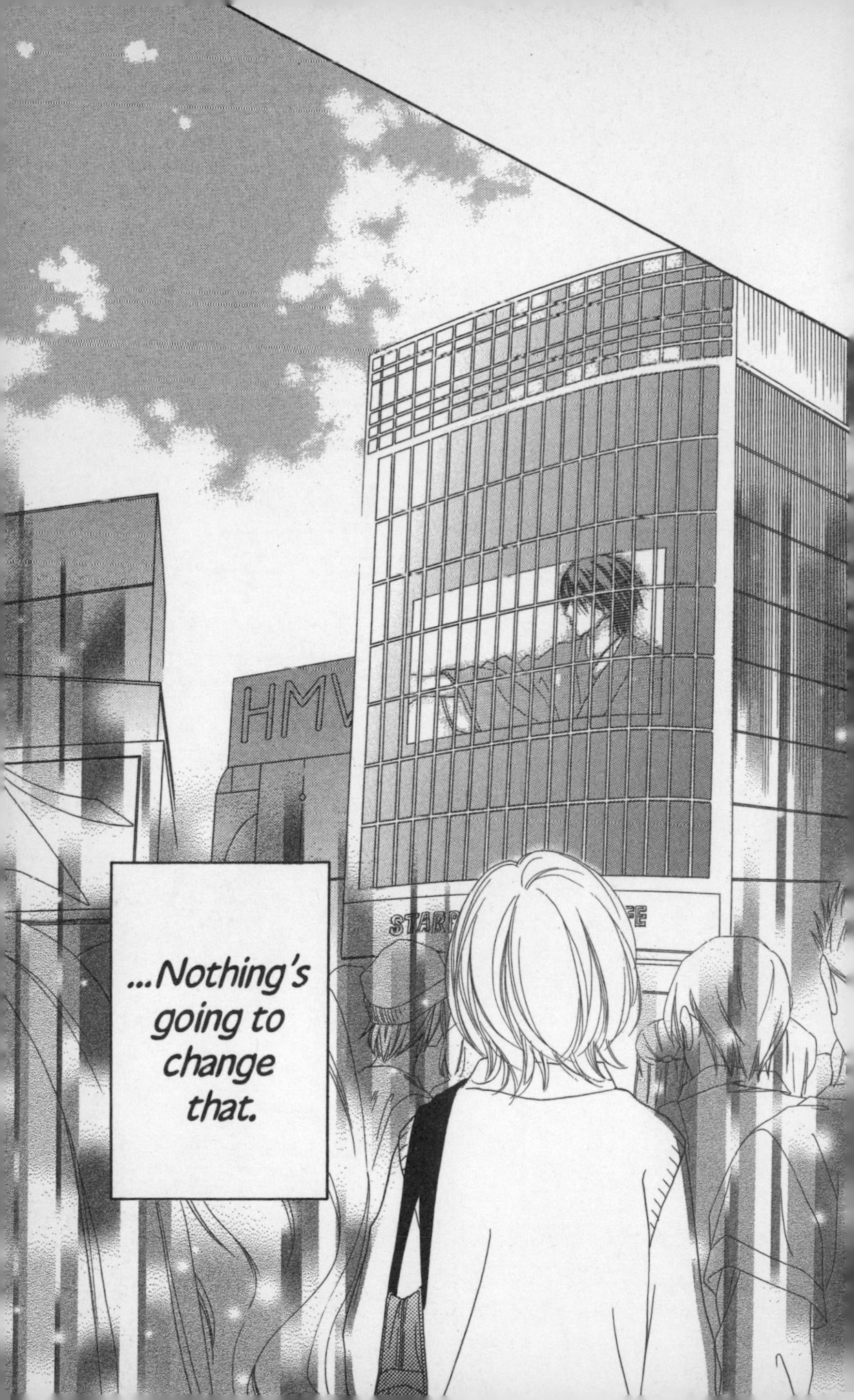
HMV
...Nothing's going to change that.

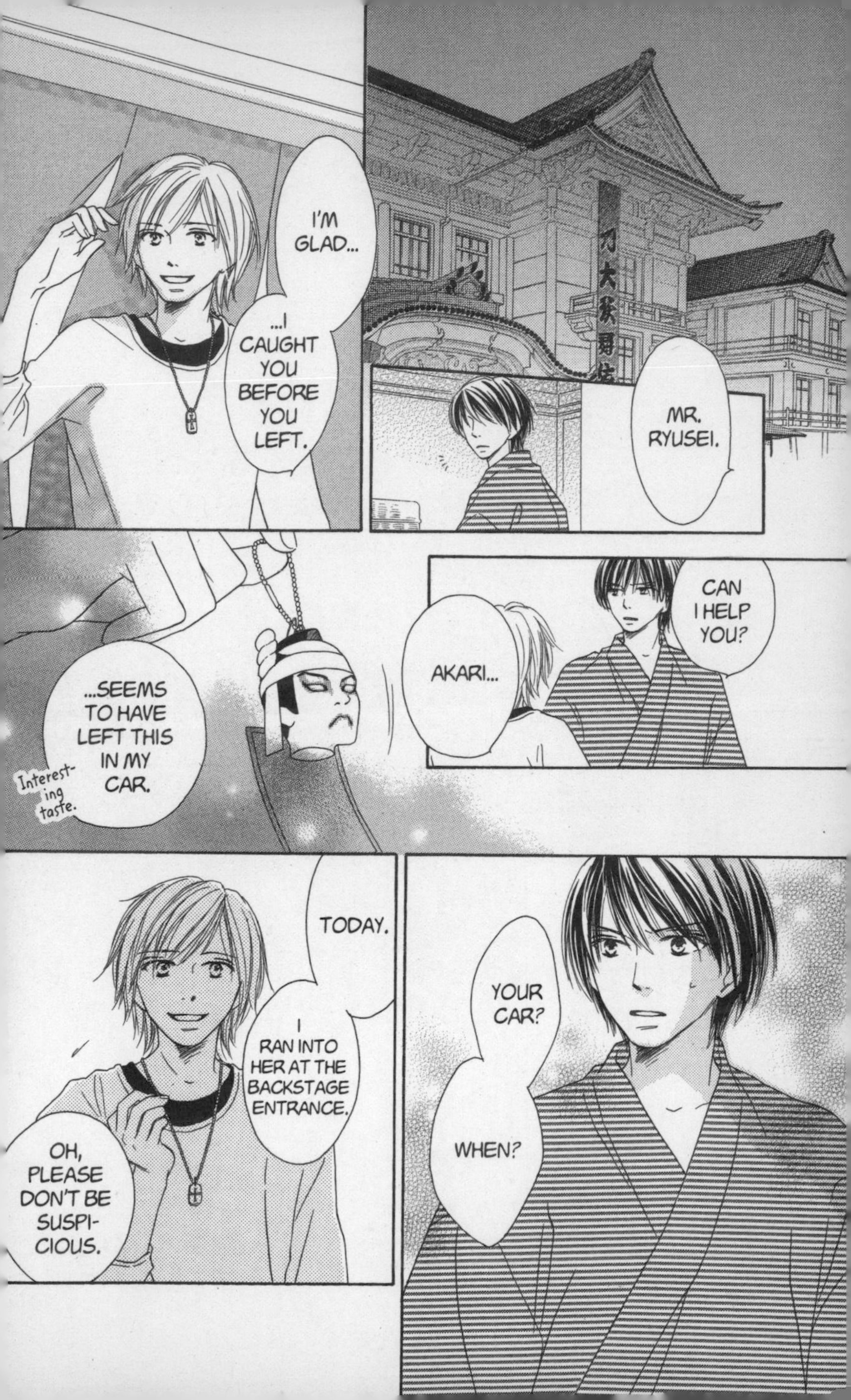
MR. RYUSEI.
I'M GLAD...
...I CAUGHT YOU BEFORE YOU LEFT.
CAN I HELP YOU?
AKARI...
...SEEMS TO HAVE LEFT THIS IN MY CAR.
Interesting taste.
YOUR CAR?
WHEN?
TODAY.
I RAN INTO HER AT THE BACKSTAGE ENTRANCE.
OH, PLEASE DON'T BE SUSPICIOUS.

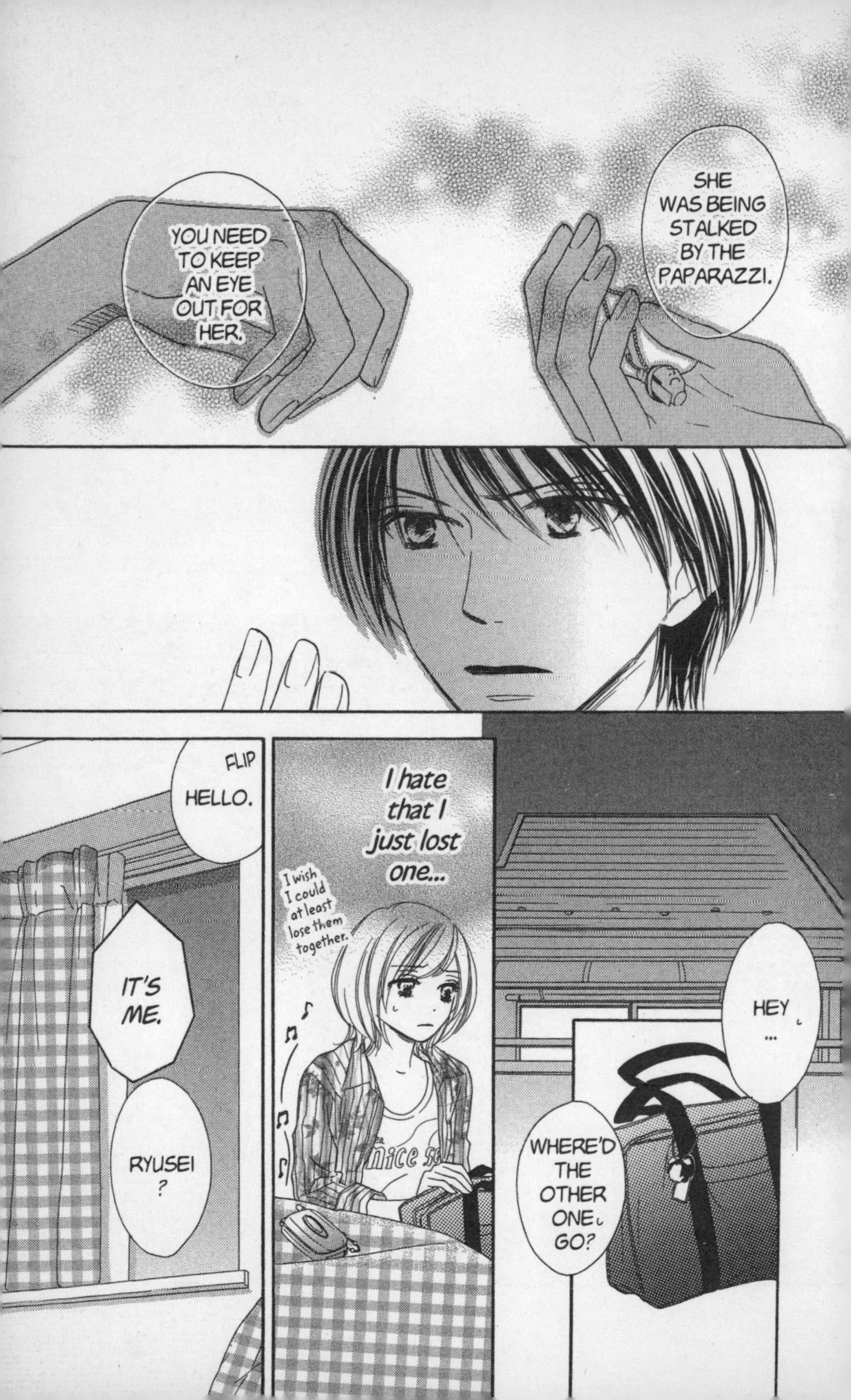
SHE WAS BEING STALKED BY THE PAPARAZZI.
YOU NEED TO KEEP AN EYE OUT FOR HER.
HEY...
WHERE'D THE OTHER ONE GO?
I hate that I just lost one...
I wish I could at least lose them together.
FLIP
HELLO.
IT'S ME.
RYUSEI?

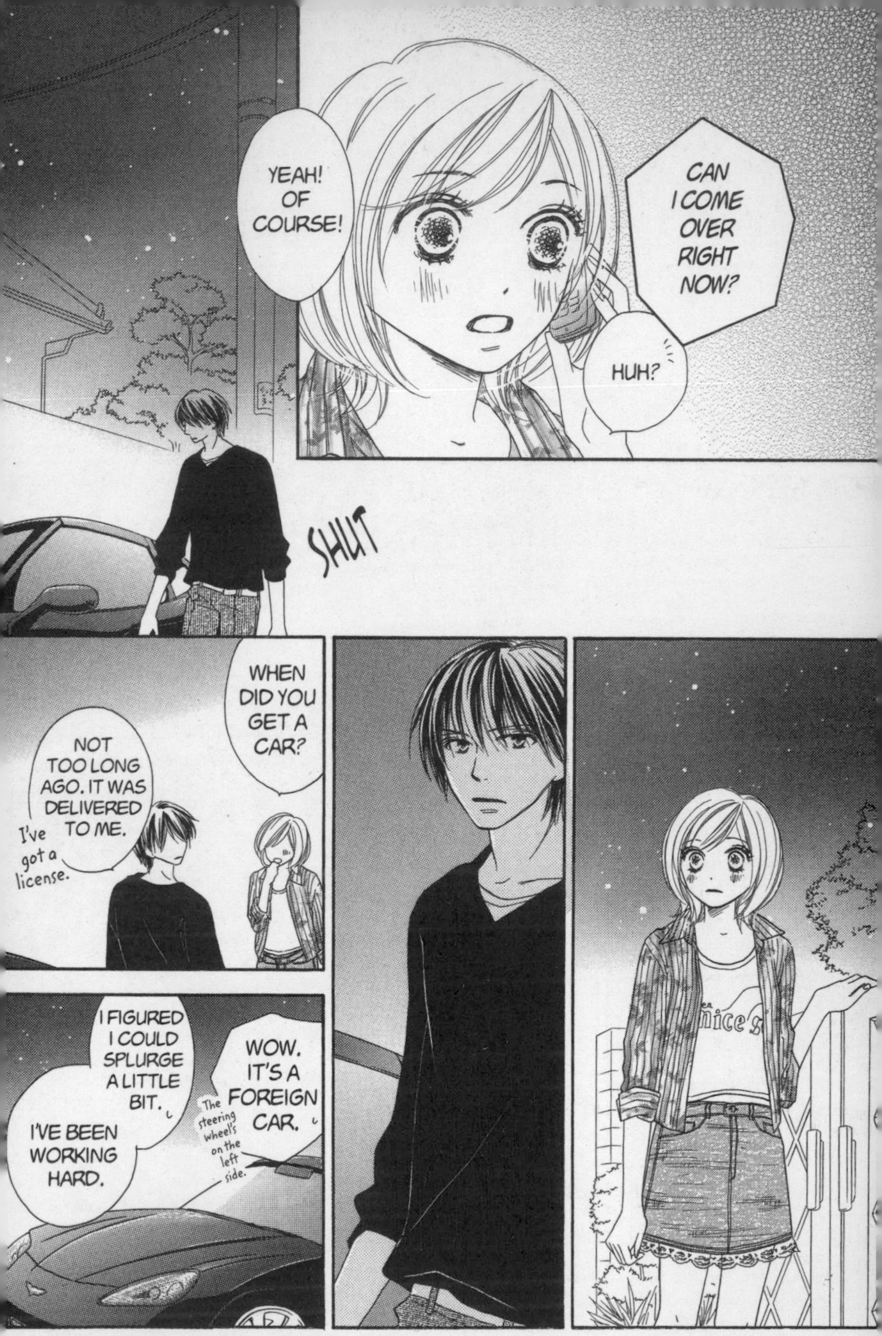
CAN I COME OVER RIGHT NOW?
HUH?
YEAH! OF COURSE!
SHUT
WHEN DID YOU GET A CAR?
NOT TOO LONG AGO. IT WAS DELIVERED TO ME.
I've got a license.
WOW. IT'S A FOREIGN CAR.
The steering wheel's on the left side.
I FIGURED I COULD SPLURGE A LITTLE BIT.
I'VE BEEN WORKING HARD.

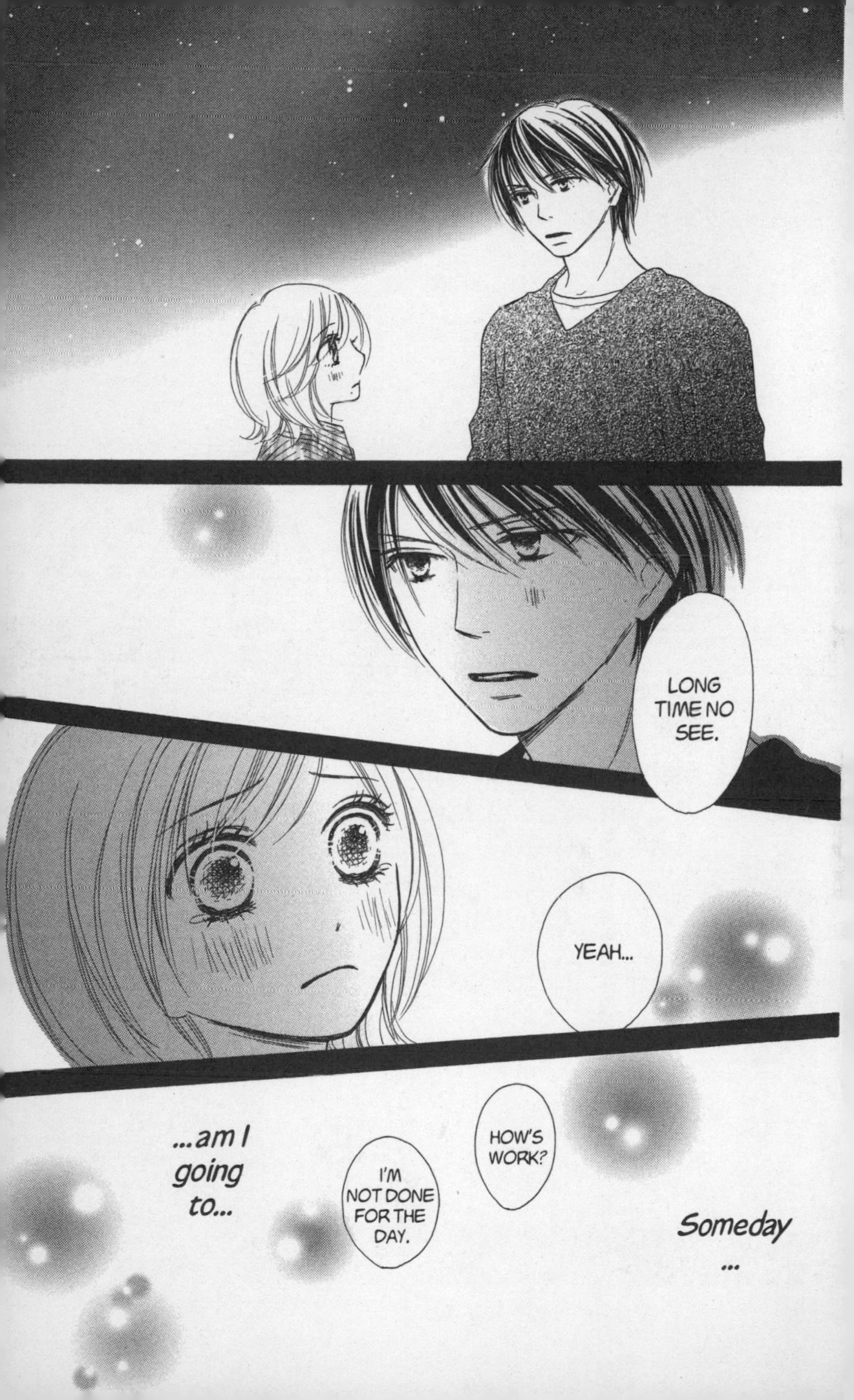
LONG TIME NO SEE.
YEAH...
Someday ...
HOW'S WORK?
I'M NOT DONE FOR THE DAY.
...am I going to...

...have to break up with him?
AKARI.
WANT TO GET MARRIED?
RIGHT NOW.
WHAT DO YOU MEAN, "RIGHT NOW"?
You and your jokes.
IT'S NOT LIKE YOU CAN'T.
YOU'RE OF LEGAL AGE.

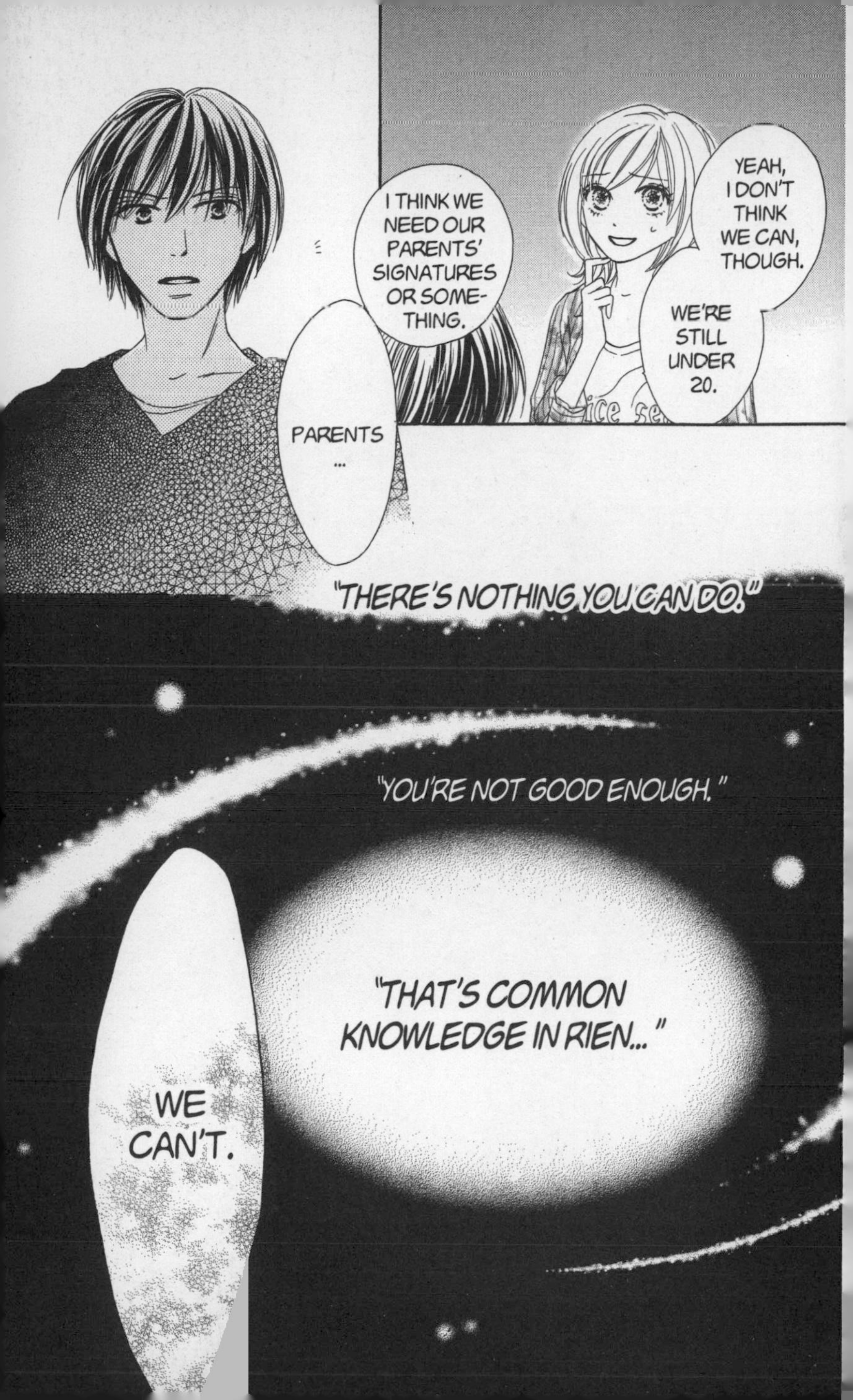
YEAH, I DON'T THINK WE CAN, THOUGH.
WE'RE STILL UNDER 20.
I THINK WE NEED OUR PARENTS' SIGNATURES OR SOME-THING.
PARENTS ...
"THERE'S NOTHING YOU CAN DO."
"YOU'RE NOT GOOD ENOUGH."
"THAT'S COMMON KNOWLEDGE IN RIEN..."
WE CAN'T.

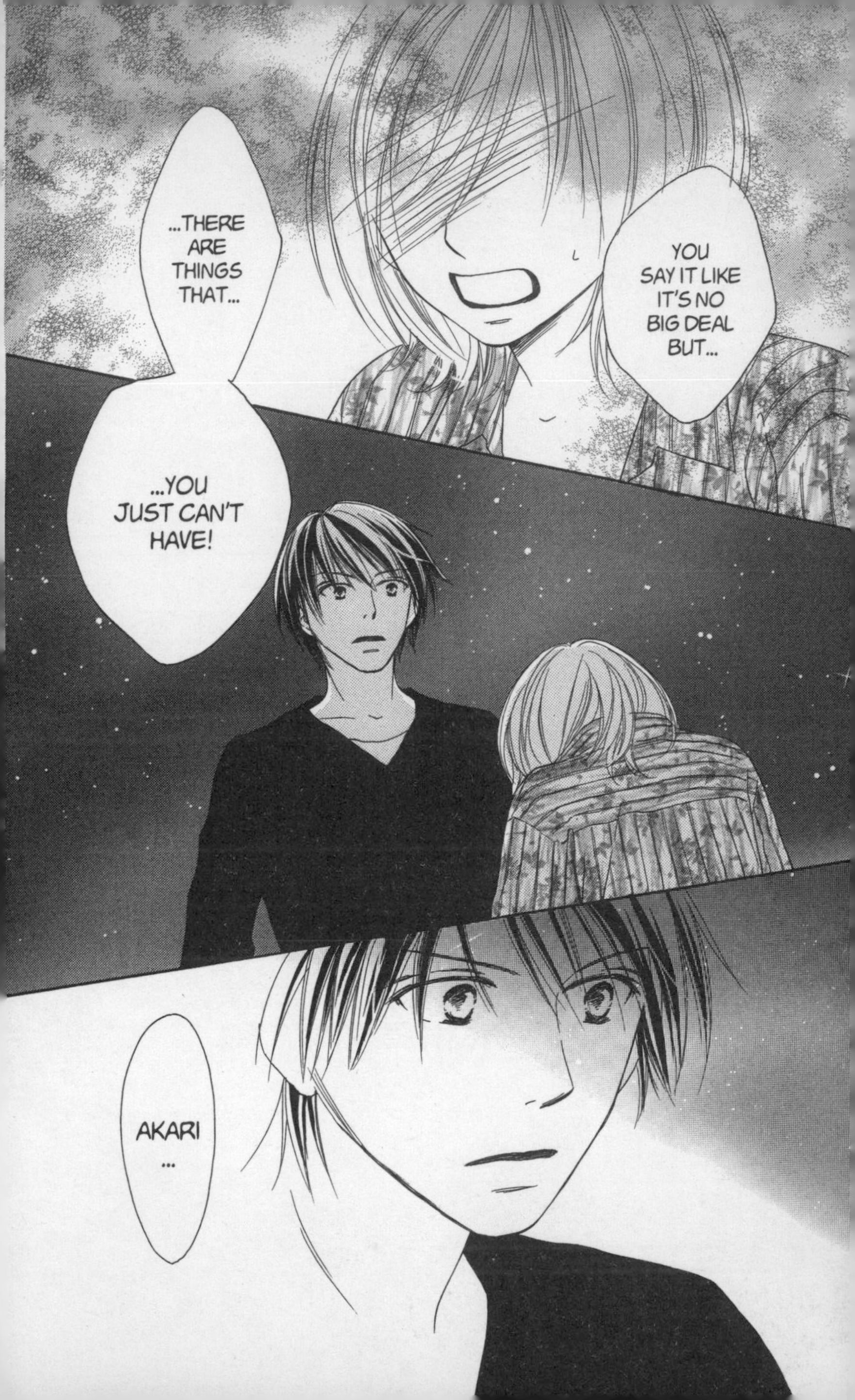
YOU SAY IT LIKE IT'S NO BIG DEAL BUT...
...THERE ARE THINGS THAT...
...YOU JUST CAN'T HAVE!
AKARI ...

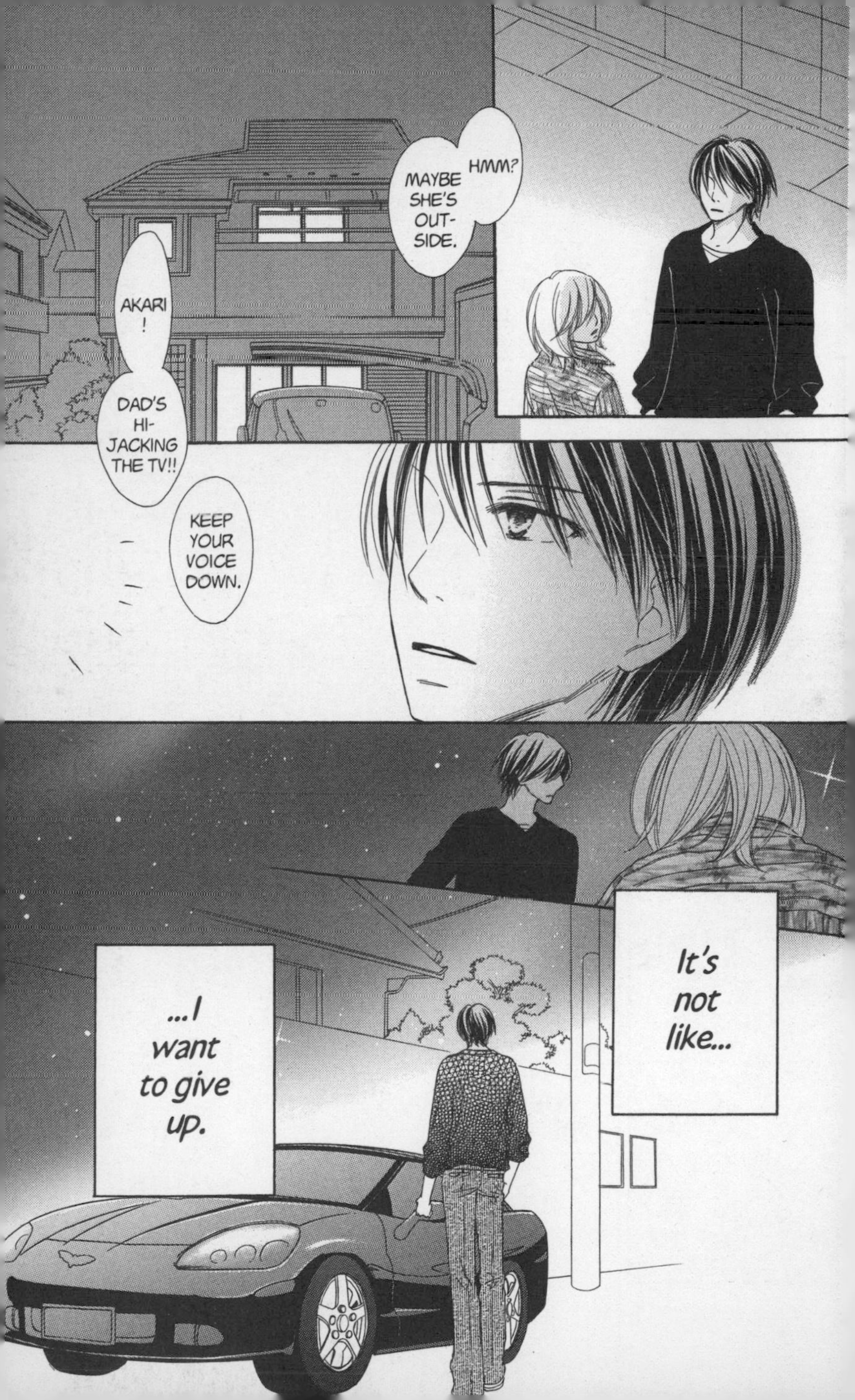
HMM?
MAYBE SHE'S OUT-SIDE.
AKARI!
DAD'S HI-JACKING THE TV!!
KEEP YOUR VOICE DOWN.
It's not like...
...I want to give up.

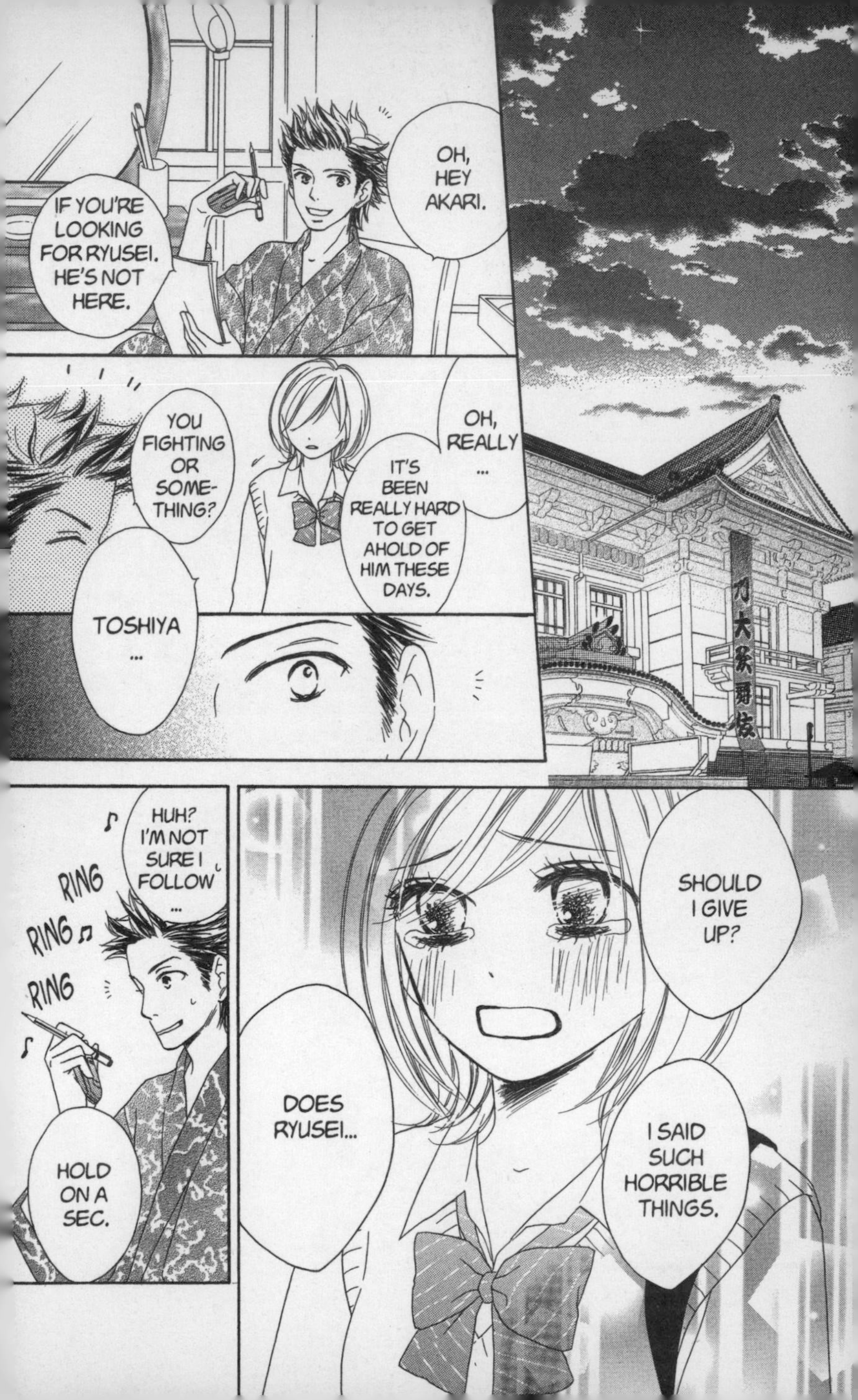
OH, HEY AKARI.
IF YOU'RE LOOKING FOR RYUSEI. HE'S NOT HERE.
OH, REALLY ...
IT'S BEEN REALLY HARD TO GET AHOLD OF HIM THESE DAYS.
YOU FIGHTING OR SOME-THING?
TOSHIYA ...
SHOULD I GIVE UP?
I SAID SUCH HORRIBLE THINGS.
DOES RYUSEI...
HUH? I'M NOT SURE I FOLLOW ...
RING
RING
RING
HOLD ON A SEC.

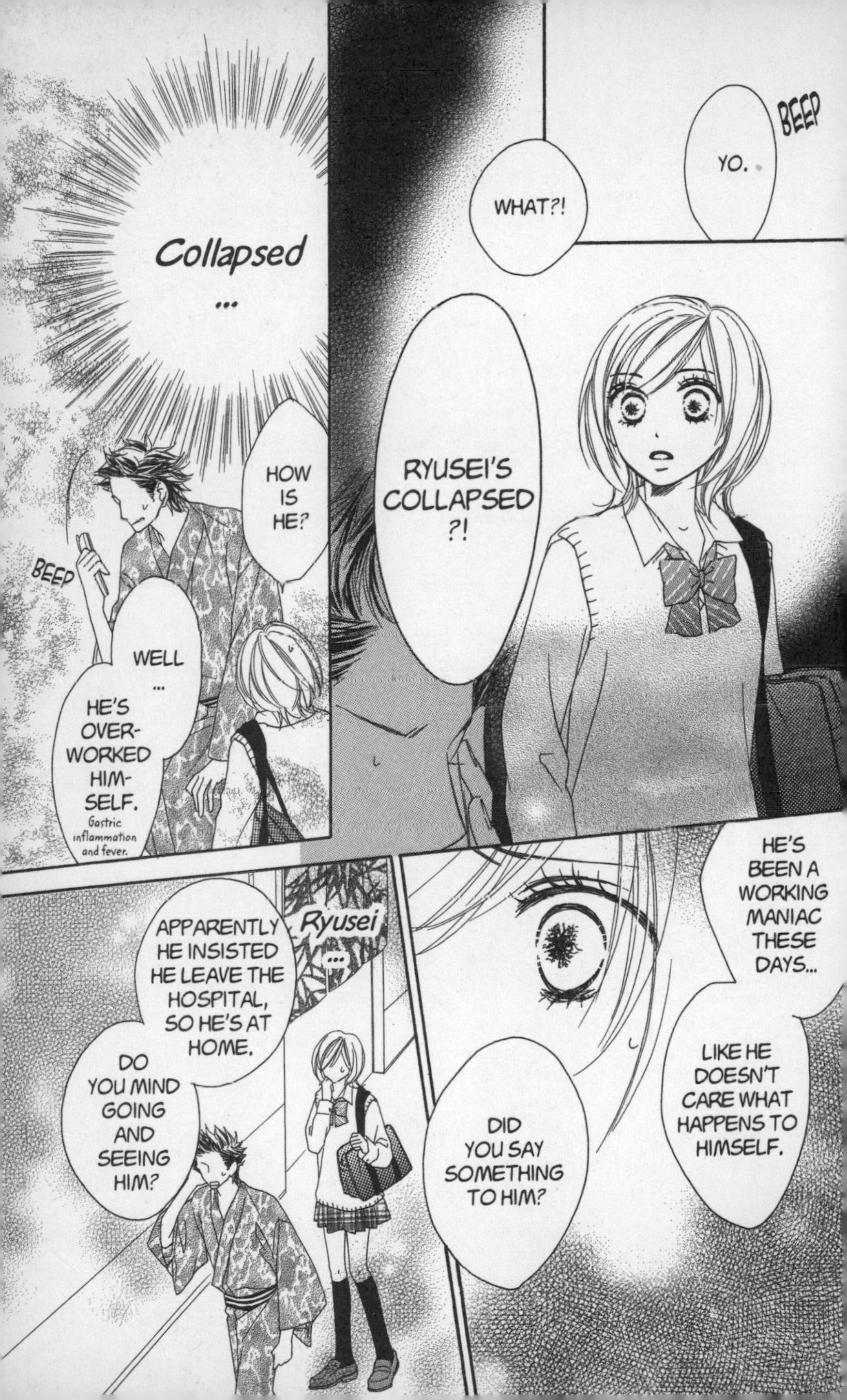
YO.
BEEP
WHAT?!
RYUSEI'S COLLAPSED ?!
Collapsed ...
HOW IS HE?
BEEP
WELL ...
HE'S OVER-WORKED HIM-SELF.
Gastric inflammation and fever.
HE'S BEEN A WORKING MANIAC THESE DAYS...
LIKE HE DOESN'T CARE WHAT HAPPENS TO HIMSELF.
DID YOU SAY SOMETHING TO HIM?
Ryusei ...
APPARENTLY HE INSISTED HE LEAVE THE HOSPITAL, SO HE'S AT HOME.
DO YOU MIND GOING AND SEEING HIM?

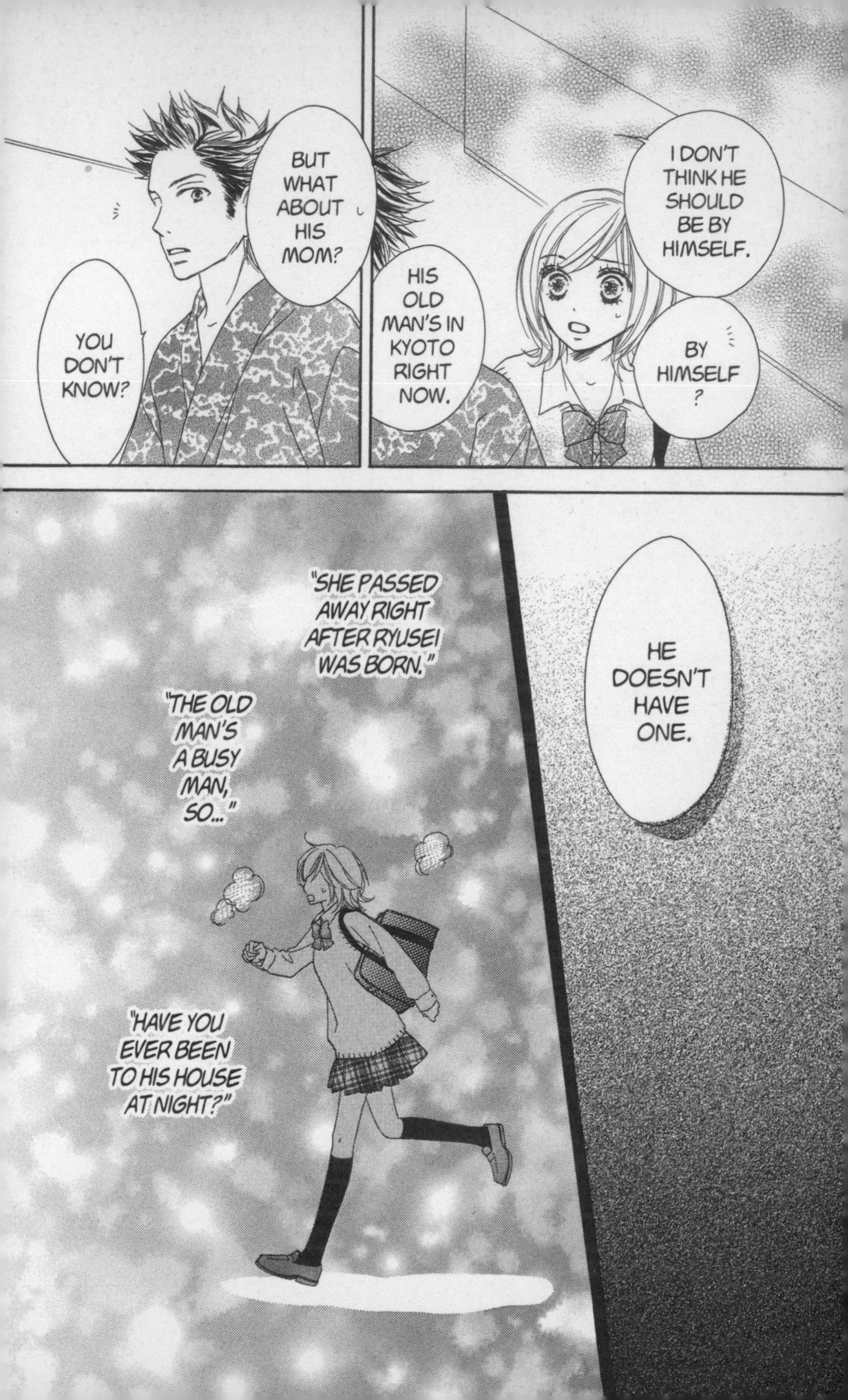
I DON'T THINK HE SHOULD BE BY HIMSELF.
BY HIMSELF?
HIS OLD MAN'S IN KYOTO RIGHT NOW.
BUT WHAT ABOUT HIS MOM?
YOU DON'T KNOW?
HE DOESN'T HAVE ONE.
"SHE PASSED AWAY RIGHT AFTER RYUSEI WAS BORN."
"THE OLD MAN'S A BUSY MAN, SO..."
"HAVE YOU EVER BEEN TO HIS HOUSE AT NIGHT?"

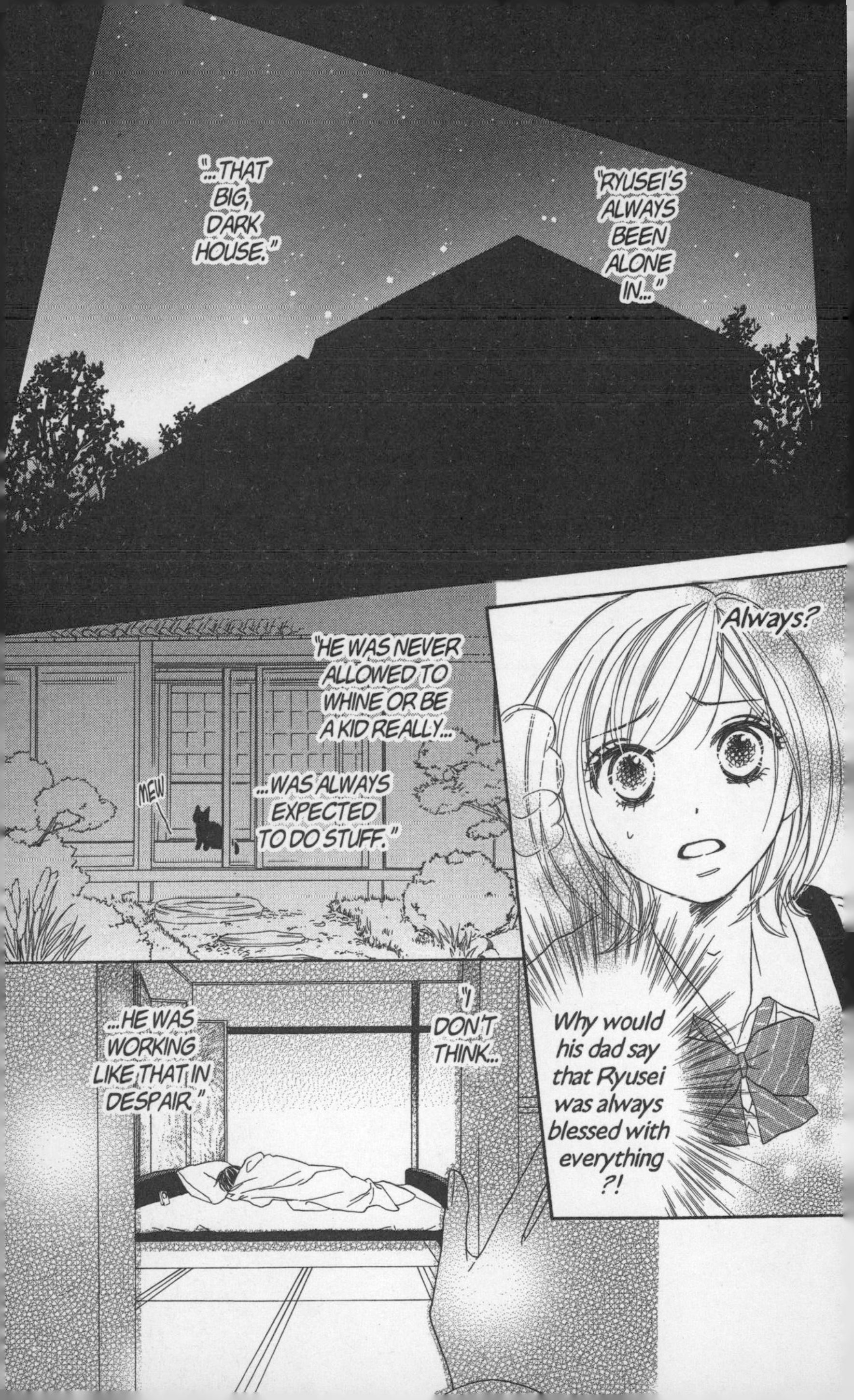
"RYUSEI'S ALWAYS BEEN ALONE IN..."
"...THAT BIG, DARK HOUSE."
Always?
Why would his dad say that Ryusei was always blessed with everything ?!
"HE WAS NEVER ALLOWED TO WHINE OR BE A KID REALLY...
...WAS ALWAYS EXPECTED TO DO STUFF."
MEW
"I DON'T THINK...
...HE WAS WORKING LIKE THAT IN DESPAIR."

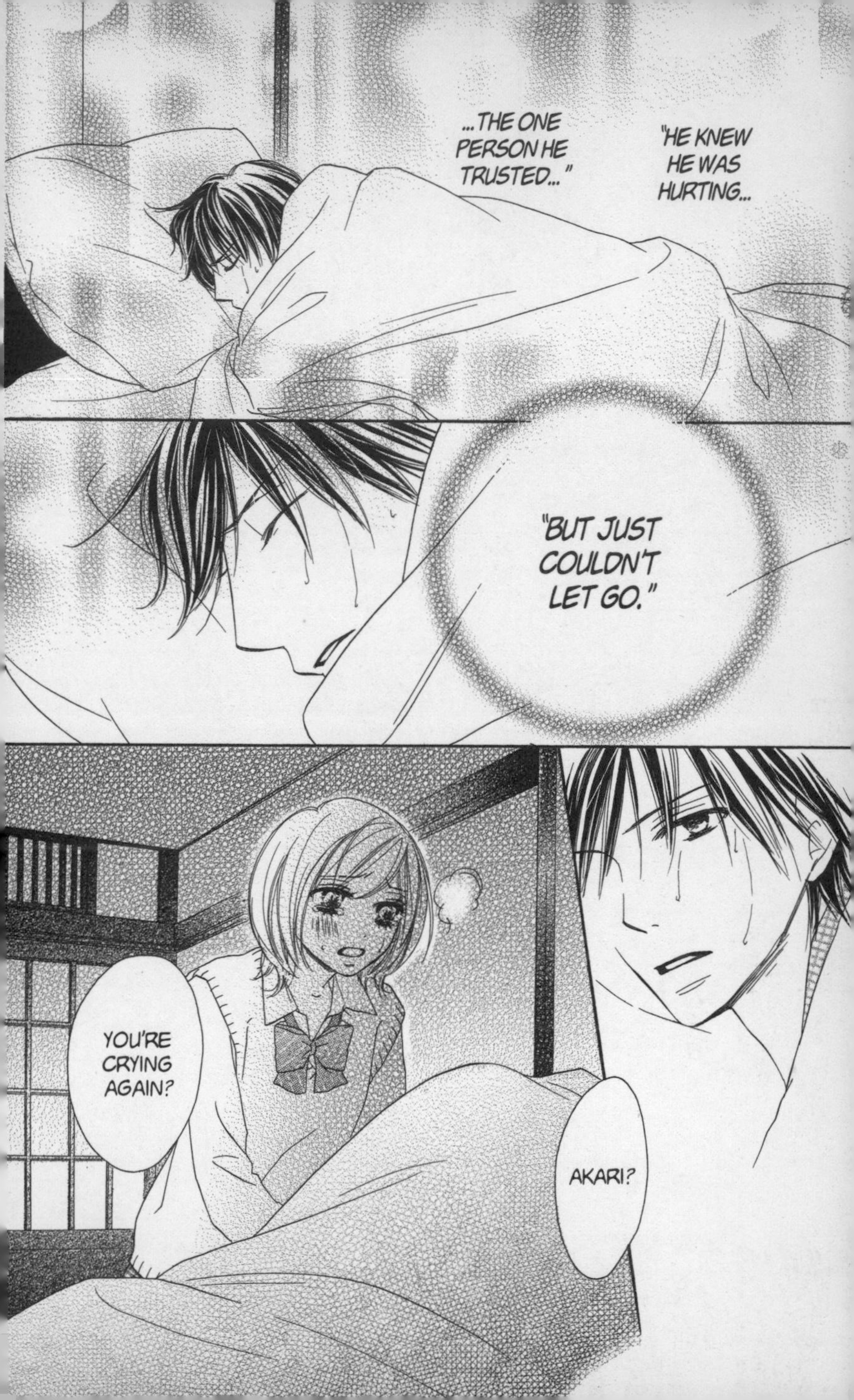
"HE KNEW HE WAS HURTING...
...THE ONE PERSON HE TRUSTED..."
"BUT JUST COULDN'T LET GO."
AKARI?
YOU'RE CRYING AGAIN?

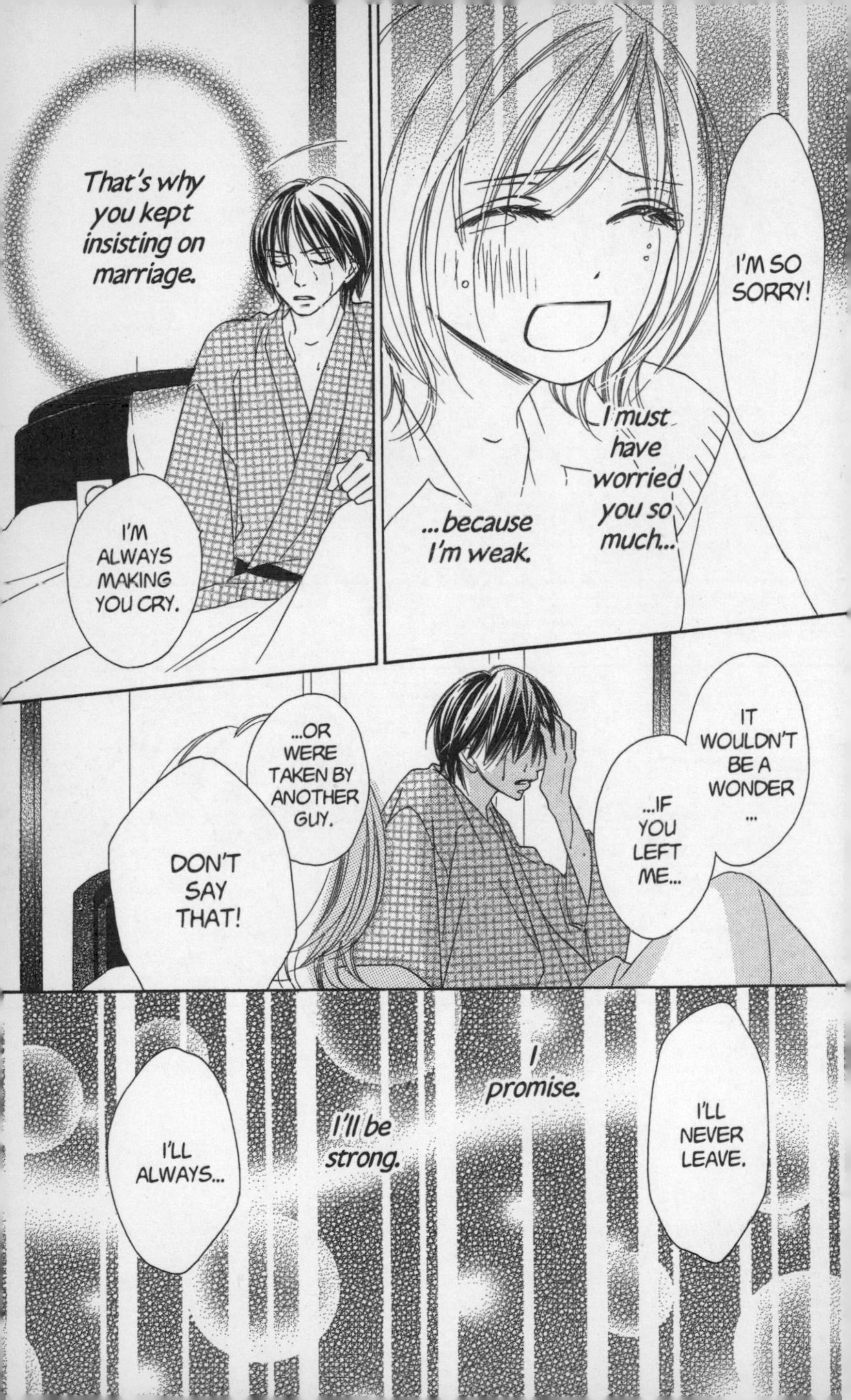
I'M SO SORRY!
I must have worried you so much...
...because I'm weak.
That's why you kept insisting on marriage.
I'M ALWAYS MAKING YOU CRY.
IT WOULDN'T BE A WONDER ...
...IF YOU LEFT ME...
...OR WERE TAKEN BY ANOTHER GUY.
DON'T SAY THAT!
I'LL NEVER LEAVE.
I promise.
I'll be strong.
I'LL ALWAYS...

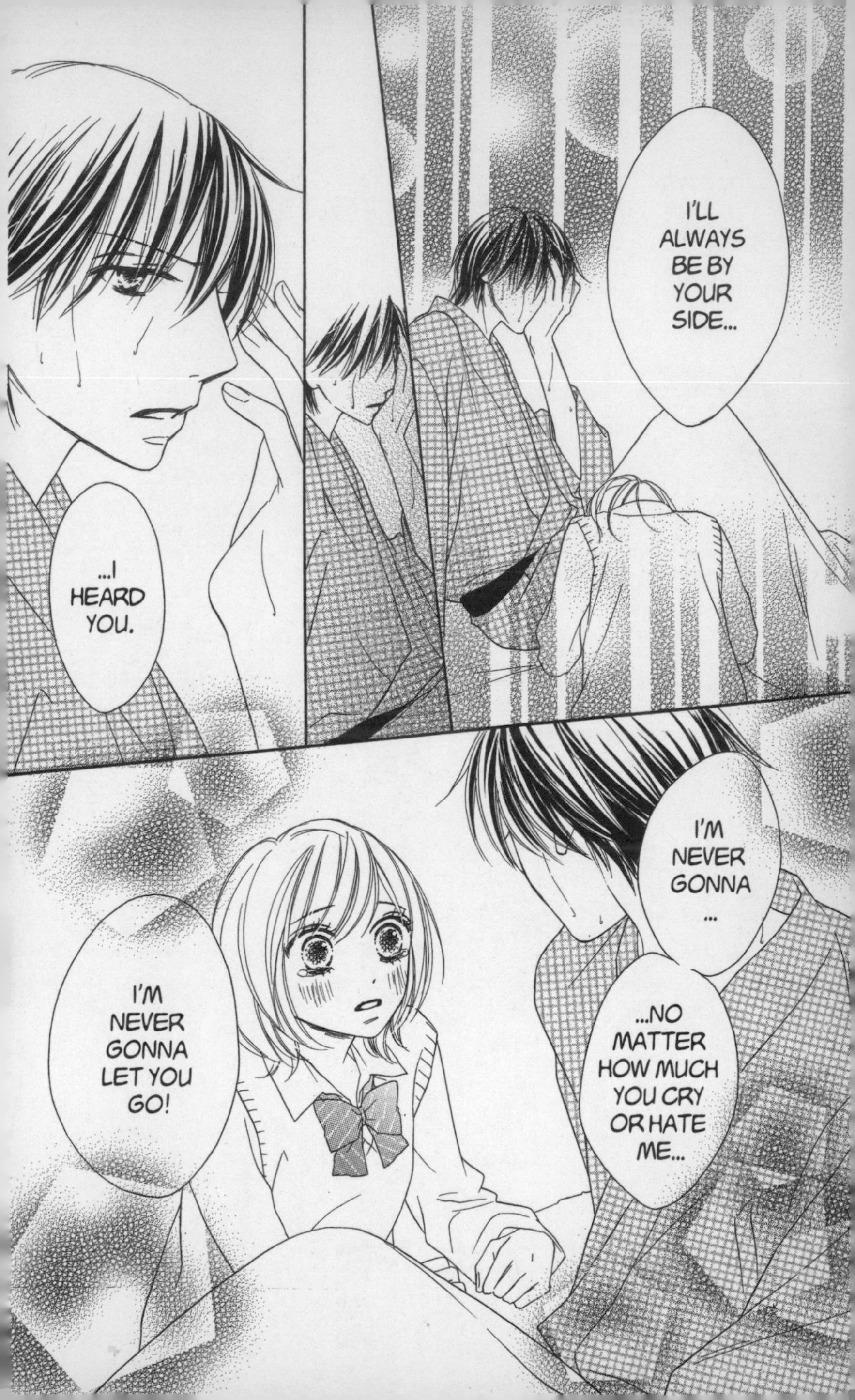
I'LL ALWAYS BE BY YOUR SIDE...
...I HEARD YOU.
I'M NEVER GONNA ...
...NO MATTER HOW MUCH YOU CRY OR HATE ME...
I'M NEVER GONNA LET YOU GO!

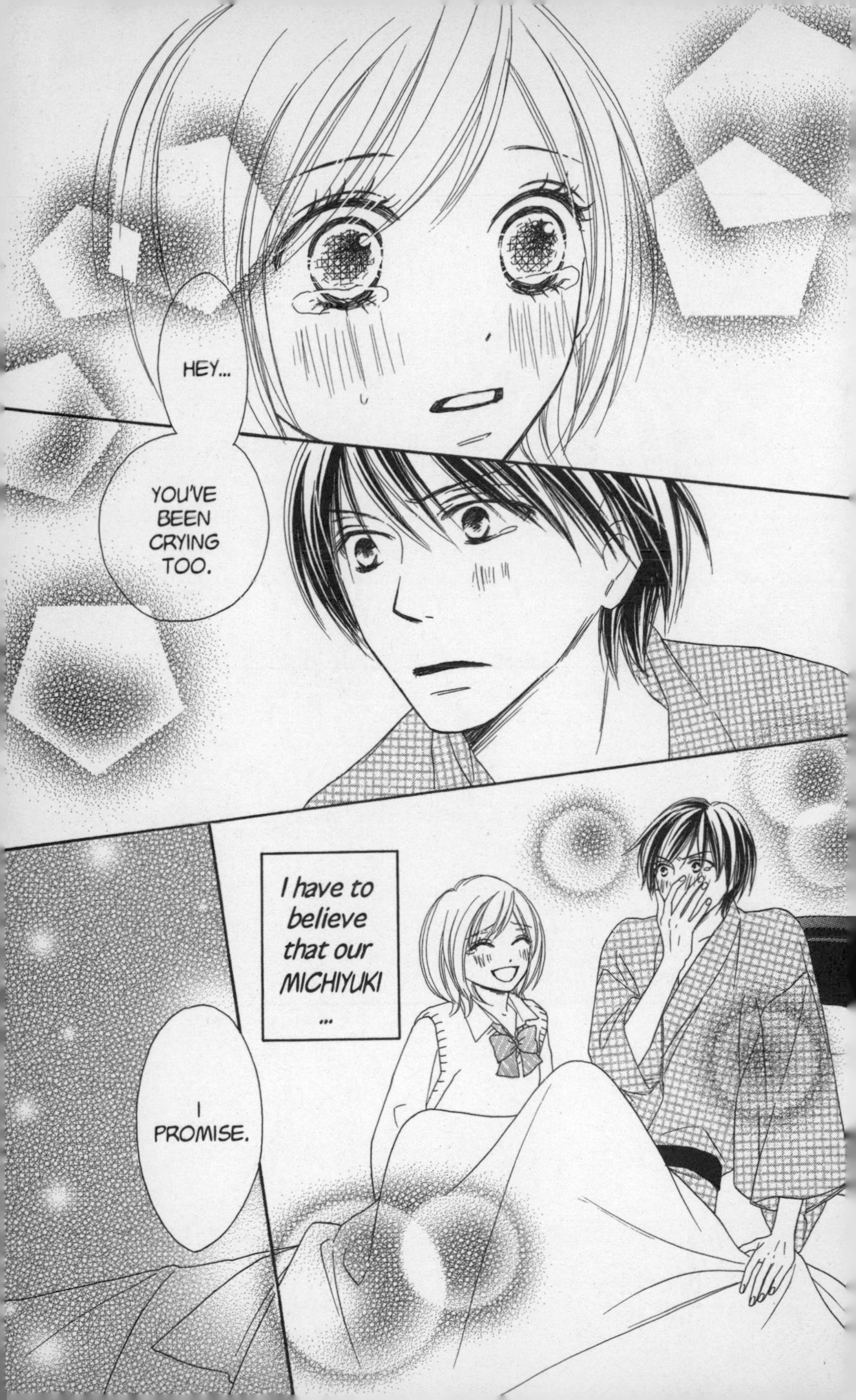
HEY...
YOU'VE BEEN CRYING TOO.
I have to believe that our MICHIYUKI ...
I PROMISE.

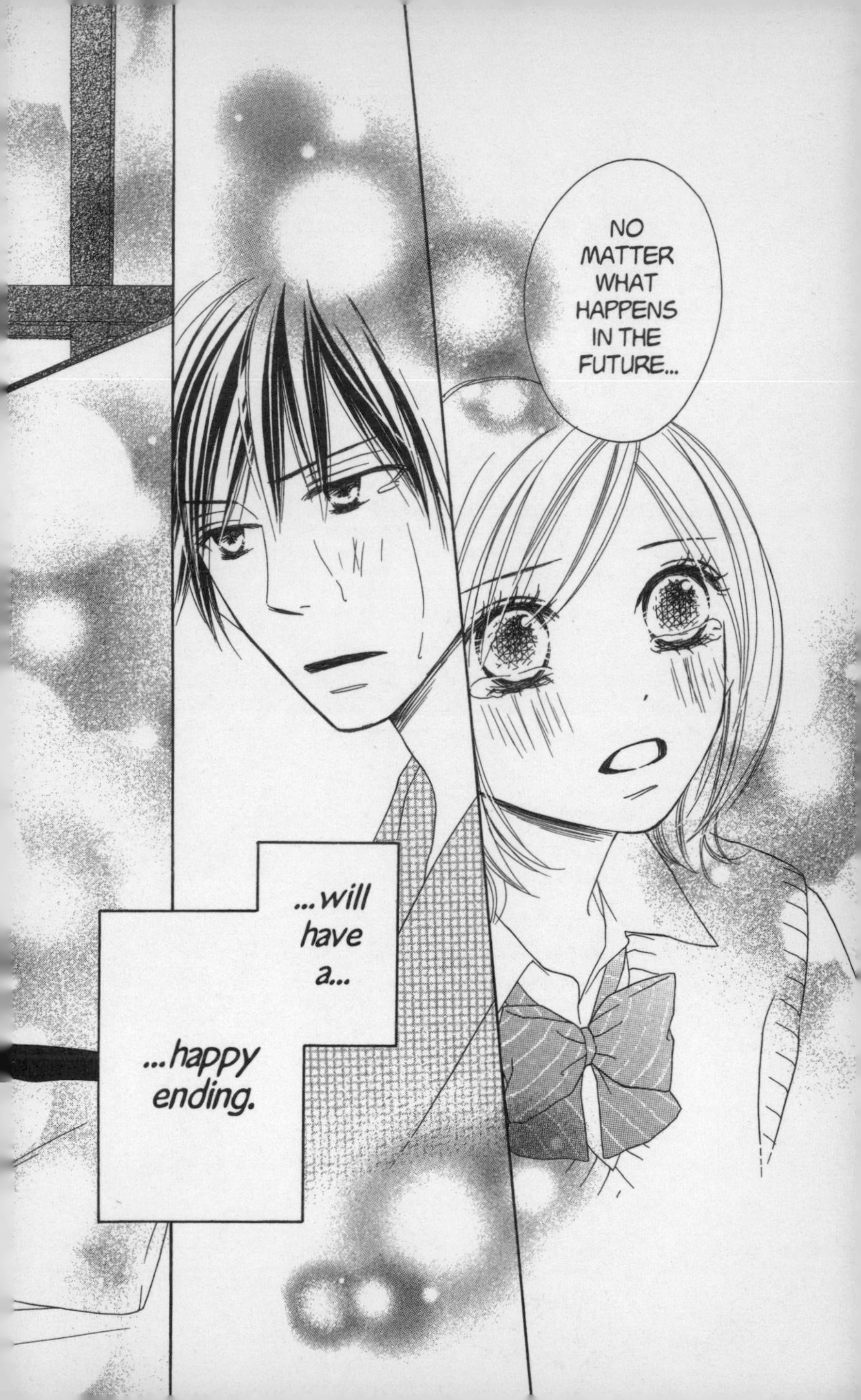
NO MATTER WHAT HAPPENS IN THE FUTURE...
...will have a...
...happy ending.

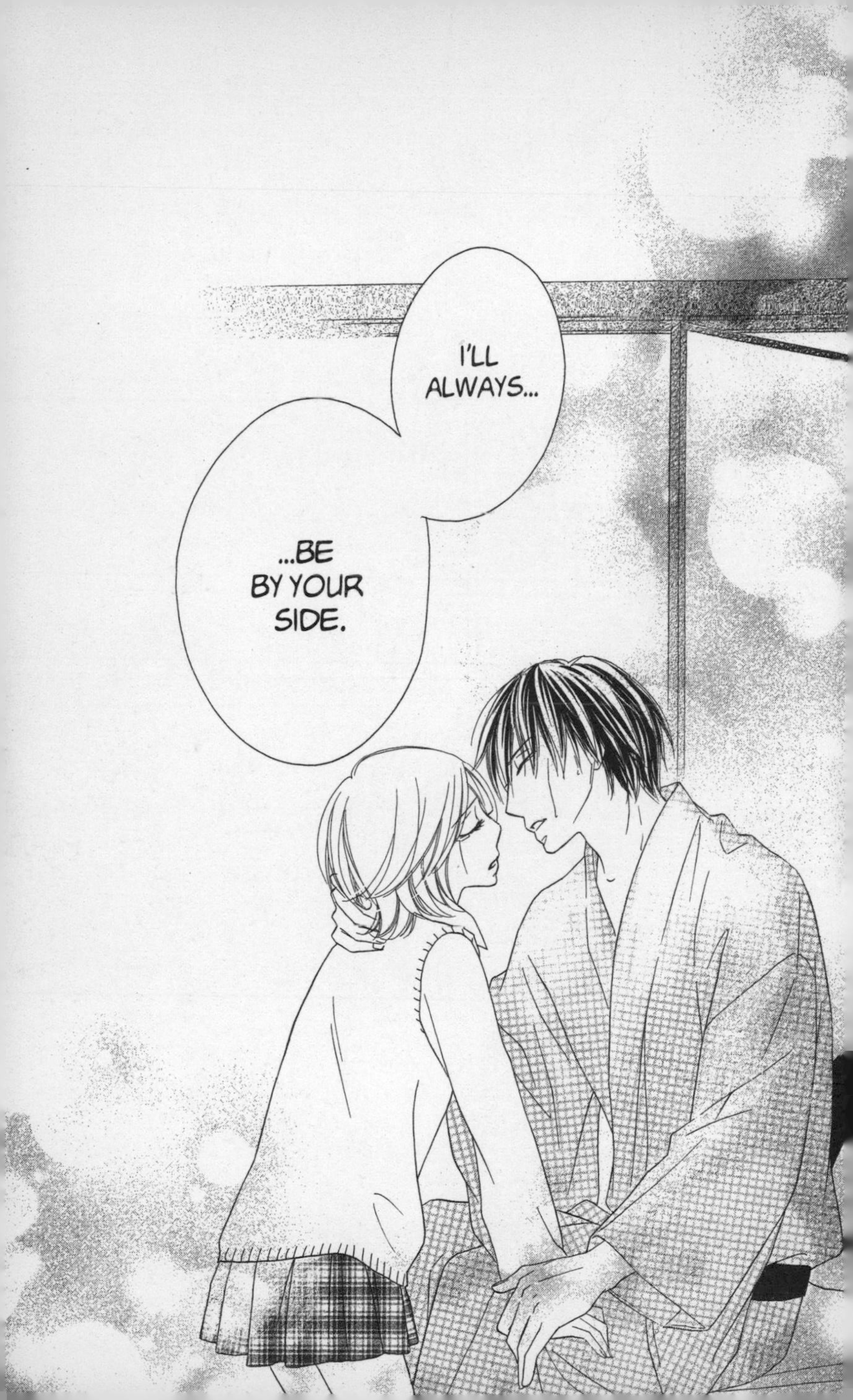
I'LL ALWAYS...
...BE BY YOUR SIDE.

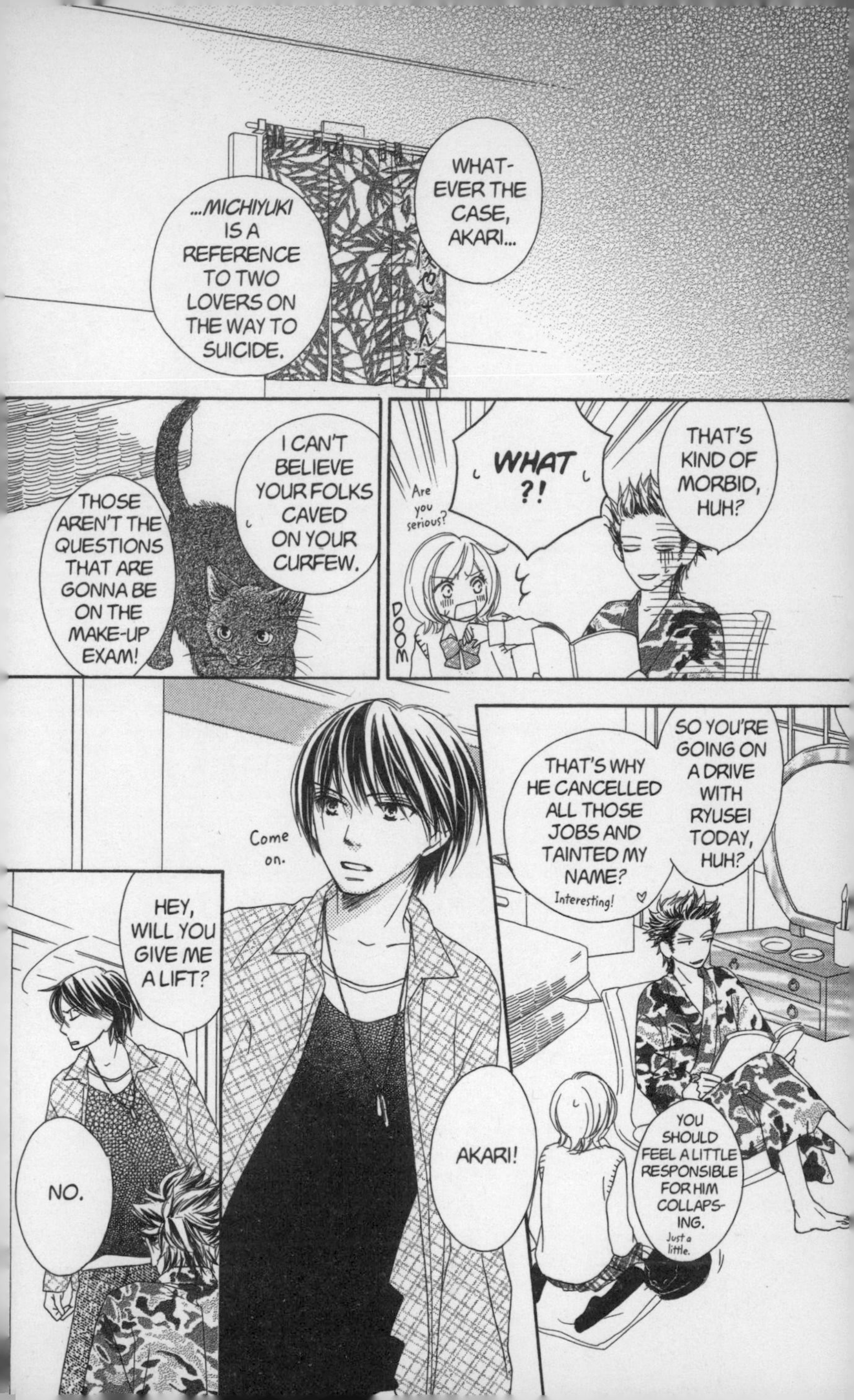
WHAT-EVER THE CASE, AKARI...
...MICHIYUKI IS A REFERENCE TO TWO LOVERS ON THE WAY TO SUICIDE.
THAT'S KIND OF MORBID, HUH?
WHAT?!
Are you serious?
DOOM
I CAN'T BELIEVE YOUR FOLKS CAVED ON YOUR CURFEW.
THOSE AREN'T THE QUESTIONS THAT ARE GONNA BE ON THE MAKE-UP EXAM!
SO YOU'RE GOING ON A DRIVE WITH RYUSEI TODAY, HUH?
THAT'S WHY HE CANCELLED ALL THOSE JOBS AND TAINTED MY NAME?
Interesting!
YOU SHOULD FEEL A LITTLE RESPONSIBLE FOR HIM COLLAPSING.
Just a little.
AKARI!
Come on.
HEY, WILL YOU GIVE ME A LIFT?
NO.

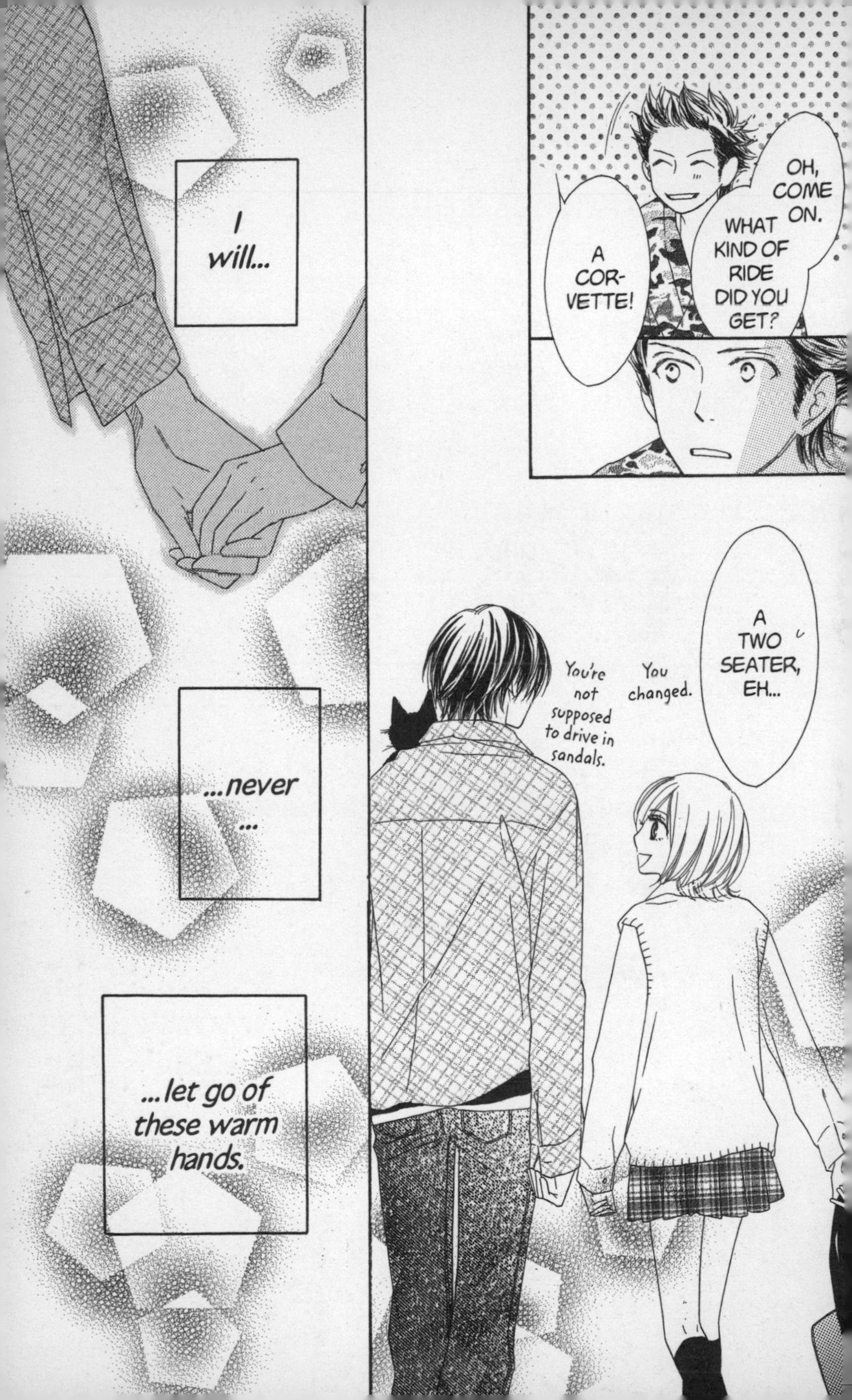
OH, COME ON.
WHAT KIND OF RIDE DID YOU GET?
A COR-VETTE!
A TWO SEATER, EH...
You changed.
You're not supposed to drive in sandals.
I will...
...never...
...let go of these warm hands.

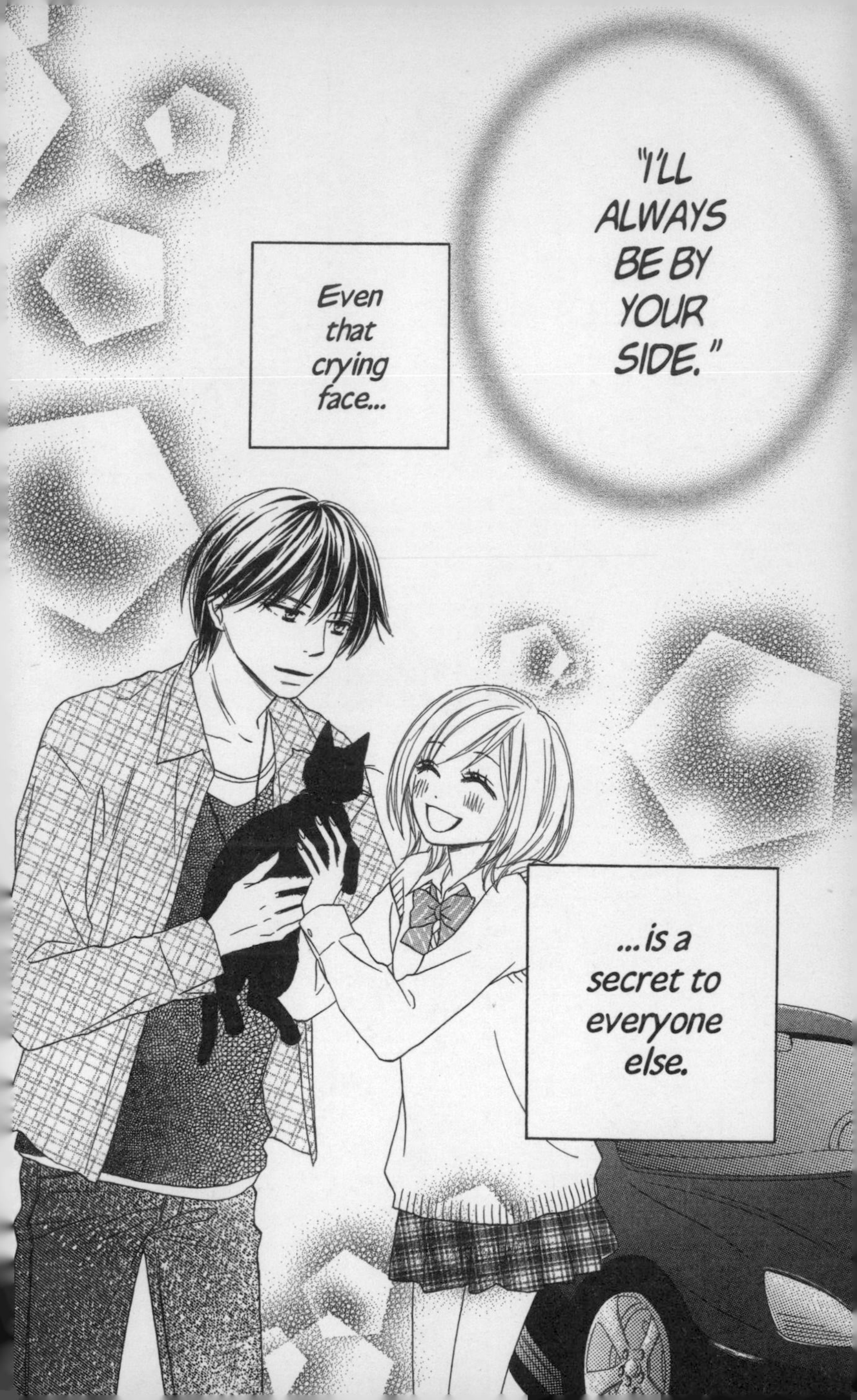
"I'LL ALWAYS BE BY YOUR SIDE."
Even that crying face...
...is a secret to everyone else.

HELLO.

THANK YOU VERY MUCH FOR
READING BACKSTAGE PRINCE.

I WISH YOU ALL HAPPINESS...

♥

Open wide.

Here ya go.

RED BEAN SOUP

Seconds, please.

THIS LOOKS LIKE A POSTCARD MY
GRANDFATHER WOULD SEND...

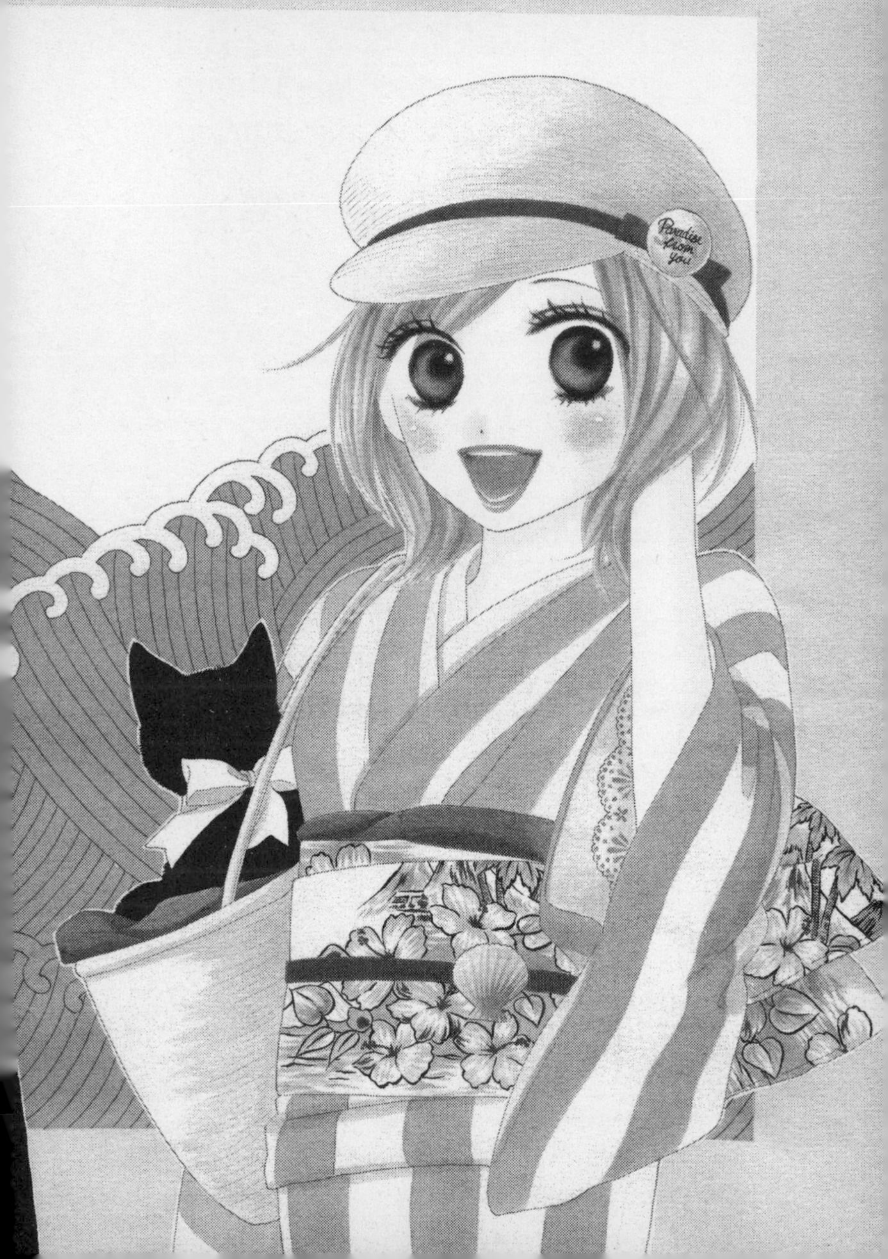
Paradise from you

ACT 2: THE SECRET OPTIONAL TOUR IN KYOTO

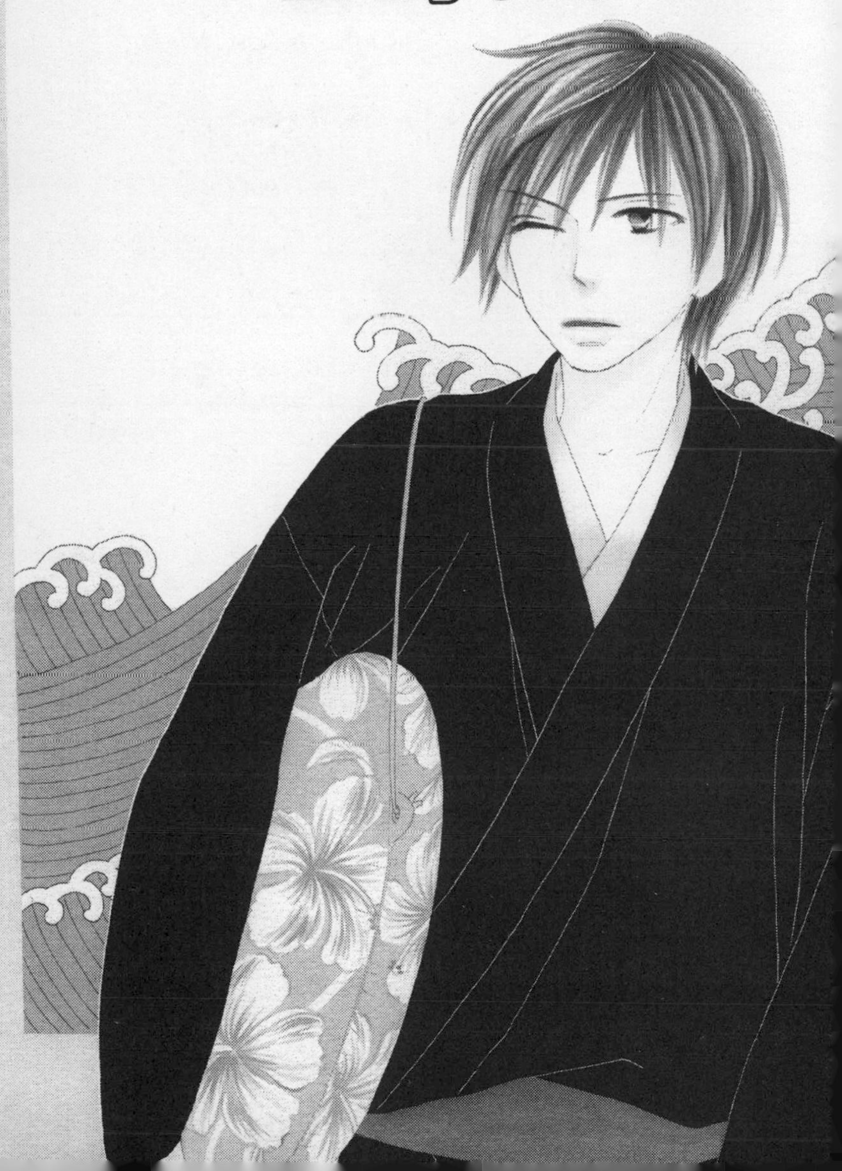

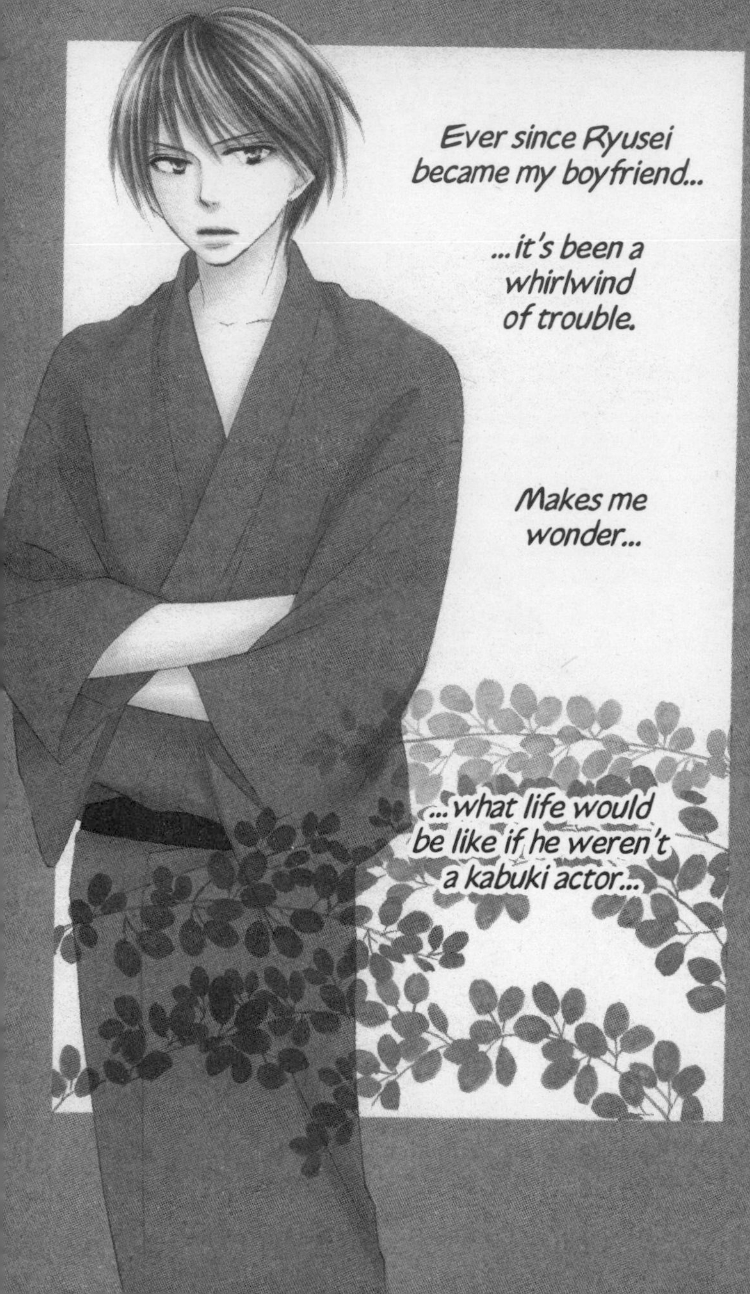
Ever since Ryusei became my boyfriend...
...it's been a whirlwind of trouble.
Makes me wonder...
...what life would be like if he weren't a kabuki actor...

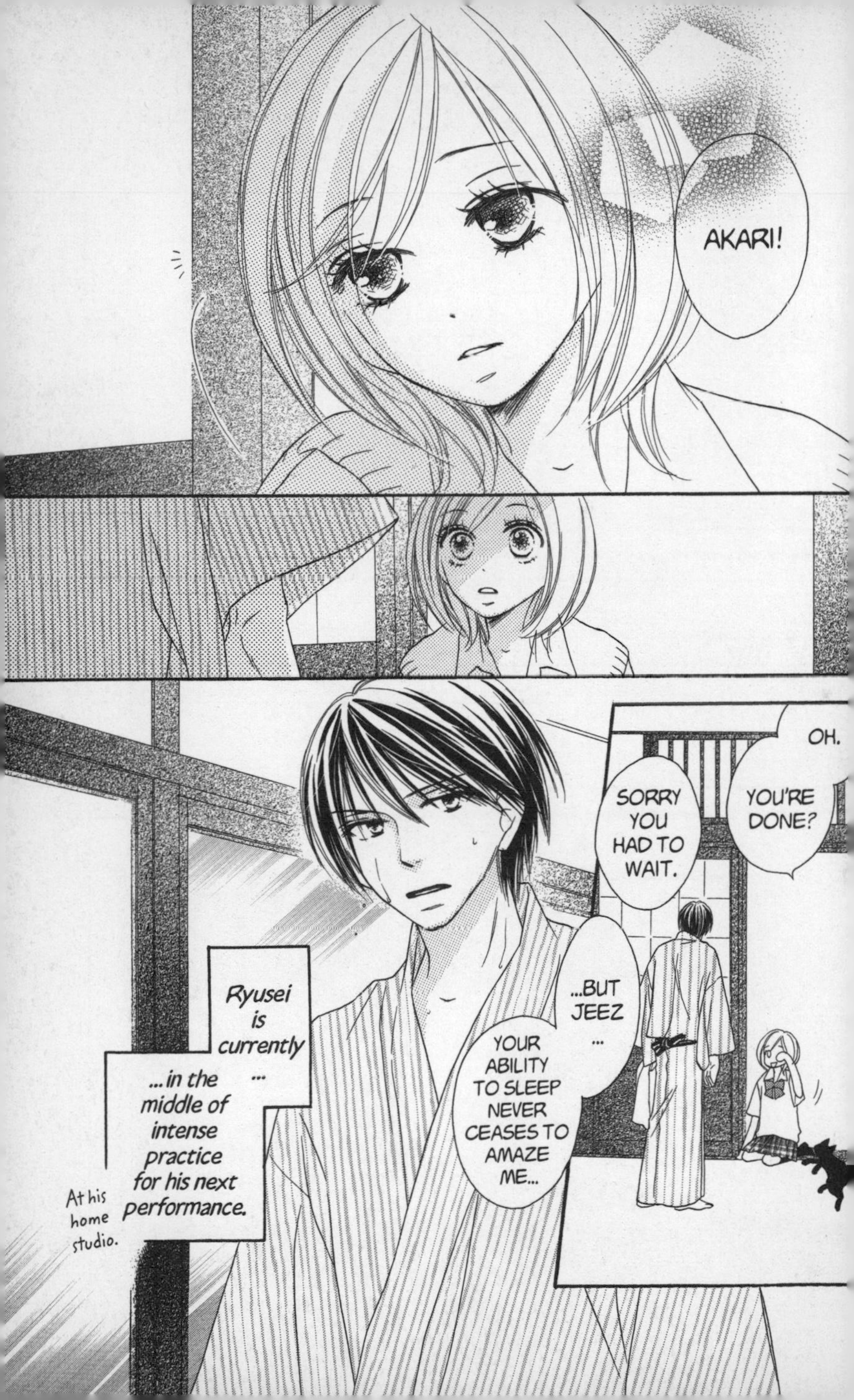
AKARI!
OH.
YOU'RE DONE?
SORRY YOU HAD TO WAIT.
...BUT JEEZ ...
YOUR ABILITY TO SLEEP NEVER CEASES TO AMAZE ME...
Ryusei is currently ...
...in the middle of intense practice for his next performance.
At his home studio.

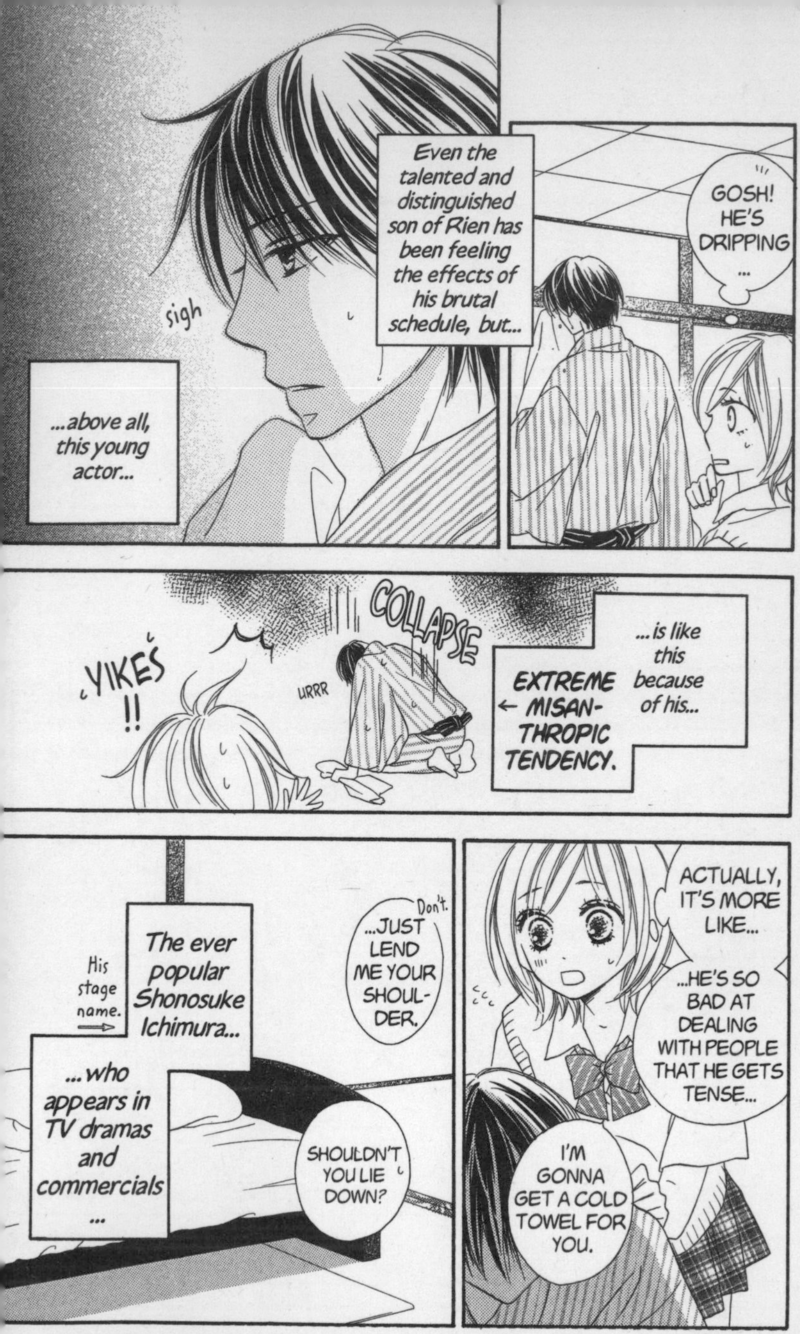
GOSH! HE'S DRIPPING ...
Even the talented and distinguished son of Rien has been feeling the effects of his brutal schedule, but...
sigh
...above all, this young actor...
...is like this because of his...
EXTREME MISAN-THROPIC TENDENCY.
COLLAPSE
URRR
YIKES !!
ACTUALLY, IT'S MORE LIKE...
...HE'S SO BAD AT DEALING WITH PEOPLE THAT HE GETS TENSE...
I'M GONNA GET A COLD TOWEL FOR YOU.
The ever popular Shonosuke Ichimura...
His stage name.
...who appears in TV dramas and commercials ...
SHOULDN'T YOU LIE DOWN?
Don't.
...JUST LEND ME YOUR SHOUL-DER.

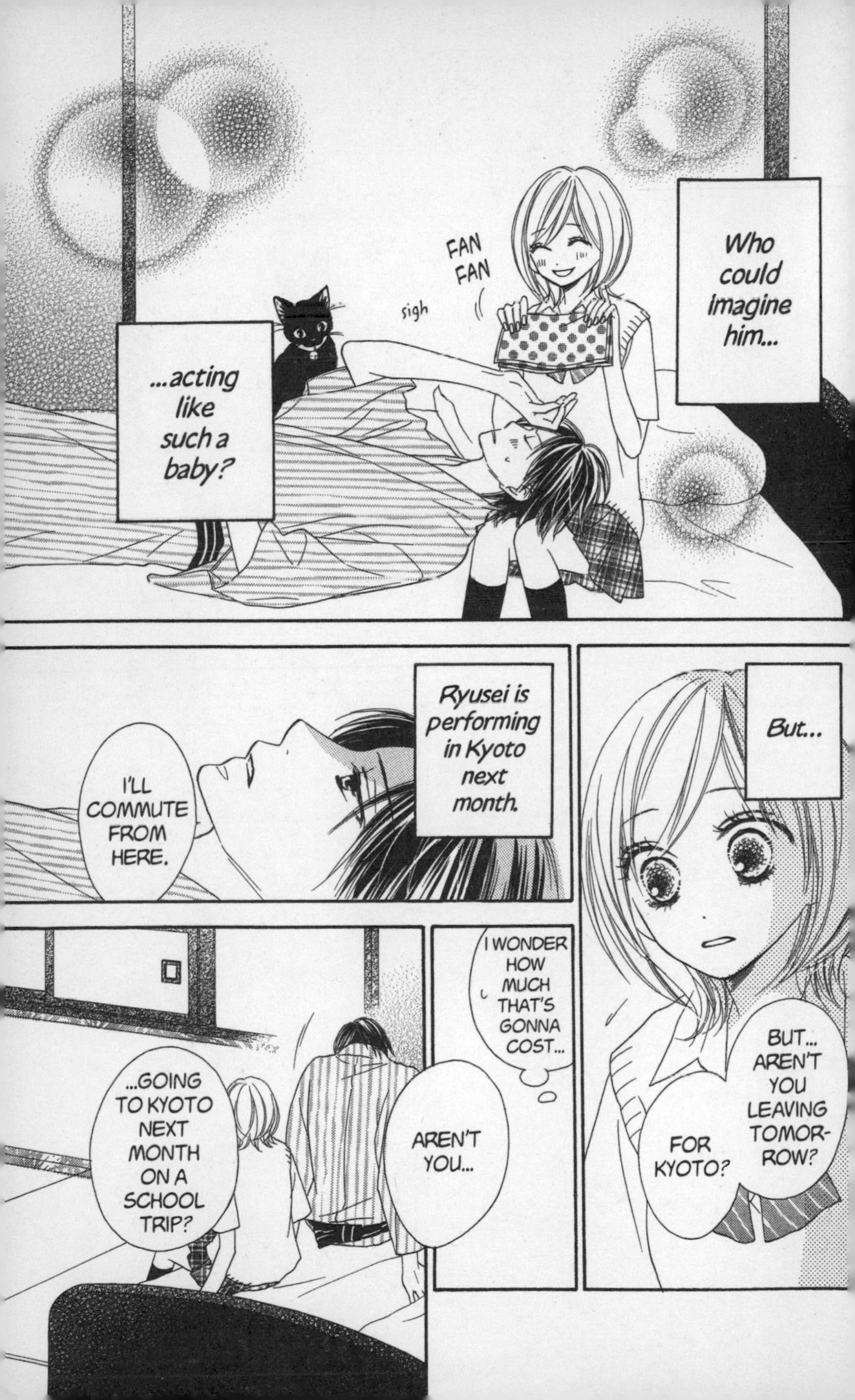
Who could imagine him...
FAN FAN
sigh
...acting like such a baby?
But...
BUT... AREN'T YOU LEAVING TOMOR-ROW?
FOR KYOTO?
Ryusei is performing in Kyoto next month.
I'LL COMMUTE FROM HERE.
I WONDER HOW MUCH THAT'S GONNA COST...
AREN'T YOU...
...GOING TO KYOTO NEXT MONTH ON A SCHOOL TRIP?

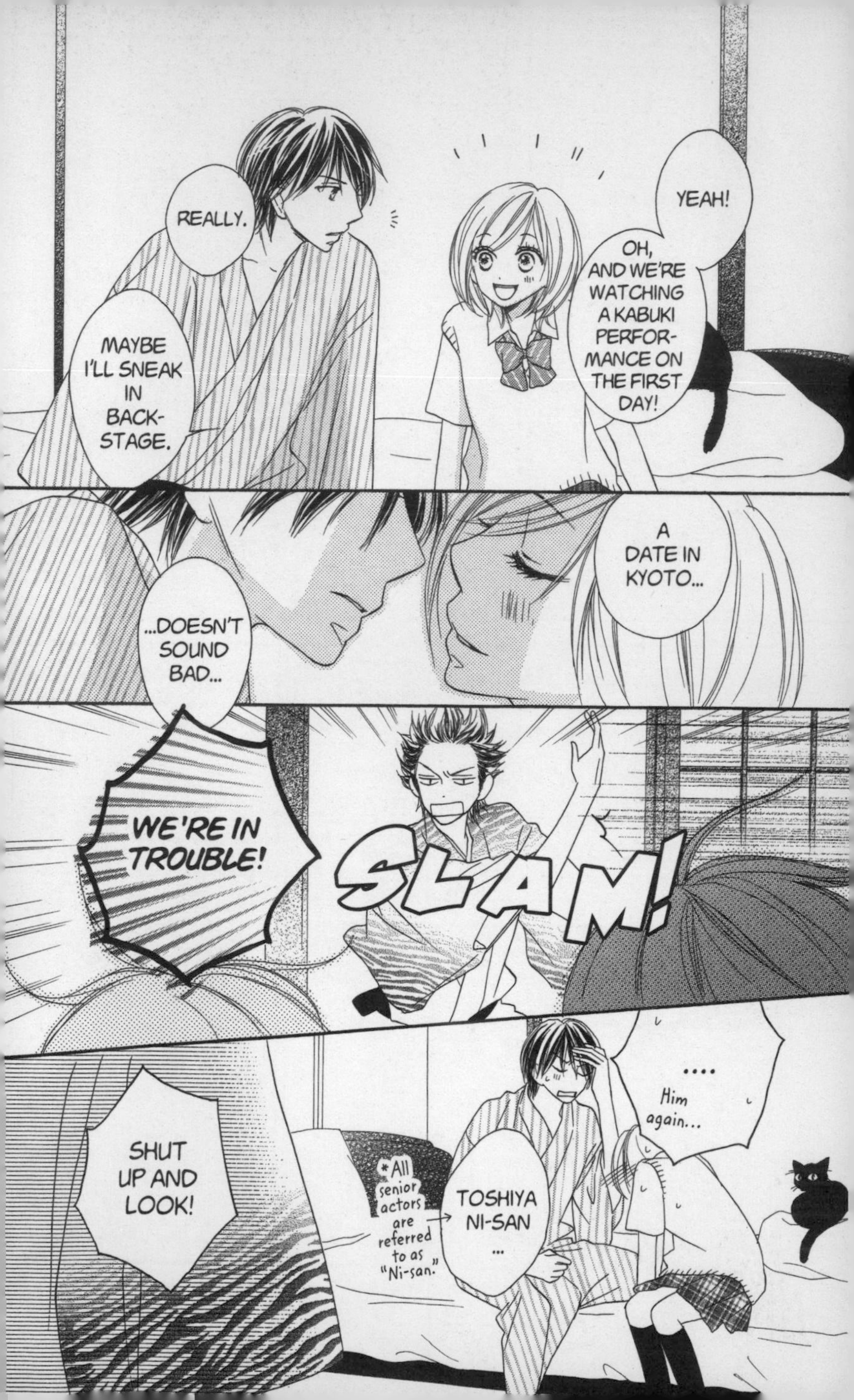
YEAH!
OH, AND WE'RE WATCHING A KABUKI PERFORMANCE ON THE FIRST DAY!
REALLY.
MAYBE I'LL SNEAK IN BACKSTAGE.
A DATE IN KYOTO...
...DOESN'T SOUND BAD...
SLAM!
WE'RE IN TROUBLE!
....
Him again...
TOSHIYA NI-SAN ...
*All senior actors are referred to as "Ni-san."
SHUT UP AND LOOK!

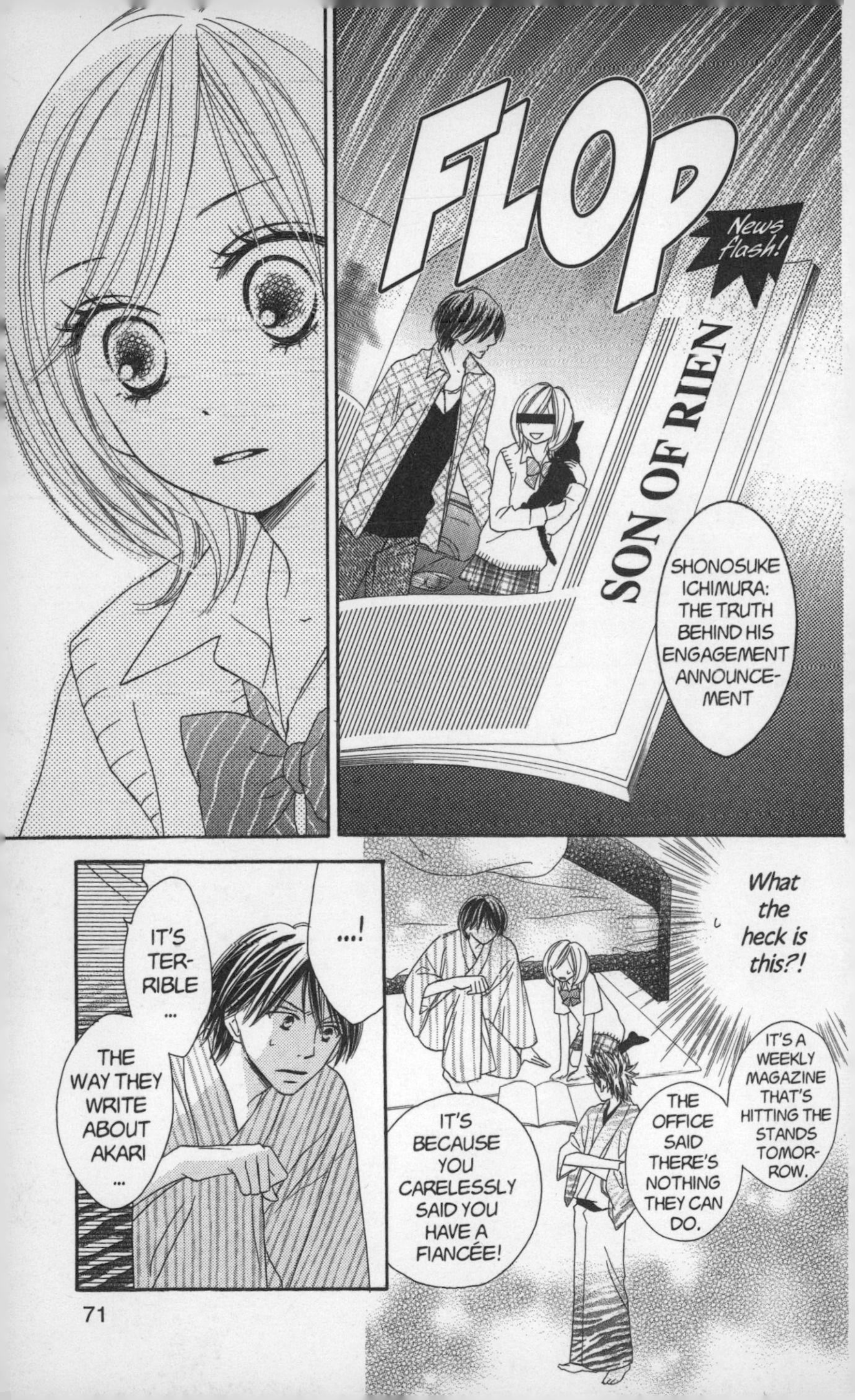
FLOP
News flash!
SON OF RIEN
SHONOSUKE ICHIMURA: THE TRUTH BEHIND HIS ENGAGEMENT ANNOUNCE-MENT
What the heck is this?!
IT'S A WEEKLY MAGAZINE THAT'S HITTING THE STANDS TOMOR-ROW.
THE OFFICE SAID THERE'S NOTHING THEY CAN DO.
IT'S BECAUSE YOU CARELESSLY SAID YOU HAVE A FIANCÉE!
...!
IT'S TER-RIBLE ...
THE WAY THEY WRITE ABOUT AKARI ...

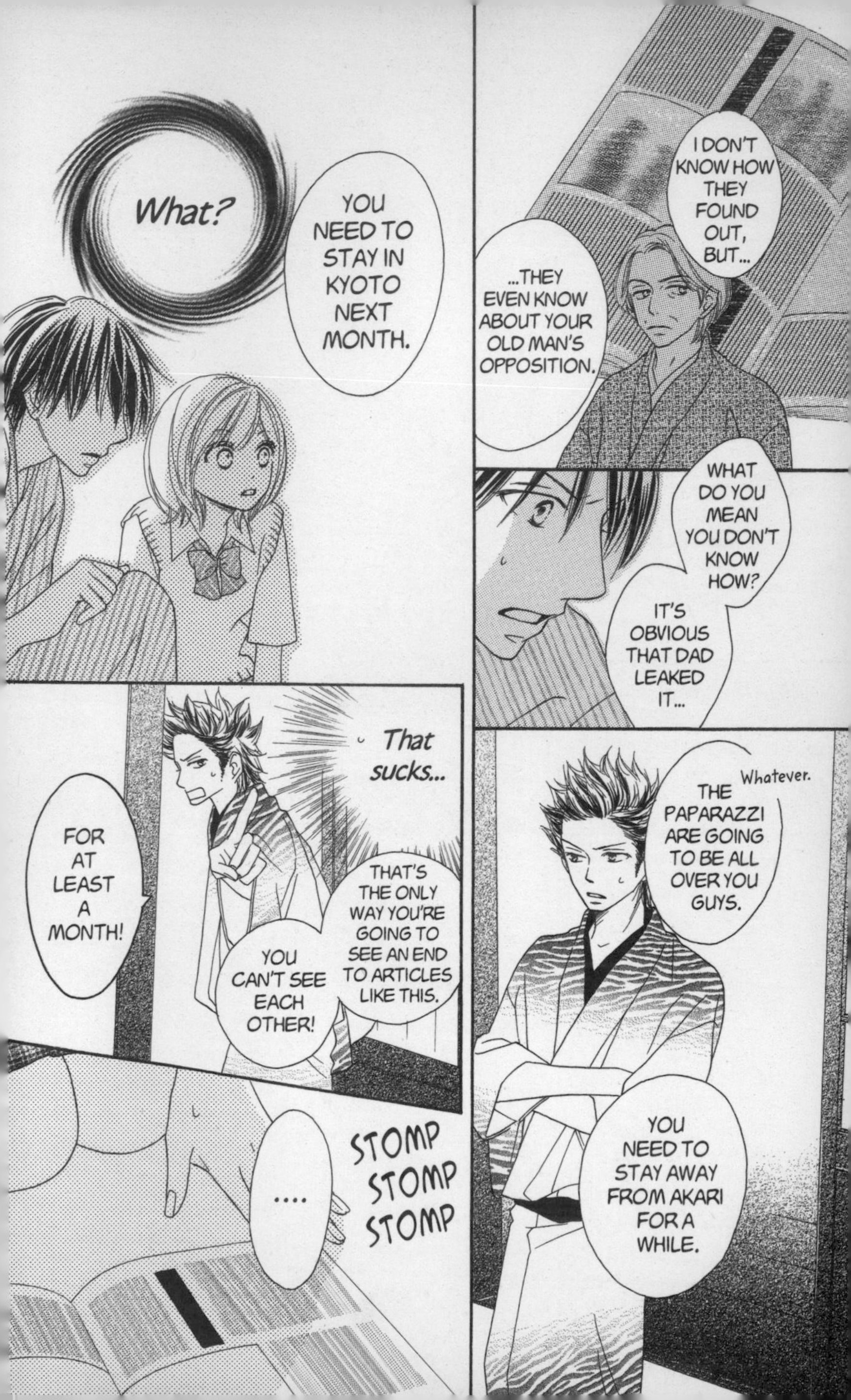
I DON'T KNOW HOW THEY FOUND OUT, BUT...
...THEY EVEN KNOW ABOUT YOUR OLD MAN'S OPPOSITION.
WHAT DO YOU MEAN YOU DON'T KNOW HOW?
IT'S OBVIOUS THAT DAD LEAKED IT...
Whatever.
THE PAPARAZZI ARE GOING TO BE ALL OVER YOU GUYS.
YOU NEED TO STAY AWAY FROM AKARI FOR A WHILE.
YOU NEED TO STAY IN KYOTO NEXT MONTH.
What?
That sucks...
THAT'S THE ONLY WAY YOU'RE GOING TO SEE AN END TO ARTICLES LIKE THIS.
YOU CAN'T SEE EACH OTHER!
FOR AT LEAST A MONTH!
....
STOMP STOMP STOMP

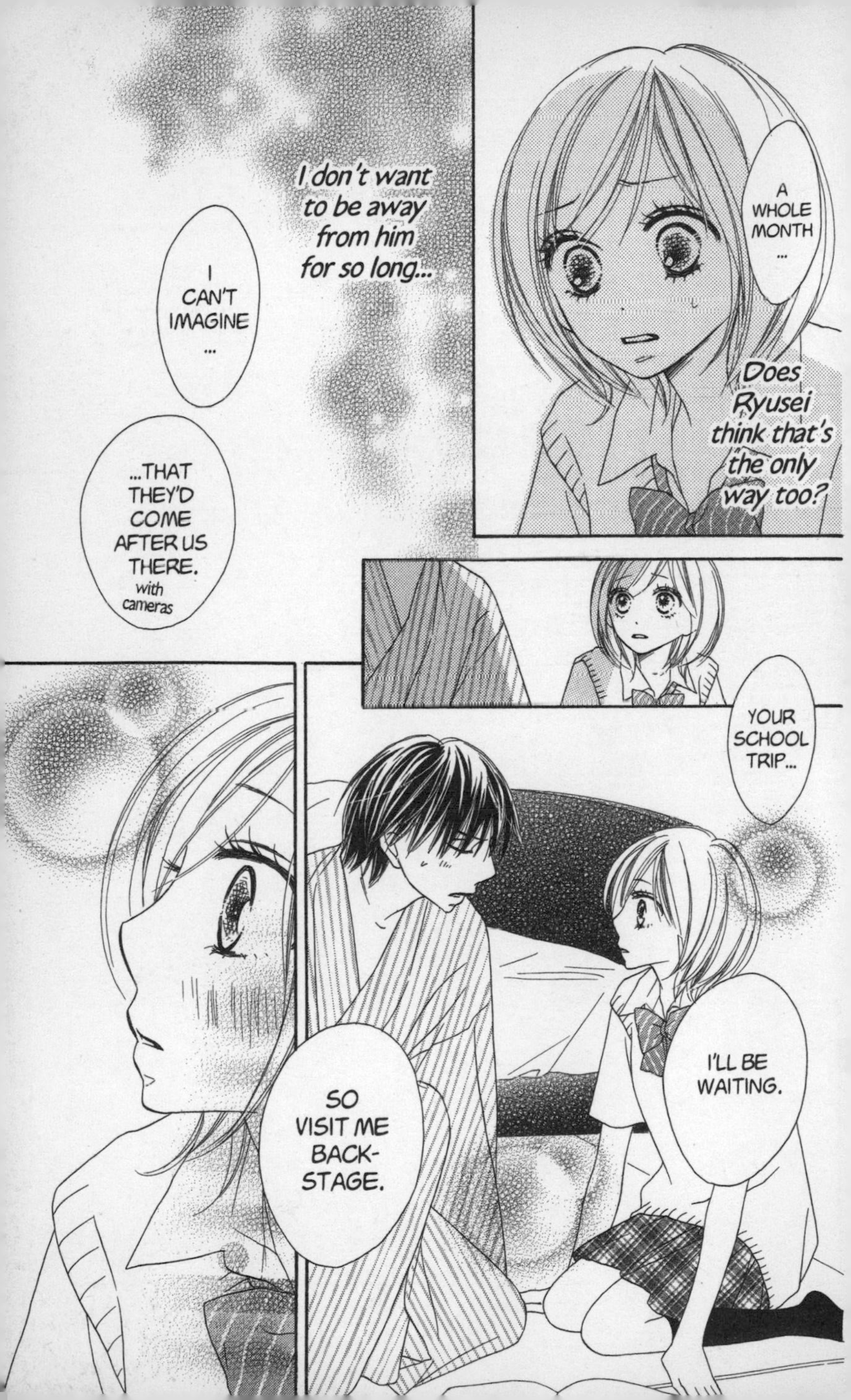
A WHOLE MONTH...
Does Ryusei think that's the only way too?
I don't want to be away from him for so long...
I CAN'T IMAGINE...
...THAT THEY'D COME AFTER US THERE.
with cameras
YOUR SCHOOL TRIP...
I'LL BE WAITING.
SO VISIT ME BACKSTAGE.

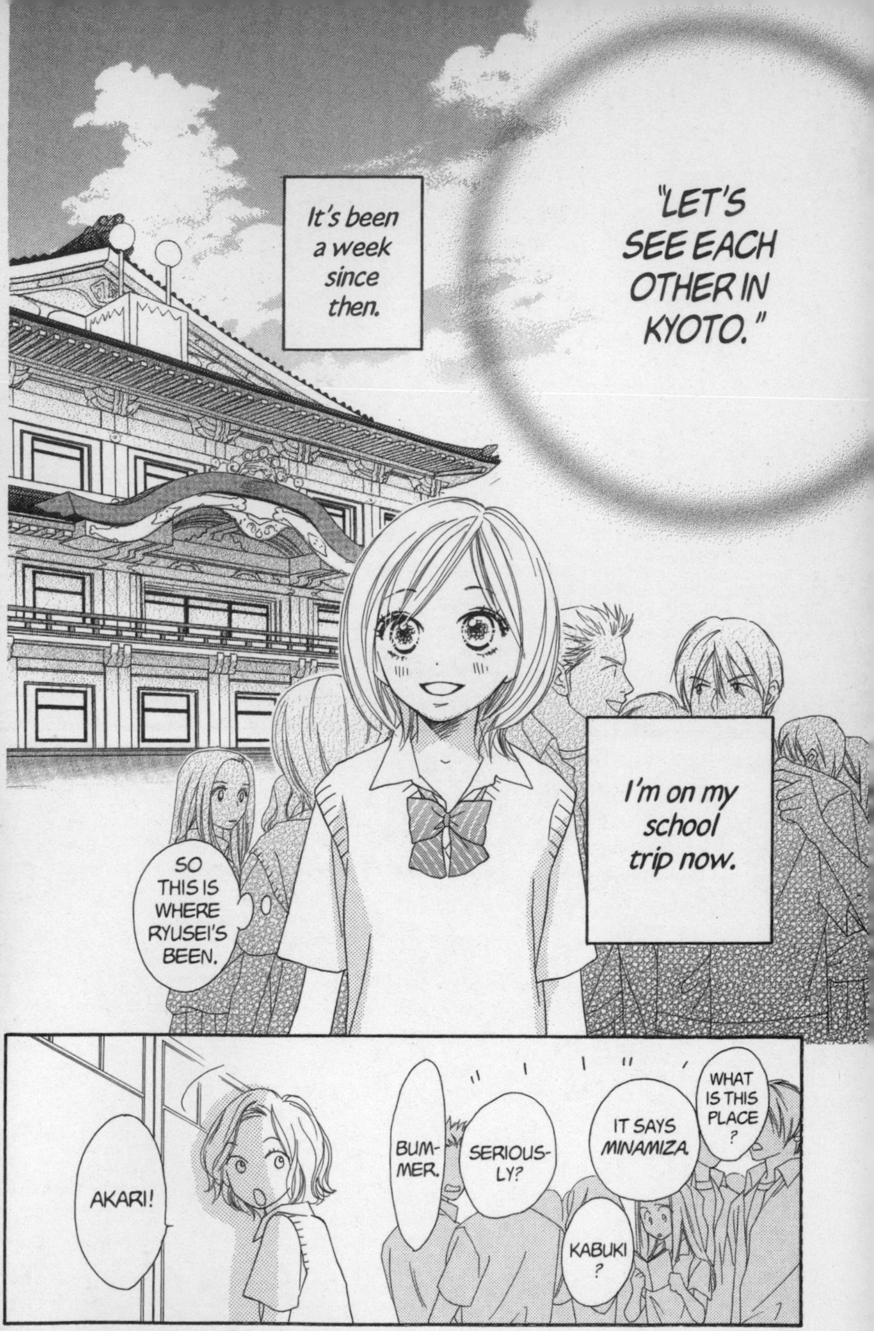
"LET'S SEE EACH OTHER IN KYOTO."
It's been a week since then.
I'm on my school trip now.
SO THIS IS WHERE RYUSEI'S BEEN.
WHAT IS THIS PLACE?
IT SAYS MINAMIZA.
KABUKI?
SERIOUSLY?
BUMMER.
AKARI!

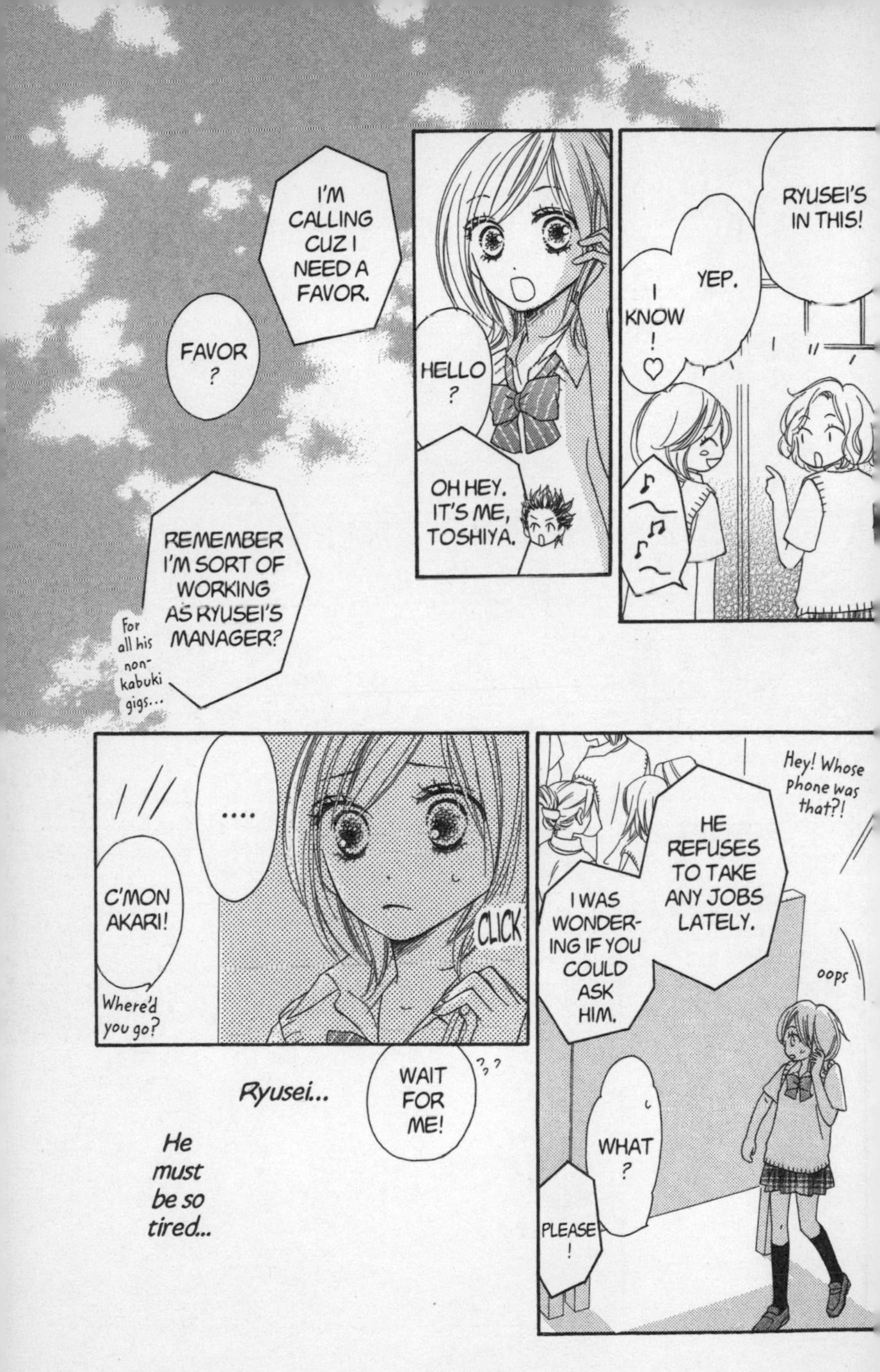
RYUSEI'S IN THIS!
YEP.
I KNOW! ♡
HELLO?
OH HEY. IT'S ME, TOSHIYA.
I'M CALLING CUZ I NEED A FAVOR.
FAVOR?
REMEMBER I'M SORT OF WORKING AS RYUSEI'S MANAGER?
For all his non-kabuki gigs...
Hey! Whose phone was that?!
oops
HE REFUSES TO TAKE ANY JOBS LATELY.
I WAS WONDERING IF YOU COULD ASK HIM.
WHAT?
PLEASE!
....
CLICK
C'MON AKARI!
Where'd you go?
WAIT FOR ME!
Ryusei...
He must be so tired...

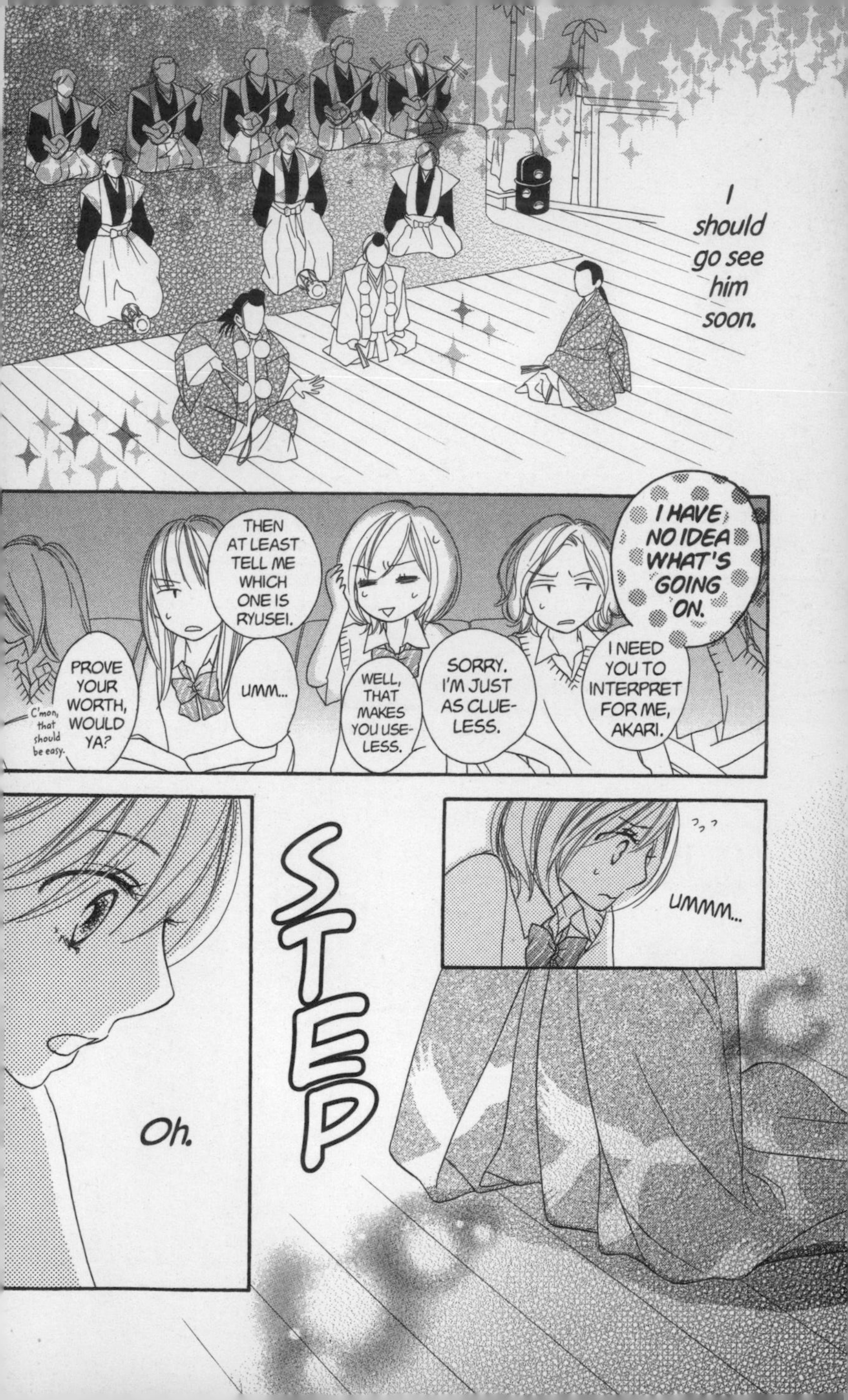
I should go see him soon.
I HAVE NO IDEA WHAT'S GOING ON.
I NEED YOU TO INTERPRET FOR ME, AKARI.
SORRY. I'M JUST AS CLUE-LESS.
WELL, THAT MAKES YOU USE-LESS.
THEN AT LEAST TELL ME WHICH ONE IS RYUSEI.
UMM...
PROVE YOUR WORTH, WOULD YA?
C'mon, that should be easy.
UMMM...
STEP
Oh.

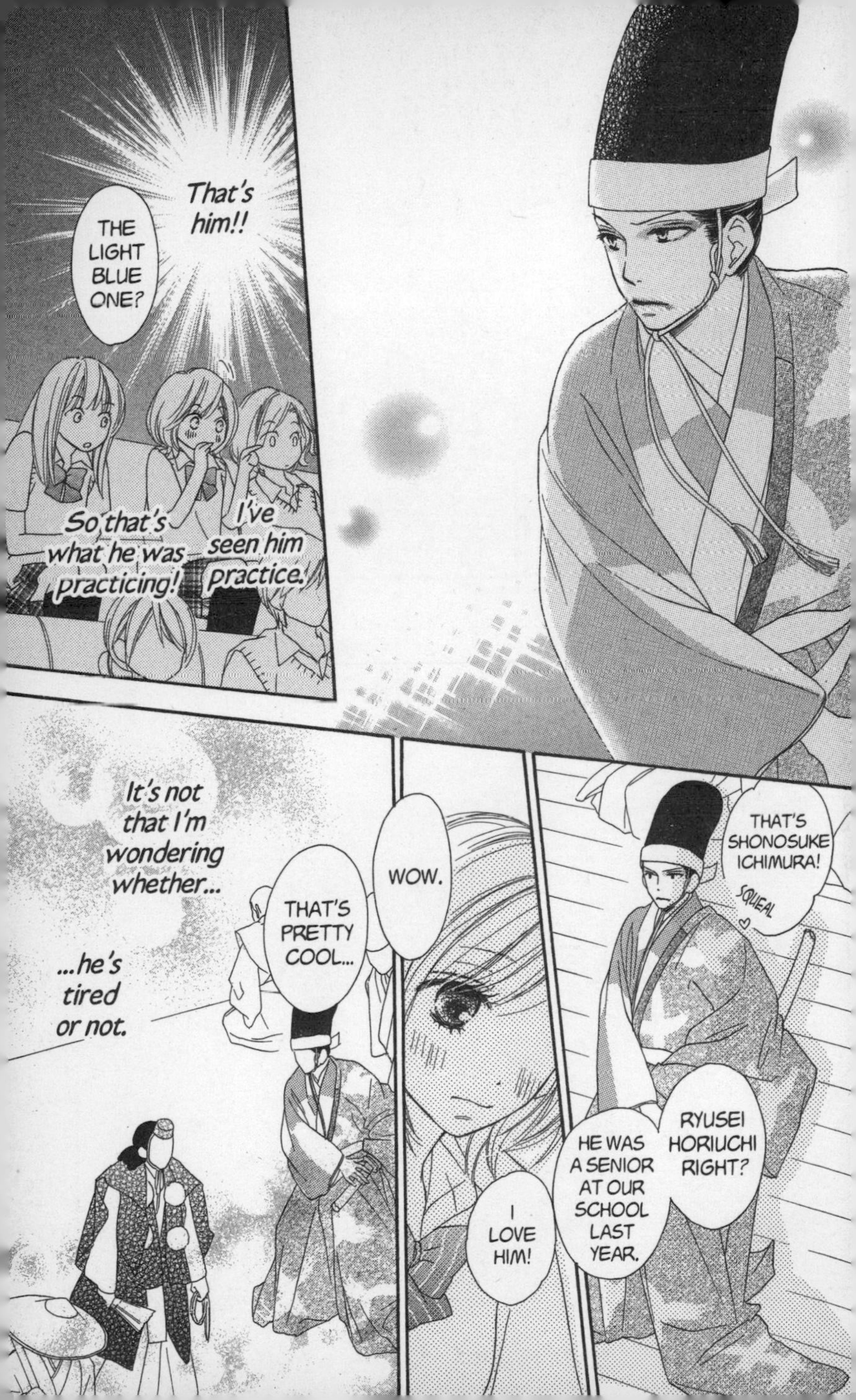
That's him!!
THE LIGHT BLUE ONE?
I've seen him practice.
So that's what he was practicing!
THAT'S SHONOSUKE ICHIMURA!
SQUEAL ♡
RYUSEI HORIUCHI RIGHT?
HE WAS A SENIOR AT OUR SCHOOL LAST YEAR.
I LOVE HIM!
WOW.
THAT'S PRETTY COOL...
It's not that I'm wondering whether...
...he's tired or not.

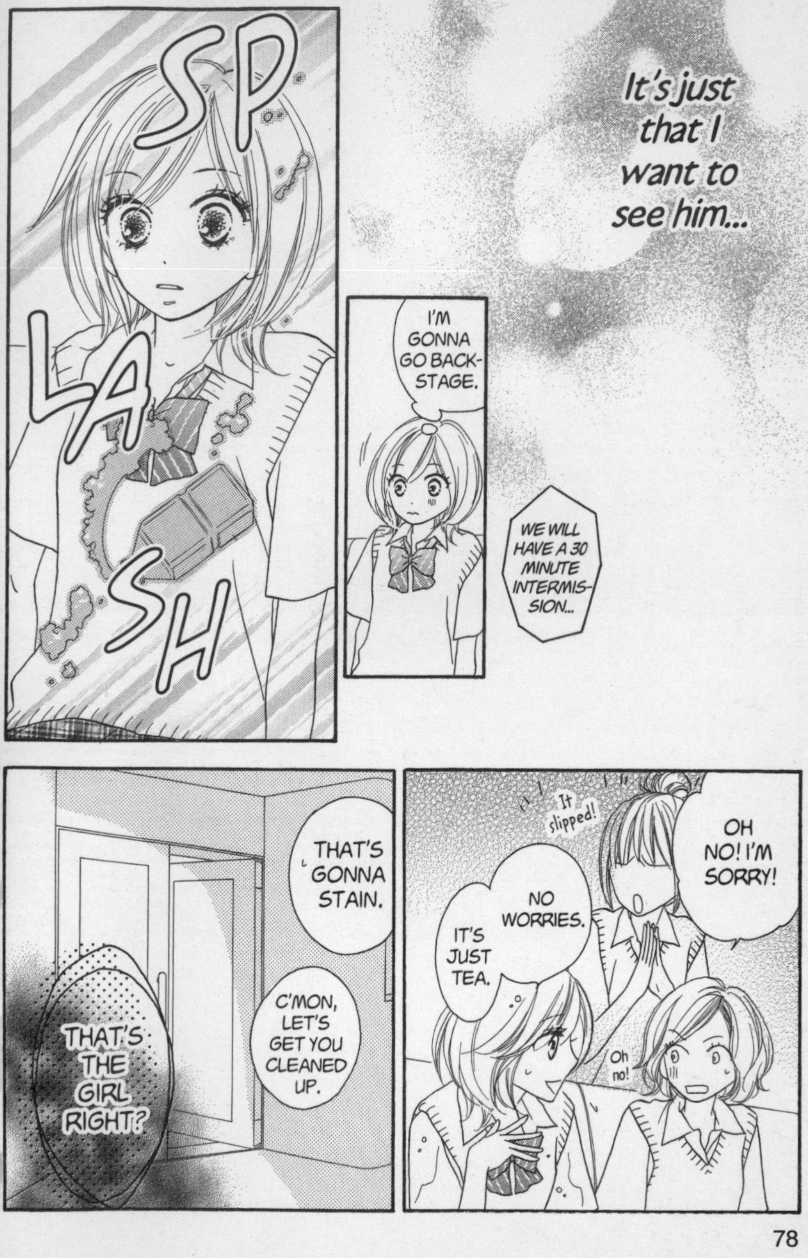
It's just that I want to see him...
WE WILL HAVE A 30 MINUTE INTERMISSION...
I'M GONNA GO BACKSTAGE.
SPLASH
It slipped!
OH NO! I'M SORRY!
NO WORRIES.
IT'S JUST TEA.
Oh no!
THAT'S GONNA STAIN.
C'MON, LET'S GET YOU CLEANED UP.
THAT'S THE GIRL RIGHT?

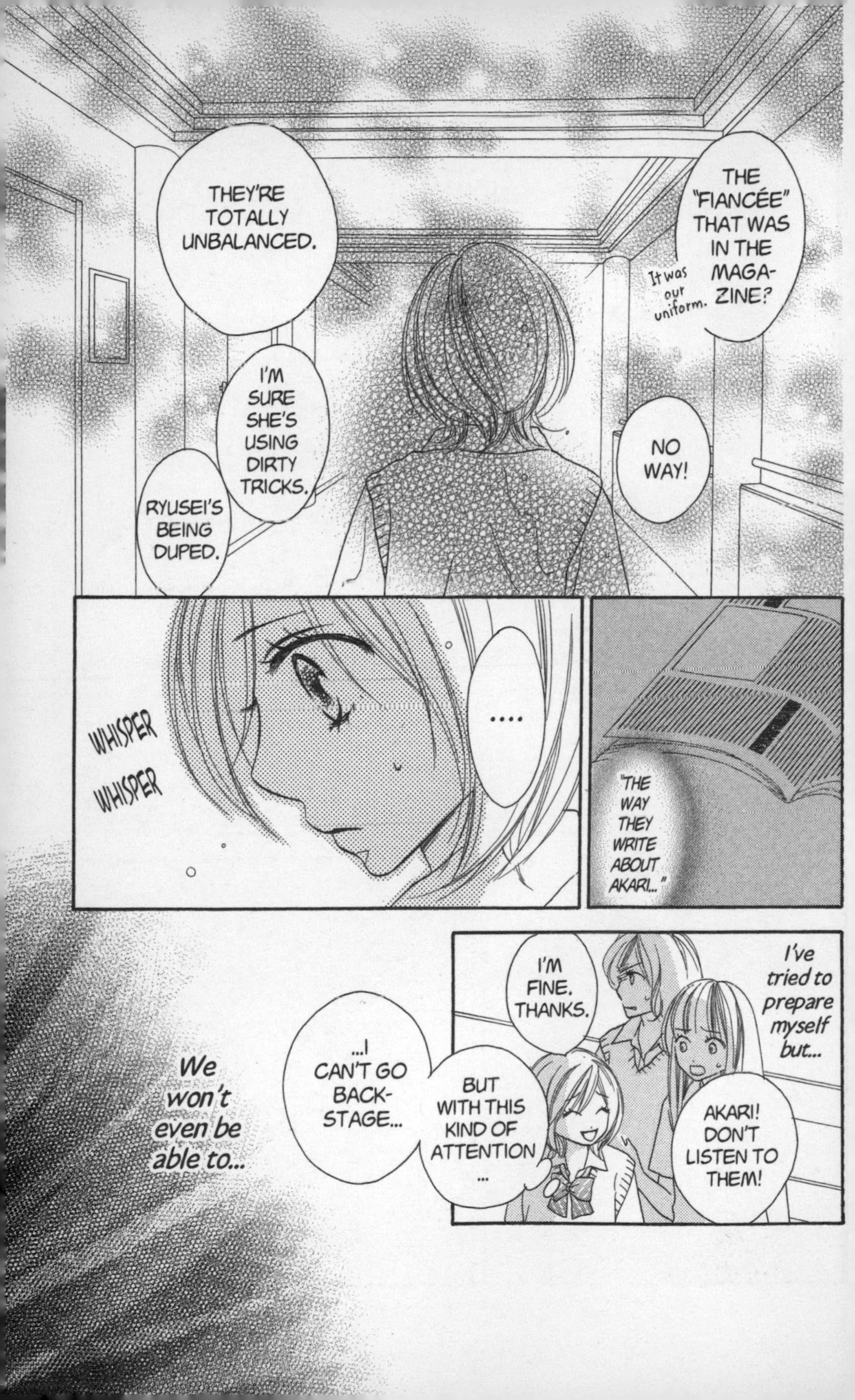
THE "FIANCÉE" THAT WAS IN THE MAGAZINE?
It was our uniform.
THEY'RE TOTALLY UNBALANCED.
NO WAY!
I'M SURE SHE'S USING DIRTY TRICKS.
RYUSEI'S BEING DUPED.
"THE WAY THEY WRITE ABOUT AKARI..."
....
WHISPER
WHISPER
I've tried to prepare myself but...
I'M FINE. THANKS.
AKARI! DON'T LISTEN TO THEM!
BUT WITH THIS KIND OF ATTENTION ...
...I CAN'T GO BACKSTAGE...
We won't even be able to...

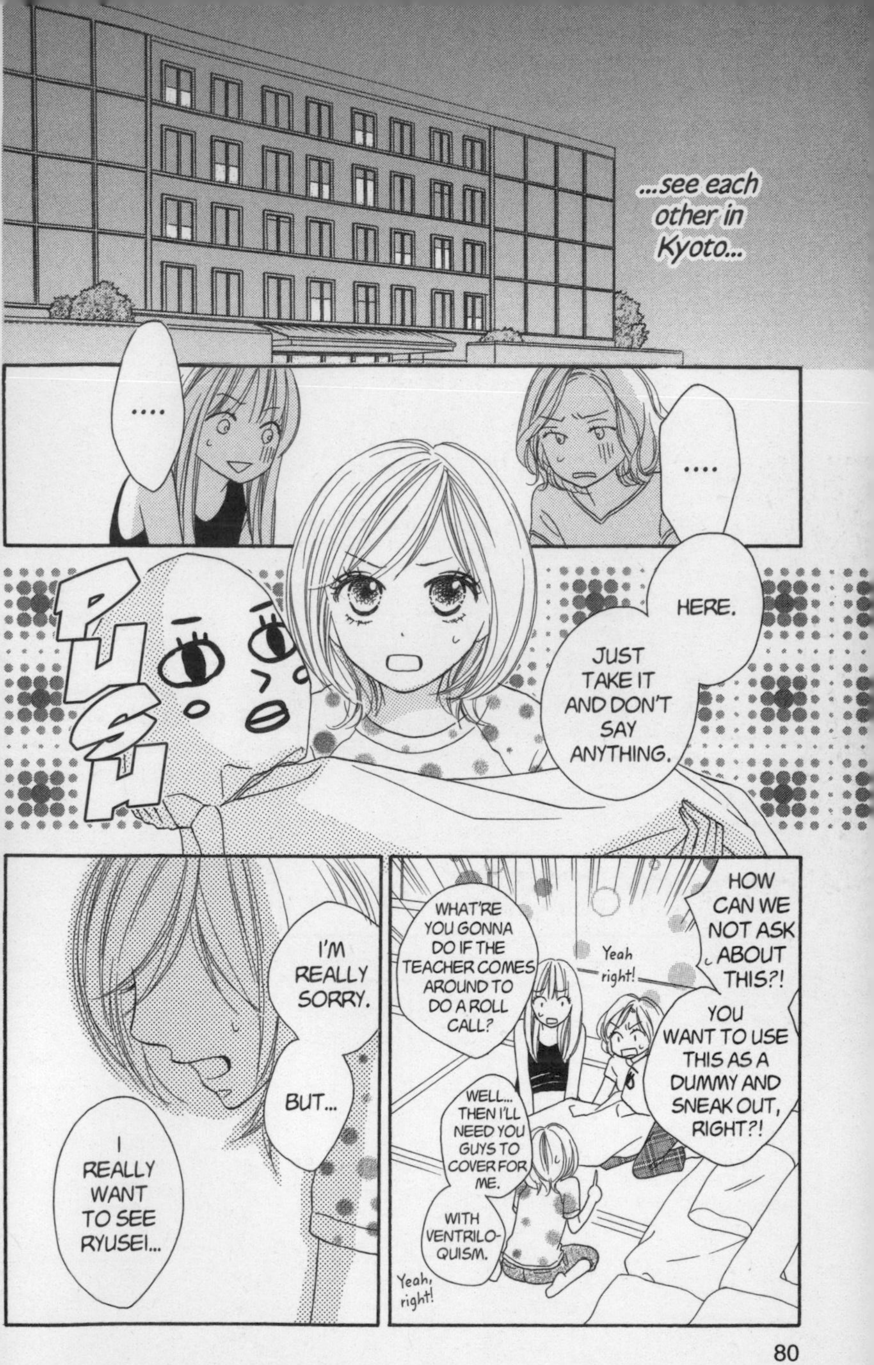
...see each other in Kyoto...
....
....
HERE.
JUST TAKE IT AND DON'T SAY ANYTHING.
PUSH
HOW CAN WE NOT ASK ABOUT THIS?!
Yeah right!
WHAT'RE YOU GONNA DO IF THE TEACHER COMES AROUND TO DO A ROLL CALL?
YOU WANT TO USE THIS AS A DUMMY AND SNEAK OUT, RIGHT?!
WELL... THEN I'LL NEED YOU GUYS TO COVER FOR ME.
WITH VENTRILO-QUISM.
Yeah, right!
I'M REALLY SORRY.
BUT...
I REALLY WANT TO SEE RYUSEI...

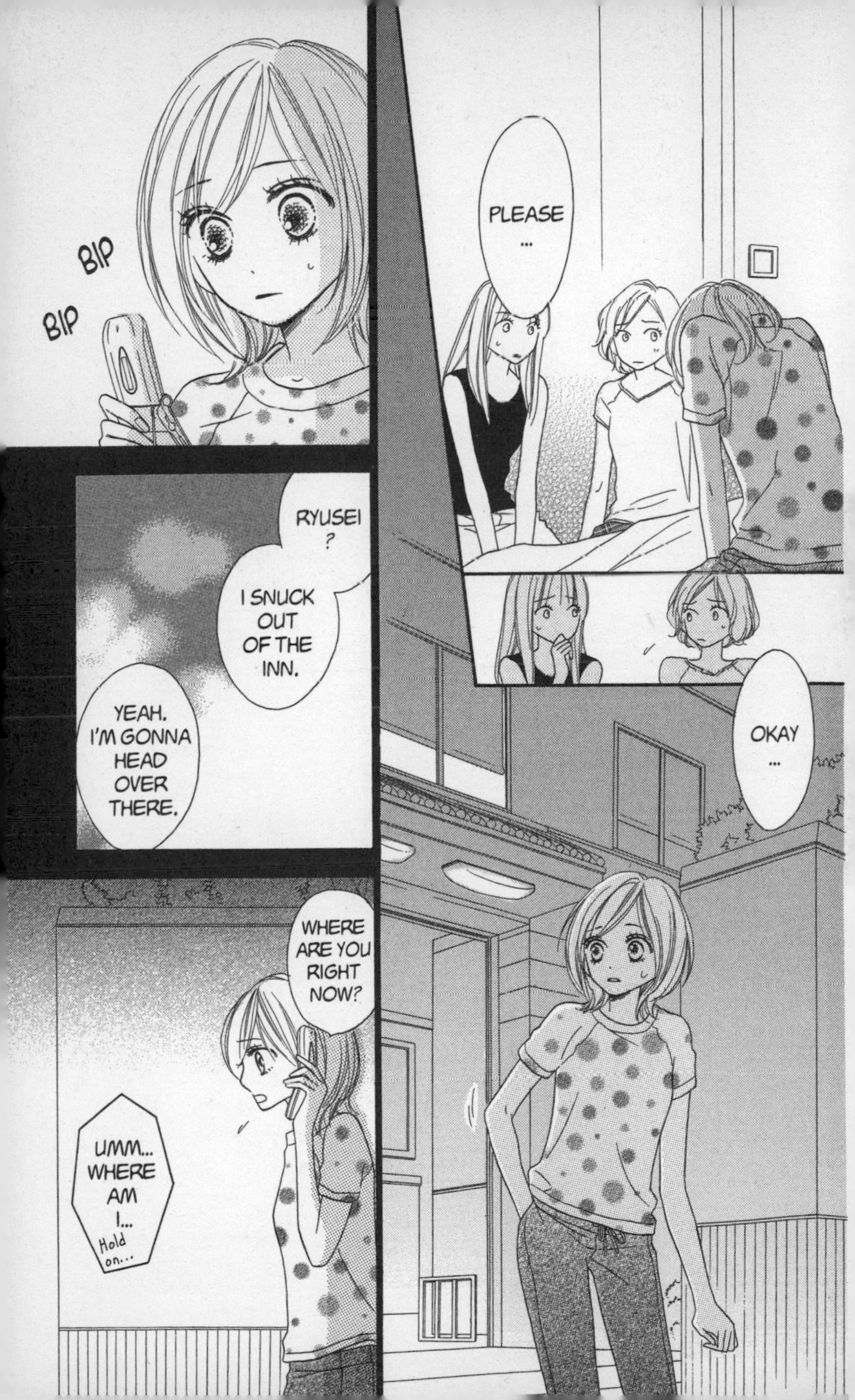
PLEASE ...
OKAY ...
BIP
BIP
RYUSEI ?
I SNUCK OUT OF THE INN.
YEAH. I'M GONNA HEAD OVER THERE.
WHERE ARE YOU RIGHT NOW?
UMM... WHERE AM I...
Hold on...

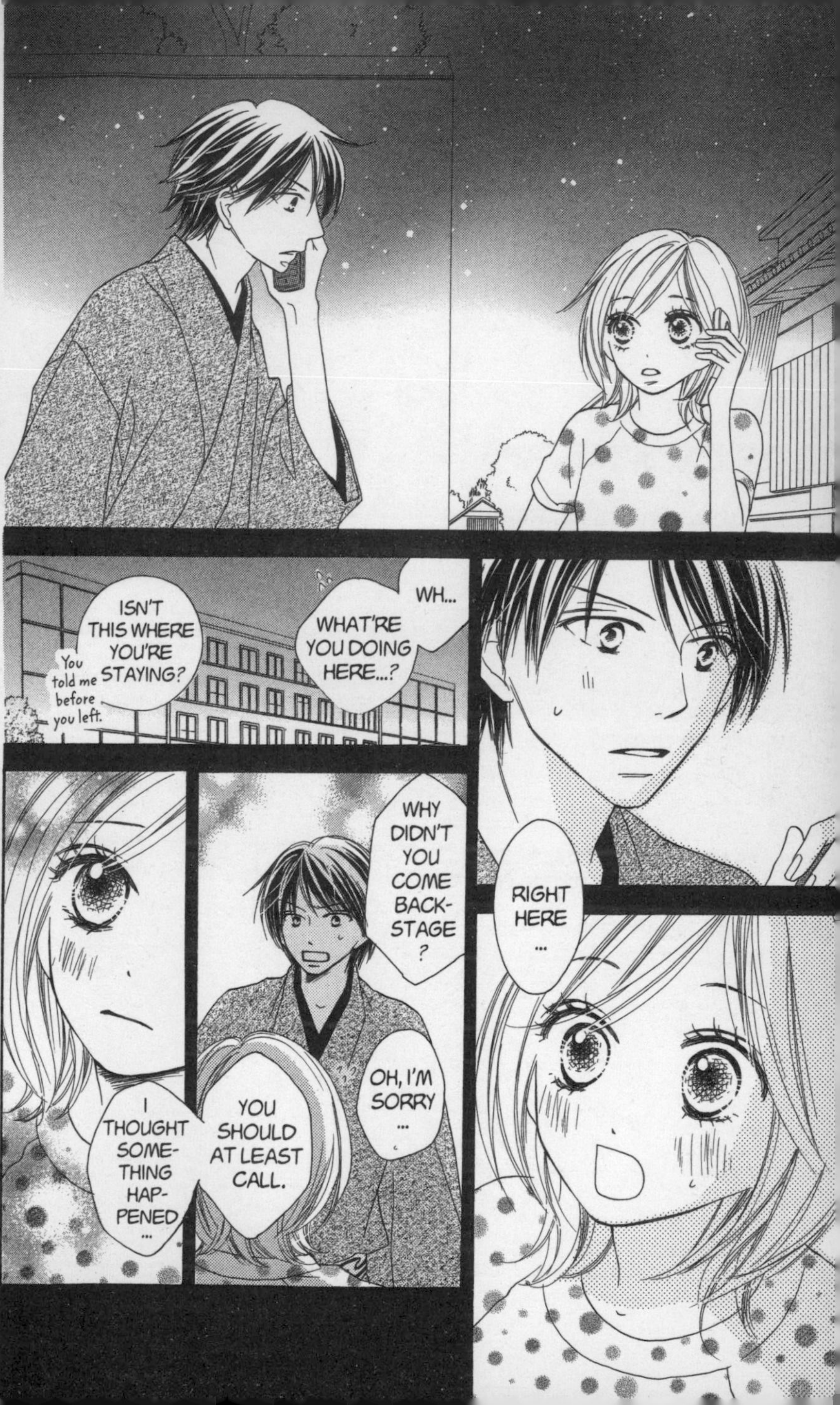
RIGHT HERE ...
WH...
WHAT'RE YOU DOING HERE...?
ISN'T THIS WHERE YOU'RE STAYING?
You told me before you left.
WHY DIDN'T YOU COME BACK-STAGE ?
OH, I'M SORRY ...
YOU SHOULD AT LEAST CALL.
I THOUGHT SOME-THING HAP-PENED ...

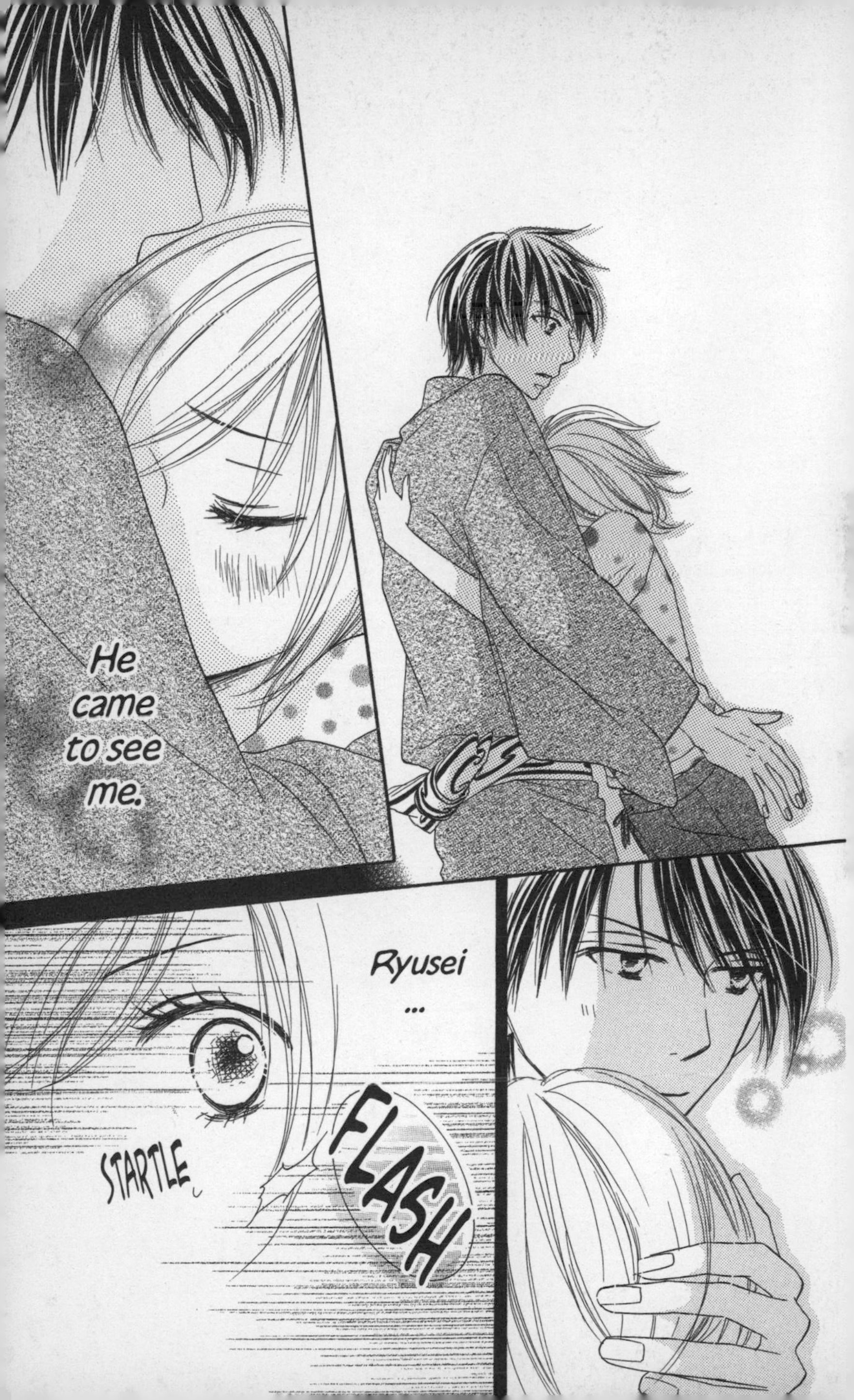
He came to see me.
Ryusei ...
FLASH
STARTLE

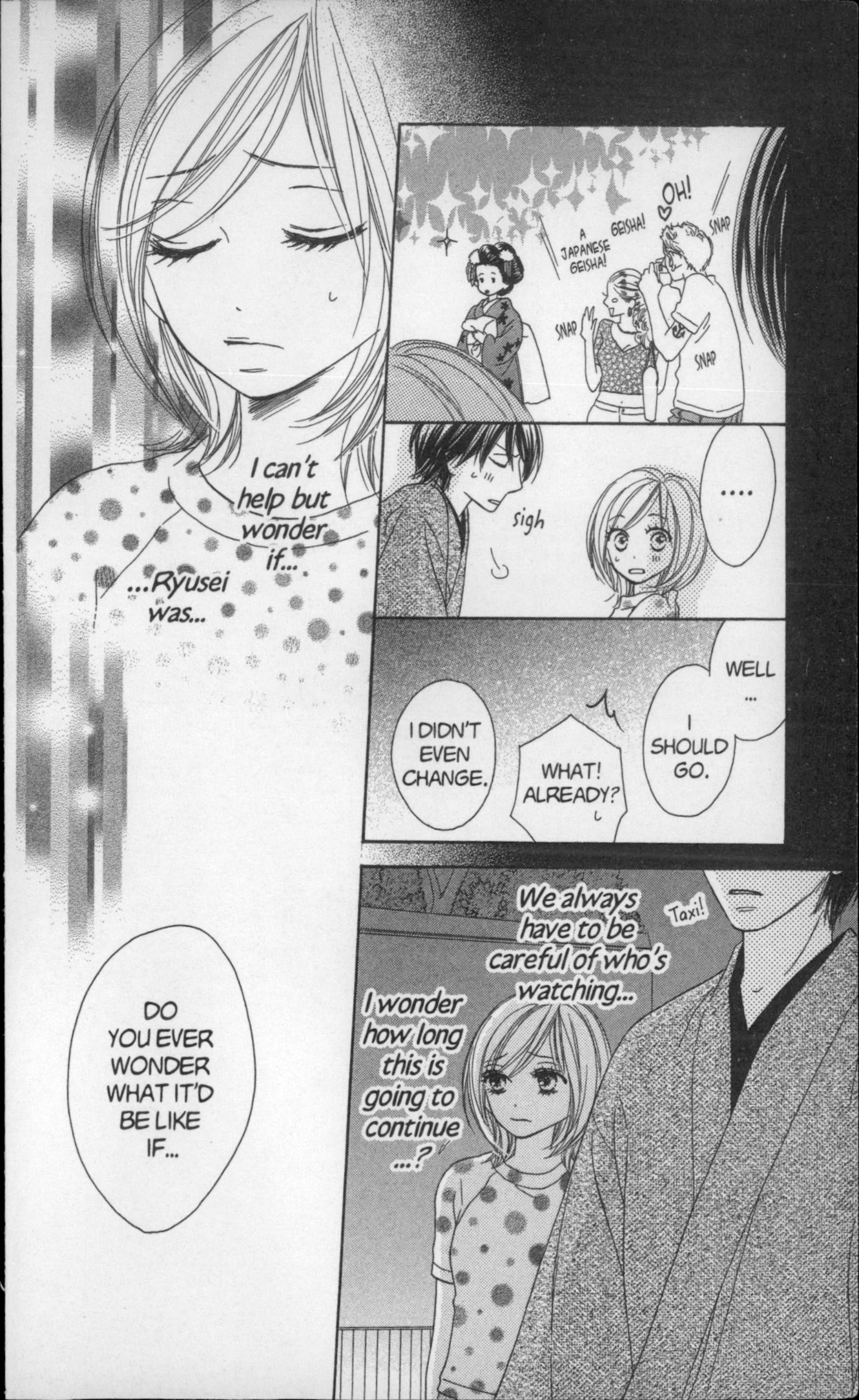
SNAP
OH!
GEISHA!
A JAPANESE GEISHA!
SNAP
SNAP
....
sigh
WELL... I SHOULD GO.
WHAT! ALREADY?
I DIDN'T EVEN CHANGE.
Taxi!
We always have to be careful of who's watching...
I wonder how long this is going to continue ...?
I can't help but wonder if...
...Ryusei was...
DO YOU EVER WONDER WHAT IT'D BE LIKE IF...

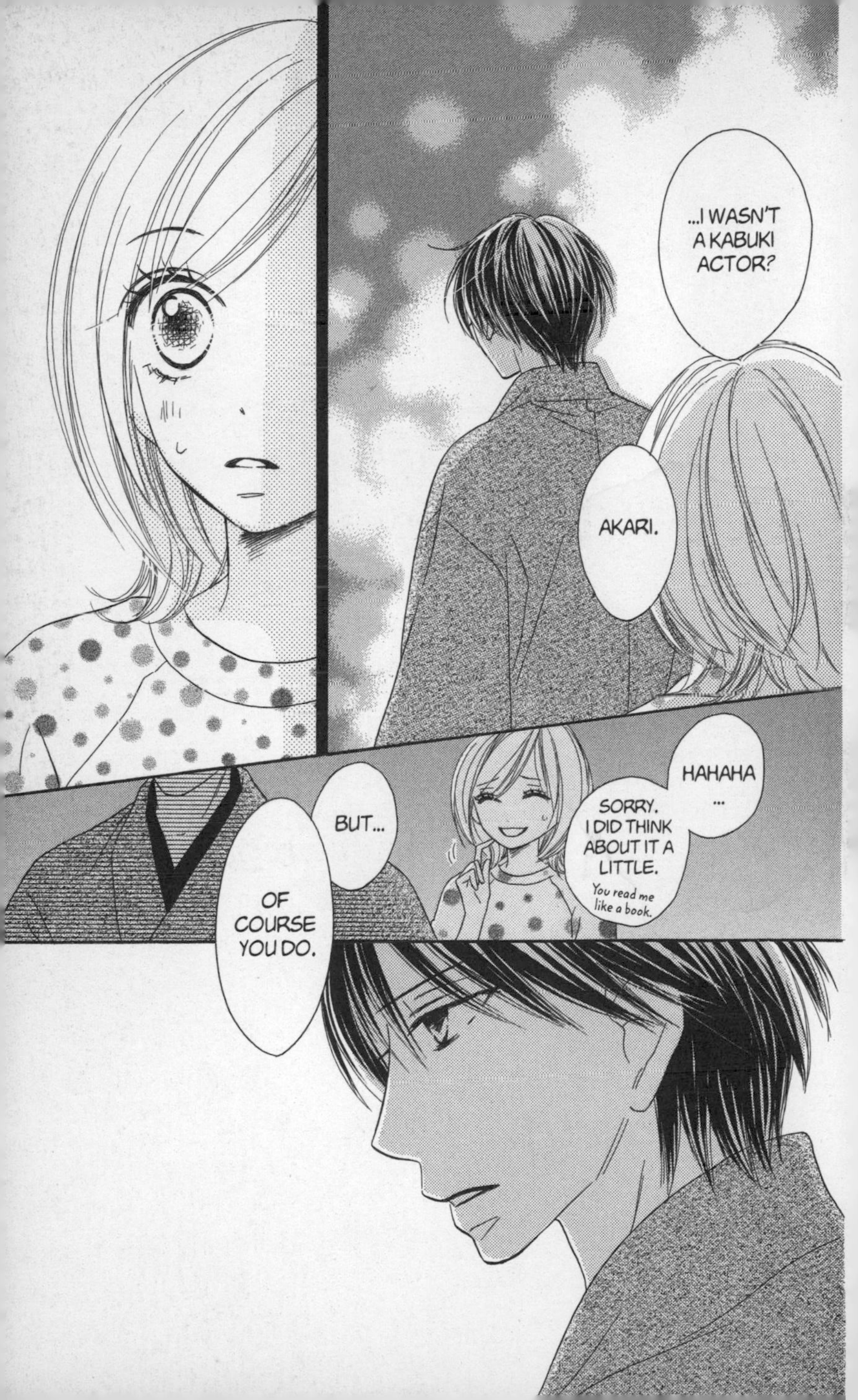
...I WASN'T A KABUKI ACTOR?
AKARI.
HAHAHA ...
SORRY. I DID THINK ABOUT IT A LITTLE.
You read me like a book.
BUT...
OF COURSE YOU DO.

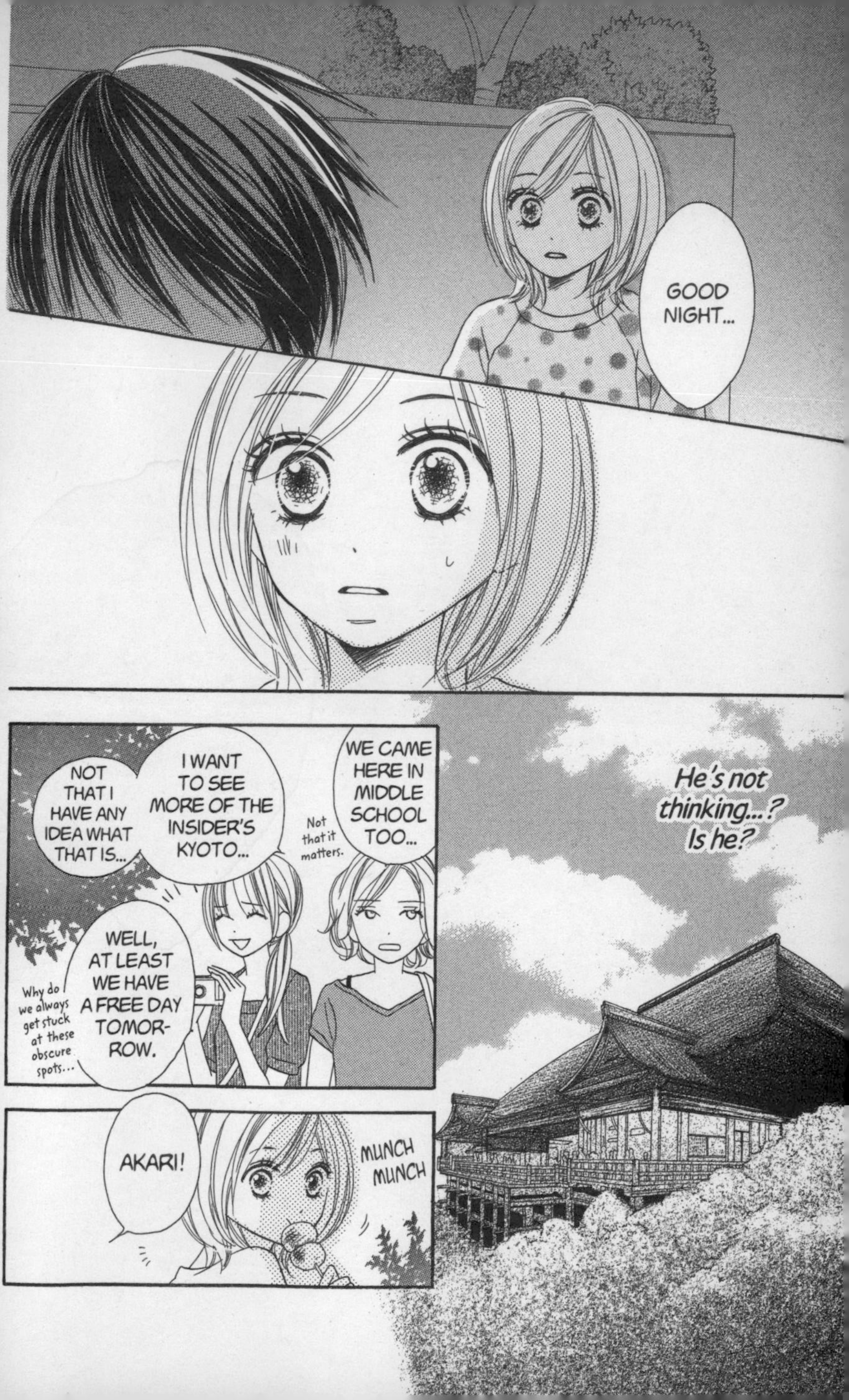
GOOD NIGHT...
He's not thinking...? Is he?
WE CAME HERE IN MIDDLE SCHOOL TOO...
Not that it matters.
I WANT TO SEE MORE OF THE INSIDER'S KYOTO...
NOT THAT I HAVE ANY IDEA WHAT THAT IS...
WELL, AT LEAST WE HAVE A FREE DAY TOMORROW.
Why do we always get stuck at these obscure spots...
MUNCH MUNCH
AKARI!

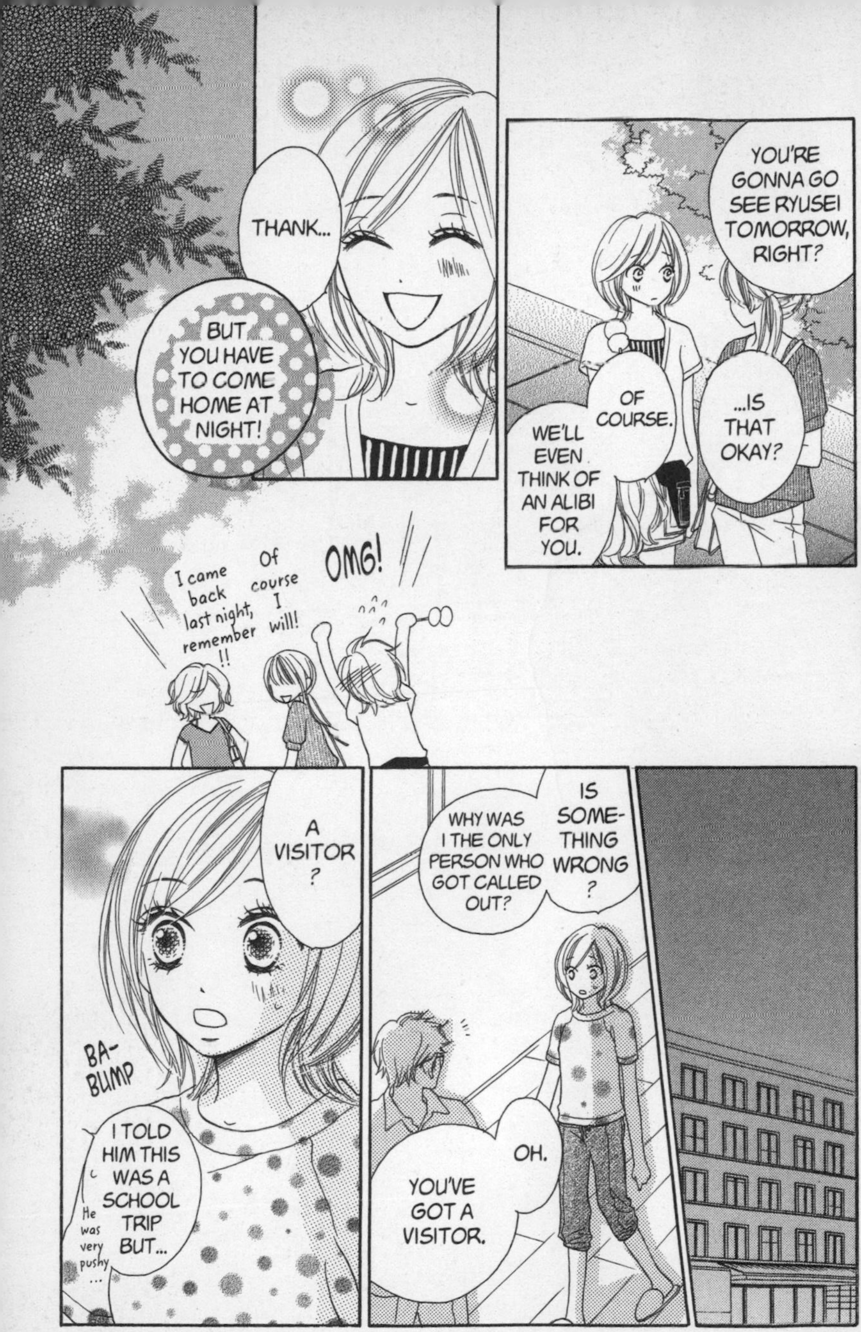
YOU'RE GONNA GO SEE RYUSEI TOMORROW, RIGHT?
...IS THAT OKAY?
OF COURSE.
WE'LL EVEN THINK OF AN ALIBI FOR YOU.
THANK...
BUT YOU HAVE TO COME HOME AT NIGHT!
OMG!
Of course I will!
I came back last night, remember!!
IS SOME-THING WRONG?
WHY WAS I THE ONLY PERSON WHO GOT CALLED OUT?
OH.
YOU'VE GOT A VISITOR.
A VISITOR?
BA-BUMP
I TOLD HIM THIS WAS A SCHOOL TRIP BUT...
He was very pushy...

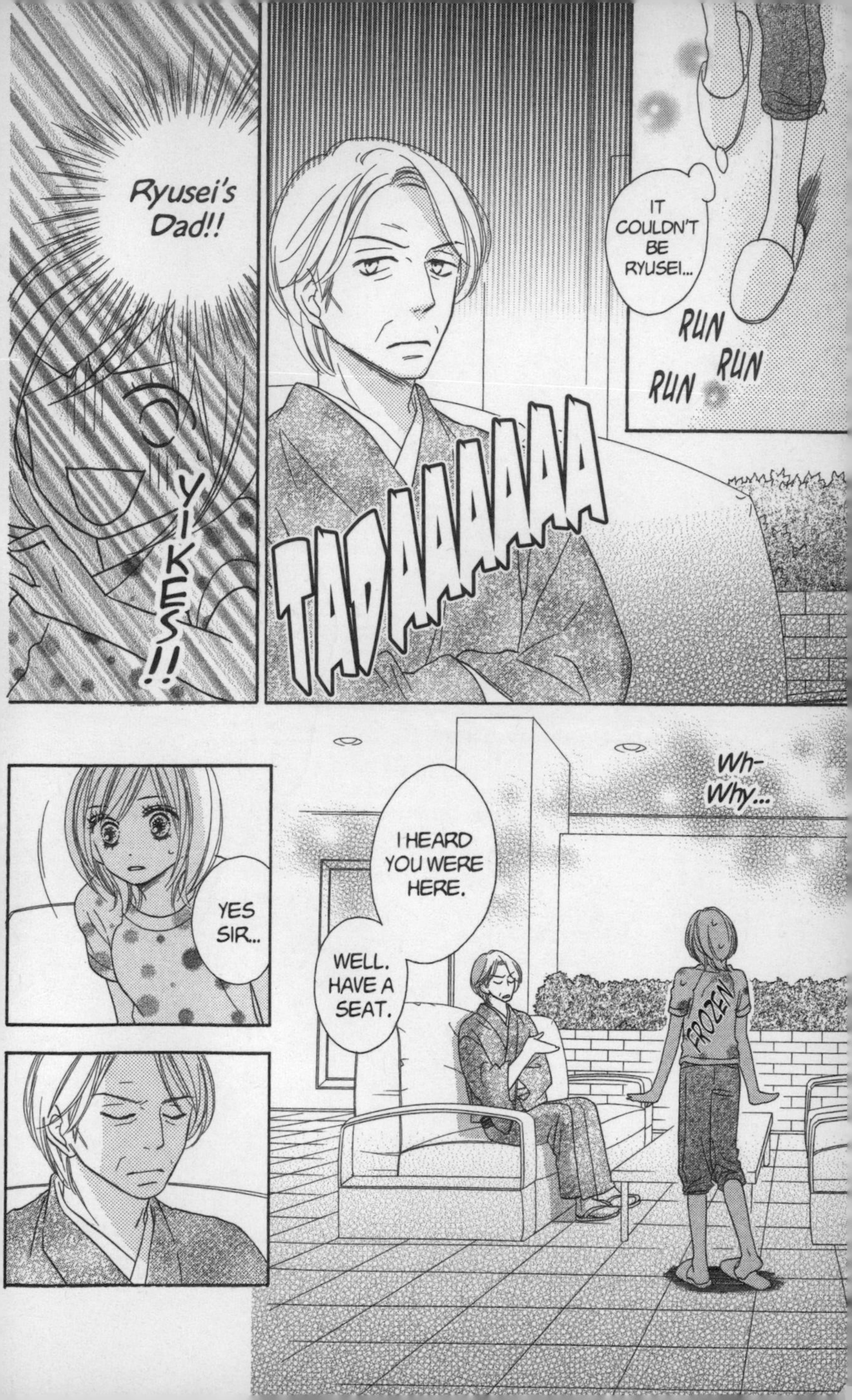
IT COULDN'T BE RYUSEI...
RUN RUN RUN
TADAAAAAAA
Ryusei's Dad!!
YIKES!!
Wh- Why...
I HEARD YOU WERE HERE.
WELL. HAVE A SEAT.
FROZEN
YES SIR...

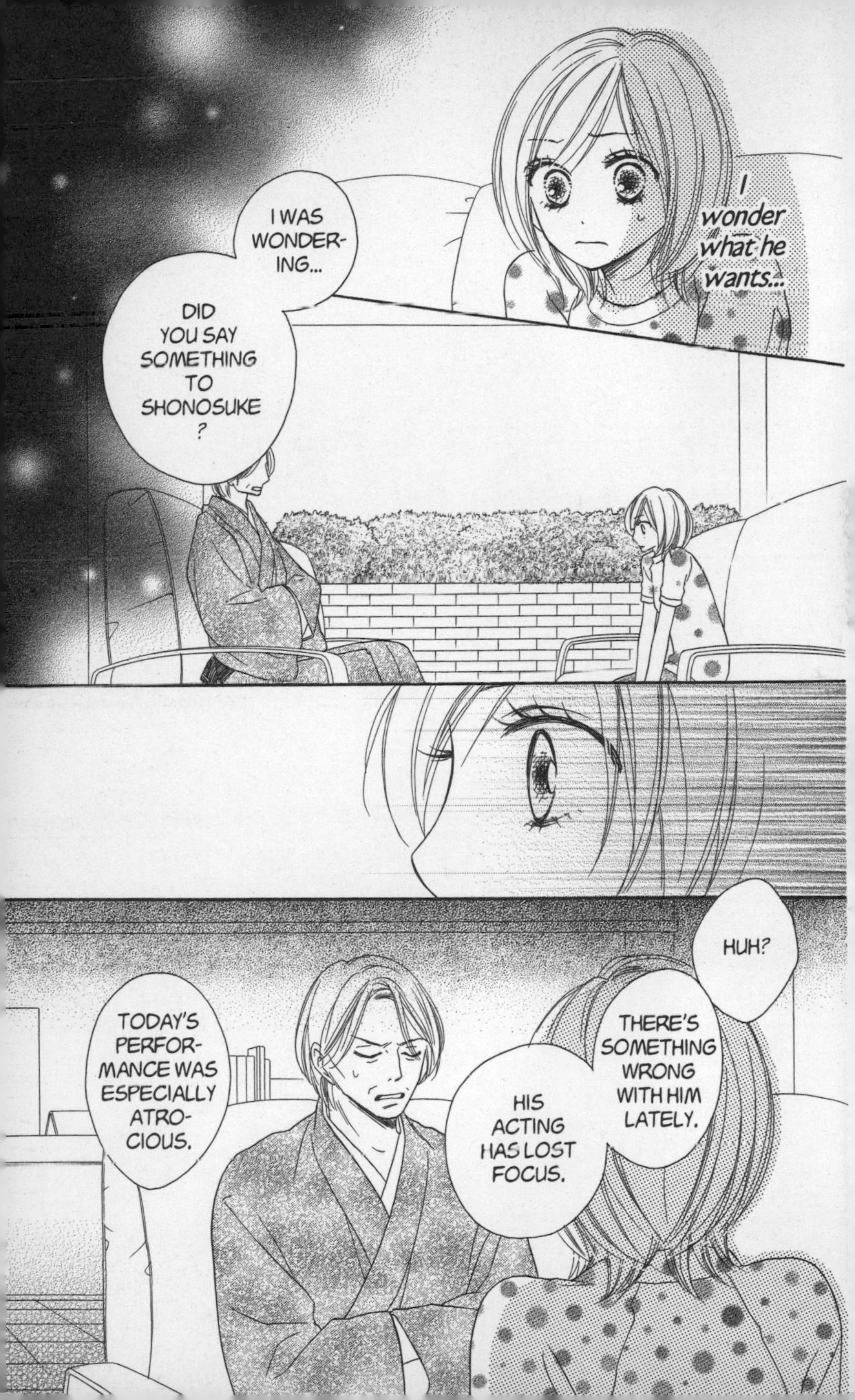
I wonder what he wants...
I WAS WONDER-ING...
DID YOU SAY SOMETHING TO SHONOSUKE?
HUH?
THERE'S SOMETHING WRONG WITH HIM LATELY.
HIS ACTING HAS LOST FOCUS.
TODAY'S PERFOR-MANCE WAS ESPECIALLY ATRO-CIOUS.

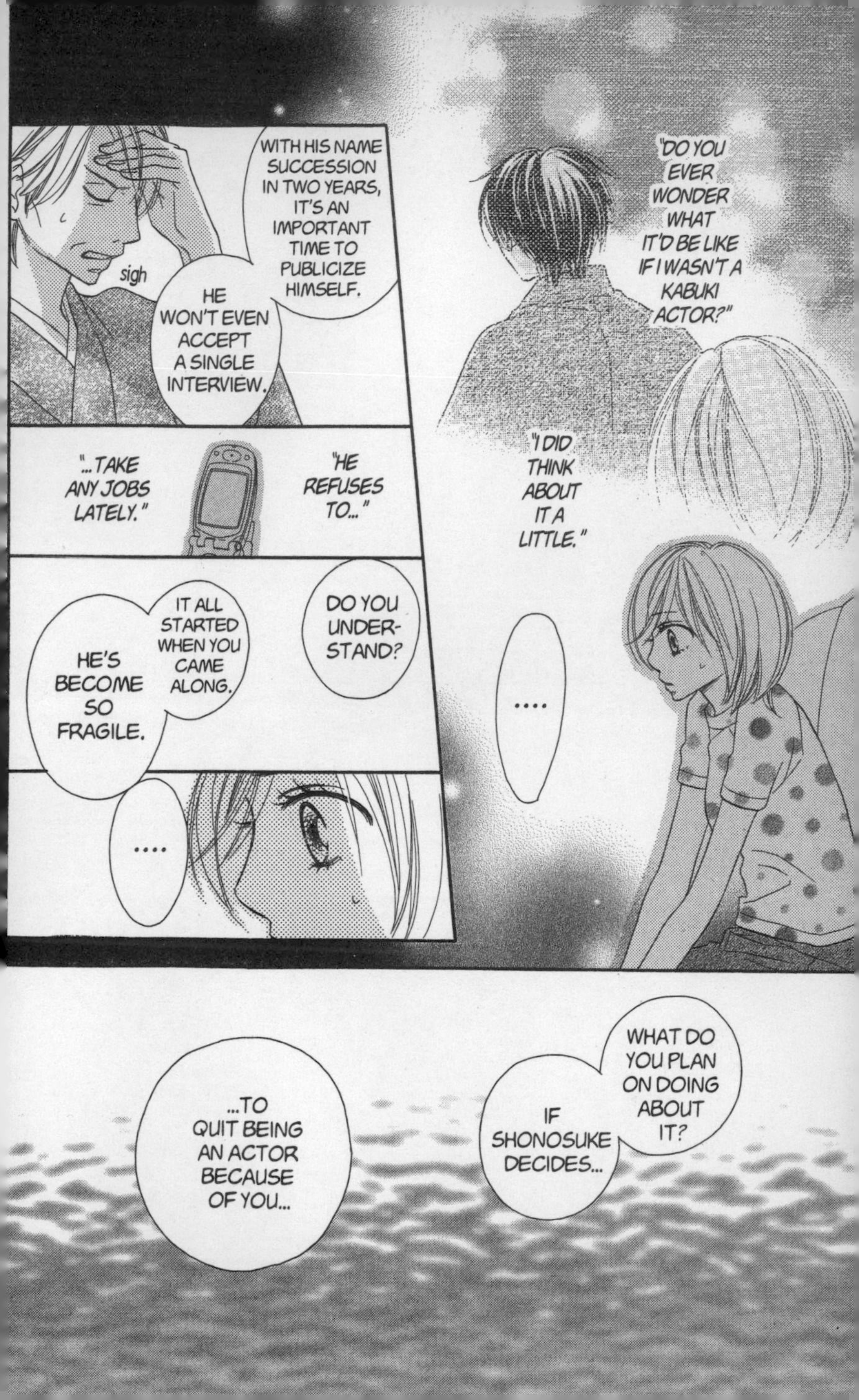
"DO YOU EVER WONDER WHAT IT'D BE LIKE IF I WASN'T A KABUKI ACTOR?"
"I DID THINK ABOUT IT A LITTLE."
....
WITH HIS NAME SUCCESSION IN TWO YEARS, IT'S AN IMPORTANT TIME TO PUBLICIZE HIMSELF.
sigh
HE WON'T EVEN ACCEPT A SINGLE INTERVIEW.
"HE REFUSES TO..."
"...TAKE ANY JOBS LATELY."
DO YOU UNDER-STAND?
IT ALL STARTED WHEN YOU CAME ALONG.
HE'S BECOME SO FRAGILE.
....
WHAT DO YOU PLAN ON DOING ABOUT IT?
IF SHONOSUKE DECIDES...
...TO QUIT BEING AN ACTOR BECAUSE OF YOU...

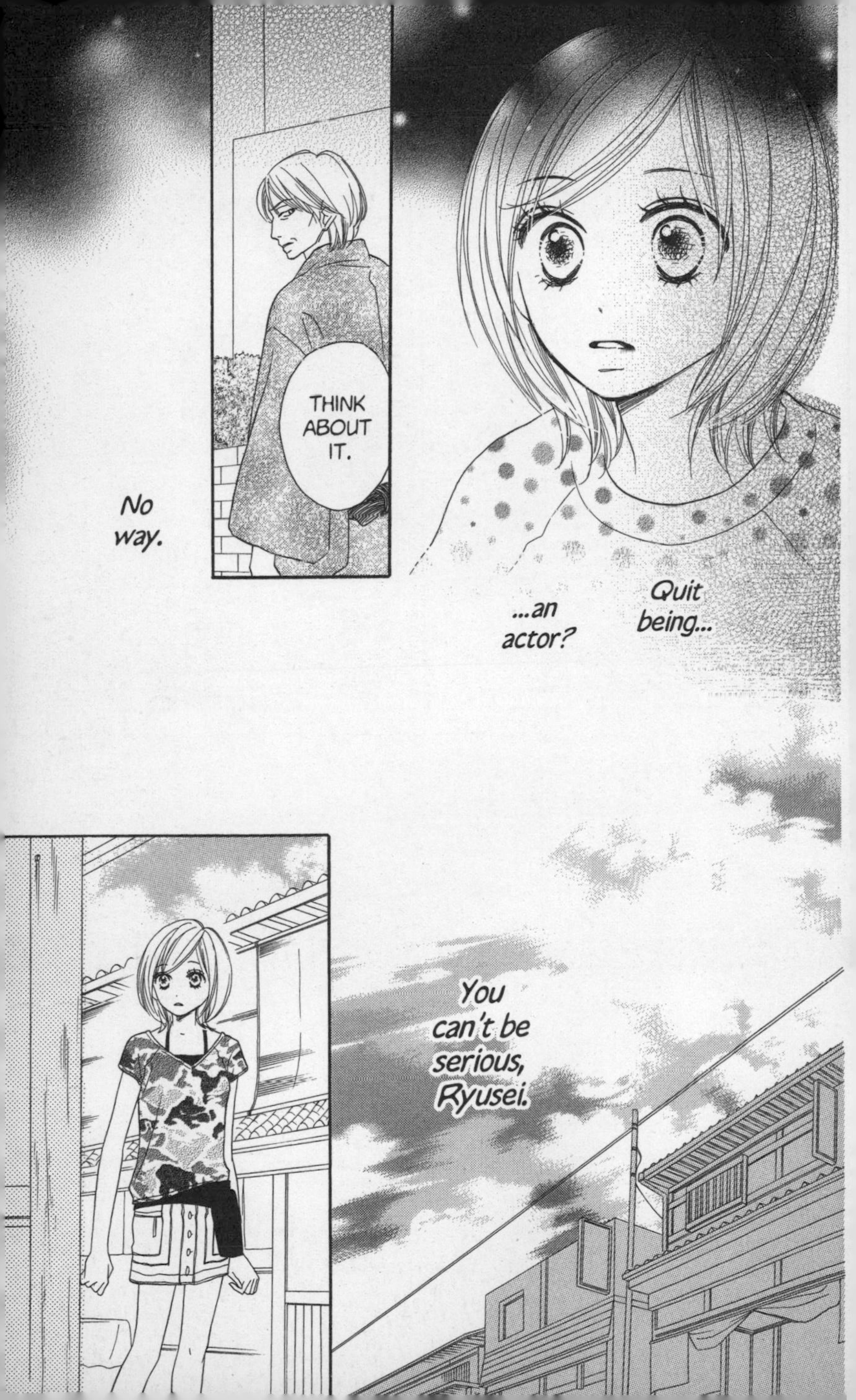
Quit being...
...an actor?
THINK ABOUT IT.
No way.
You can't be serious, Ryusei.

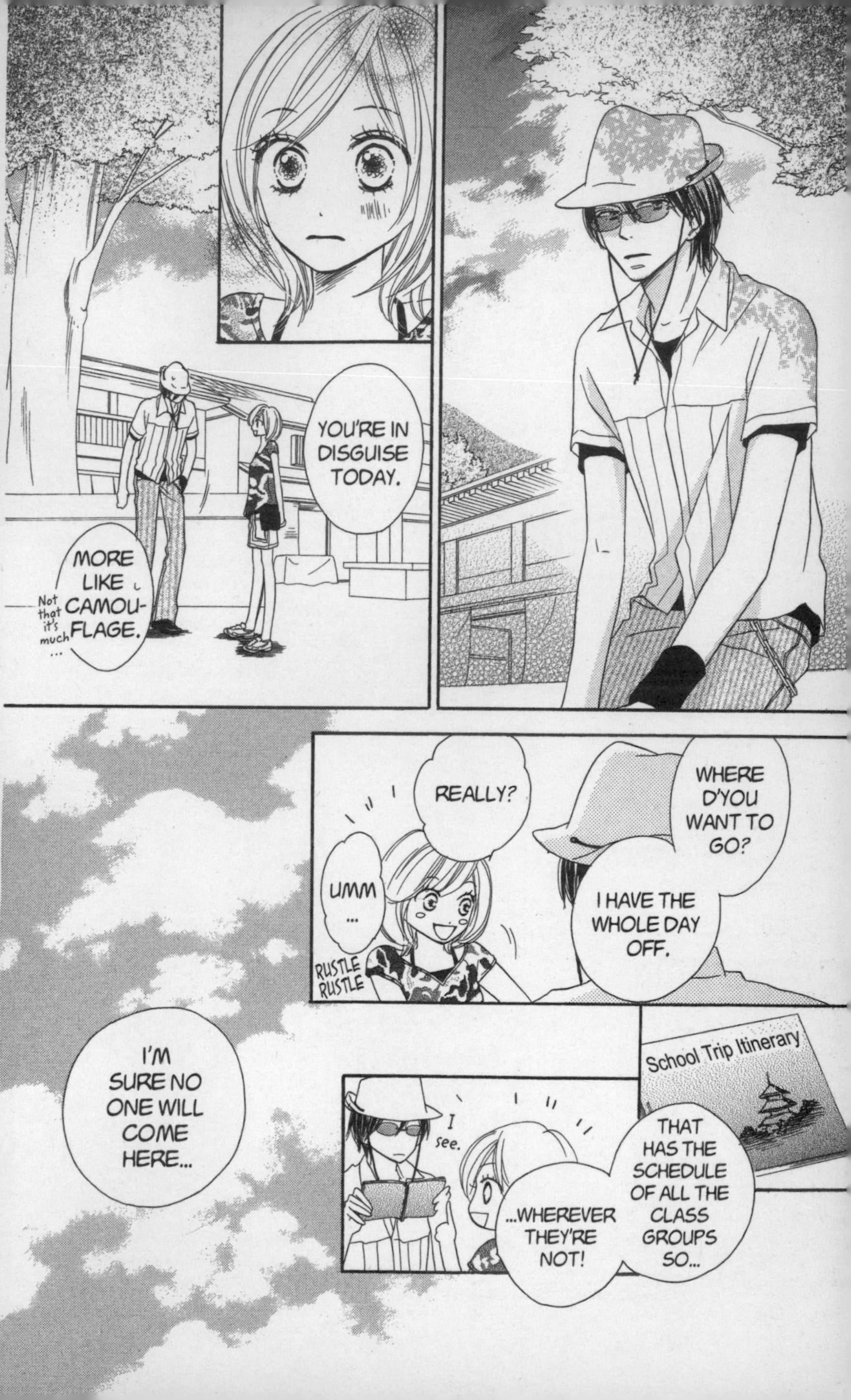
YOU'RE IN DISGUISE TODAY.
MORE LIKE CAMOUFLAGE.
Not that it's much...
WHERE D'YOU WANT TO GO?
I HAVE THE WHOLE DAY OFF.
REALLY?
UMM...
RUSTLE RUSTLE
School Trip Itinerary
THAT HAS THE SCHEDULE OF ALL THE CLASS GROUPS SO...
...WHEREVER THEY'RE NOT!
I see.
I'M SURE NO ONE WILL COME HERE...

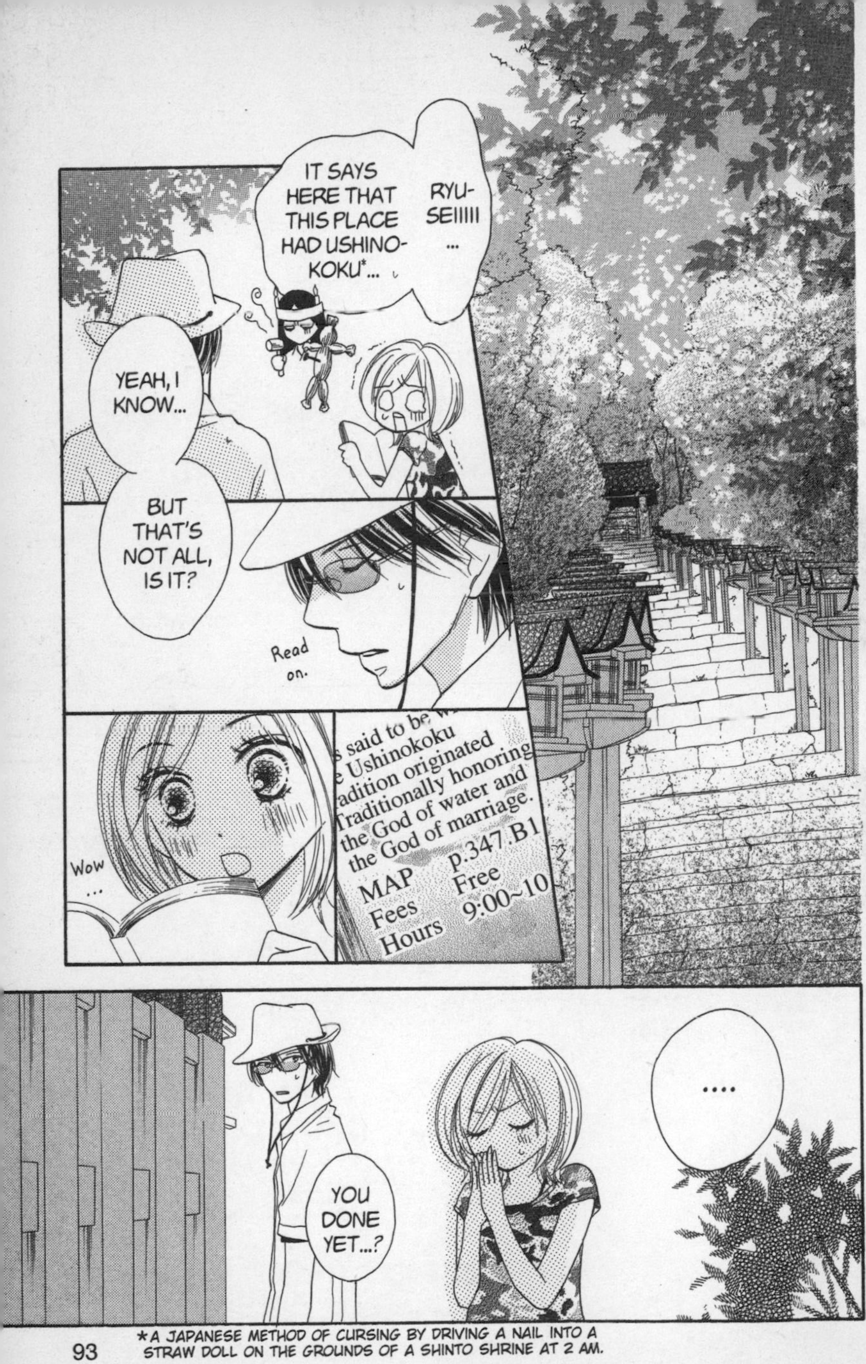
RYU-SEIIIII ...
IT SAYS HERE THAT THIS PLACE HAD USHINO-KOKU*...
YEAH, I KNOW...
BUT THAT'S NOT ALL, IS IT?
Read on.
s said to be
e Ushinokoku
adition originated
Traditionally honoring
the God of water and
the God of marriage.
MAP p.347 B1
Fees Free
Hours 9:00~10
Wow ...
....
YOU DONE YET...?

*A JAPANESE METHOD OF CURSING BY DRIVING A NAIL INTO A STRAW DOLL ON THE GROUNDS OF A SHINTO SHRINE AT 2 AM.

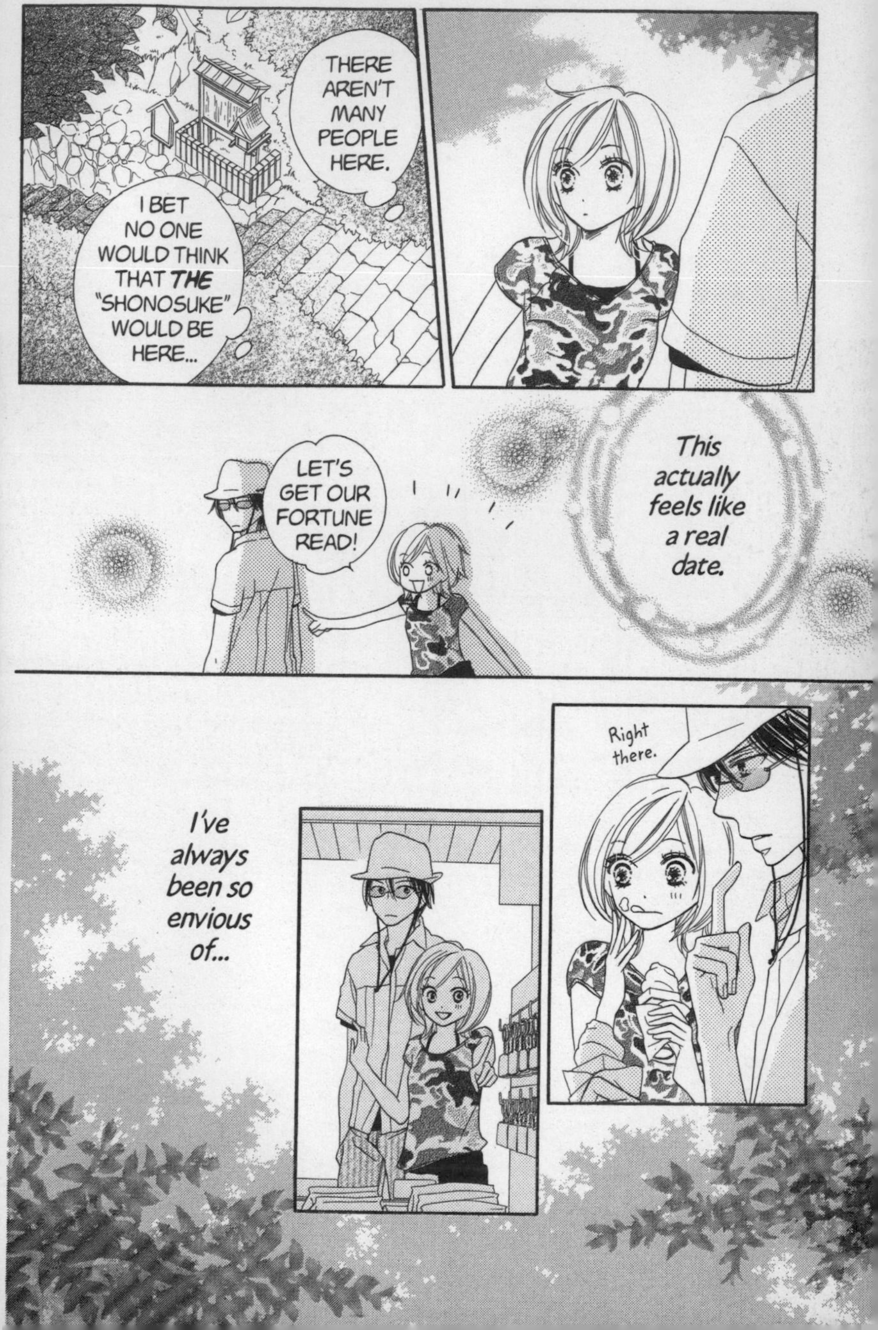
THERE AREN'T MANY PEOPLE HERE.
I BET NO ONE WOULD THINK THAT THE "SHONOSUKE" WOULD BE HERE...
This actually feels like a real date.
LET'S GET OUR FORTUNE READ!
Right there.
I've always been so envious of...

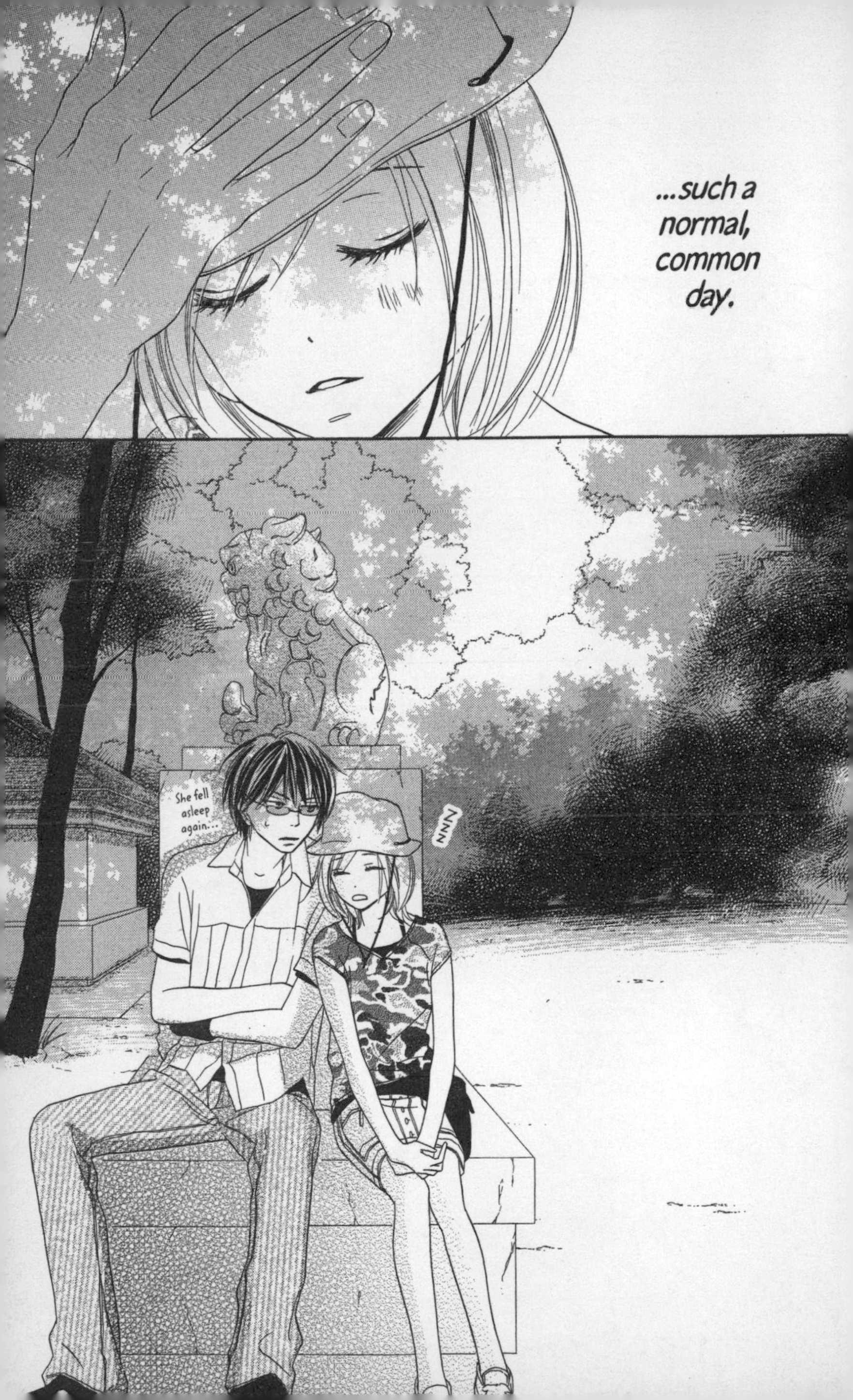
...such a normal, common day.
ZZZ
She fell asleep again...

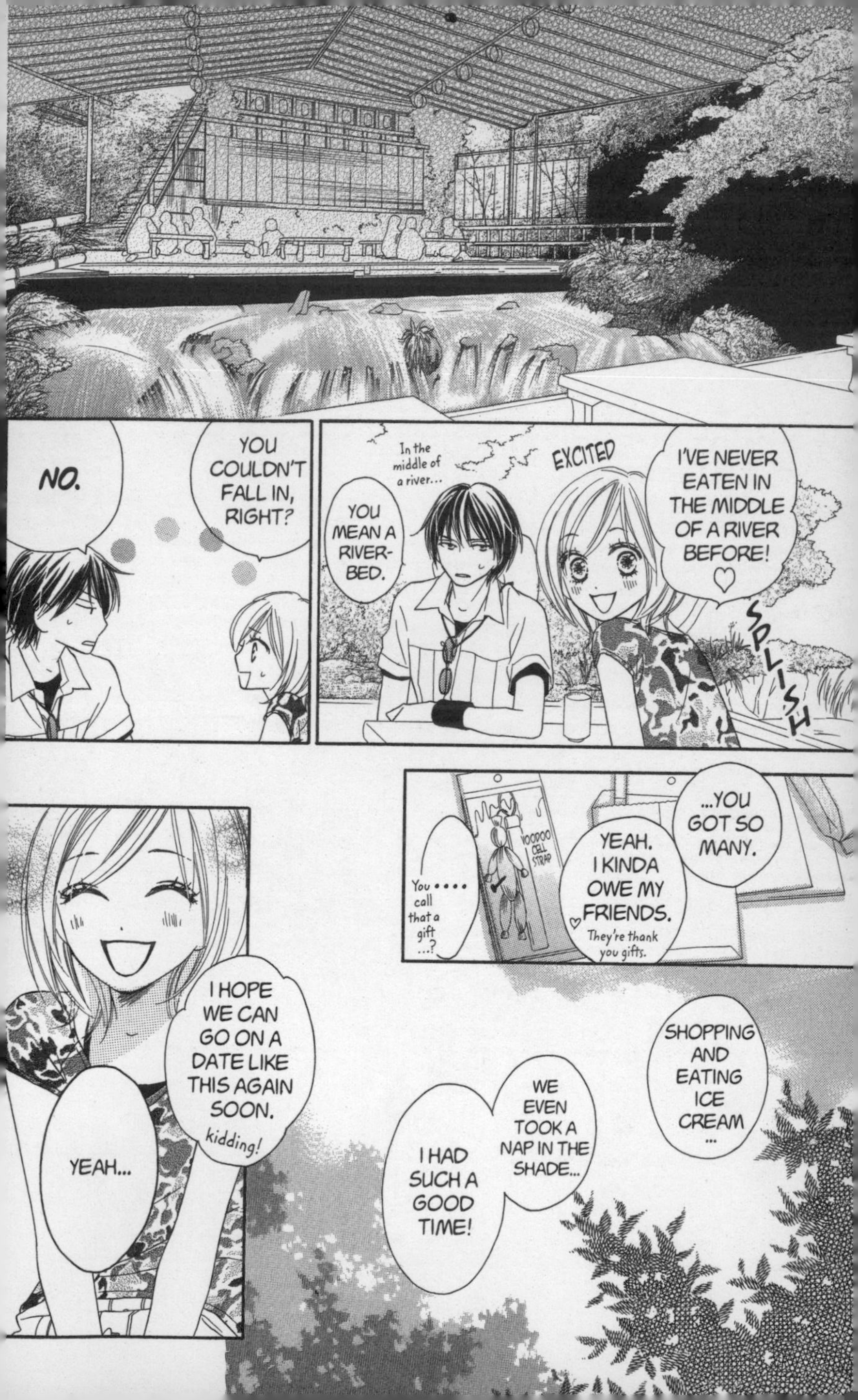
EXCITED
I'VE NEVER EATEN IN THE MIDDLE OF A RIVER BEFORE! ♡
SPLISH
In the middle of a river...
YOU MEAN A RIVER-BED.
YOU COULDN'T FALL IN, RIGHT?
NO.
...YOU GOT SO MANY.
YEAH. I KINDA OWE MY FRIENDS. ♡
They're thank you gifts.
VOODOO CELL STRAP
You.... call that a gift...?
SHOPPING AND EATING ICE CREAM...
WE EVEN TOOK A NAP IN THE SHADE...
I HAD SUCH A GOOD TIME!
I HOPE WE CAN GO ON A DATE LIKE THIS AGAIN SOON.
kidding!
YEAH...

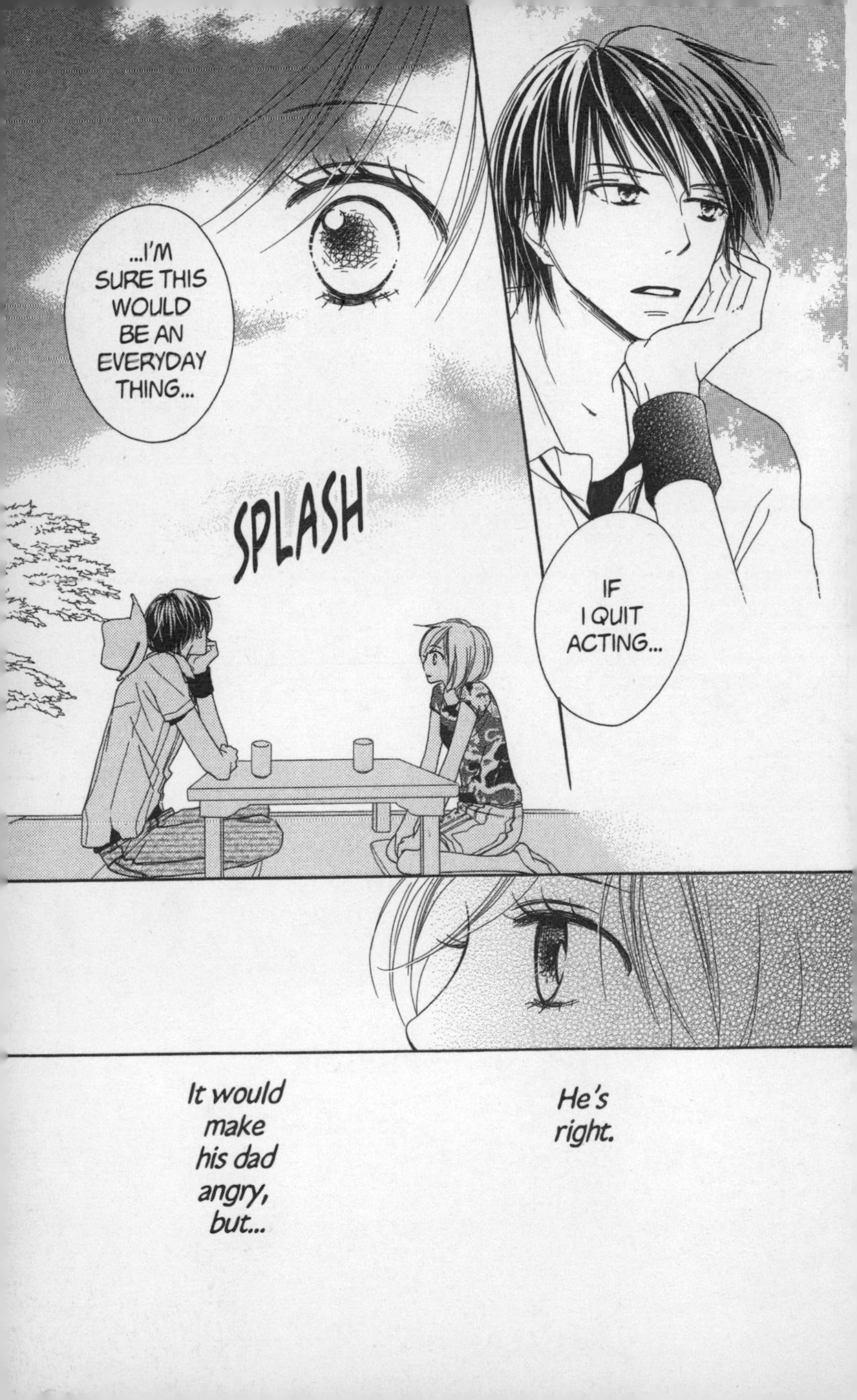
IF I QUIT ACTING...
...I'M SURE THIS WOULD BE AN EVERYDAY THING...
SPLASH
He's right.
It would make his dad angry, but...

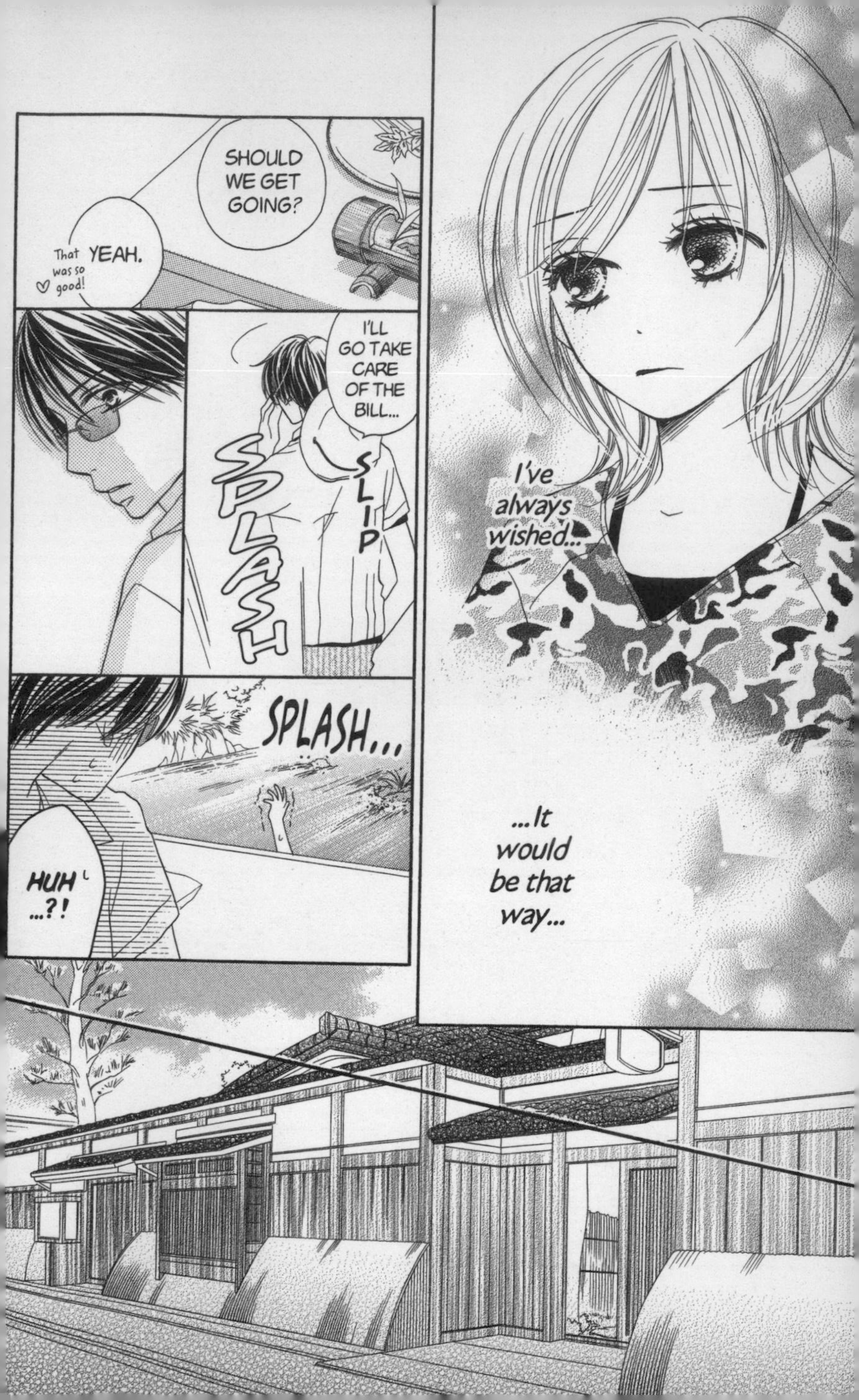
I've always wished...
...It would be that way...
SHOULD WE GET GOING?
YEAH.
That was so good! ♡
I'LL GO TAKE CARE OF THE BILL...
SLIP
SPLASH
SPLASH...
HUH ...?!

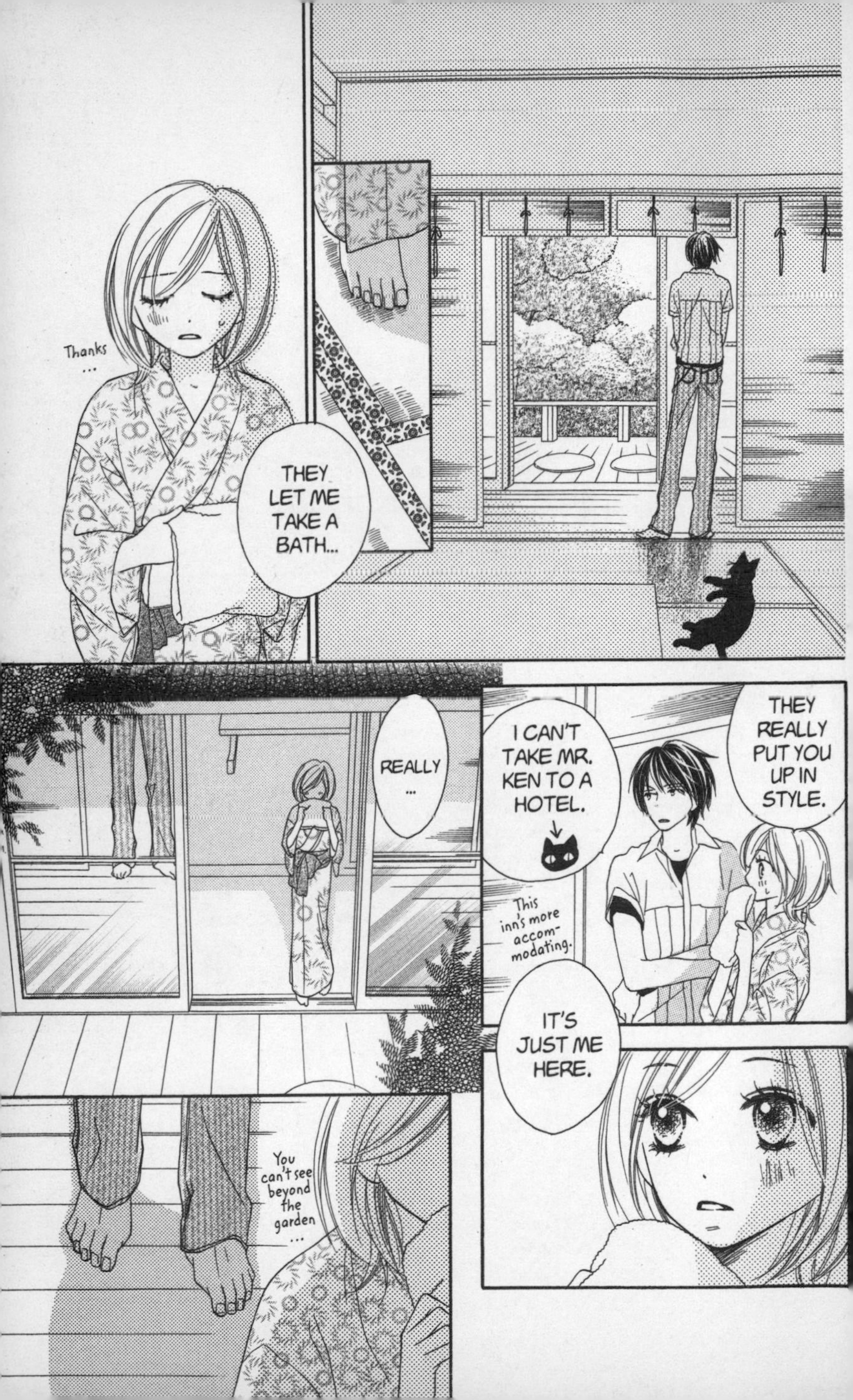
THEY LET ME TAKE A BATH...
Thanks...
THEY REALLY PUT YOU UP IN STYLE.
I CAN'T TAKE MR. KEN TO A HOTEL.
This inn's more accommodating.
REALLY...
IT'S JUST ME HERE.
You can't see beyond the garden...

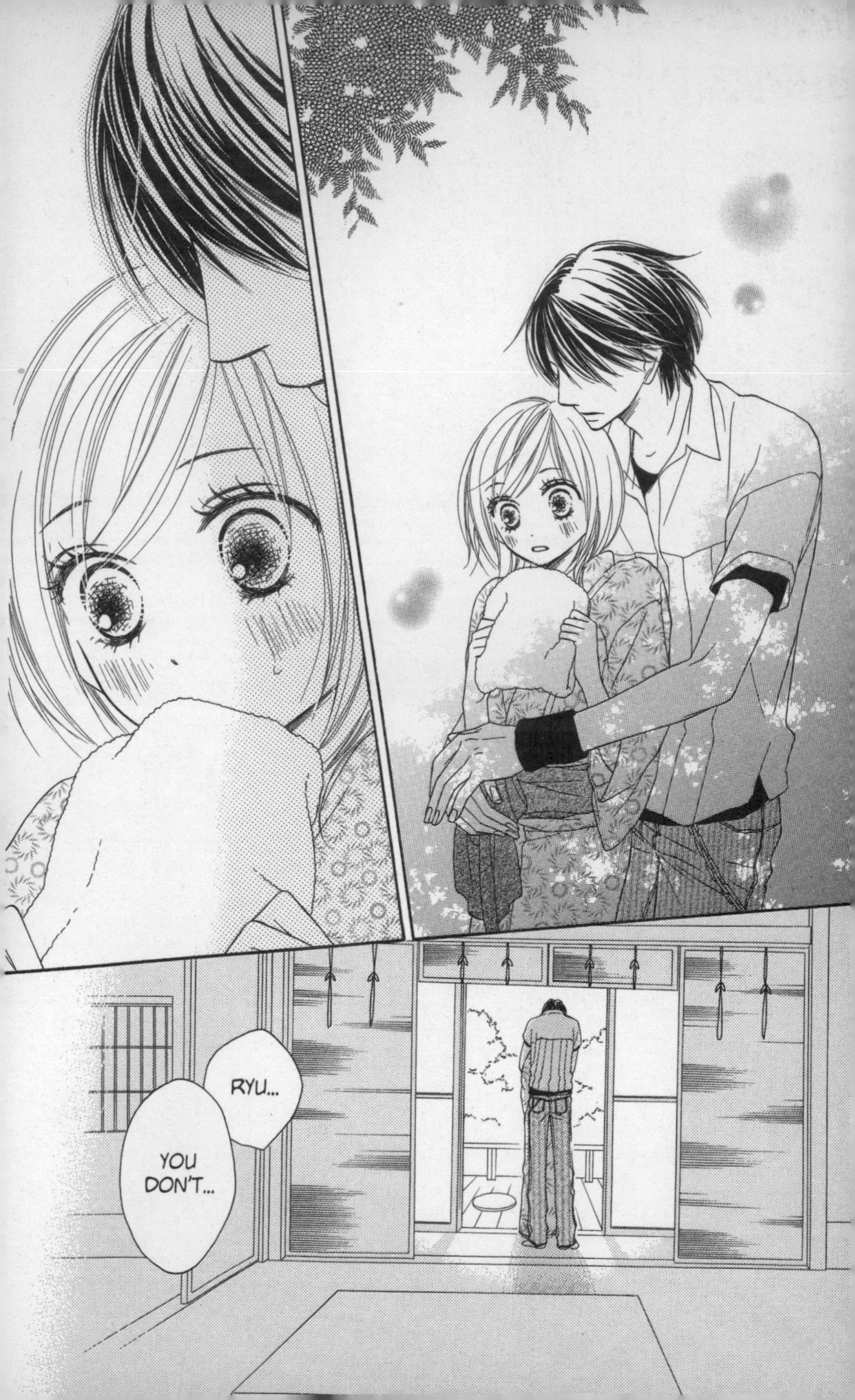
RYU...
YOU DON'T...

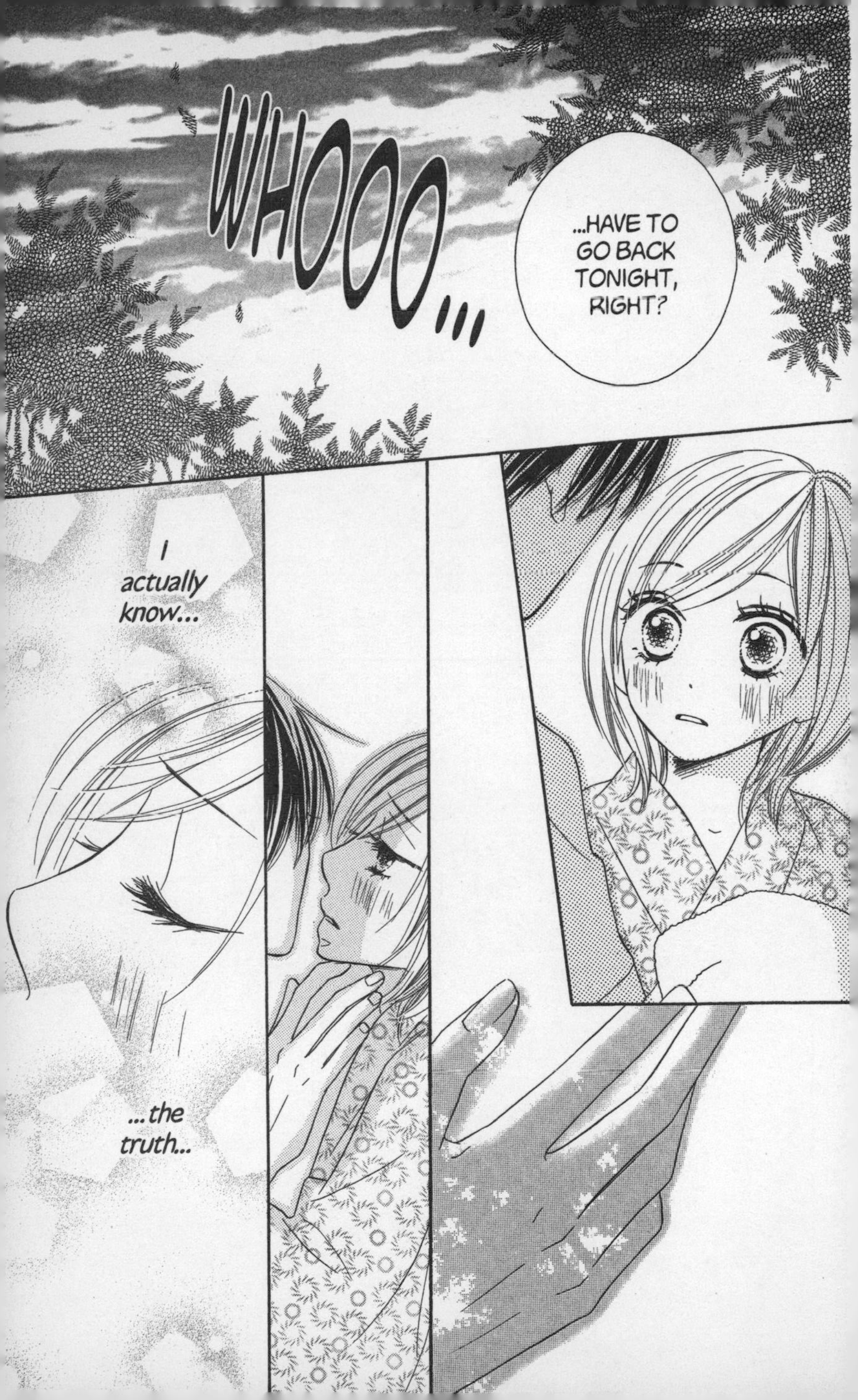
...HAVE TO GO BACK TONIGHT, RIGHT?
WHOOO...
I actually know...
...the truth...

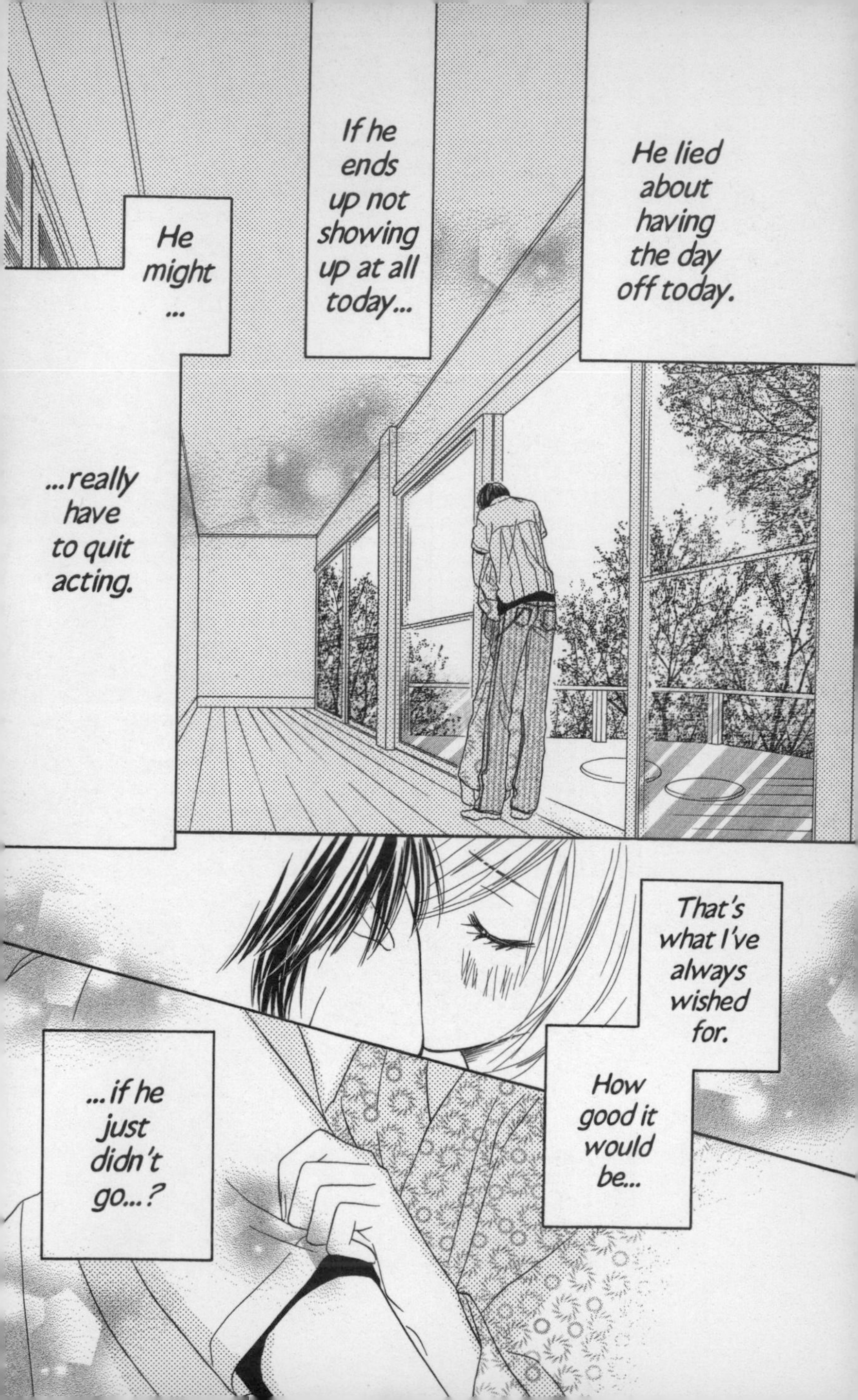
He lied about having the day off today.
If he ends up not showing up at all today...
He might...
...really have to quit acting.
That's what I've always wished for.
How good it would be...
...if he just didn't go...?

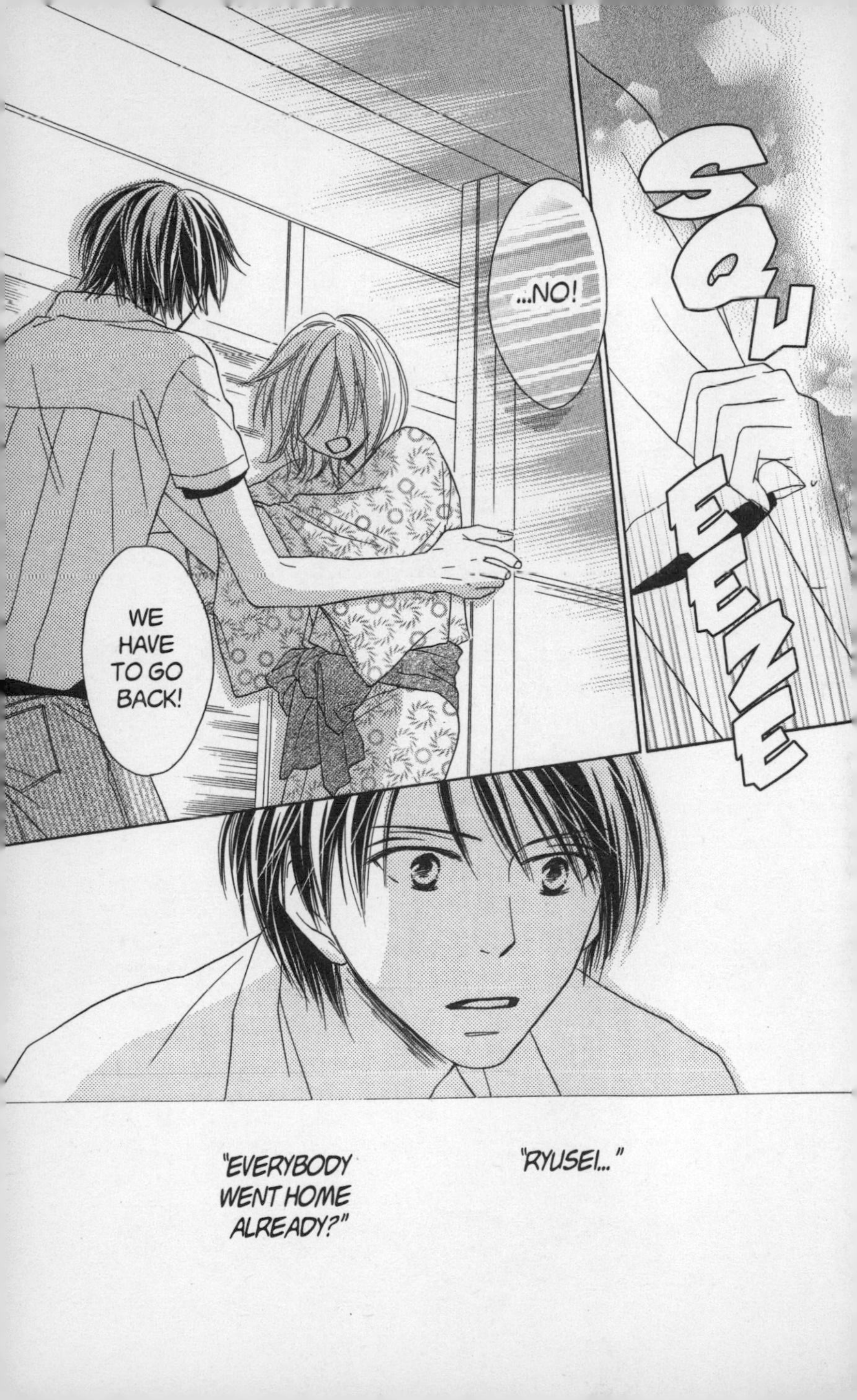
SQUEEZE
...NO!
WE HAVE TO GO BACK!
"RYUSEI..."
"EVERYBODY WENT HOME ALREADY?"

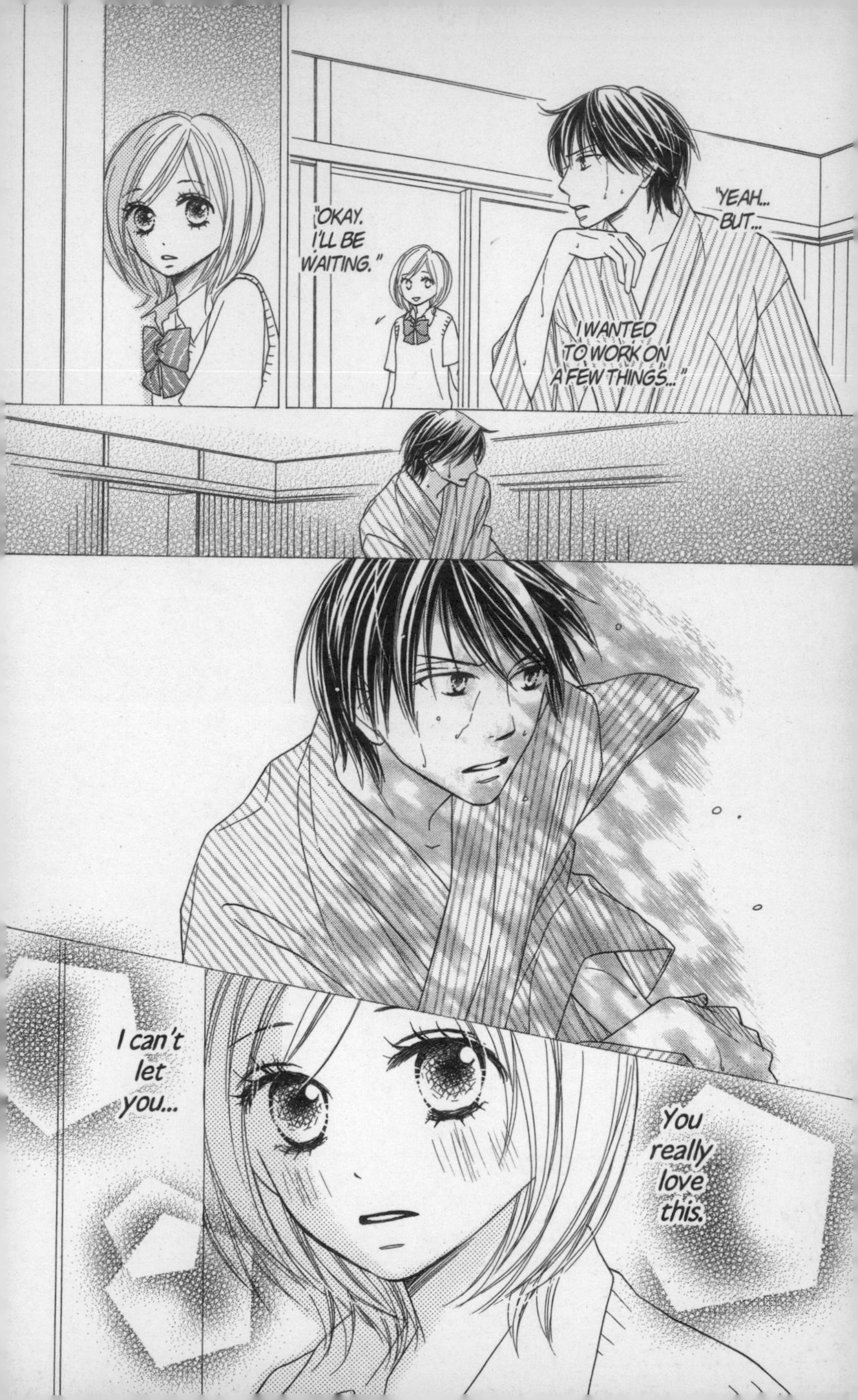
"YEAH... BUT...
I WANTED TO WORK ON A FEW THINGS..."
"OKAY. I'LL BE WAITING."
You really love this.
I can't let you...

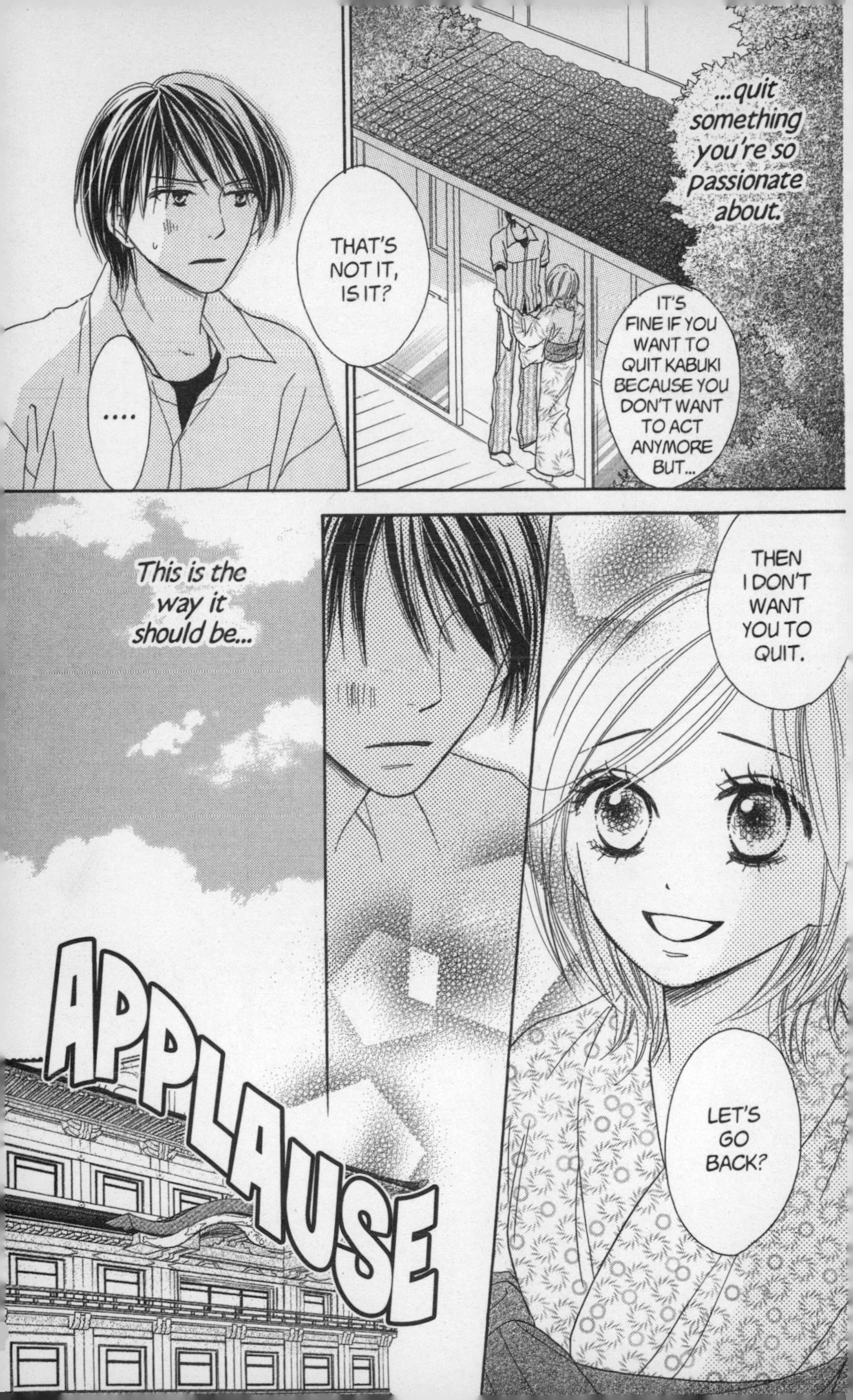
...quit something you're so passionate about.
IT'S FINE IF YOU WANT TO QUIT KABUKI BECAUSE YOU DON'T WANT TO ACT ANYMORE BUT...
THAT'S NOT IT, IS IT?
....
THEN I DON'T WANT YOU TO QUIT.
LET'S GO BACK?
This is the way it should be...
APPLAUSE

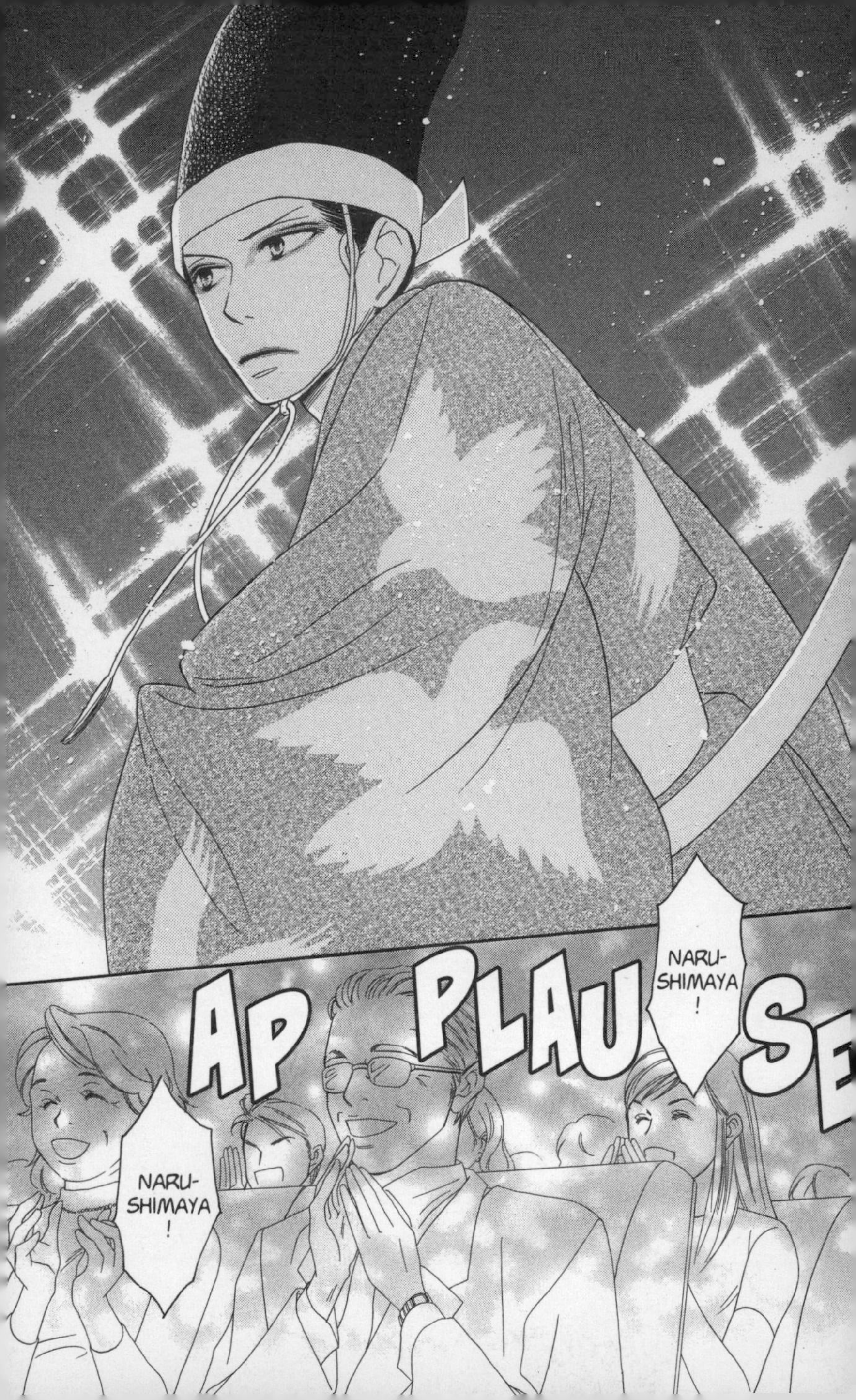
NARU-SHIMAYA!
AP PLAU SE
NARU-SHIMAYA!

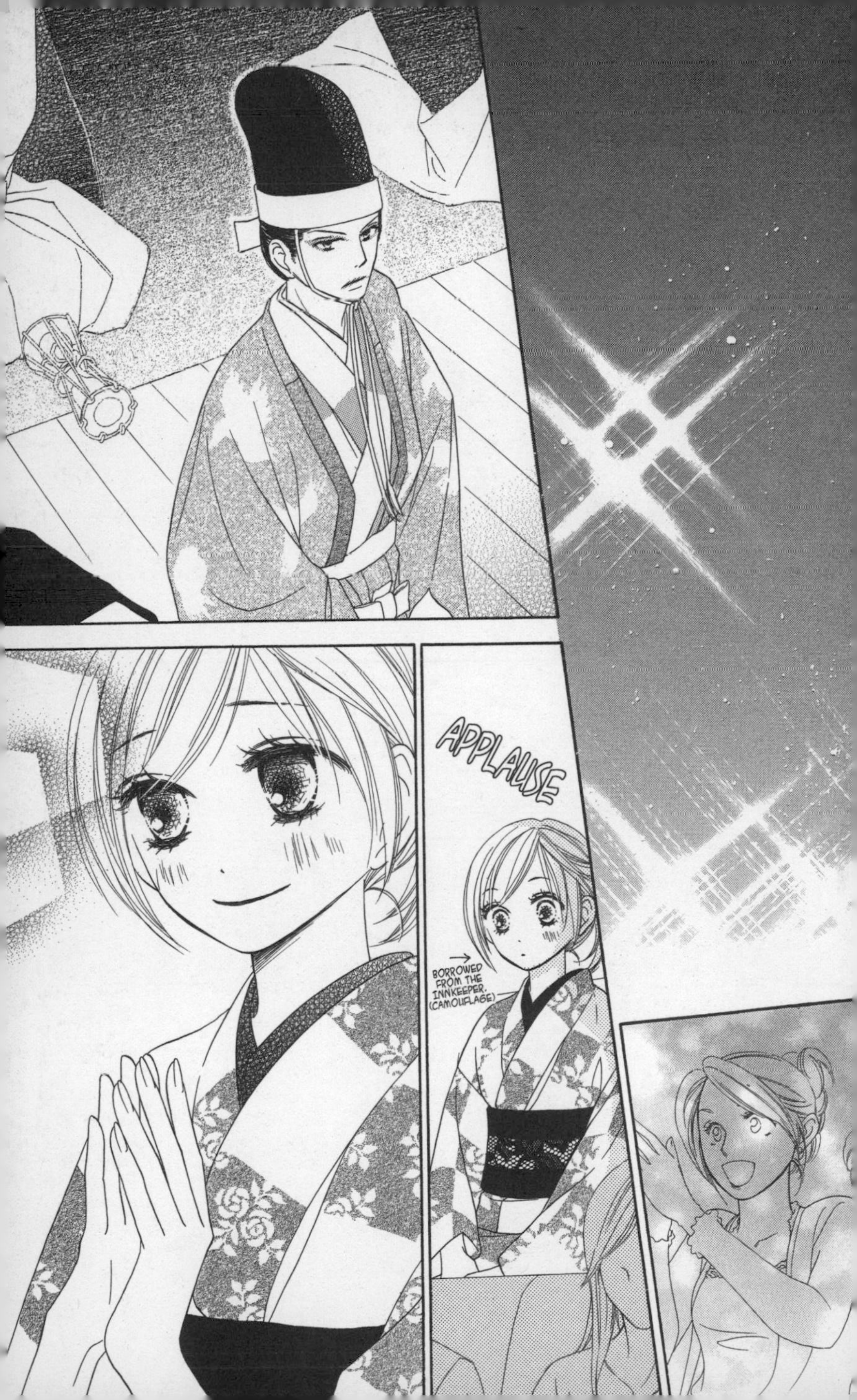
APPLAUSE
BORROWED FROM THE INNKEEPER. (CAMOUFLAGE)

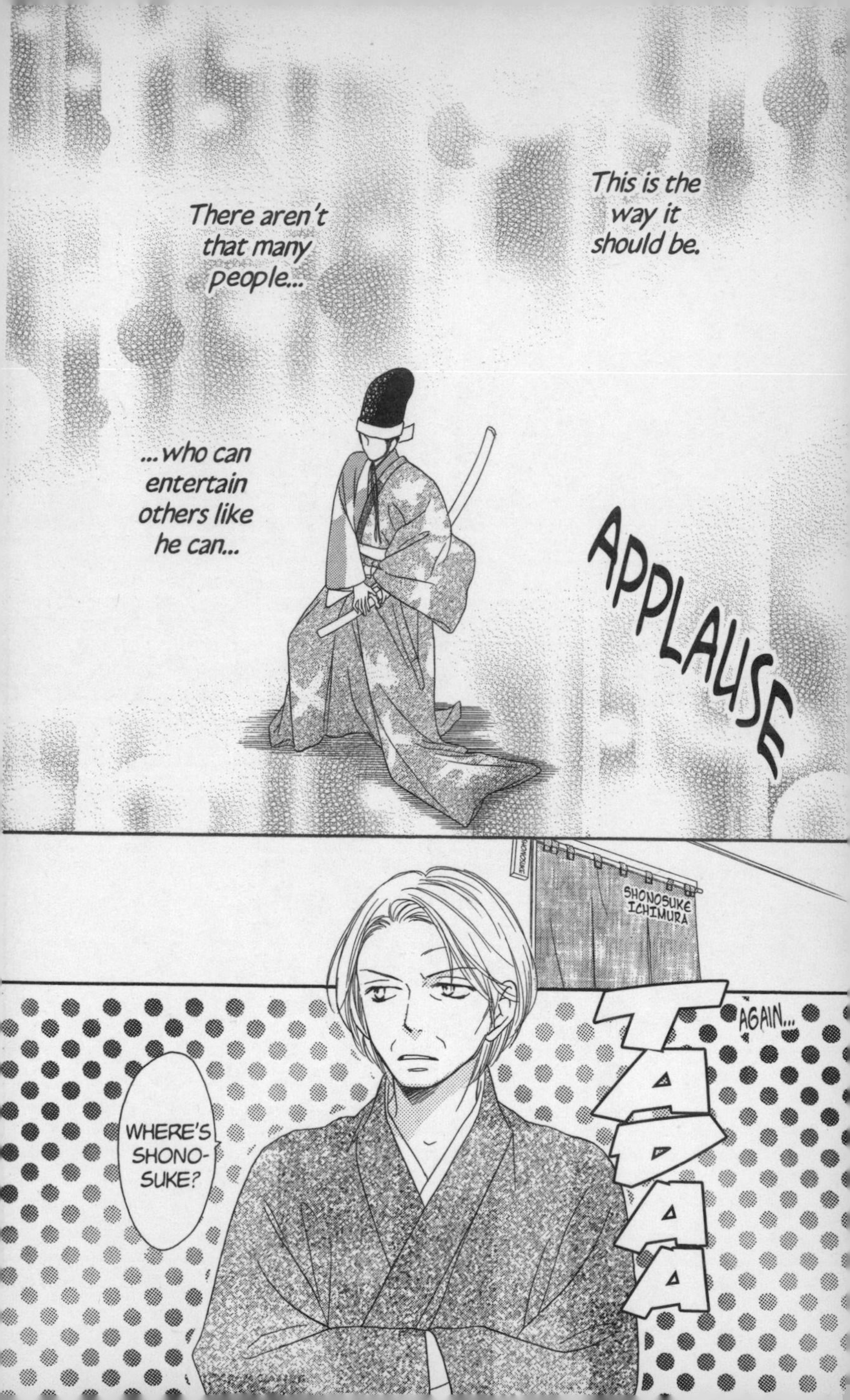
This is the way it should be.
There aren't that many people...
...who can entertain others like he can...
APPLAUSE
SHONOSUKE ICHIMURA
AGAIN...
TADAAA
WHERE'S SHONOSUKE?

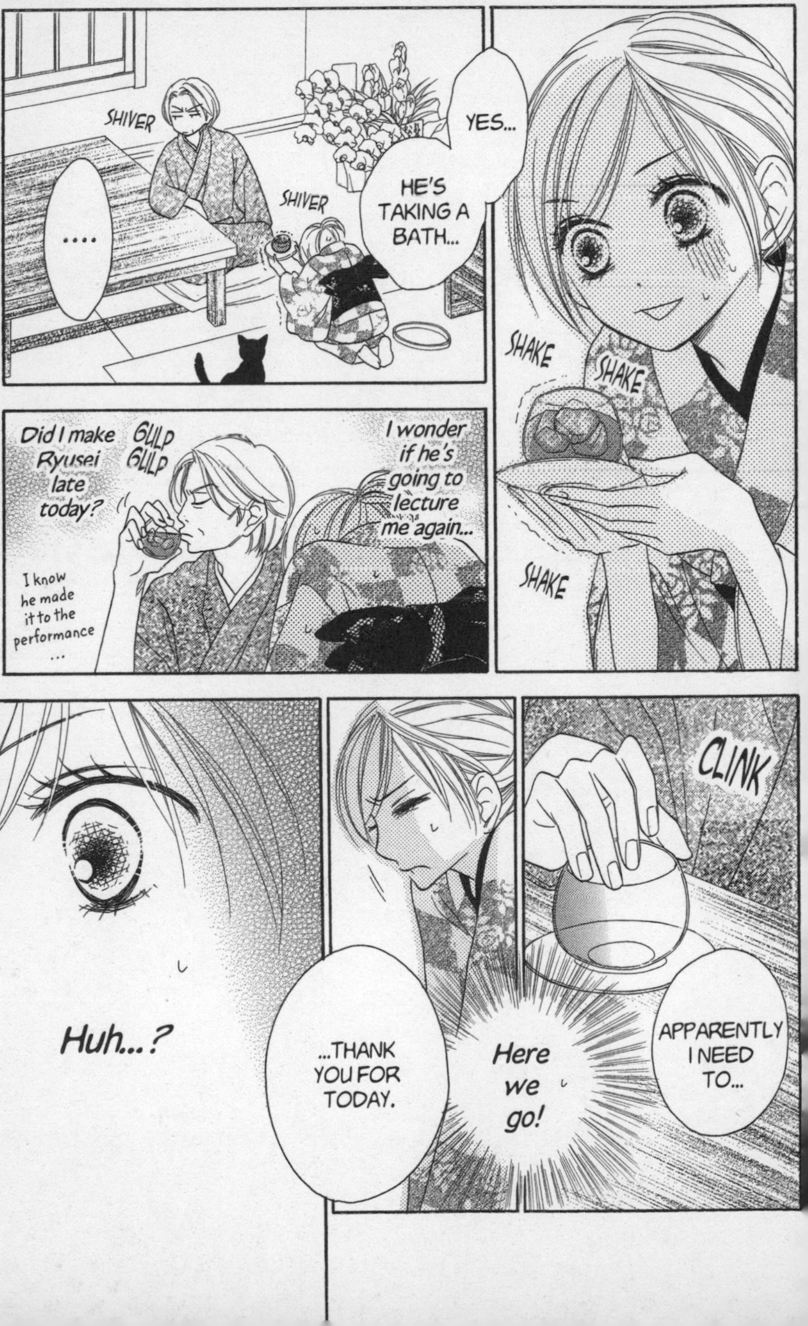
YES...
HE'S TAKING A BATH...
SHAKE
SHAKE
SHAKE
SHIVER
....
SHIVER
I wonder if he's going to lecture me again...
GULP GULP
Did I make Ryusei late today?
I know he made it to the performance ...
CLINK
APPARENTLY I NEED TO...
Here we go!
...THANK YOU FOR TODAY.
Huh...?

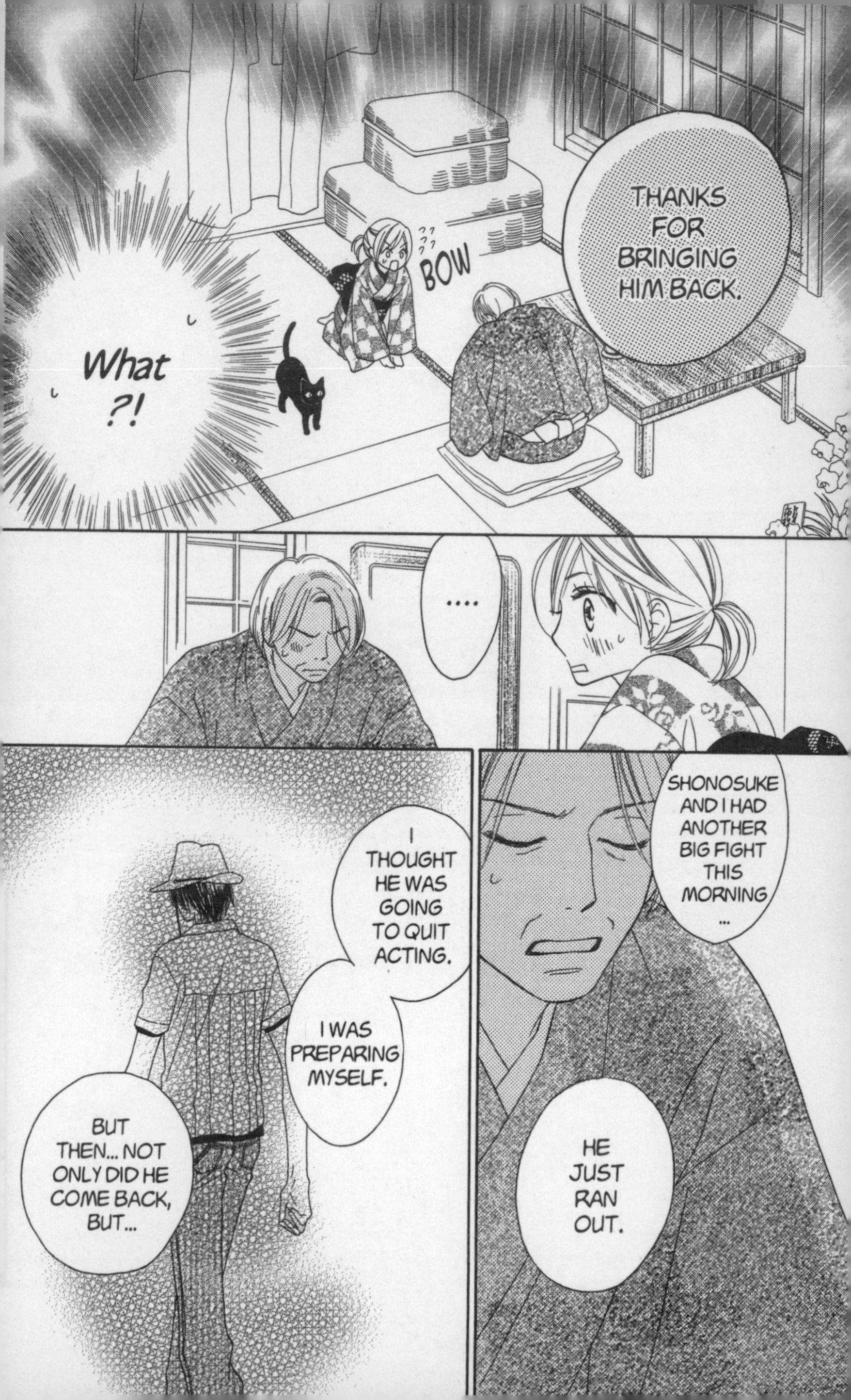
THANKS FOR BRINGING HIM BACK.
BOW
What ?!
....
SHONOSUKE AND I HAD ANOTHER BIG FIGHT THIS MORNING ...
HE JUST RAN OUT.
I THOUGHT HE WAS GOING TO QUIT ACTING.
I WAS PREPARING MYSELF.
BUT THEN... NOT ONLY DID HE COME BACK, BUT...

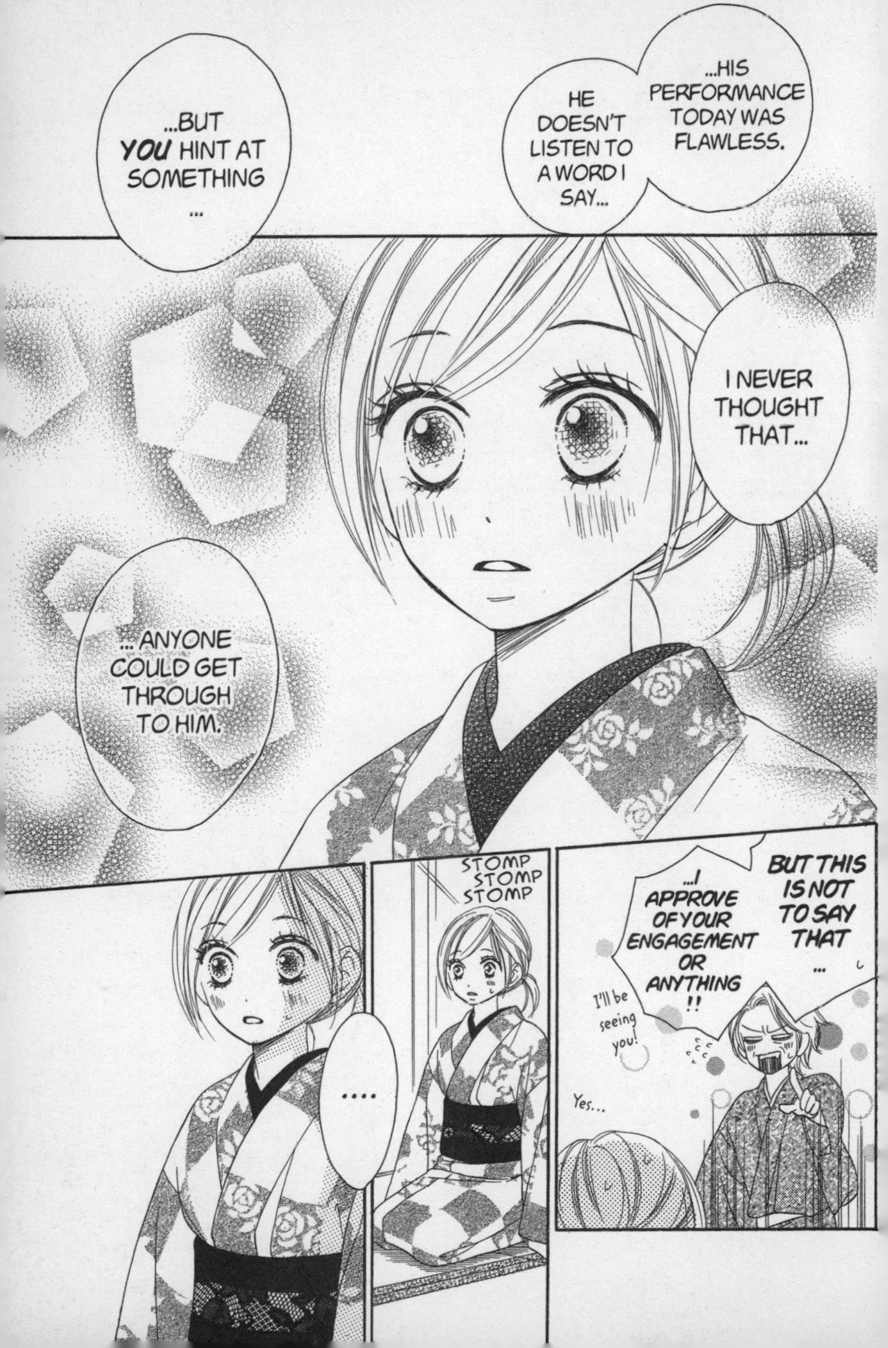
...HIS PERFORMANCE TODAY WAS FLAWLESS.
HE DOESN'T LISTEN TO A WORD I SAY...
...BUT YOU HINT AT SOMETHING ...
I NEVER THOUGHT THAT...
... ANYONE COULD GET THROUGH TO HIM.
BUT THIS IS NOT TO SAY THAT ...
...I APPROVE OF YOUR ENGAGEMENT OR ANYTHING !!
I'll be seeing you!
Yes...
STOMP STOMP STOMP
....

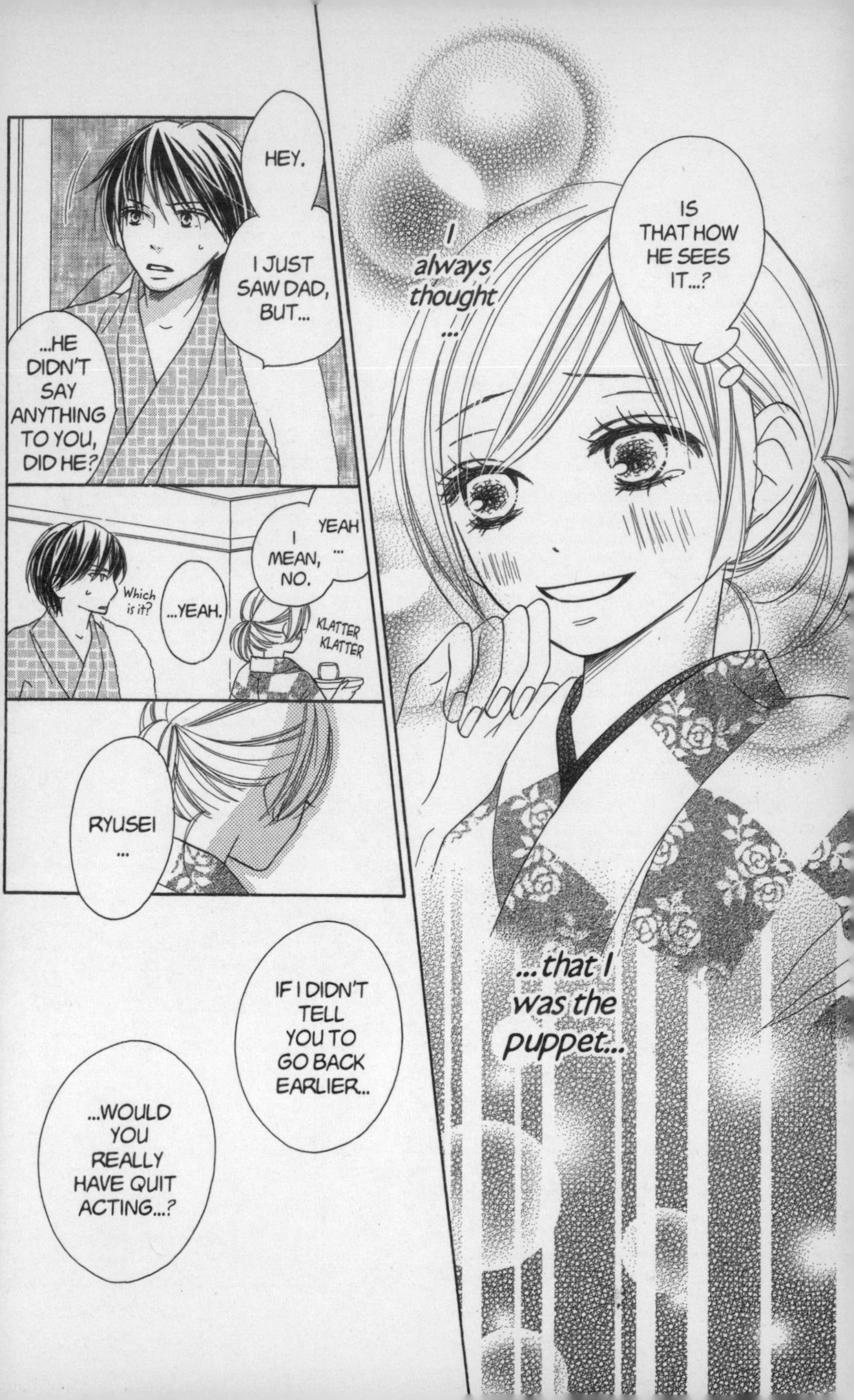
IS THAT HOW HE SEES IT...?
I always thought ...
...that I was the puppet...
HEY.
I JUST SAW DAD, BUT...
...HE DIDN'T SAY ANYTHING TO YOU, DID HE?
YEAH ...
I MEAN, NO.
KLATTER KLATTER
...YEAH.
Which is it?
RYUSEI ...
IF I DIDN'T TELL YOU TO GO BACK EARLIER..
...WOULD YOU REALLY HAVE QUIT ACTING...?

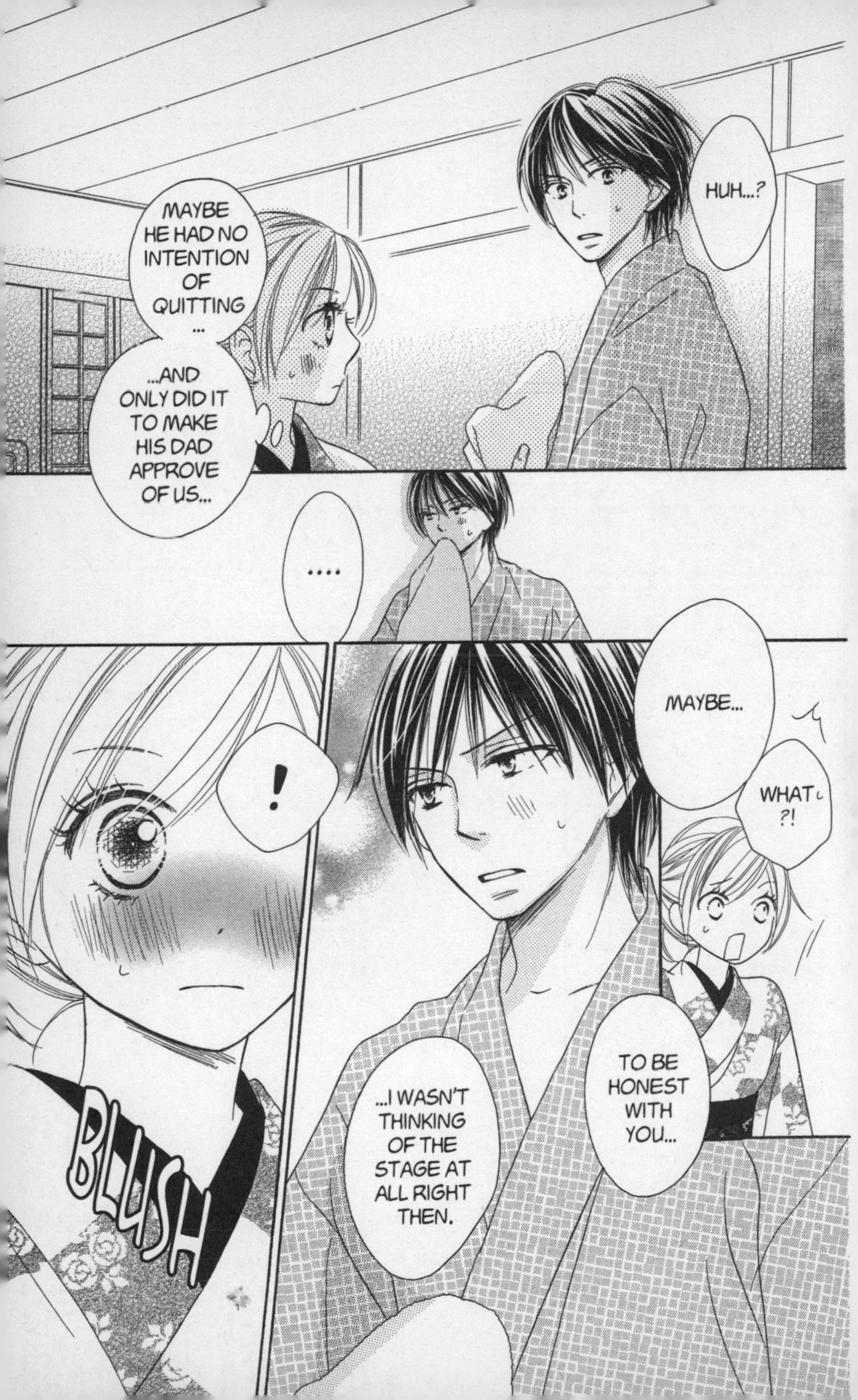
HUH...?
MAYBE HE HAD NO INTENTION OF QUITTING...
...AND ONLY DID IT TO MAKE HIS DAD APPROVE OF US...
....
MAYBE...
WHAT?!
TO BE HONEST WITH YOU...
...I WASN'T THINKING OF THE STAGE AT ALL RIGHT THEN.
!
BLUSH

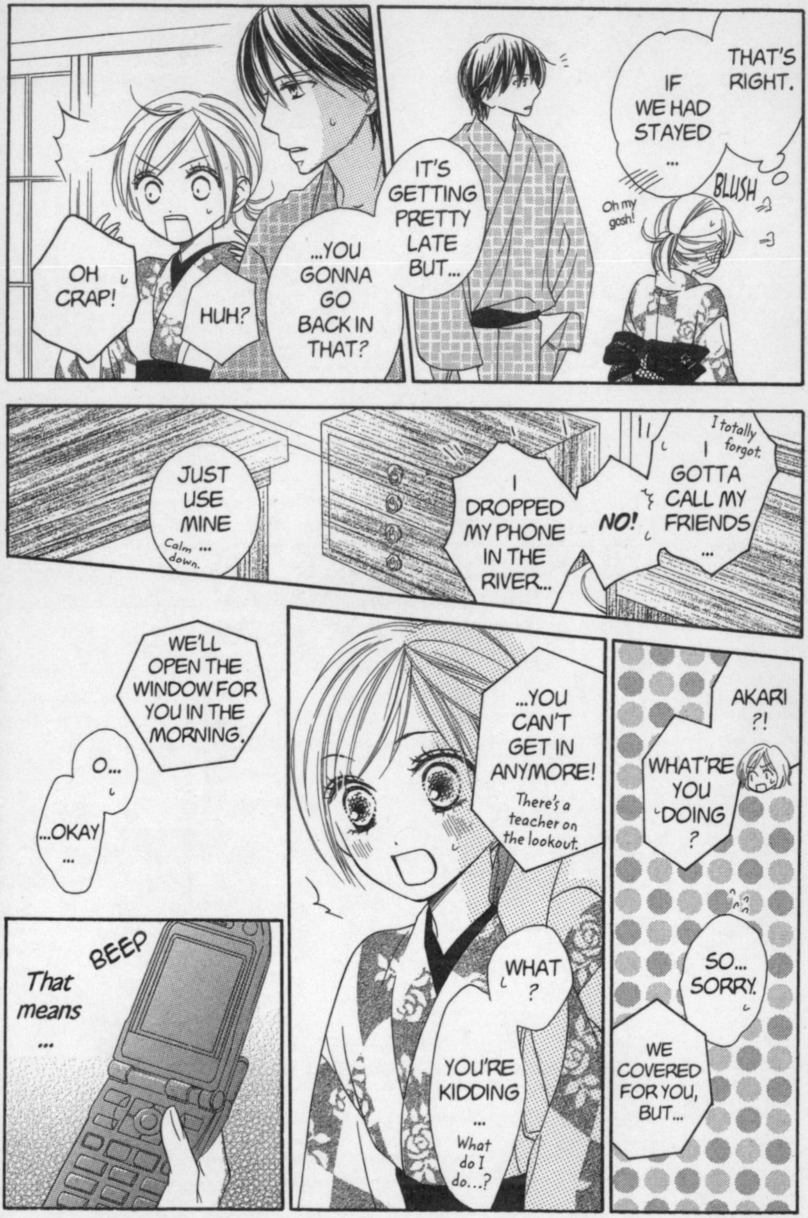
THAT'S RIGHT.
IF WE HAD STAYED ...
IT'S GETTING PRETTY LATE BUT...
BLUSH
Oh my gosh!
...YOU GONNA GO BACK IN THAT?
HUH?
OH CRAP!
I totally forgot.
I GOTTA CALL MY FRIENDS ...
NO!
I DROPPED MY PHONE IN THE RIVER...
JUST USE MINE
Calm ... down.
AKARI ?!
WHAT'RE YOU DOING ?
SO... SORRY.
WE COVERED FOR YOU, BUT...
...YOU CAN'T GET IN ANYMORE!
There's a teacher on the lookout.
WHAT ?
YOU'RE KIDDING ...
What do I do...?
WE'LL OPEN THE WINDOW FOR YOU IN THE MORNING.
O...
...OKAY ...
BEEP
That means ...

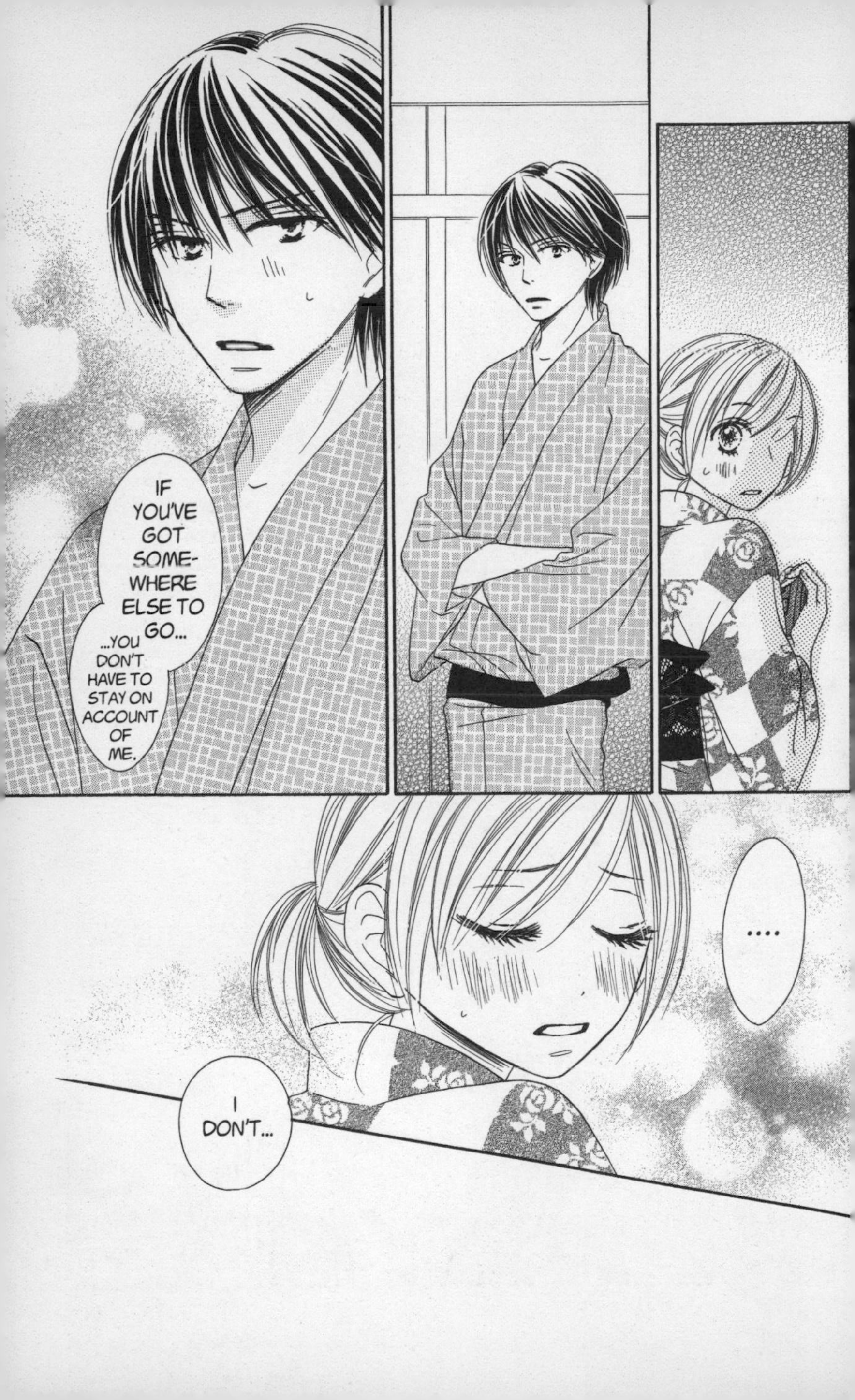
IF YOU'VE GOT SOME-WHERE ELSE TO GO...
...YOU DON'T HAVE TO STAY ON ACCOUNT OF ME.
....
I DON'T...

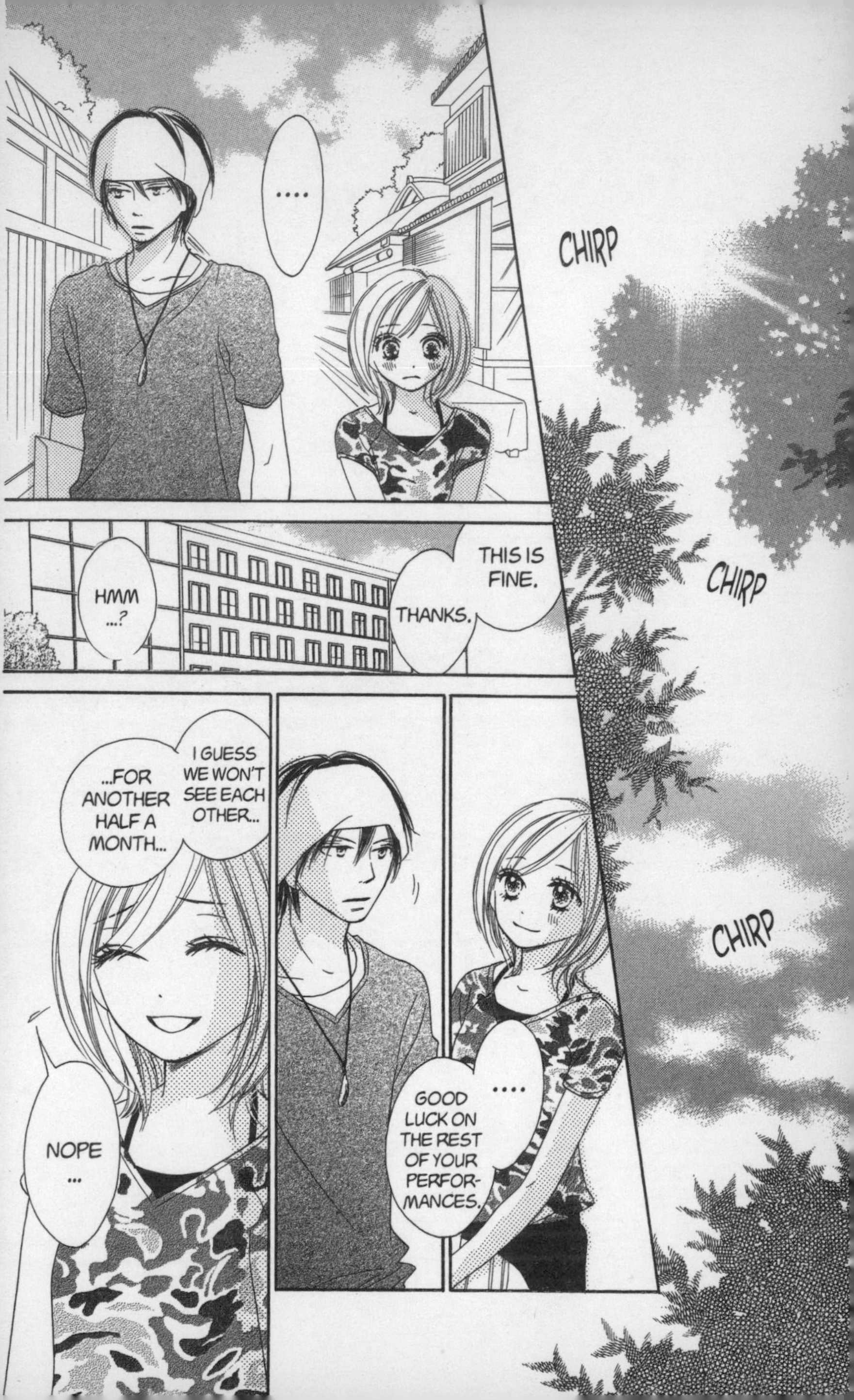
CHIRP
CHIRP
CHIRP
....
THIS IS FINE. THANKS.
HMM ...?
....
GOOD LUCK ON THE REST OF YOUR PERFOR-MANCES.
I GUESS WE WON'T SEE EACH OTHER...
...FOR ANOTHER HALF A MONTH...
NOPE ...

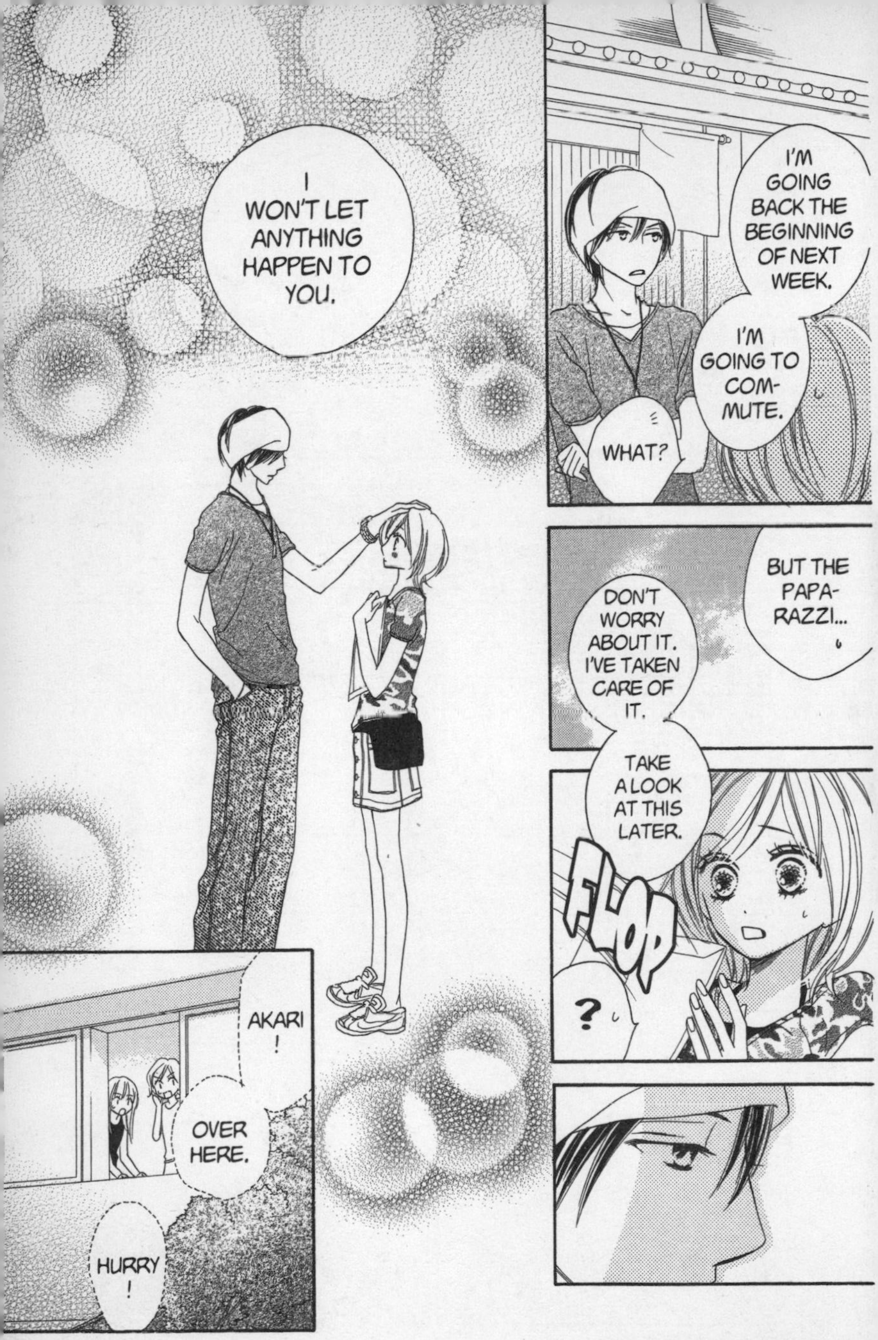
I'M GOING BACK THE BEGINNING OF NEXT WEEK.
I'M GOING TO COM-MUTE.
WHAT?
BUT THE PAPA-RAZZI...
DON'T WORRY ABOUT IT. I'VE TAKEN CARE OF IT.
TAKE A LOOK AT THIS LATER.
FLOP
?
I WON'T LET ANYTHING HAPPEN TO YOU.
AKARI!
OVER HERE.
HURRY!

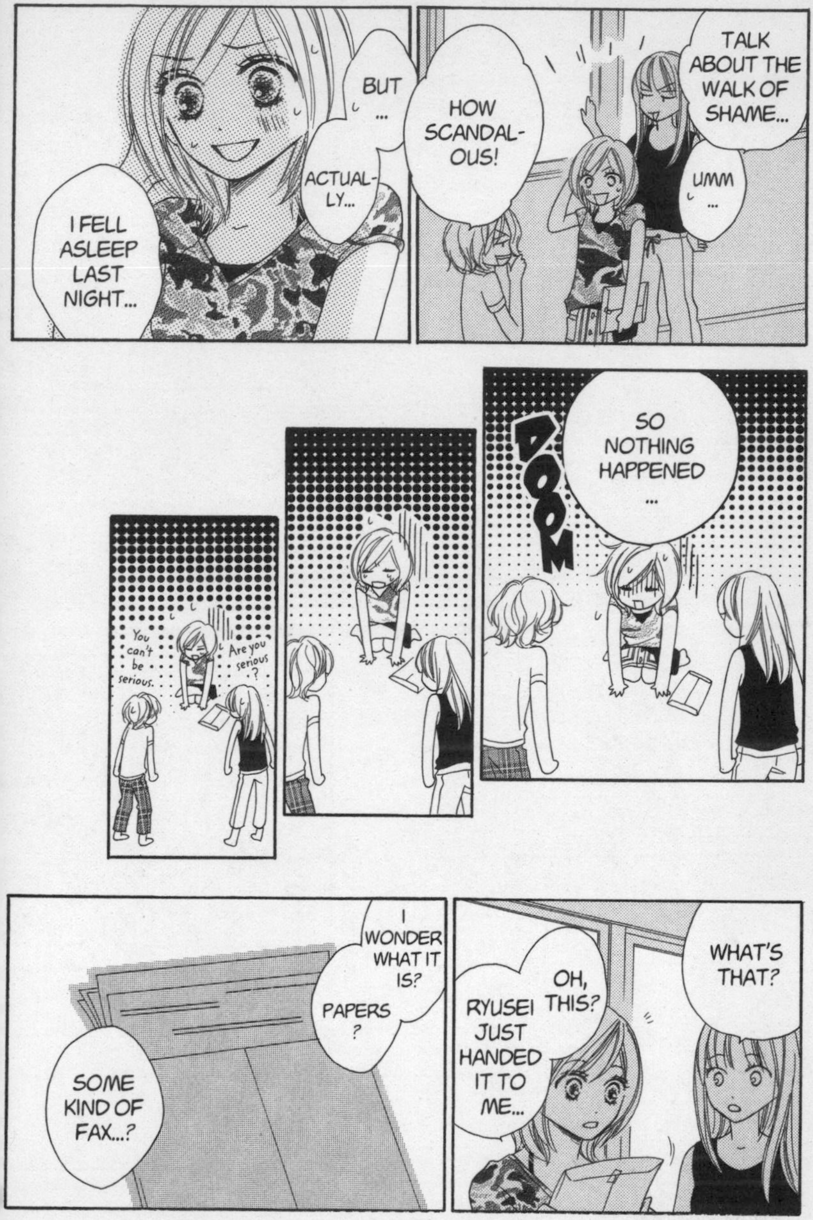
TALK ABOUT THE WALK OF SHAME...
HOW SCANDAL-OUS!
UMM...
BUT...
ACTUAL-LY...
I FELL ASLEEP LAST NIGHT...
DOOM
SO NOTHING HAPPENED...
Are you serious?
You can't be serious.
WHAT'S THAT?
OH, THIS?
RYUSEI JUST HANDED IT TO ME...
I WONDER WHAT IT IS?
PAPERS?
SOME KIND OF FAX...?

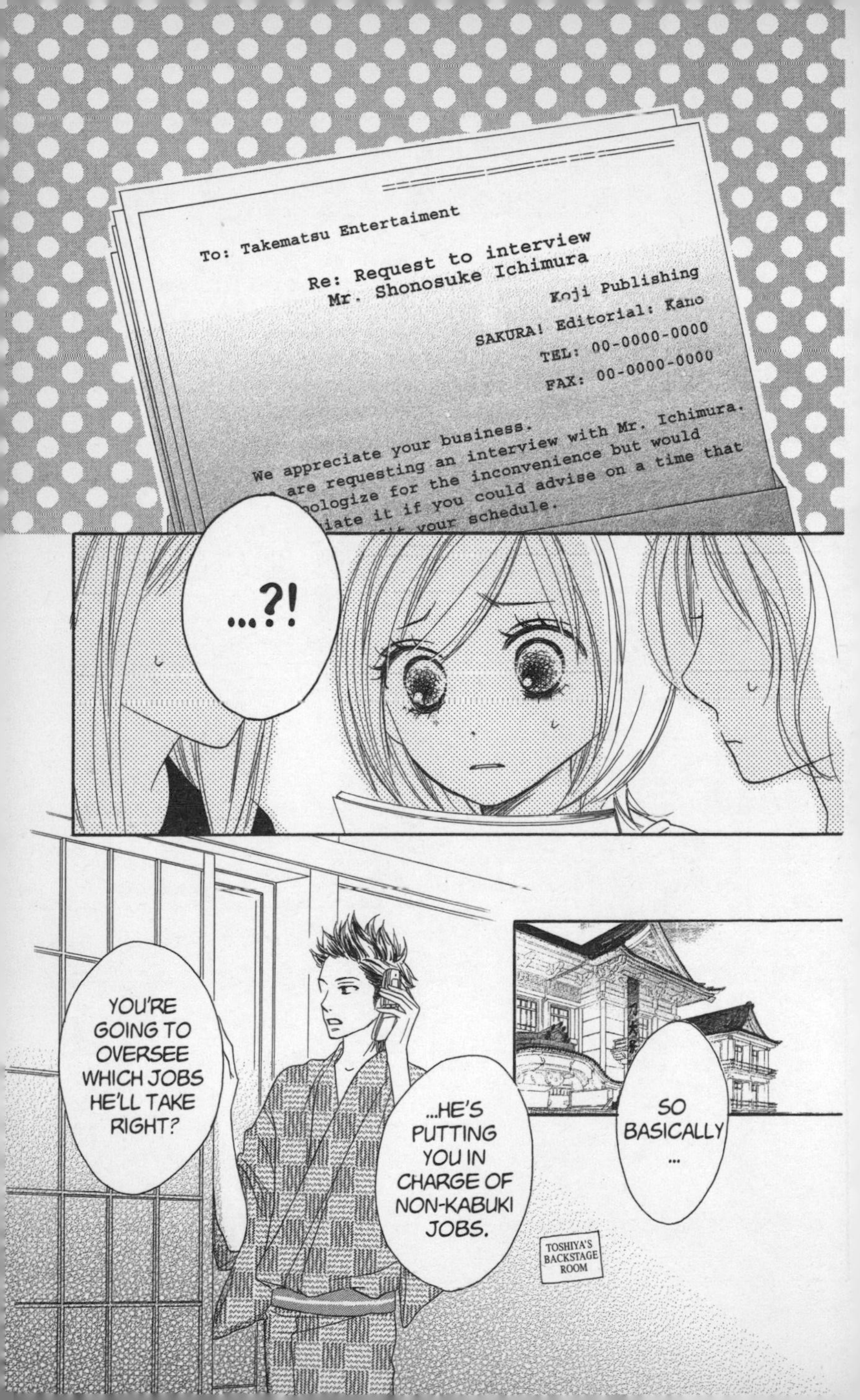
To: Takematsu Entertaiment
Re: Request to interview
Mr. Shonosuke Ichimura
Koji Publishing
SAKURA! Editorial: Kano
TEL: 00-0000-0000
FAX: 00-0000-0000
We appreciate your business.
are requesting an interview with Mr. Ichimura.
pologize for the inconvenience but would
iate it if you could advise on a time that
your schedule.
...?!
TOSHIYA'S BACKSTAGE ROOM
SO BASICALLY ...
...HE'S PUTTING YOU IN CHARGE OF NON-KABUKI JOBS.
YOU'RE GOING TO OVERSEE WHICH JOBS HE'LL TAKE RIGHT?

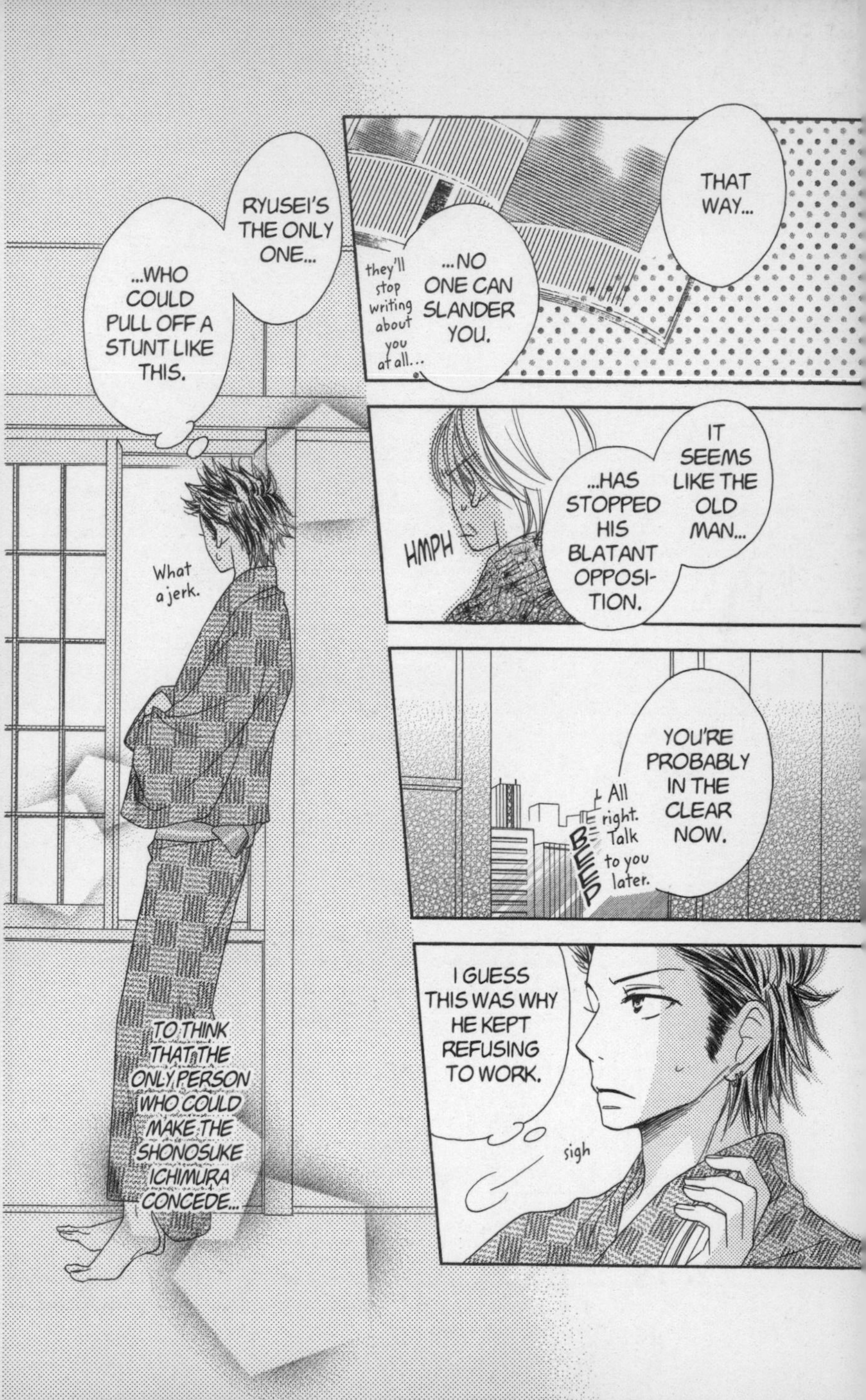
THAT WAY...
...NO ONE CAN SLANDER YOU.
they'll stop writing about you at all...
IT SEEMS LIKE THE OLD MAN...
...HAS STOPPED HIS BLATANT OPPOSITION.
HMPH
YOU'RE PROBABLY IN THE CLEAR NOW.
All right. Talk to you later.
BEEP
I GUESS THIS WAS WHY HE KEPT REFUSING TO WORK.
sigh
RYUSEI'S THE ONLY ONE...
...WHO COULD PULL OFF A STUNT LIKE THIS.
What a jerk.
TO THINK THAT THE ONLY PERSON WHO COULD MAKE THE SHONOSUKE ICHIMURA CONCEDE...

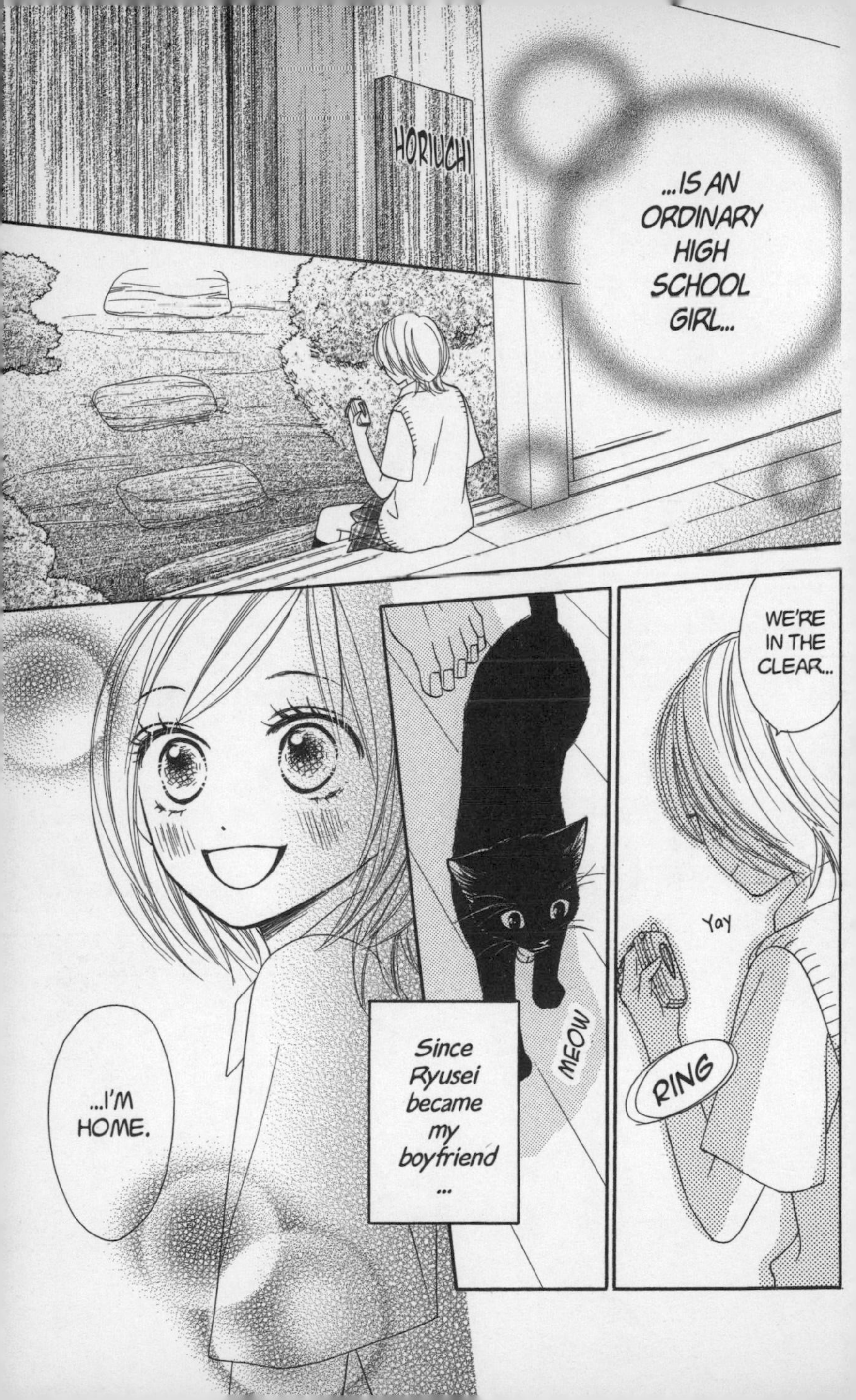
HORIUCHI
...IS AN ORDINARY HIGH SCHOOL GIRL...
WE'RE IN THE CLEAR...
Yay
RING
MEOW
Since Ryusei became my boyfriend ...
...I'M HOME.

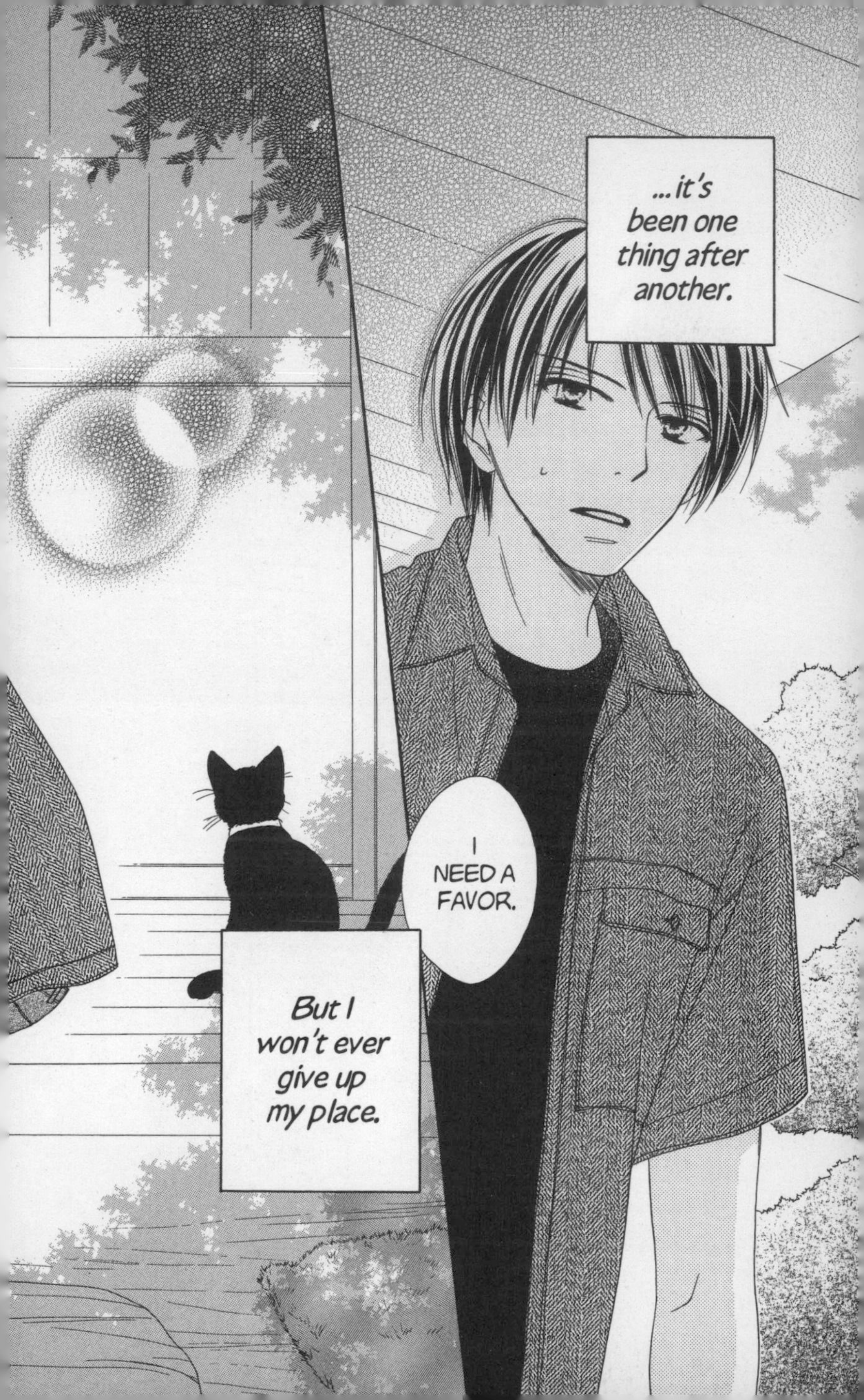
...it's been one thing after another.
I NEED A FAVOR.
But I won't ever give up my place.

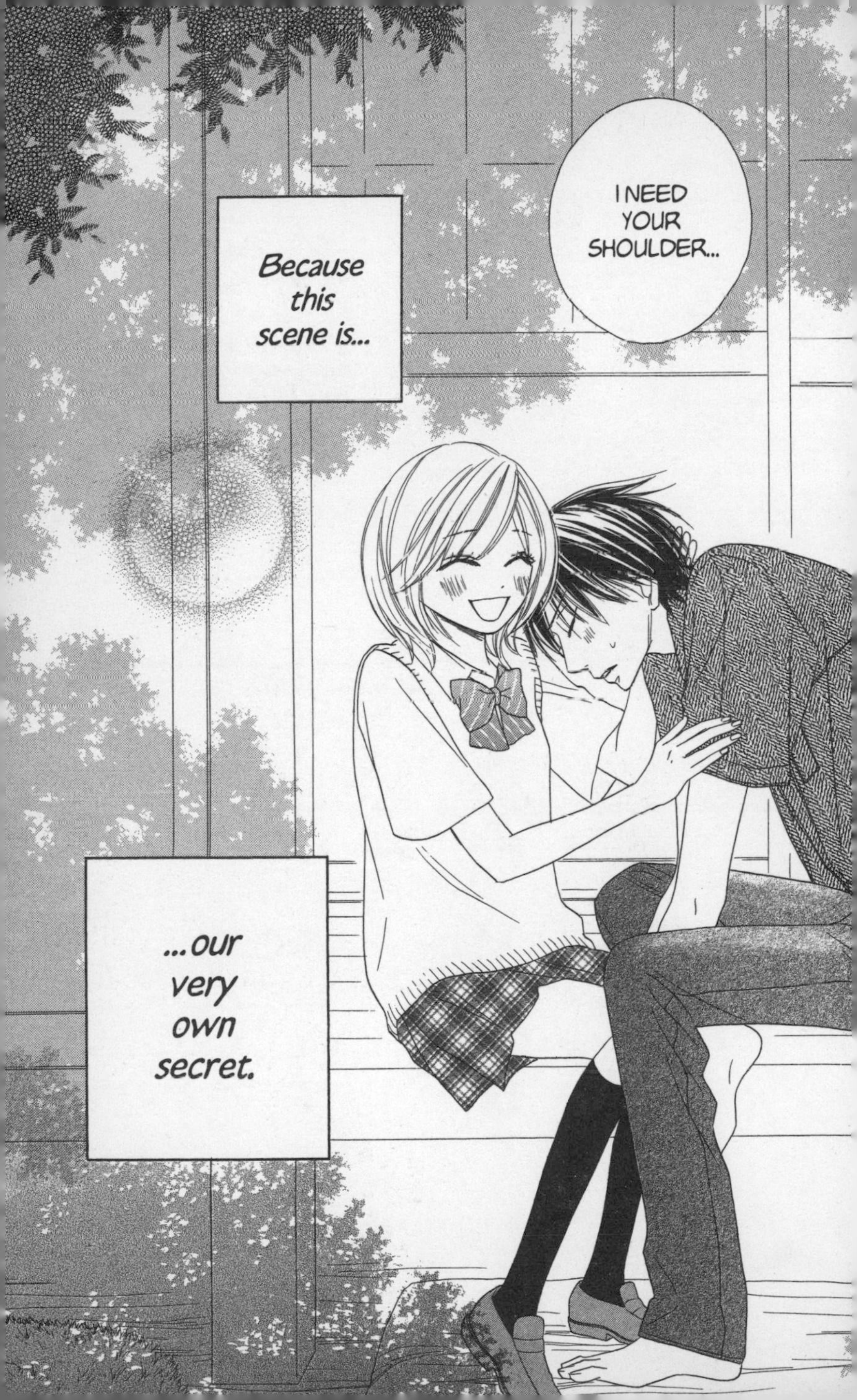
I NEED YOUR SHOULDER...
Because this scene is...
...our very own secret.

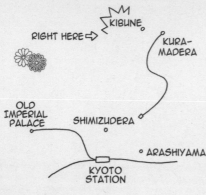

THE MAKING OF BACKSTAGE PRINCE

AKARI AND RYUSEI'S DATE SPOT WAS IN KIBUNE, WHICH IS NORTH OF KYOTO.

KIBUNE
RIGHT HERE
KURA-MADERA
OLD IMPERIAL PALACE
SHIMIZUDERA
ARASHIYAMA
KYOTO STATION

IT'S SO GREEN AND COOL IN THE SUMMER. KIBUNE SHRINE IS JUST A GREAT PLACE TO GO.

YOU CAN GO TO A RIVERBED RESTAURANT AT THE PARLOR BUILT ON THE KIBUNE RIVER. (A PRICY ONE?)

I'D JUST LIKE TO SAY FOR THE RECORD...

YOU CAN ONLY FALL IN IF YOU TRY.

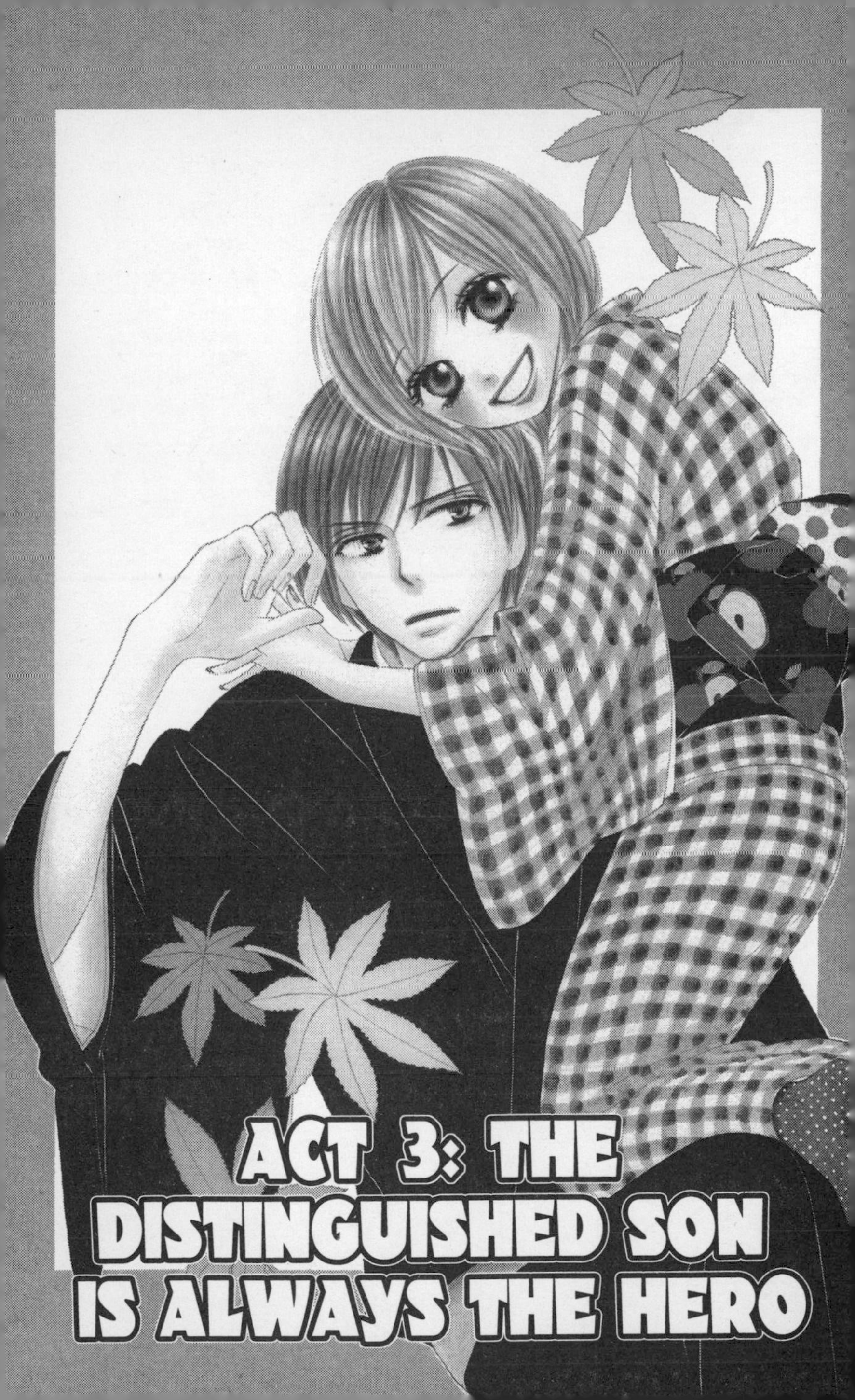

ACT 3: THE DISTINGUISHED SON IS ALWAYS THE HERO

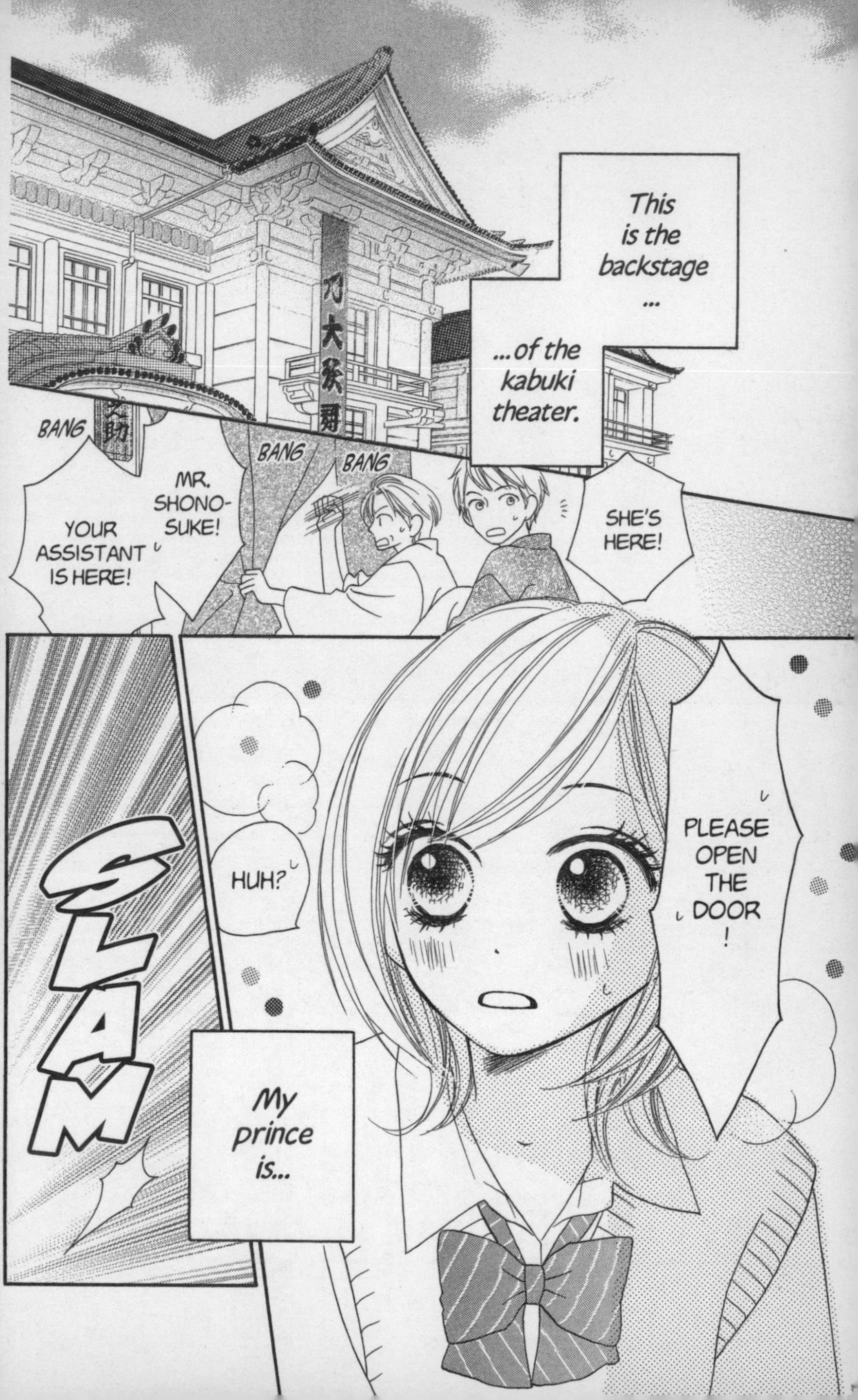
This is the backstage ...
...of the kabuki theater.
BANG
BANG
BANG
SHE'S HERE!
MR. SHONOSUKE!
YOUR ASSISTANT IS HERE!
PLEASE OPEN THE DOOR!
HUH?
My prince is...
SLAM

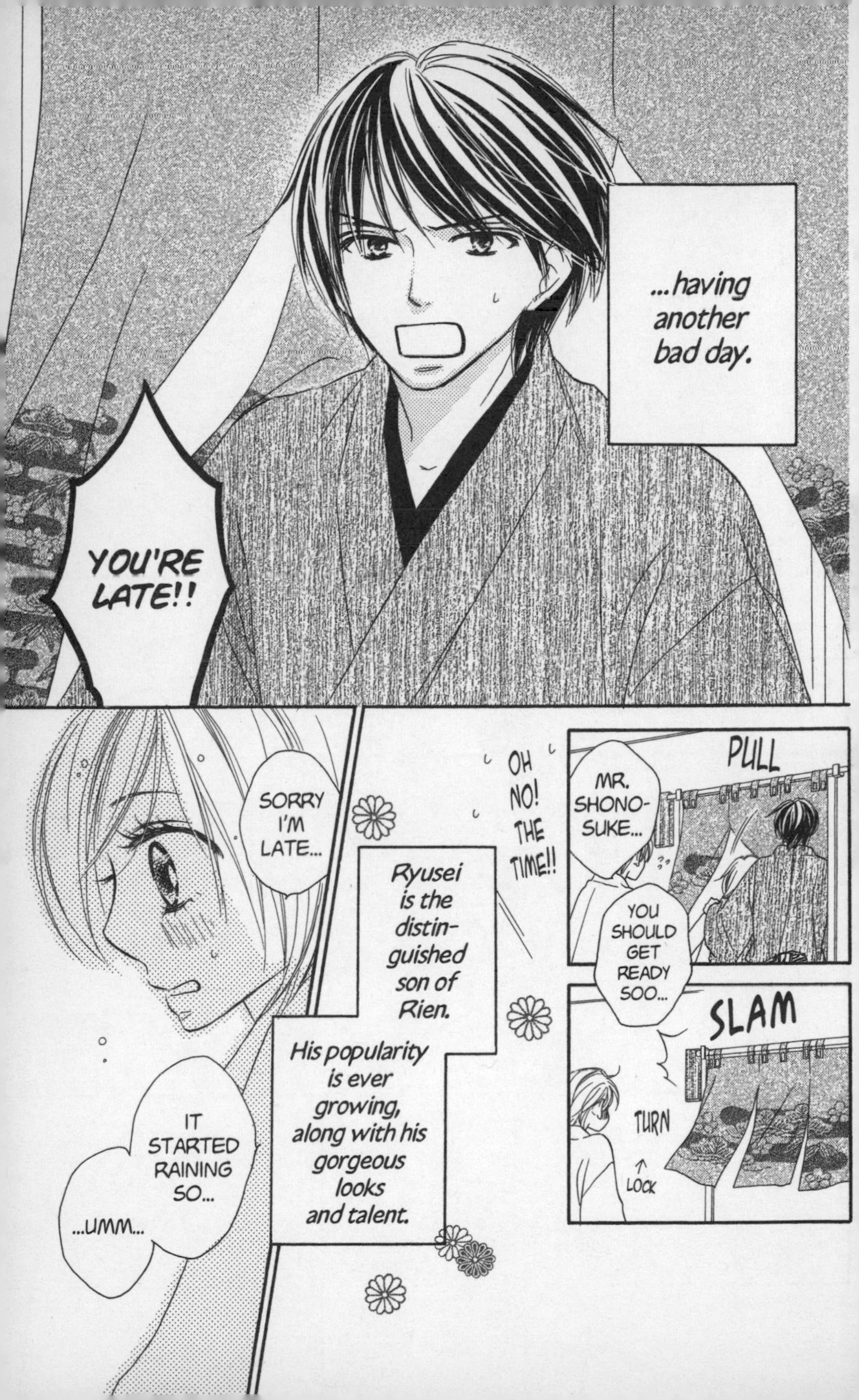
...having another bad day.
YOU'RE LATE!!
PULL
MR. SHONOSUKE...
YOU SHOULD GET READY SOO...
SLAM
TURN
↑ LOCK
OH NO! THE TIME!!
Ryusei is the distinguished son of Rien.
His popularity is ever growing, along with his gorgeous looks and talent.
SORRY I'M LATE...
IT STARTED RAINING SO...
...UMM...

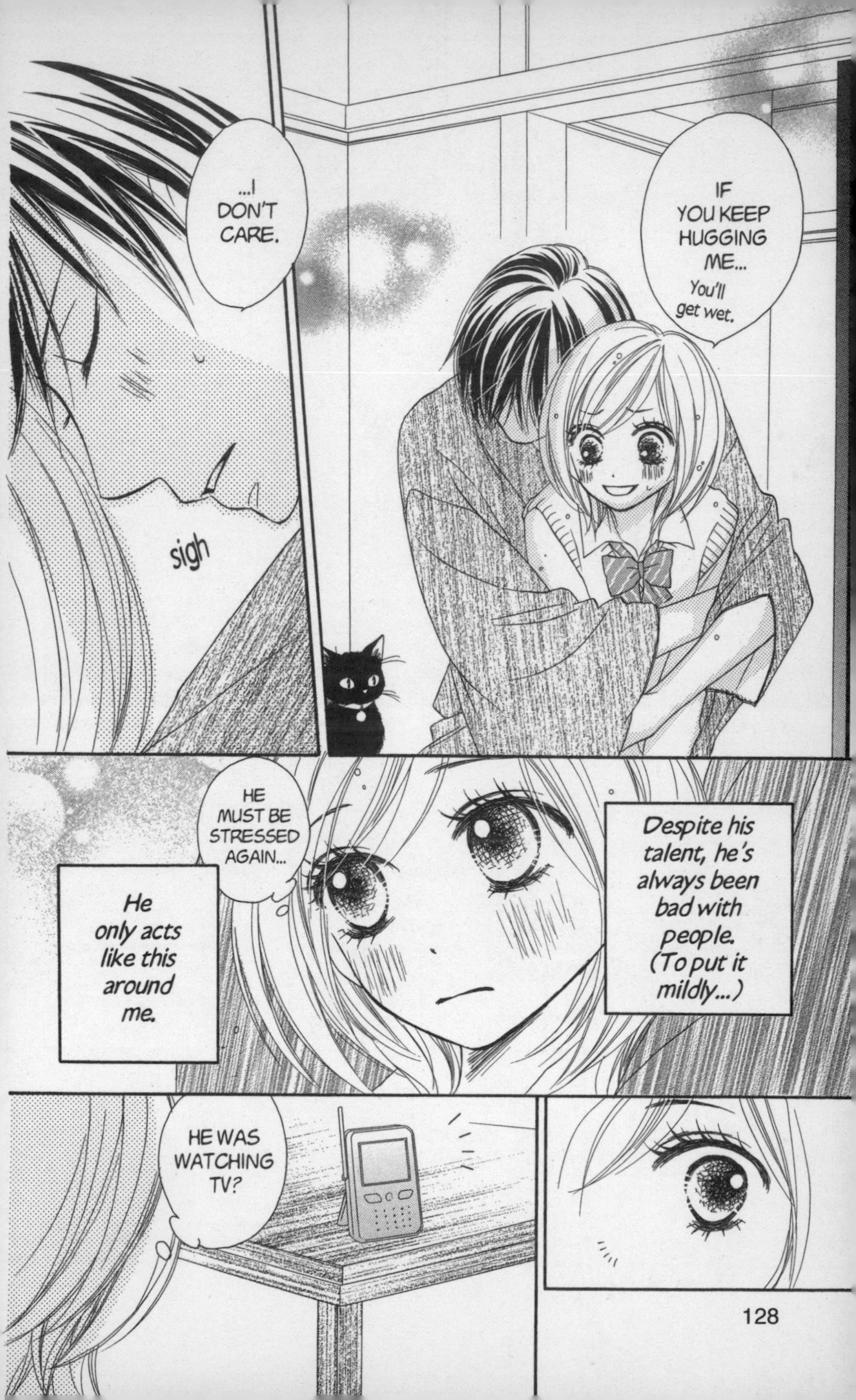
IF YOU KEEP HUGGING ME... You'll get wet.
...I DON'T CARE.
sigh
Despite his talent, he's always been bad with people. (To put it mildly...)
HE MUST BE STRESSED AGAIN...
He only acts like this around me.
HE WAS WATCHING TV?

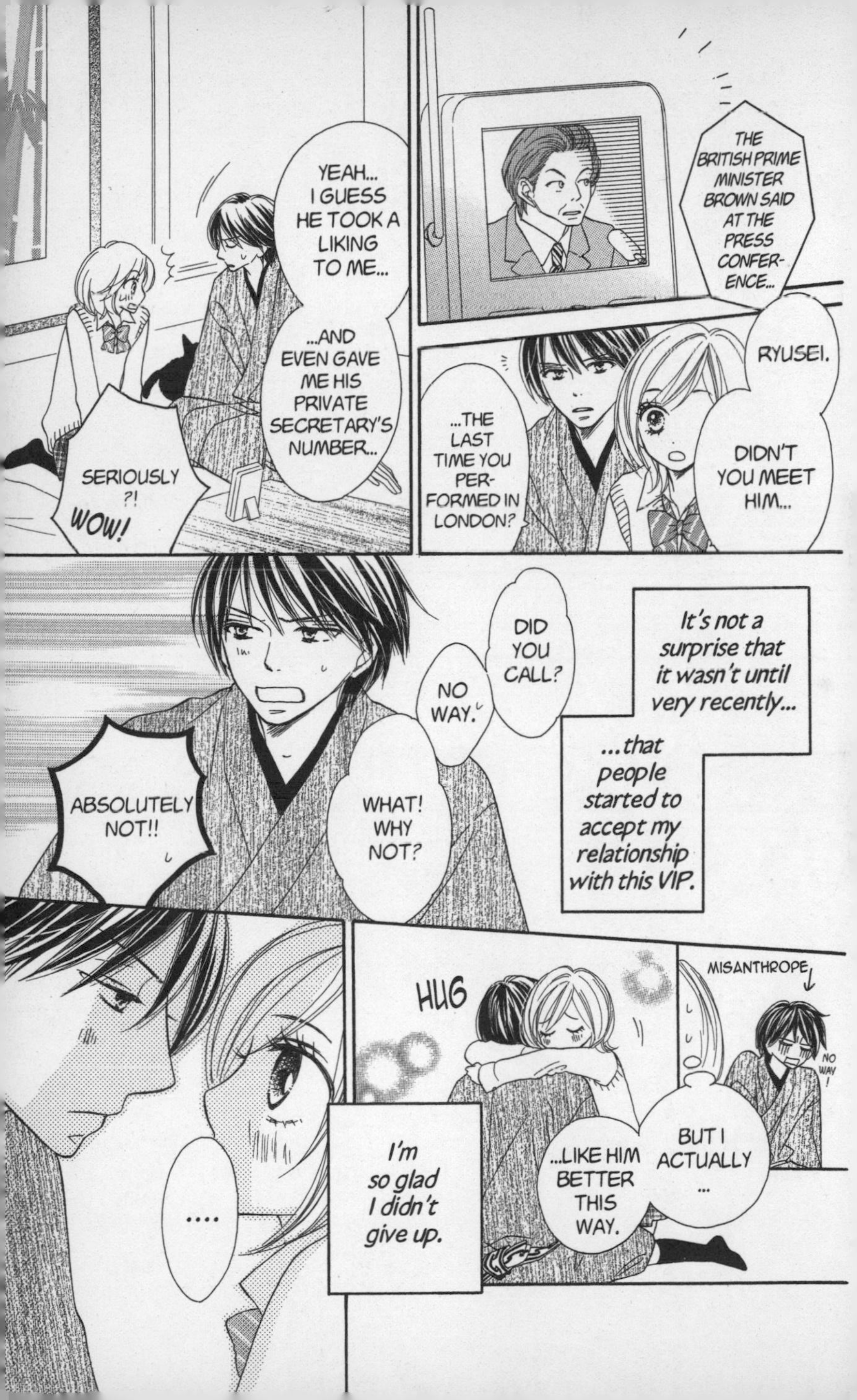
THE BRITISH PRIME MINISTER BROWN SAID AT THE PRESS CONFERENCE...
RYUSEI.
DIDN'T YOU MEET HIM...
...THE LAST TIME YOU PERFORMED IN LONDON?
YEAH... I GUESS HE TOOK A LIKING TO ME...
...AND EVEN GAVE ME HIS PRIVATE SECRETARY'S NUMBER...
SERIOUSLY?!
WOW!
It's not a surprise that it wasn't until very recently...
...that people started to accept my relationship with this VIP.
DID YOU CALL?
NO WAY.
WHAT! WHY NOT?
ABSOLUTELY NOT!!
MISANTHROPE
NO WAY!
HUG
BUT I ACTUALLY...
...LIKE HIM BETTER THIS WAY.
I'm so glad I didn't give up.
....

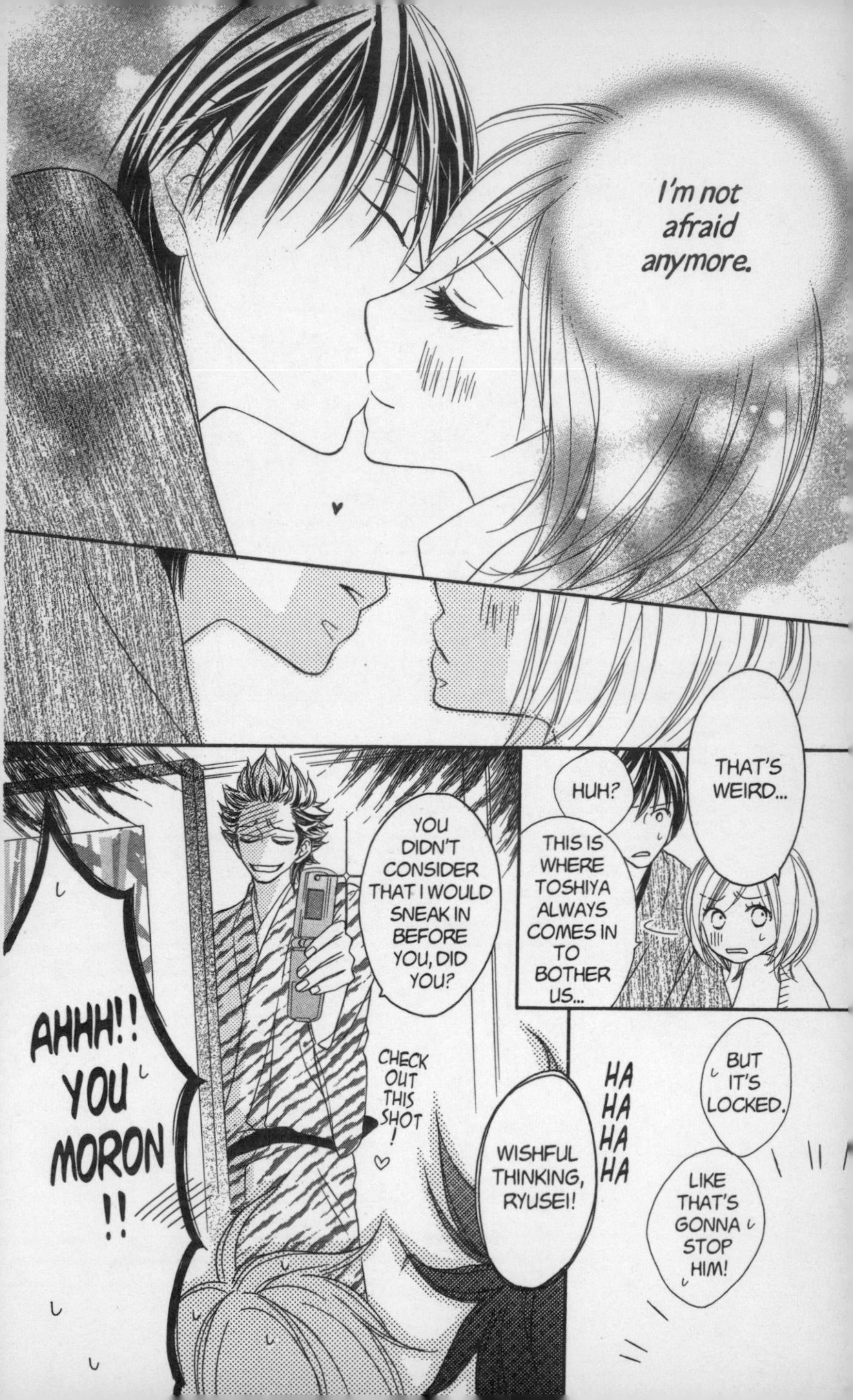
I'm not afraid anymore.
THAT'S WEIRD...
HUH?
THIS IS WHERE TOSHIYA ALWAYS COMES IN TO BOTHER US...
BUT IT'S LOCKED.
LIKE THAT'S GONNA STOP HIM!
HA HA HA HA
WISHFUL THINKING, RYUSEI!
YOU DIDN'T CONSIDER THAT I WOULD SNEAK IN BEFORE YOU, DID YOU?
CHECK OUT THIS SHOT!
AHHH!! YOU MORON!!

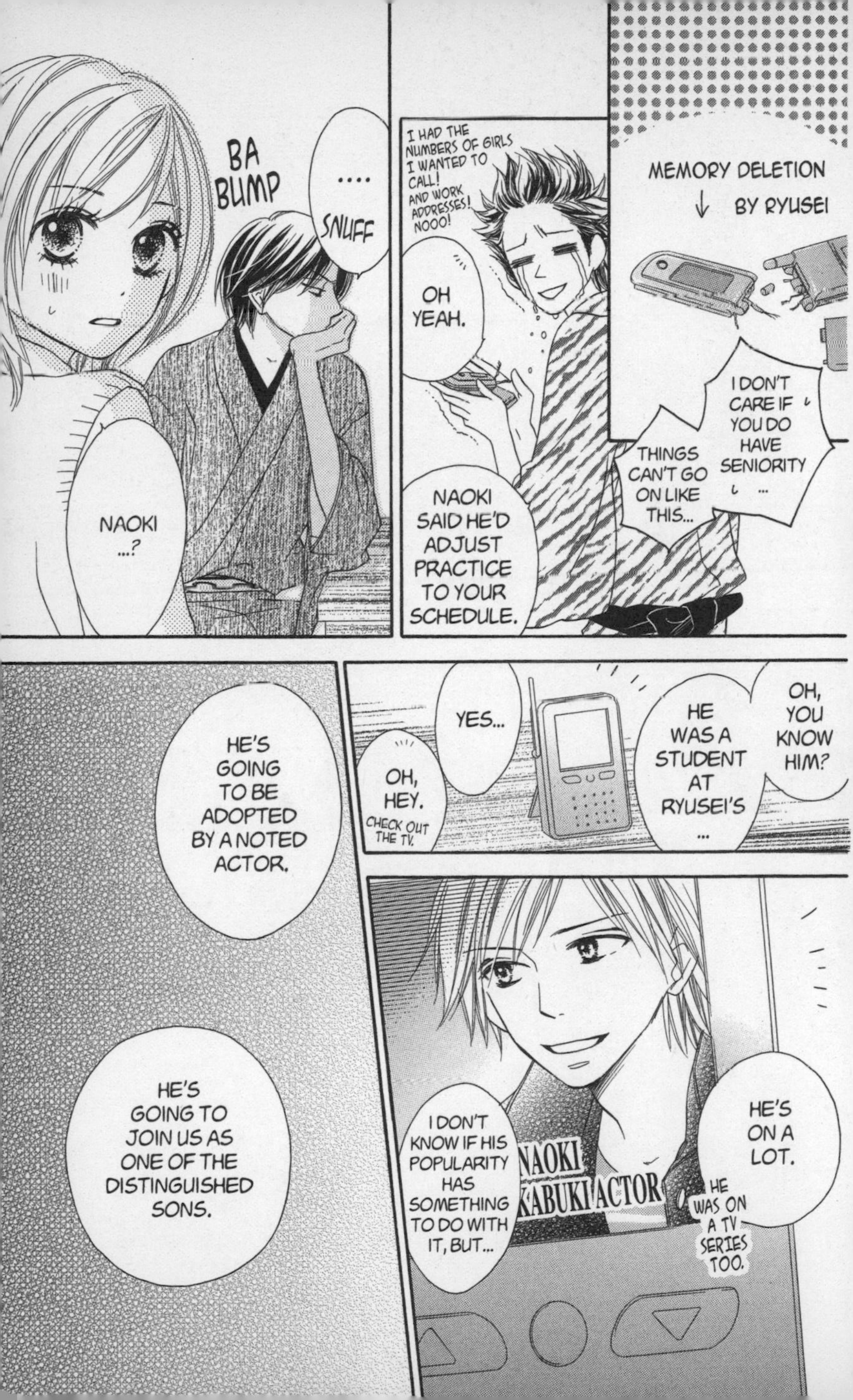
MEMORY DELETION
↓ BY RYUSEI
I DON'T CARE IF YOU DO HAVE SENIORITY...
THINGS CAN'T GO ON LIKE THIS...
I HAD THE NUMBERS OF GIRLS I WANTED TO CALL! AND WORK ADDRESSES! NOOO!
OH YEAH.
NAOKI SAID HE'D ADJUST PRACTICE TO YOUR SCHEDULE.
BA BUMP
....
SNUFF
NAOKI ...?
OH, YOU KNOW HIM?
HE WAS A STUDENT AT RYUSEI'S ...
YES...
OH, HEY.
CHECK OUT THE TV.
HE'S ON A LOT.
HE WAS ON A TV SERIES TOO.
NAOKI
KABUKI ACTOR
I DON'T KNOW IF HIS POPULARITY HAS SOMETHING TO DO WITH IT, BUT...
HE'S GOING TO BE ADOPTED BY A NOTED ACTOR.
HE'S GOING TO JOIN US AS ONE OF THE DISTINGUISHED SONS.

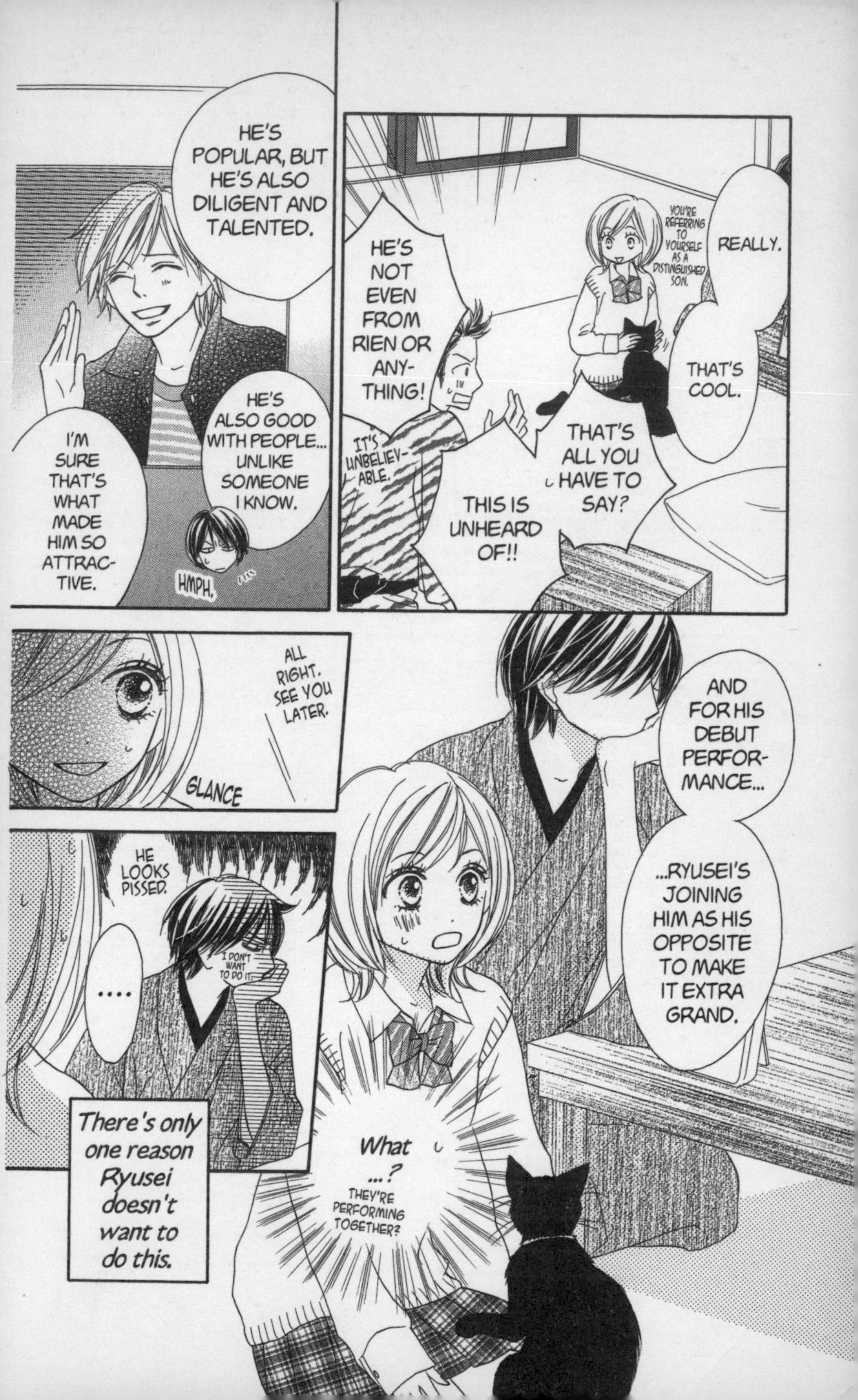
REALLY.
YOU'RE REFERRING TO YOURSELF AS A DISTINGUISHED SON.
THAT'S COOL.
HE'S NOT EVEN FROM RIEN OR ANY-THING!
THAT'S ALL YOU HAVE TO SAY?
IT'S UNBELIEV-ABLE.
THIS IS UNHEARD OF!!
HE'S POPULAR, BUT HE'S ALSO DILIGENT AND TALENTED.
HE'S ALSO GOOD WITH PEOPLE... UNLIKE SOMEONE I KNOW.
I'M SURE THAT'S WHAT MADE HIM SO ATTRAC-TIVE.
HMPH.
AND FOR HIS DEBUT PERFOR-MANCE...
...RYUSEI'S JOINING HIM AS HIS OPPOSITE TO MAKE IT EXTRA GRAND.
What ...?
THEY'RE PERFORMING TOGETHER?
ALL RIGHT. SEE YOU LATER.
GLANCE
HE LOOKS PISSED.
I DON'T WANT TO DO IT.
....
There's only one reason Ryusei doesn't want to do this.

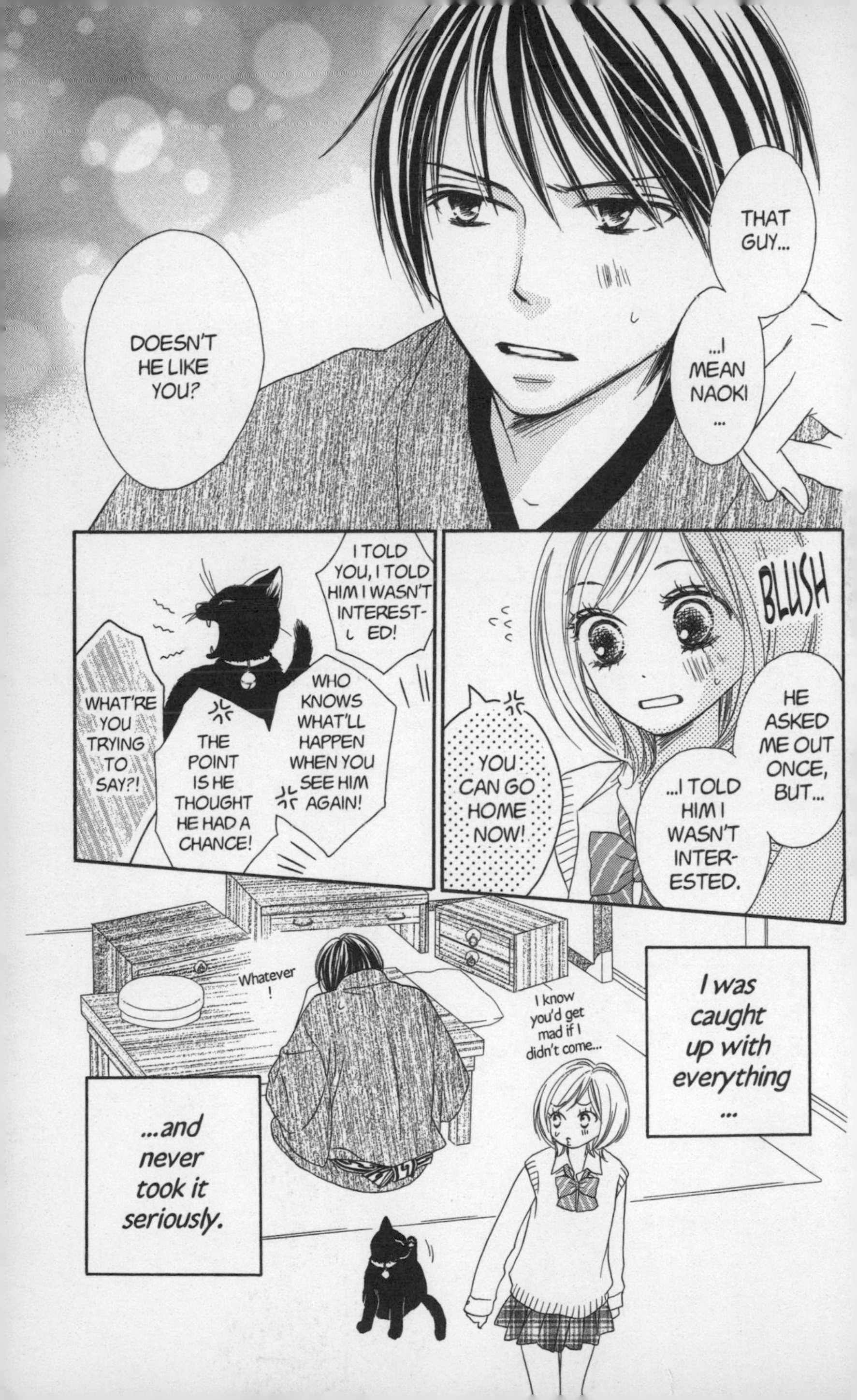
THAT GUY...
...I MEAN NAOKI ...
DOESN'T HE LIKE YOU?
BLUSH
HE ASKED ME OUT ONCE, BUT...
...I TOLD HIM I WASN'T INTERESTED.
YOU CAN GO HOME NOW!
I TOLD YOU, I TOLD HIM I WASN'T INTEREST-ED!
WHO KNOWS WHAT'LL HAPPEN WHEN YOU SEE HIM AGAIN!
THE POINT IS HE THOUGHT HE HAD A CHANCE!
WHAT'RE YOU TRYING TO SAY?!
I was caught up with everything ...
I know you'd get mad if I didn't come...
Whatever!
...and never took it seriously.

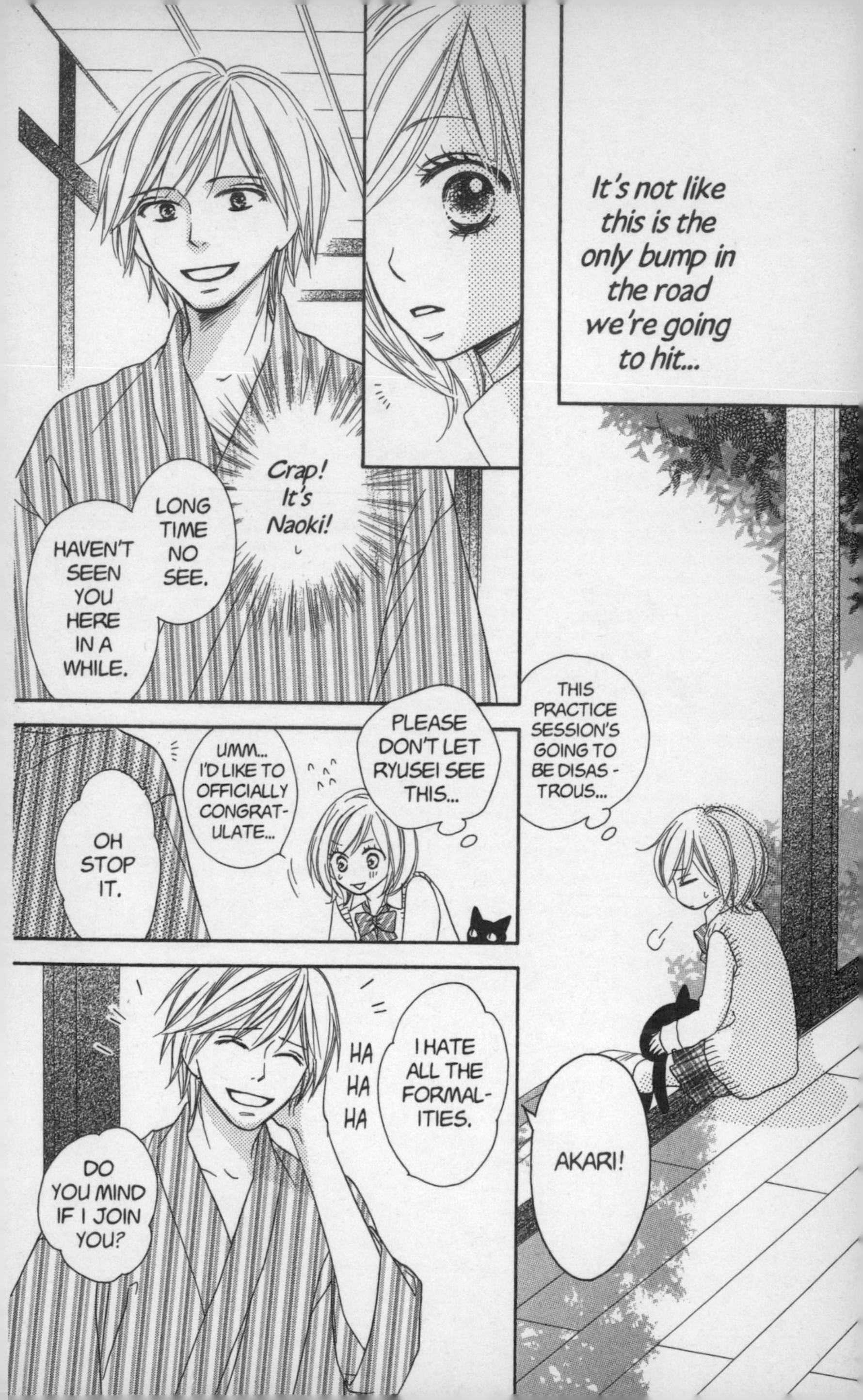
It's not like this is the only bump in the road we're going to hit...
THIS PRACTICE SESSION'S GOING TO BE DISAS-TROUS...
AKARI!
Crap! It's Naoki!
LONG TIME NO SEE.
HAVEN'T SEEN YOU HERE IN A WHILE.
PLEASE DON'T LET RYUSEI SEE THIS...
UMM... I'D LIKE TO OFFICIALLY CONGRAT-ULATE...
OH STOP IT.
I HATE ALL THE FORMAL-ITIES.
HA HA HA
DO YOU MIND IF I JOIN YOU?

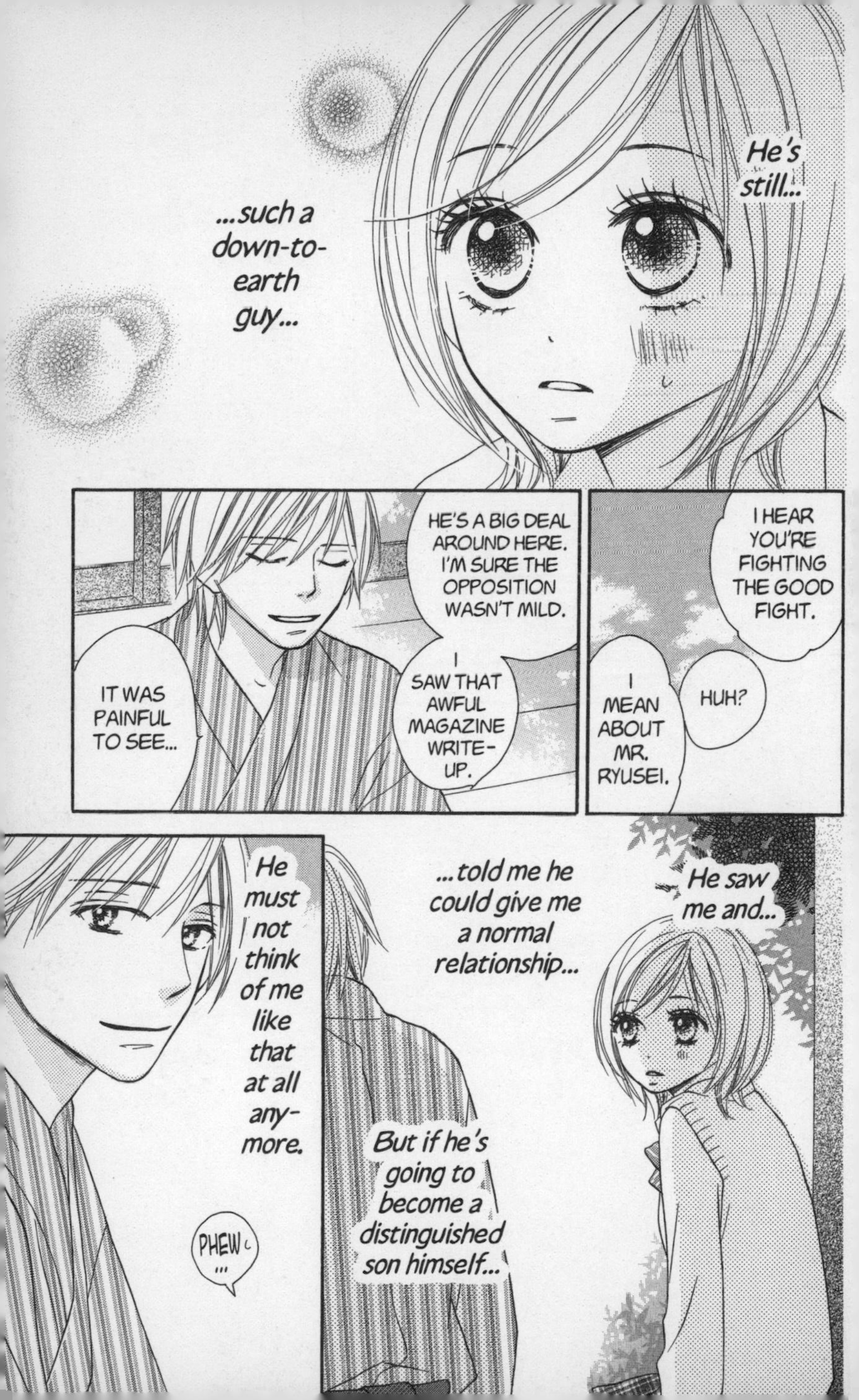
He's still...
...such a down-to-earth guy...
I HEAR YOU'RE FIGHTING THE GOOD FIGHT.
HUH?
I MEAN ABOUT MR. RYUSEI.
HE'S A BIG DEAL AROUND HERE. I'M SURE THE OPPOSITION WASN'T MILD.
I SAW THAT AWFUL MAGAZINE WRITE-UP.
IT WAS PAINFUL TO SEE...
He saw me and...
...told me he could give me a normal relationship...
But if he's going to become a distinguished son himself...
He must not think of me like that at all anymore.
PHEW...

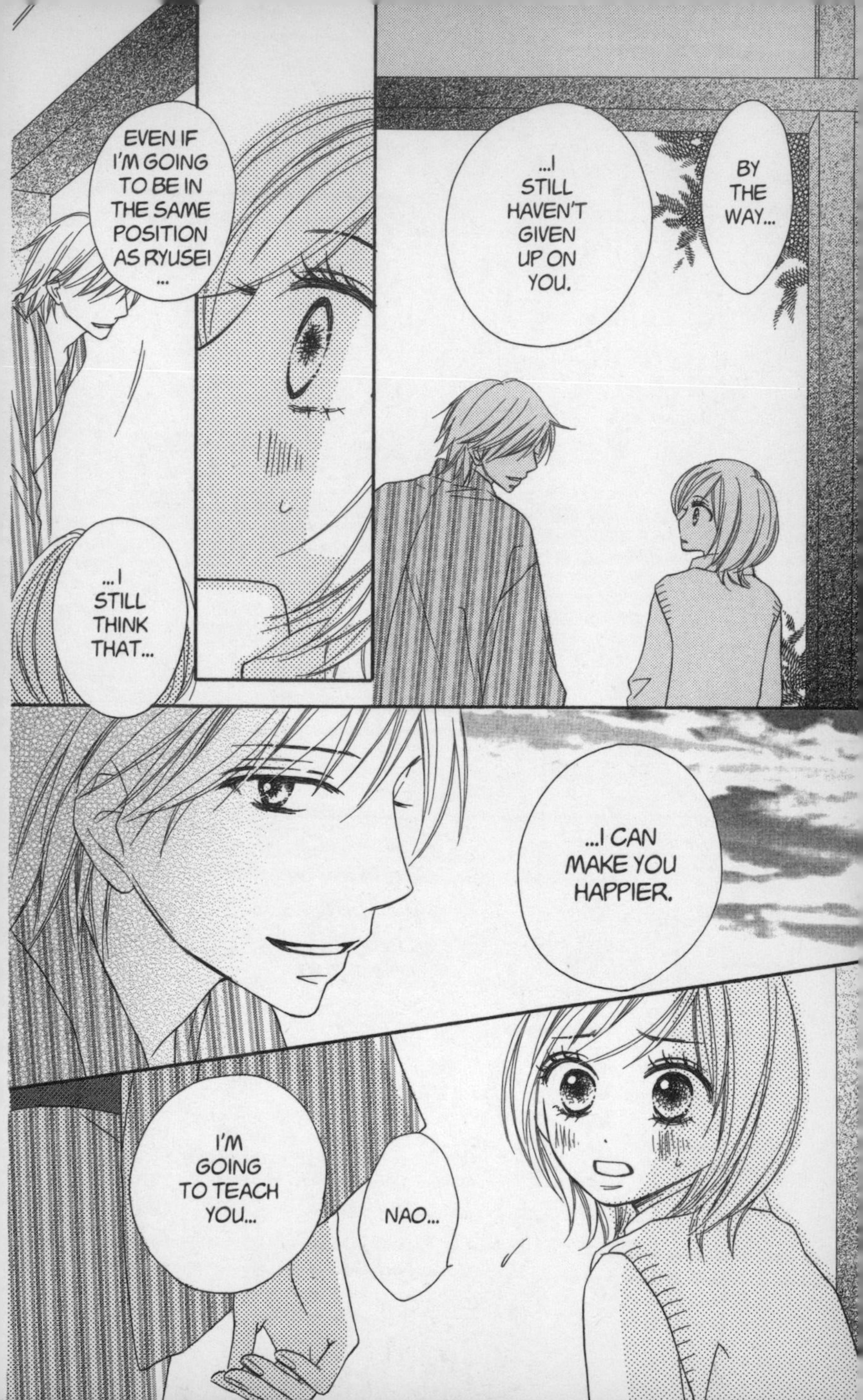
BY THE WAY...
...I STILL HAVEN'T GIVEN UP ON YOU.
EVEN IF I'M GOING TO BE IN THE SAME POSITION AS RYUSEI ...
...I STILL THINK THAT...
...I CAN MAKE YOU HAPPIER.
NAO...
I'M GOING TO TEACH YOU...

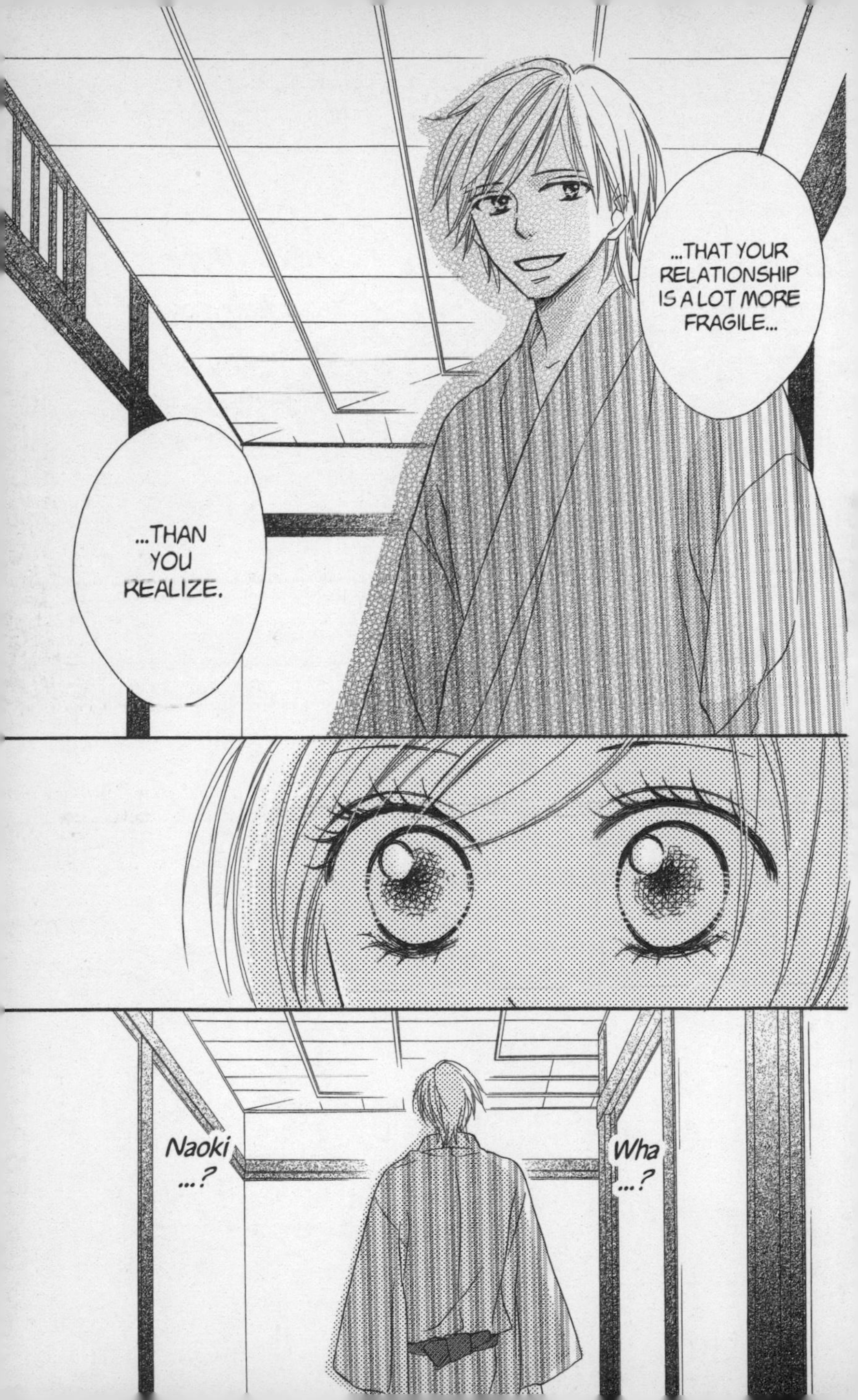
...THAT YOUR RELATIONSHIP IS A LOT MORE FRAGILE...
...THAN YOU REALIZE.
Wha ...?
Naoki ...?

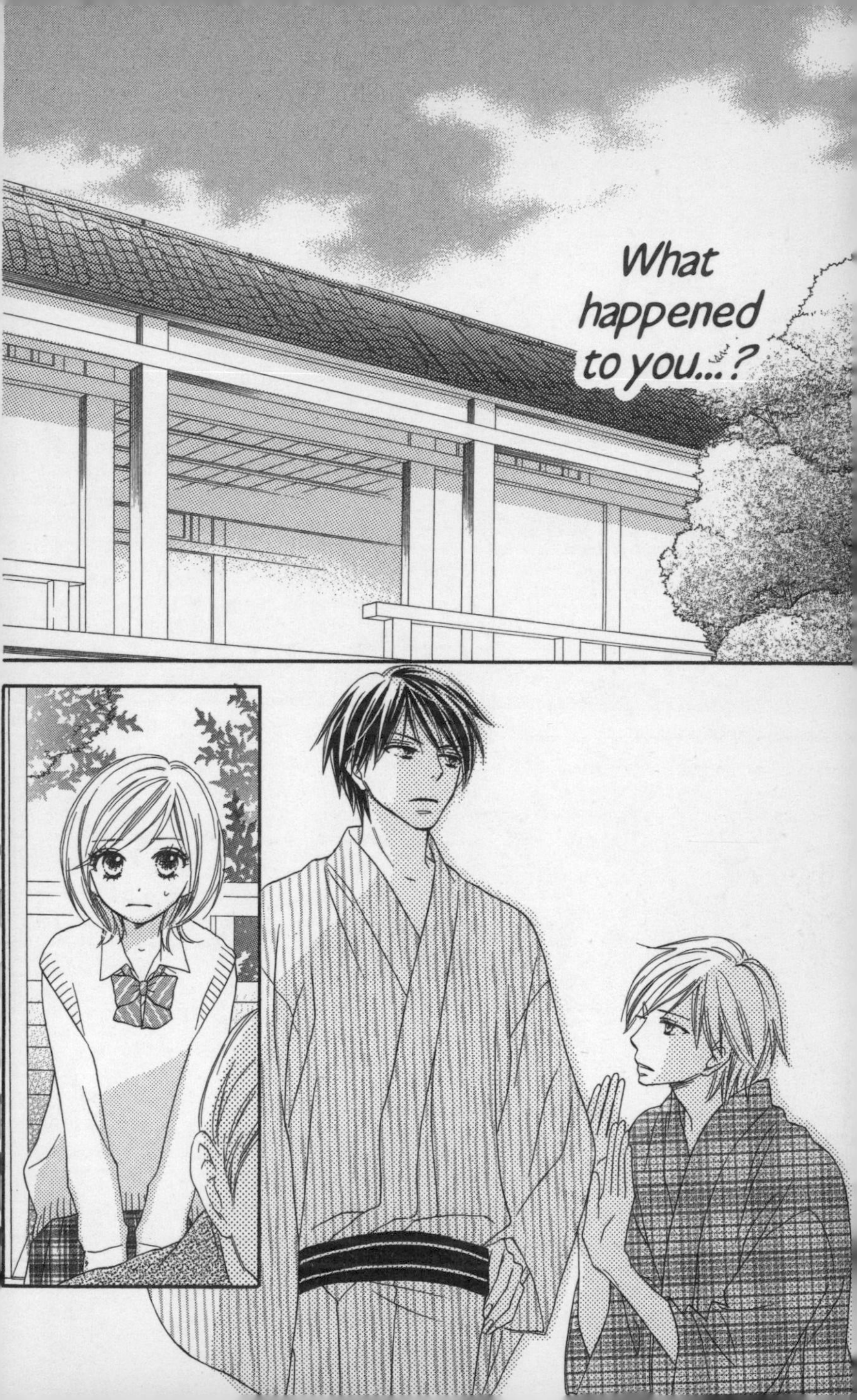
What happened to you...?

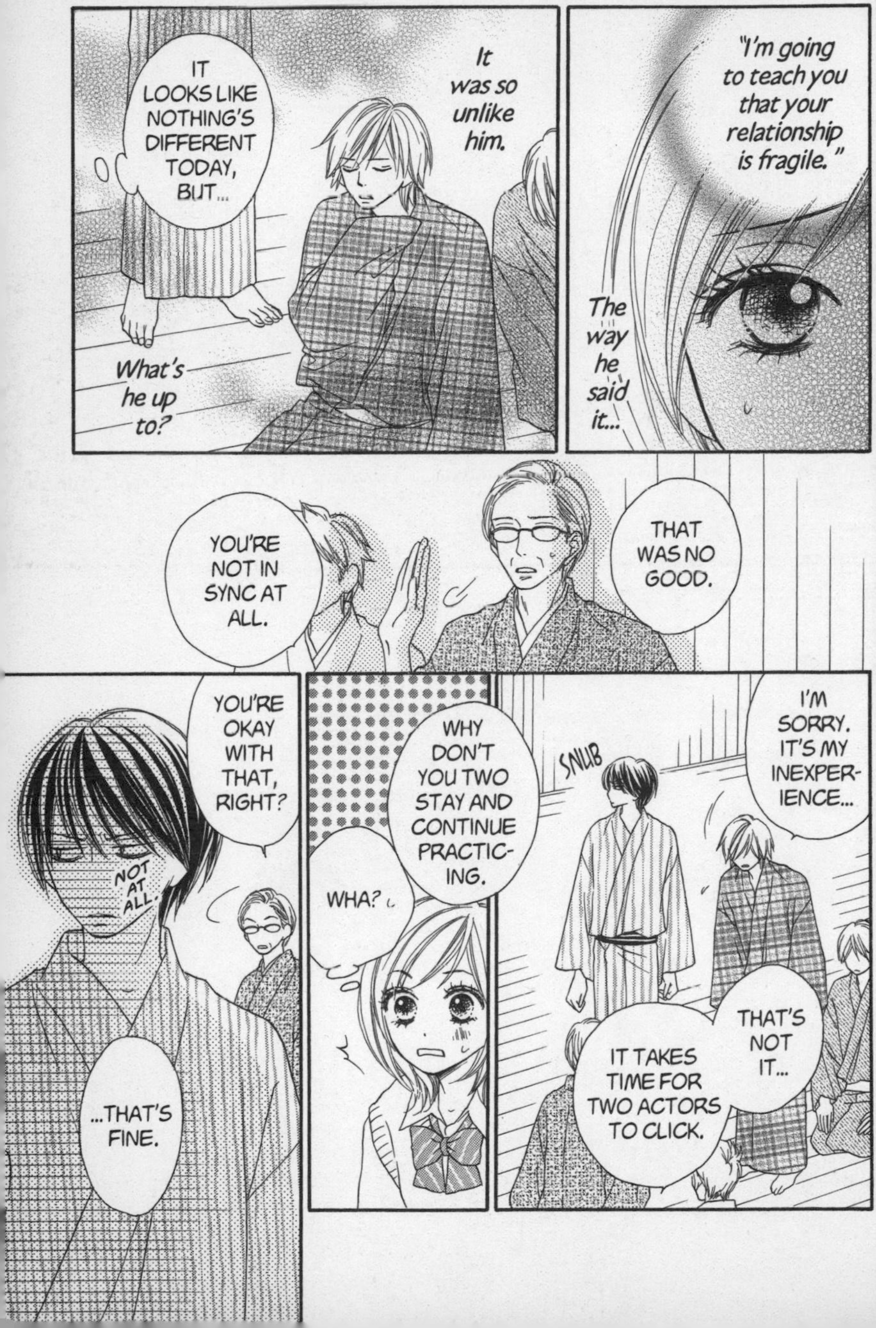

"I'm going to teach you that your relationship is fragile."
The way he said it...
It was so unlike him.
IT LOOKS LIKE NOTHING'S DIFFERENT TODAY, BUT...
What's he up to?
THAT WAS NO GOOD.
YOU'RE NOT IN SYNC AT ALL.
I'M SORRY. IT'S MY INEXPERIENCE...
SNUB
THAT'S NOT IT...
IT TAKES TIME FOR TWO ACTORS TO CLICK.
WHY DON'T YOU TWO STAY AND CONTINUE PRACTICING.
WHA?
YOU'RE OKAY WITH THAT, RIGHT?
NOT AT ALL.
...THAT'S FINE.

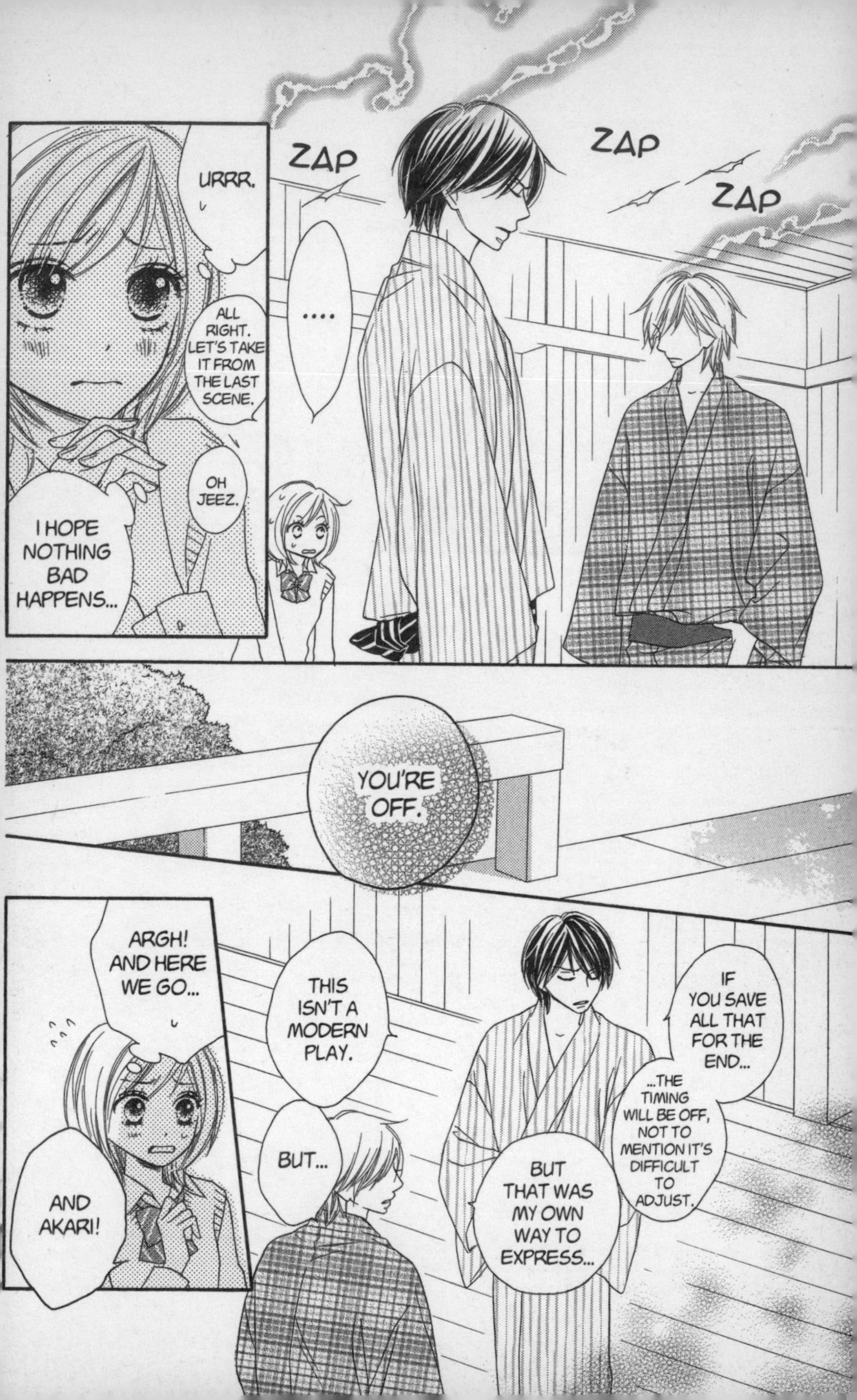
ZAP
ZAP
ZAP
....
ALL RIGHT. LET'S TAKE IT FROM THE LAST SCENE.
URRR.
OH JEEZ.
I HOPE NOTHING BAD HAPPENS...
YOU'RE OFF.
IF YOU SAVE ALL THAT FOR THE END...
...THE TIMING WILL BE OFF, NOT TO MENTION IT'S DIFFICULT TO ADJUST.
THIS ISN'T A MODERN PLAY.
BUT THAT WAS MY OWN WAY TO EXPRESS...
BUT...
ARGH! AND HERE WE GO...
AND AKARI!

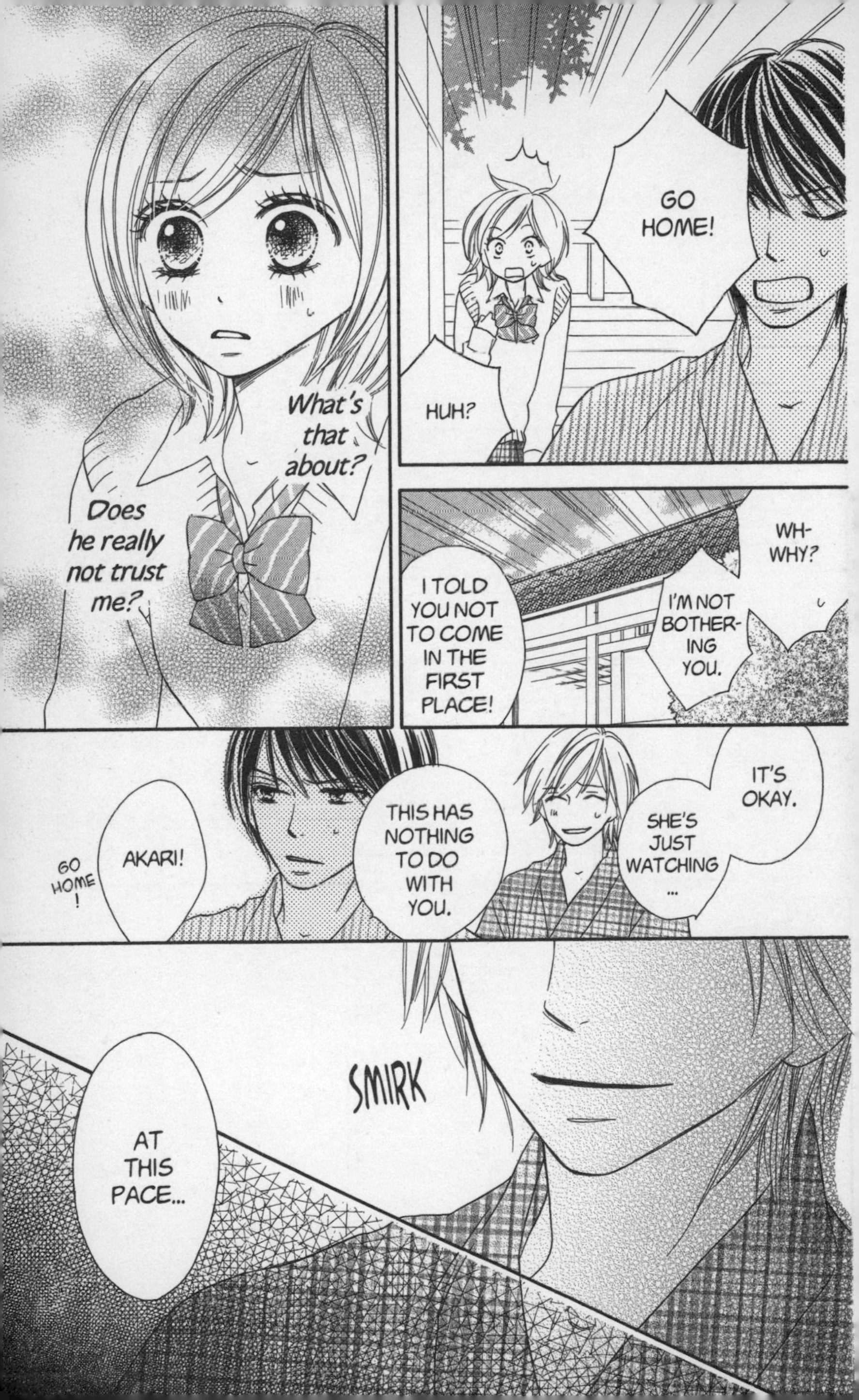
GO HOME!
HUH?
WH-WHY?
I'M NOT BOTHERING YOU.
I TOLD YOU NOT TO COME IN THE FIRST PLACE!
What's that about?
Does he really not trust me?
IT'S OKAY.
SHE'S JUST WATCHING ...
THIS HAS NOTHING TO DO WITH YOU.
AKARI!
GO HOME!
SMIRK
AT THIS PACE...

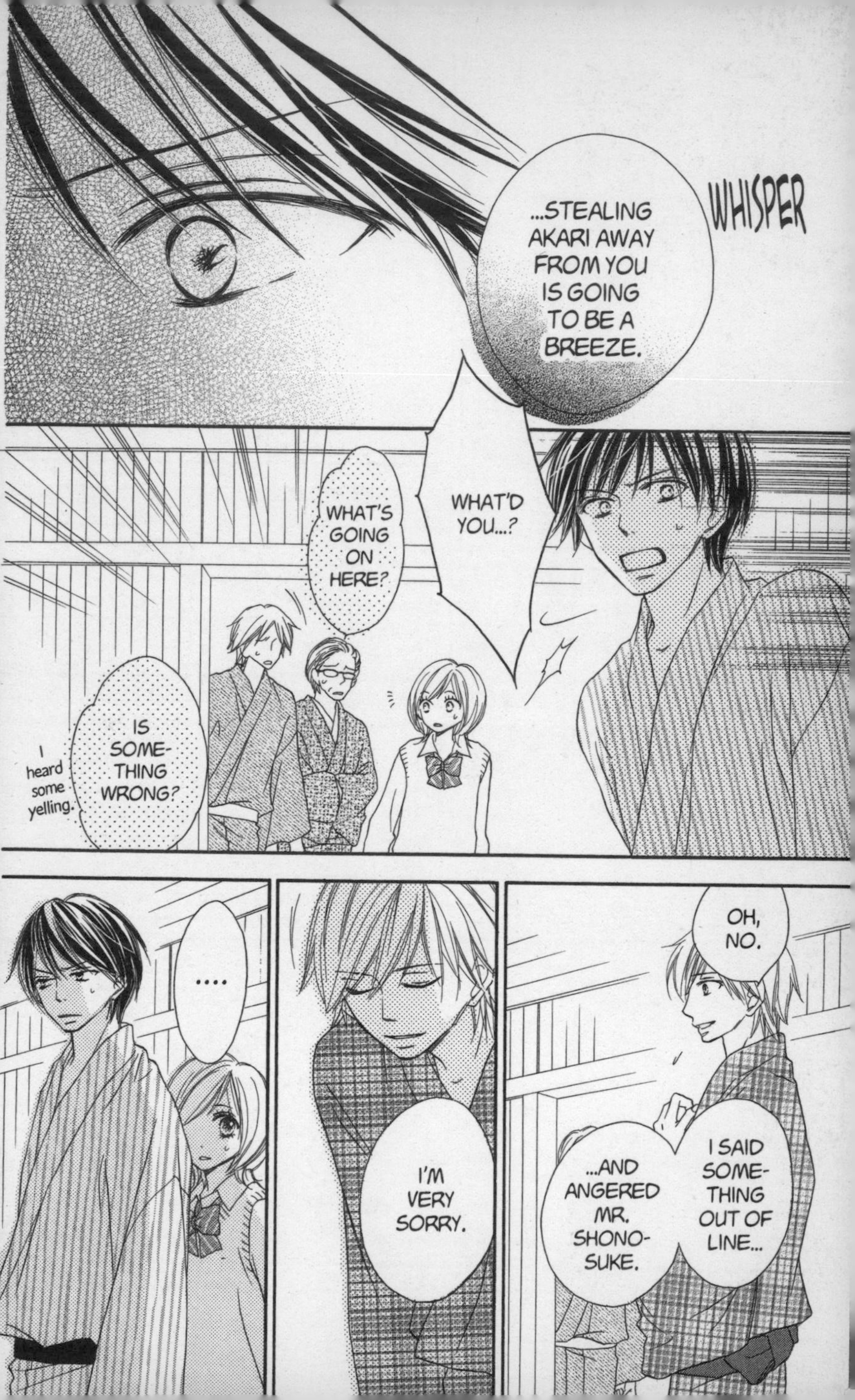
WHISPER
...STEALING AKARI AWAY FROM YOU IS GOING TO BE A BREEZE.
WHAT'D YOU...?
WHAT'S GOING ON HERE?
IS SOME-THING WRONG?
I heard some yelling.
OH, NO.
I SAID SOME-THING OUT OF LINE...
...AND ANGERED MR. SHONO-SUKE.
I'M VERY SORRY.
....

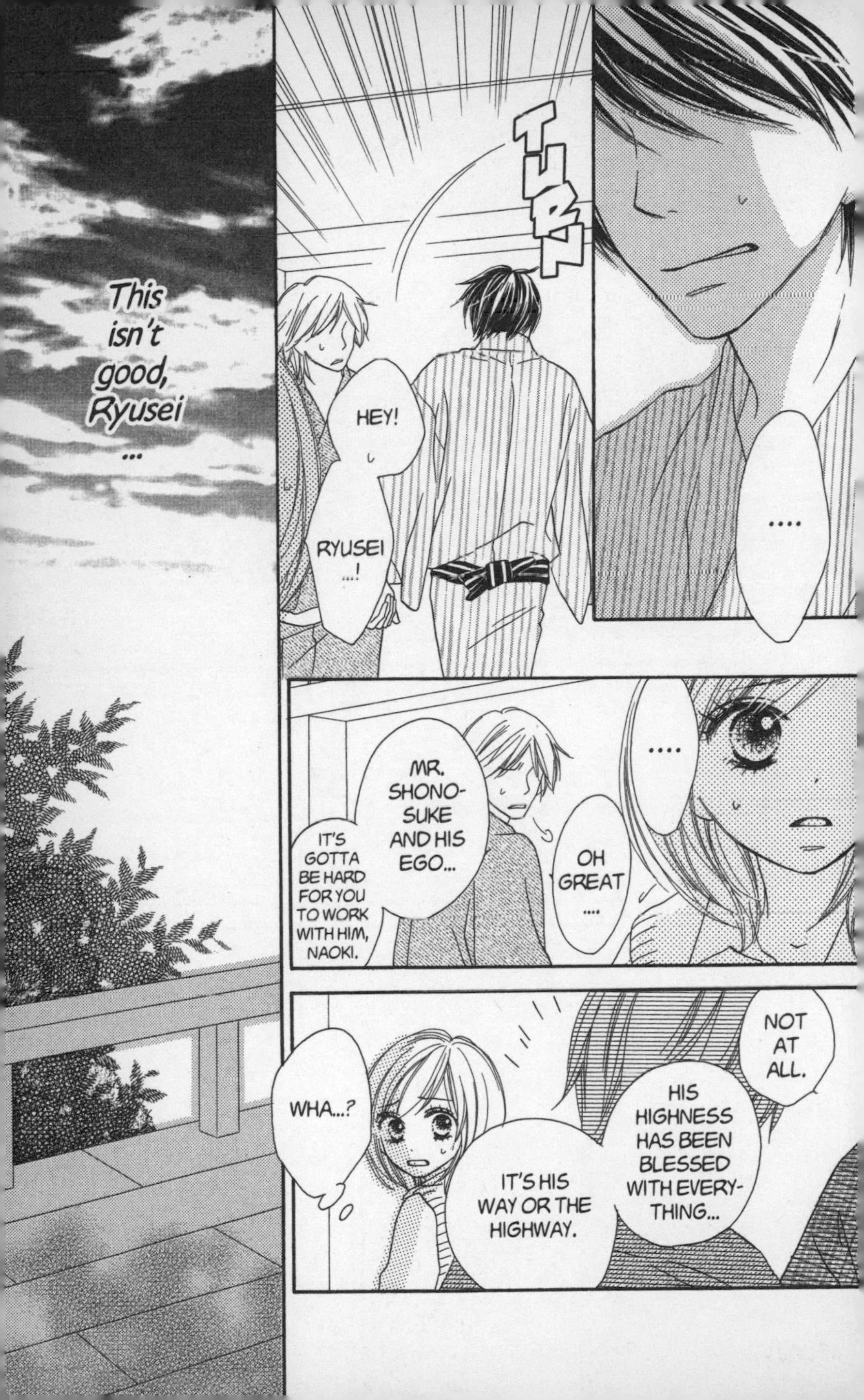
....
TURN
HEY!
RYUSEI ...!
....
OH GREAT ....
MR. SHONOSUKE AND HIS EGO...
IT'S GOTTA BE HARD FOR YOU TO WORK WITH HIM, NAOKI.
NOT AT ALL.
HIS HIGHNESS HAS BEEN BLESSED WITH EVERYTHING...
IT'S HIS WAY OR THE HIGHWAY.
WHA...?
This isn't good, Ryusei ...

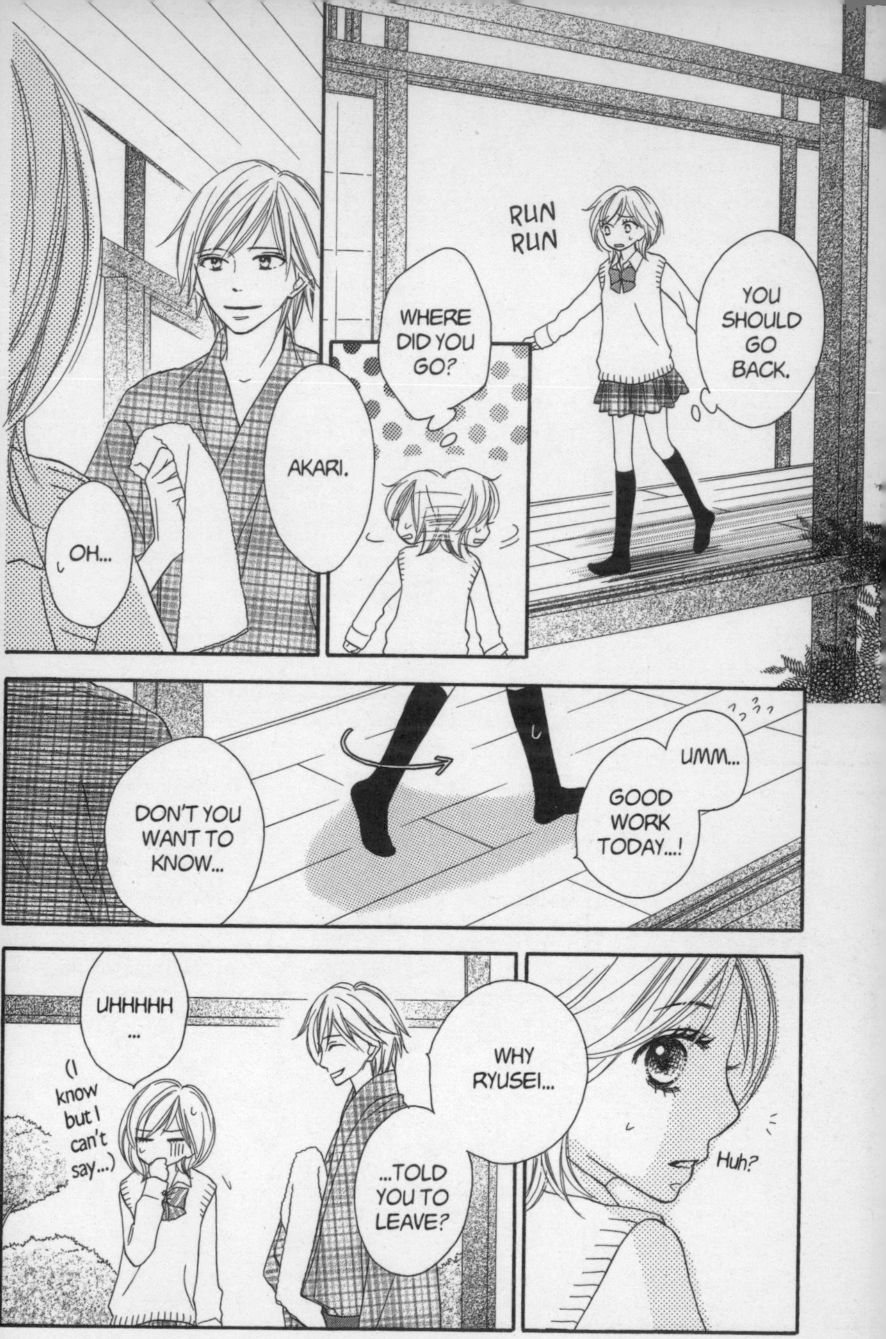
RUN RUN
YOU SHOULD GO BACK.
WHERE DID YOU GO?
AKARI.
OH...
UMM...
GOOD WORK TODAY...!
DON'T YOU WANT TO KNOW...
Huh?
WHY RYUSEI...
...TOLD YOU TO LEAVE?
UHHHHH ...
(I know but I can't say...)

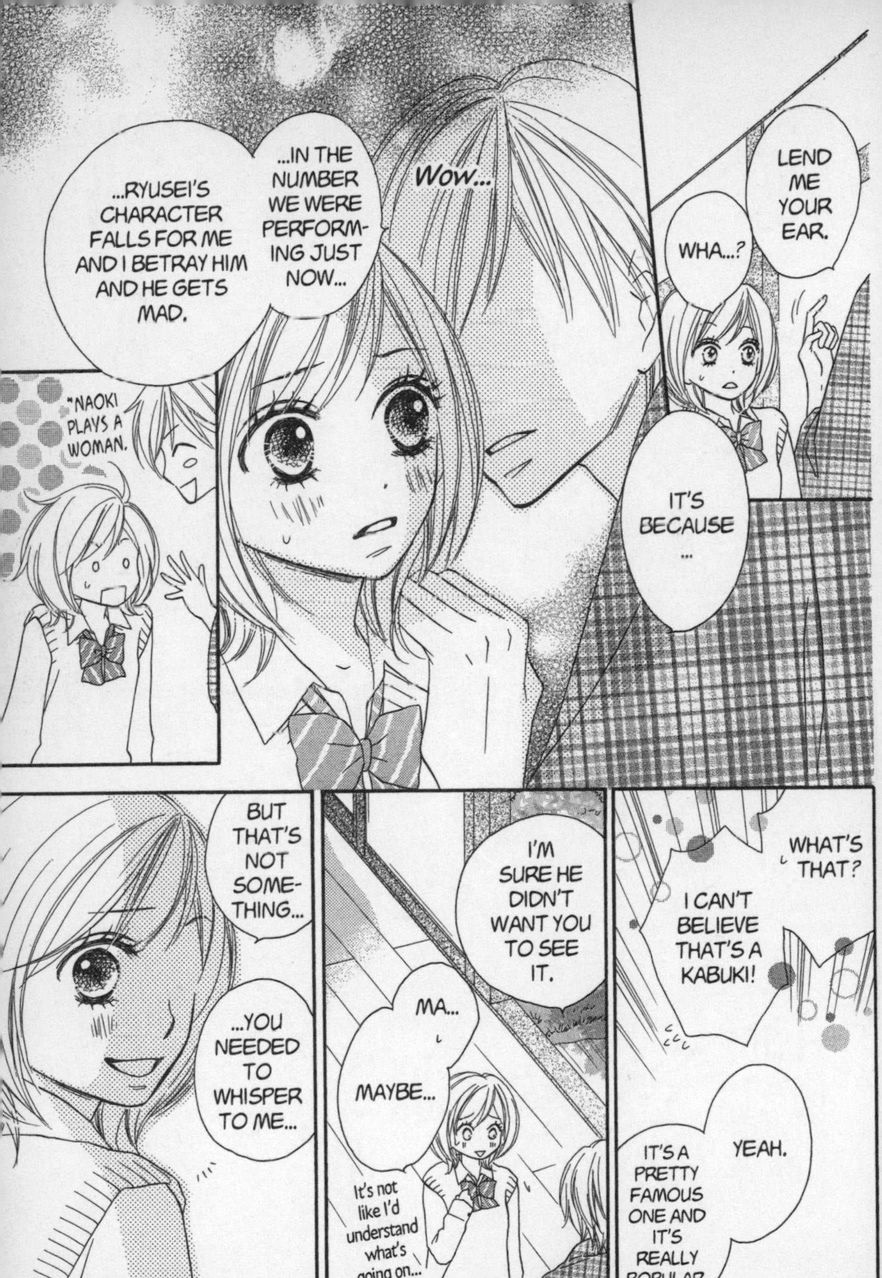
LEND ME YOUR EAR.
WHA...?
IT'S BECAUSE...
Wow...
...IN THE NUMBER WE WERE PERFORMING JUST NOW...
...RYUSEI'S CHARACTER FALLS FOR ME AND I BETRAY HIM AND HE GETS MAD.
*NAOKI PLAYS A WOMAN.
WHAT'S THAT?
I CAN'T BELIEVE THAT'S A KABUKI!
YEAH.
IT'S A PRETTY FAMOUS ONE AND IT'S REALLY POPULAR.
I'M SURE HE DIDN'T WANT YOU TO SEE IT.
MA...
MAYBE...
It's not like I'd understand what's going on...
BUT THAT'S NOT SOMETHING...
...YOU NEEDED TO WHISPER TO ME...

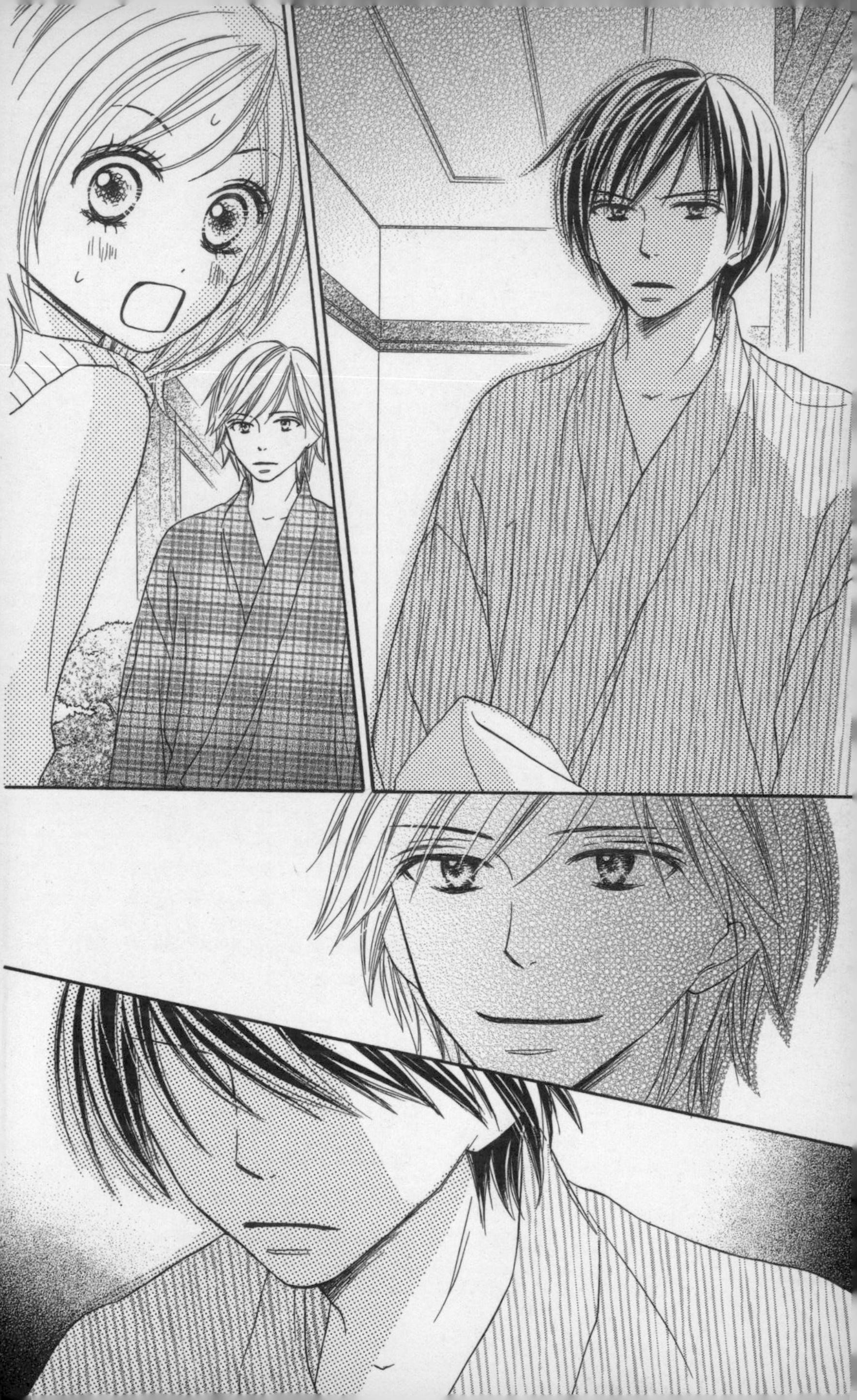

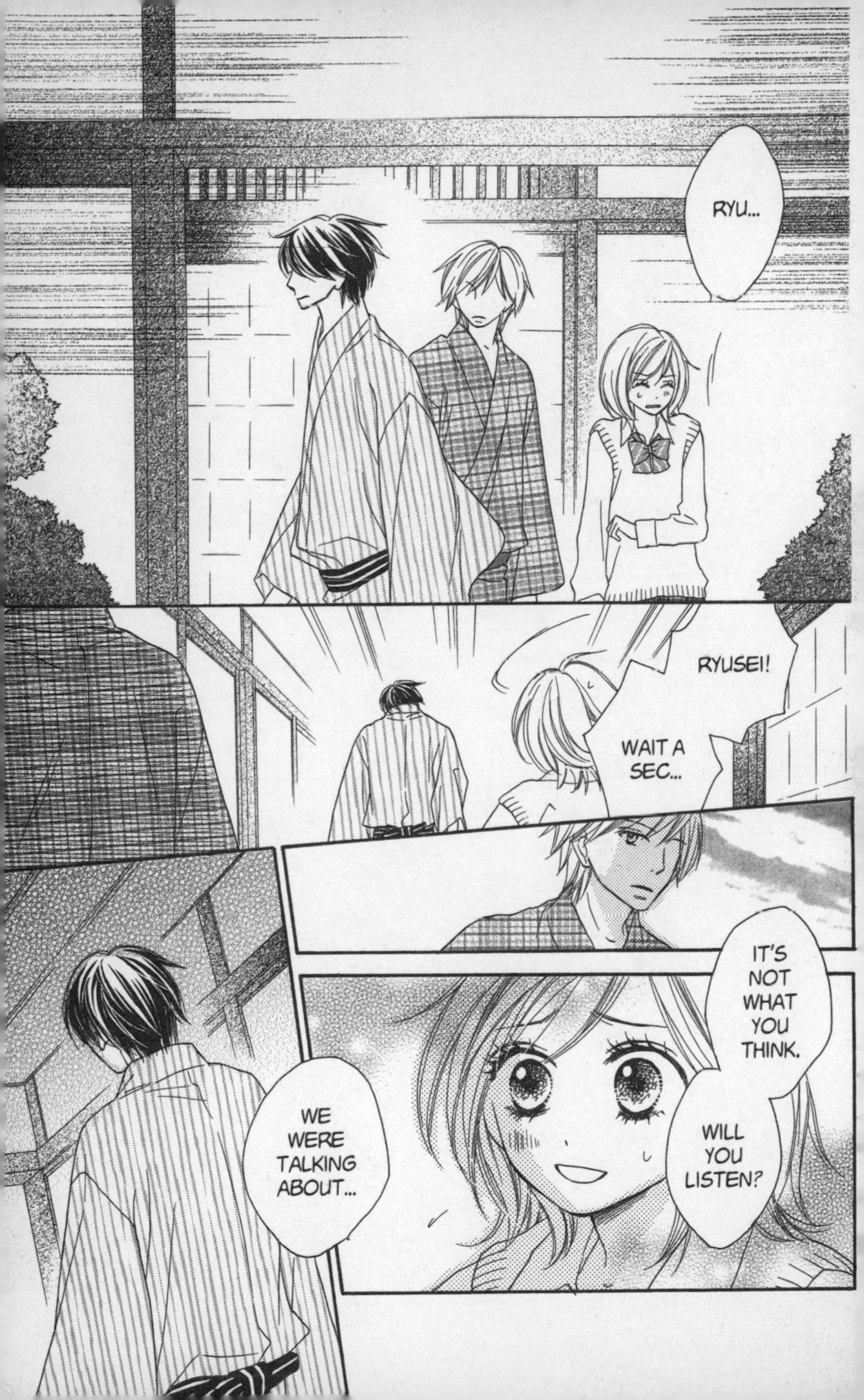
RYU...
RYUSEI!
WAIT A SEC...
IT'S NOT WHAT YOU THINK.
WILL YOU LISTEN?
WE WERE TALKING ABOUT...

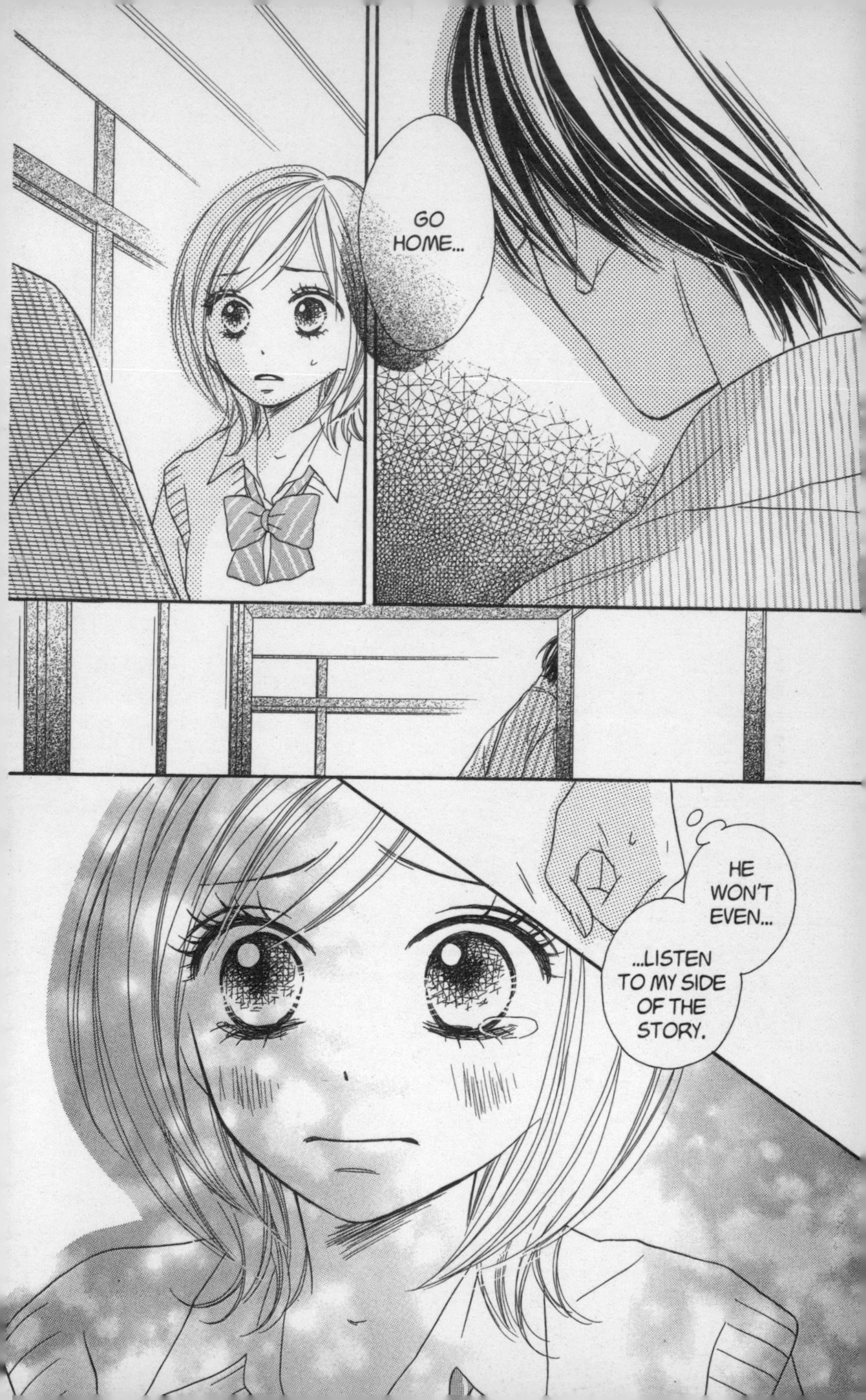
GO HOME...
HE WON'T EVEN...
...LISTEN TO MY SIDE OF THE STORY.

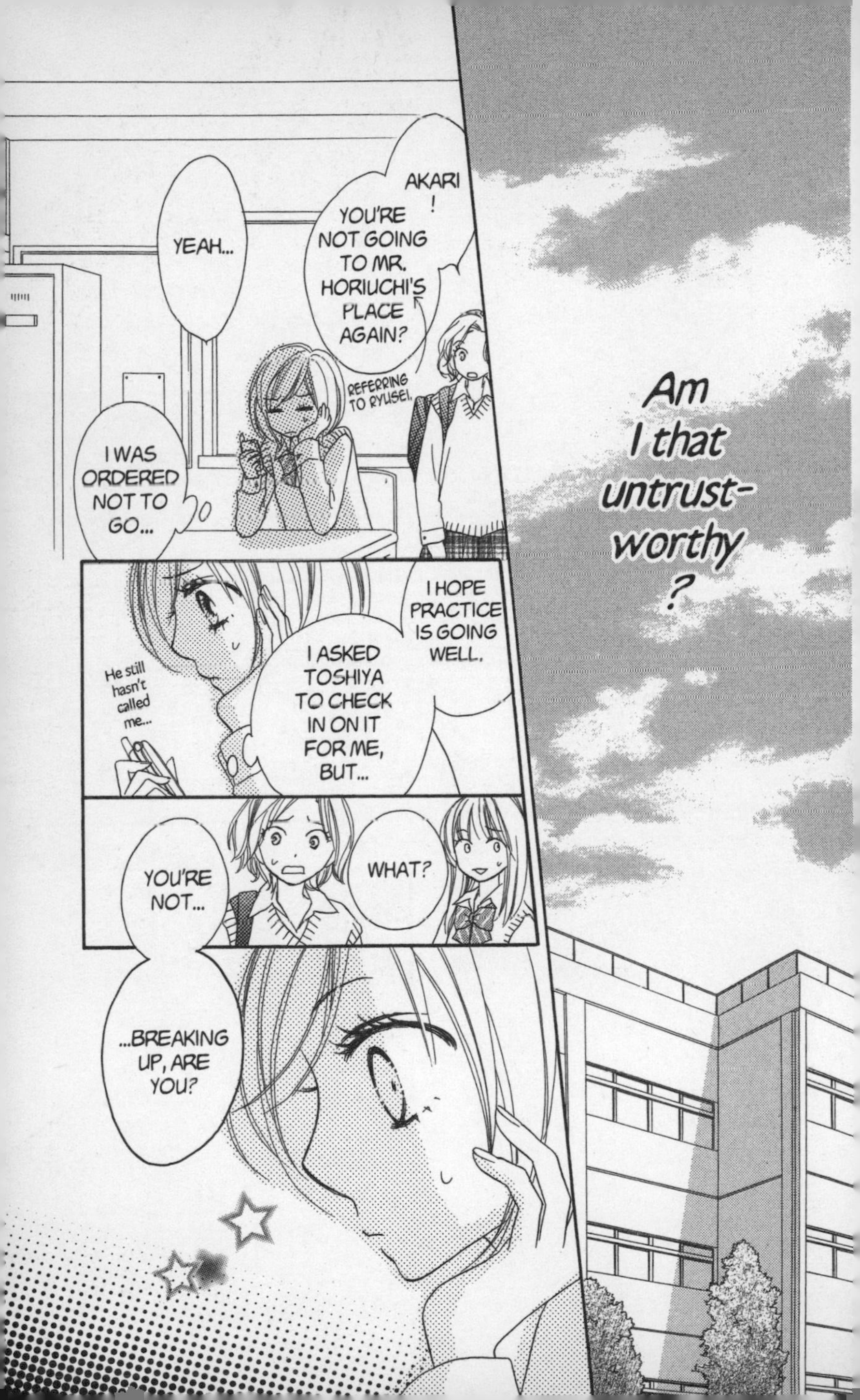
Am I that untrust-worthy?
AKARI! YOU'RE NOT GOING TO MR. HORIUCHI'S PLACE AGAIN?
REFERRING TO RYUSEI.
YEAH...
I WAS ORDERED NOT TO GO...
I HOPE PRACTICE IS GOING WELL.
I ASKED TOSHIYA TO CHECK IN ON IT FOR ME, BUT...
He still hasn't called me...
WHAT?
YOU'RE NOT...
...BREAKING UP, ARE YOU?

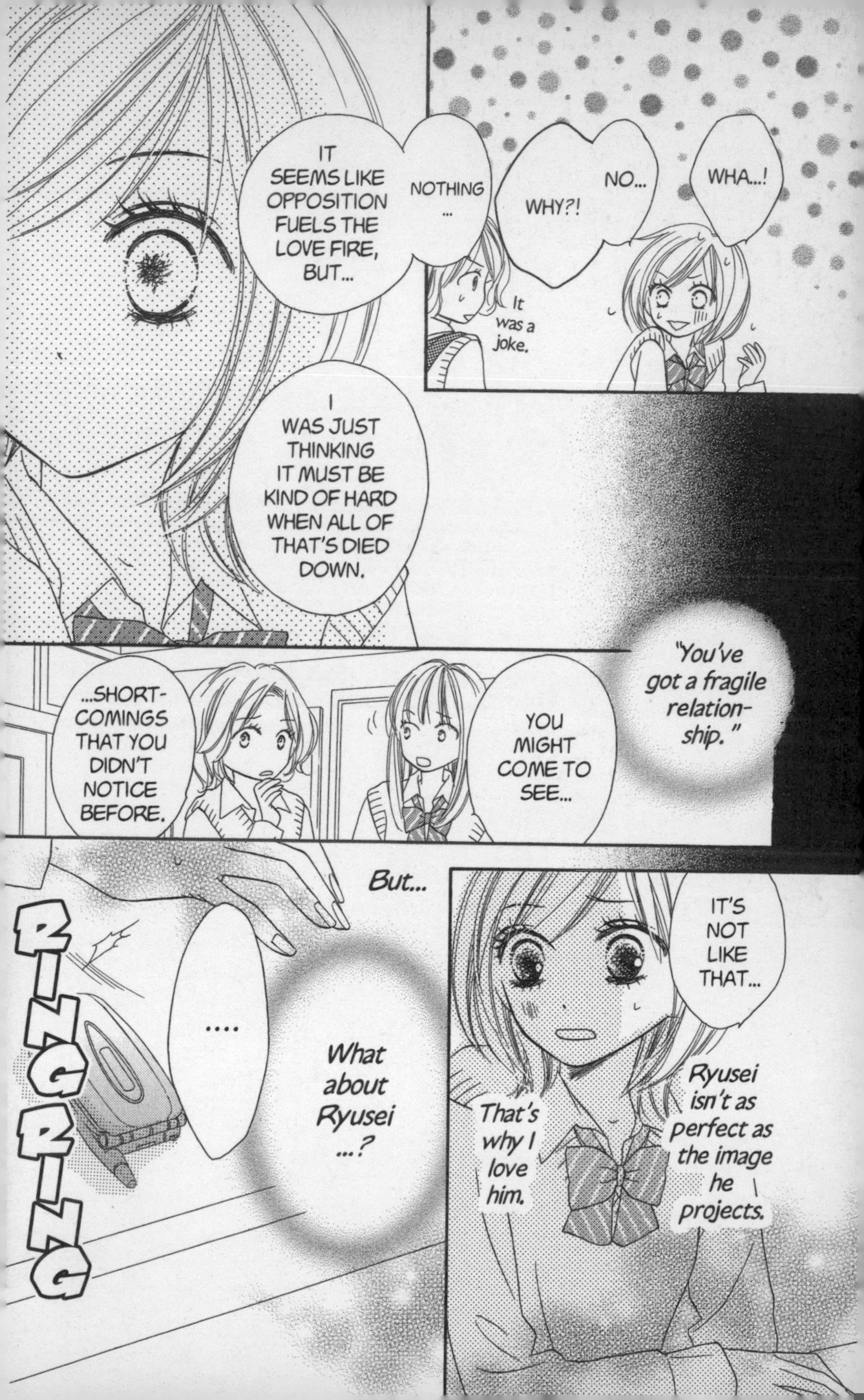
WHA...!
NO...
WHY?!
It was a joke.
NOTHING...
IT SEEMS LIKE OPPOSITION FUELS THE LOVE FIRE, BUT...
I WAS JUST THINKING IT MUST BE KIND OF HARD WHEN ALL OF THAT'S DIED DOWN.
"You've got a fragile relationship."
YOU MIGHT COME TO SEE...
...SHORT-COMINGS THAT YOU DIDN'T NOTICE BEFORE.
IT'S NOT LIKE THAT...
Ryusei isn't as perfect as the image he projects.
That's why I love him.
But...
What about Ryusei ...?
....
RING RING

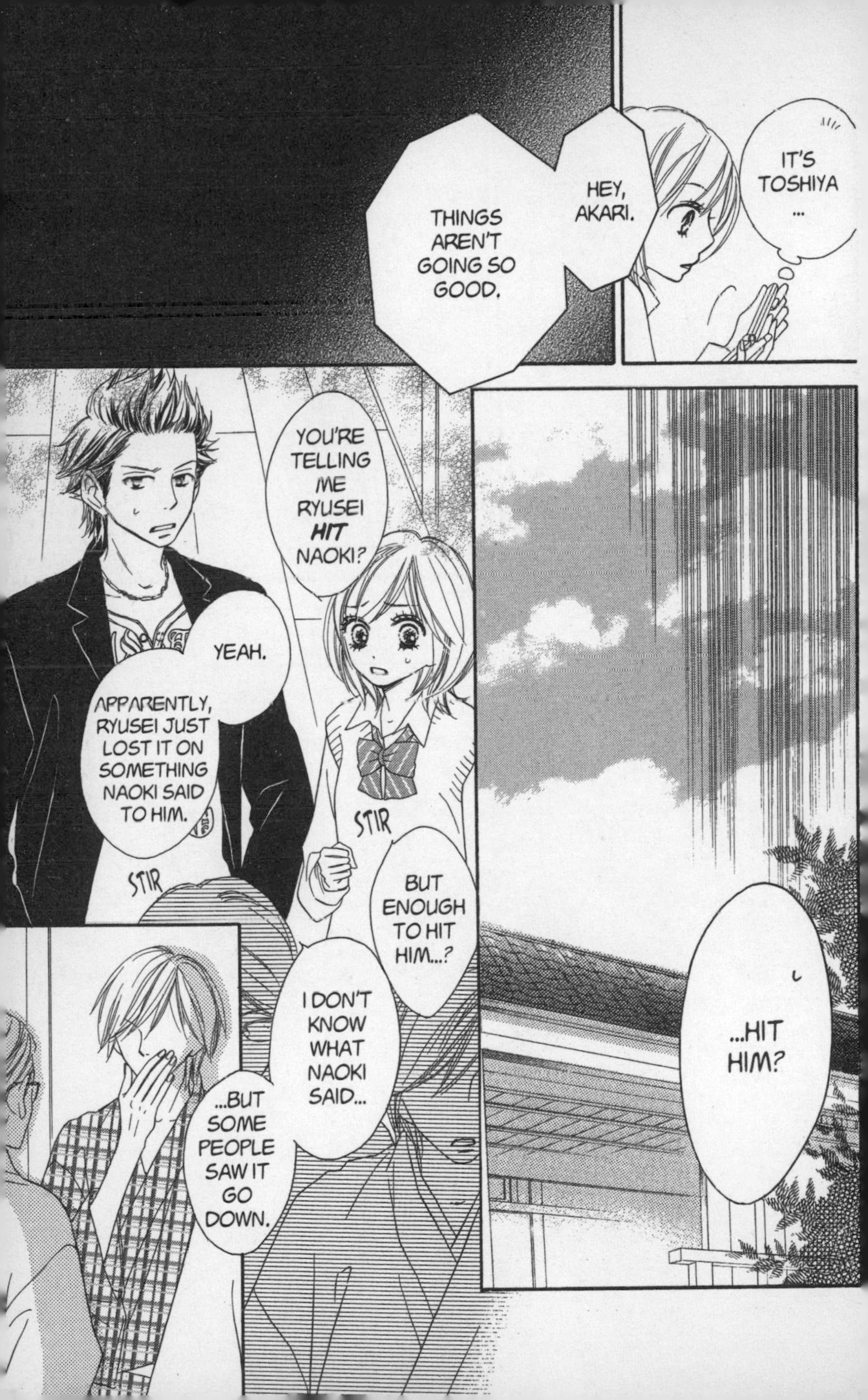
IT'S TOSHIYA ...
HEY, AKARI.
THINGS AREN'T GOING SO GOOD.
...HIT HIM?
YOU'RE TELLING ME RYUSEI HIT NAOKI?
YEAH.
APPARENTLY, RYUSEI JUST LOST IT ON SOMETHING NAOKI SAID TO HIM.
STIR
STIR
BUT ENOUGH TO HIT HIM...?
I DON'T KNOW WHAT NAOKI SAID...
...BUT SOME PEOPLE SAW IT GO DOWN.

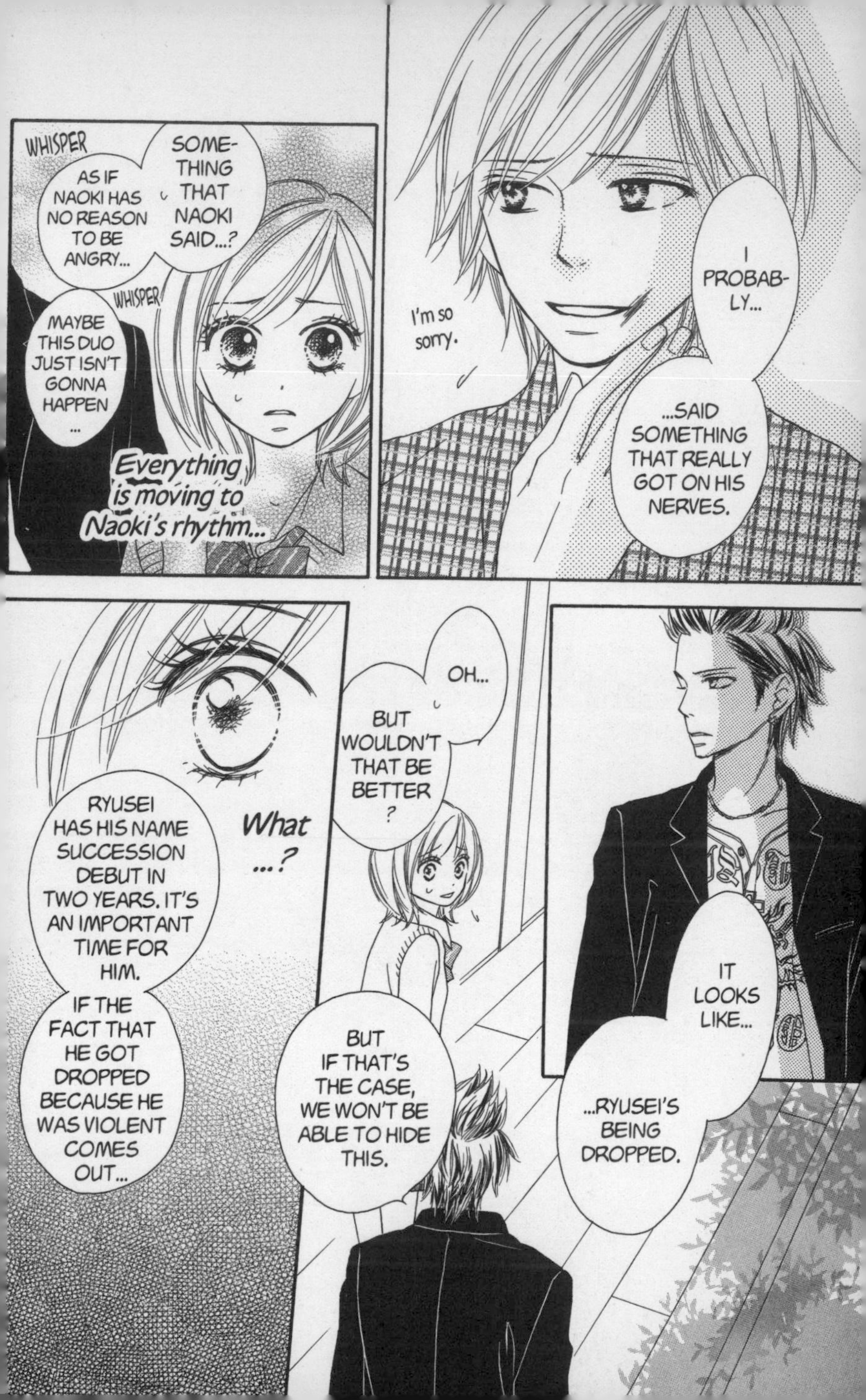
I PROBABLY...
...SAID SOMETHING THAT REALLY GOT ON HIS NERVES.
I'm so sorry.
SOMETHING THAT NAOKI SAID...?
WHISPER
AS IF NAOKI HAS NO REASON TO BE ANGRY...
WHISPER
MAYBE THIS DUO JUST ISN'T GONNA HAPPEN...
Everything is moving to Naoki's rhythm...
IT LOOKS LIKE...
...RYUSEI'S BEING DROPPED.
OH...
BUT WOULDN'T THAT BE BETTER?
BUT IF THAT'S THE CASE, WE WON'T BE ABLE TO HIDE THIS.
What...?
RYUSEI HAS HIS NAME SUCCESSION DEBUT IN TWO YEARS. IT'S AN IMPORTANT TIME FOR HIM.
IF THE FACT THAT HE GOT DROPPED BECAUSE HE WAS VIOLENT COMES OUT...

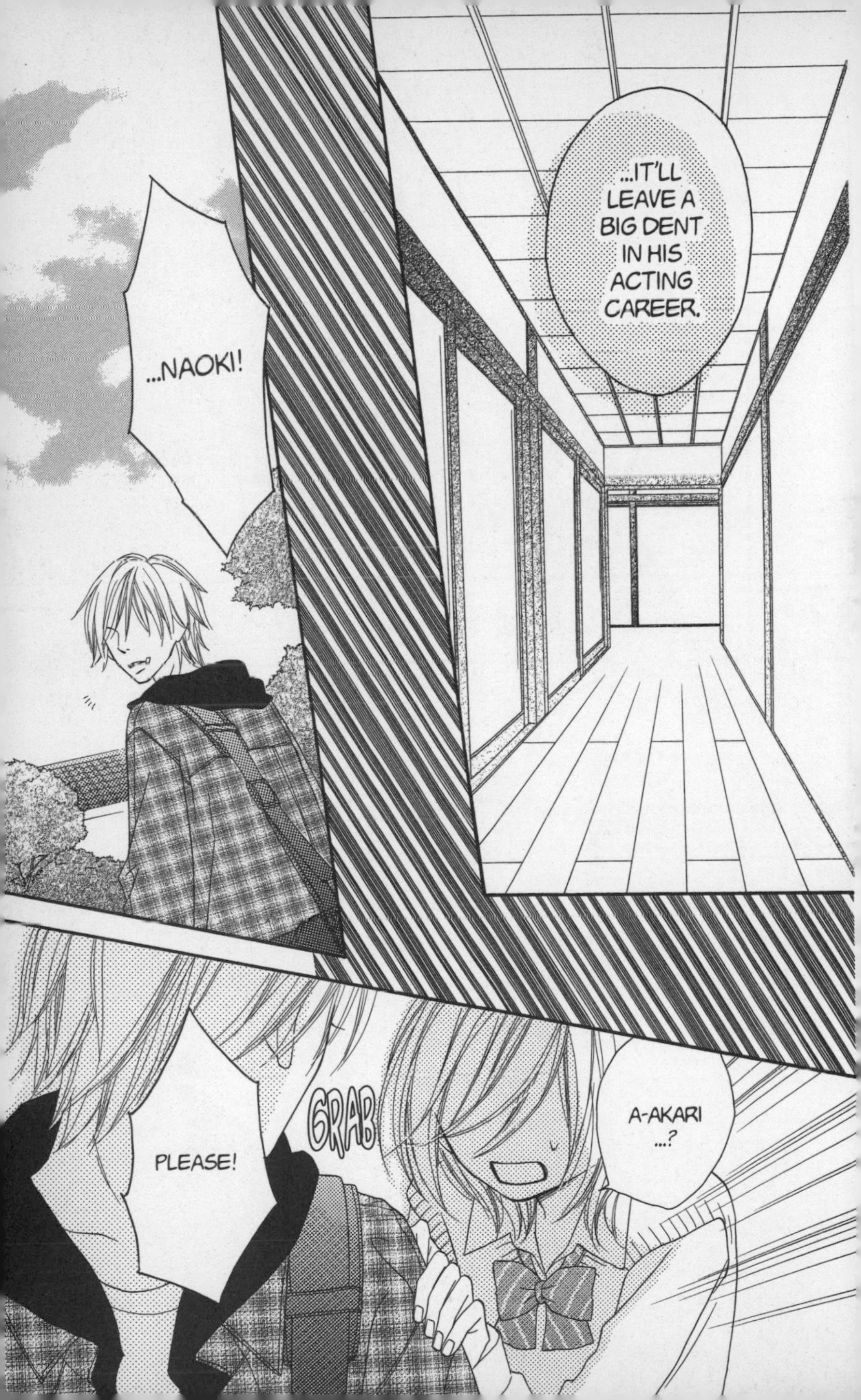
...IT'LL LEAVE A BIG DENT IN HIS ACTING CAREER.
...NAOKI!
A-AKARI ...?
GRAB
PLEASE!

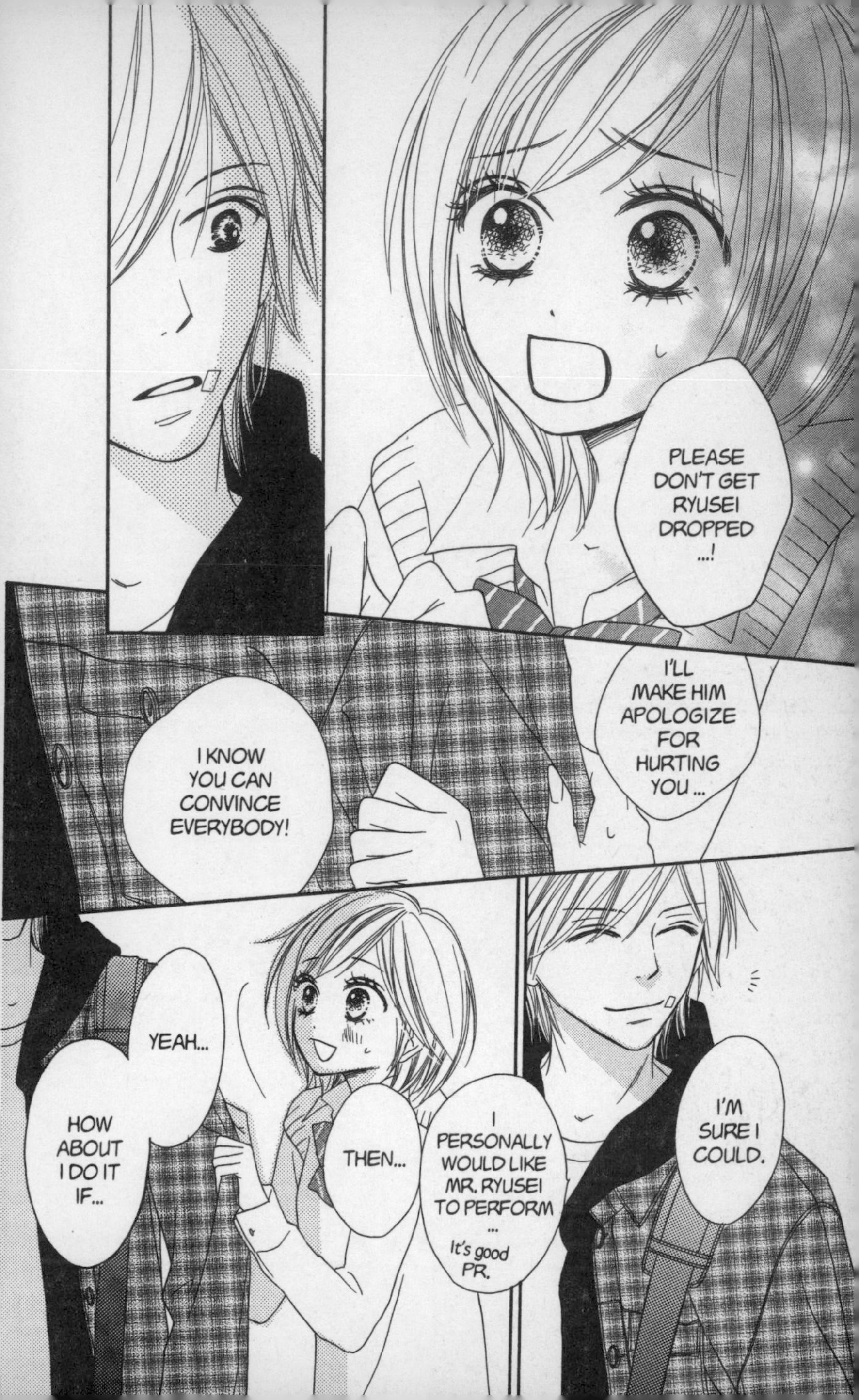
PLEASE DON'T GET RYUSEI DROPPED ...!
I'LL MAKE HIM APOLOGIZE FOR HURTING YOU ...
I KNOW YOU CAN CONVINCE EVERYBODY!
I'M SURE I COULD.
I PERSONALLY WOULD LIKE MR. RYUSEI TO PERFORM ...
It's good PR.
THEN...
YEAH...
HOW ABOUT I DO IT IF...

...YOU AGREE TO BE MY GIRLFRIEND?
WHY DON'T YOU DISCUSS IT WITH RYUSEI AND...
...DECIDE WHETHER HE'S GOING TO HAVE HIS LIFE AS AN ACTOR, OR YOU.
Why?
I CAN'T BELIEVE HOW EASY IT WAS TO BAIT HIM.
How did this happen ...?

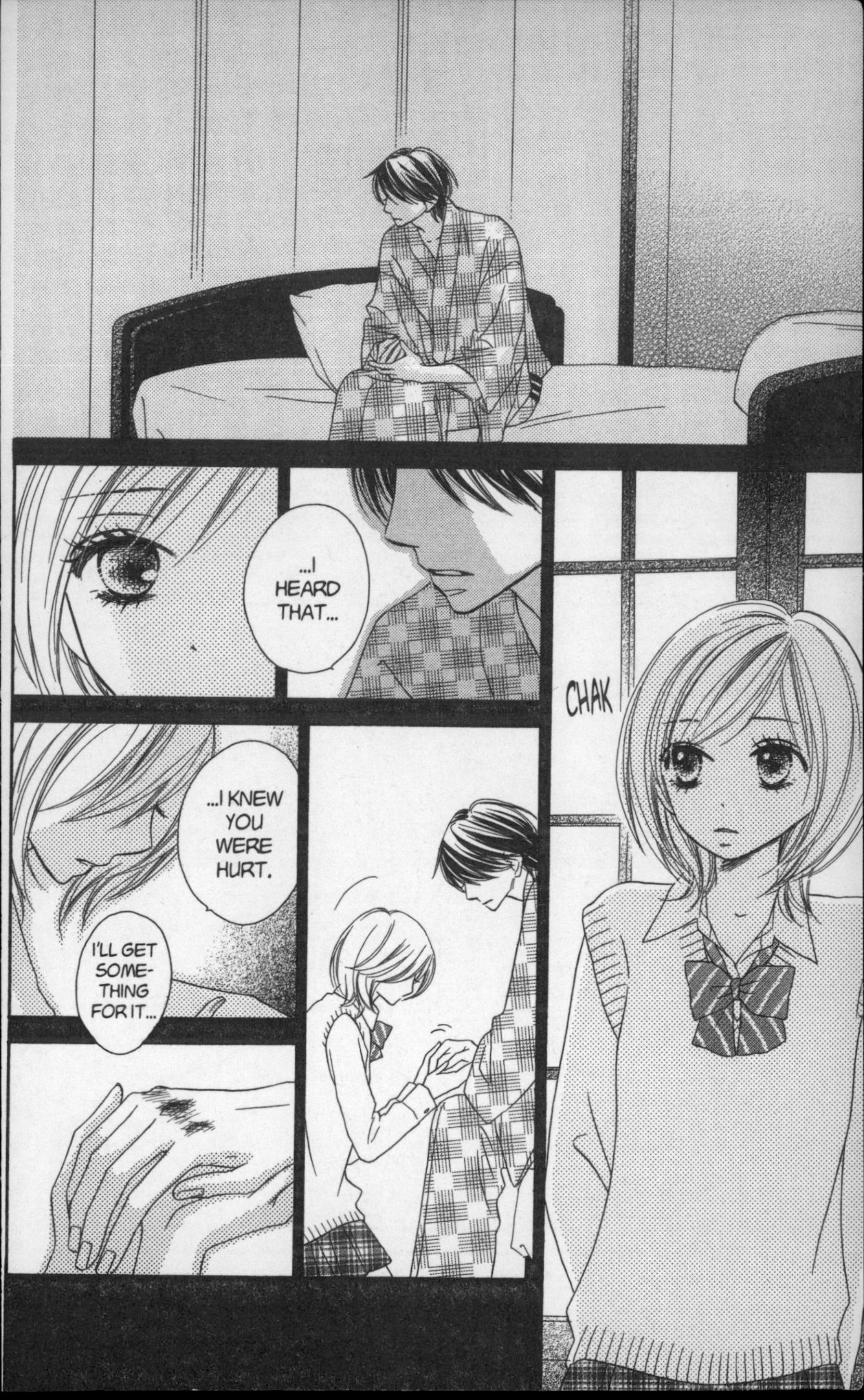
CHAK
...I HEARD THAT...
...I KNEW YOU WERE HURT.
I'LL GET SOME-THING FOR IT...

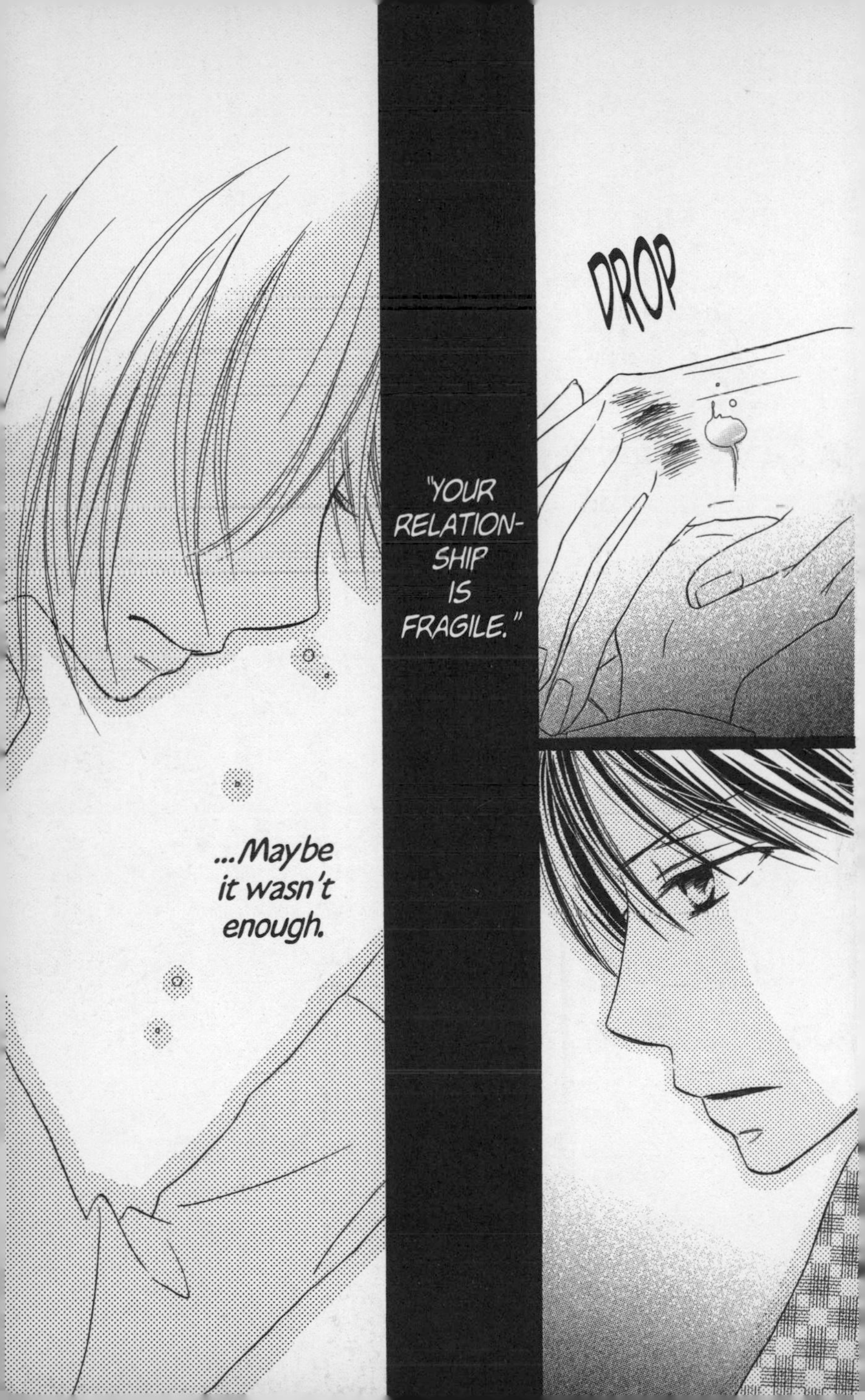
DROP
"YOUR RELATION-SHIP IS FRAGILE."
...Maybe it wasn't enough.

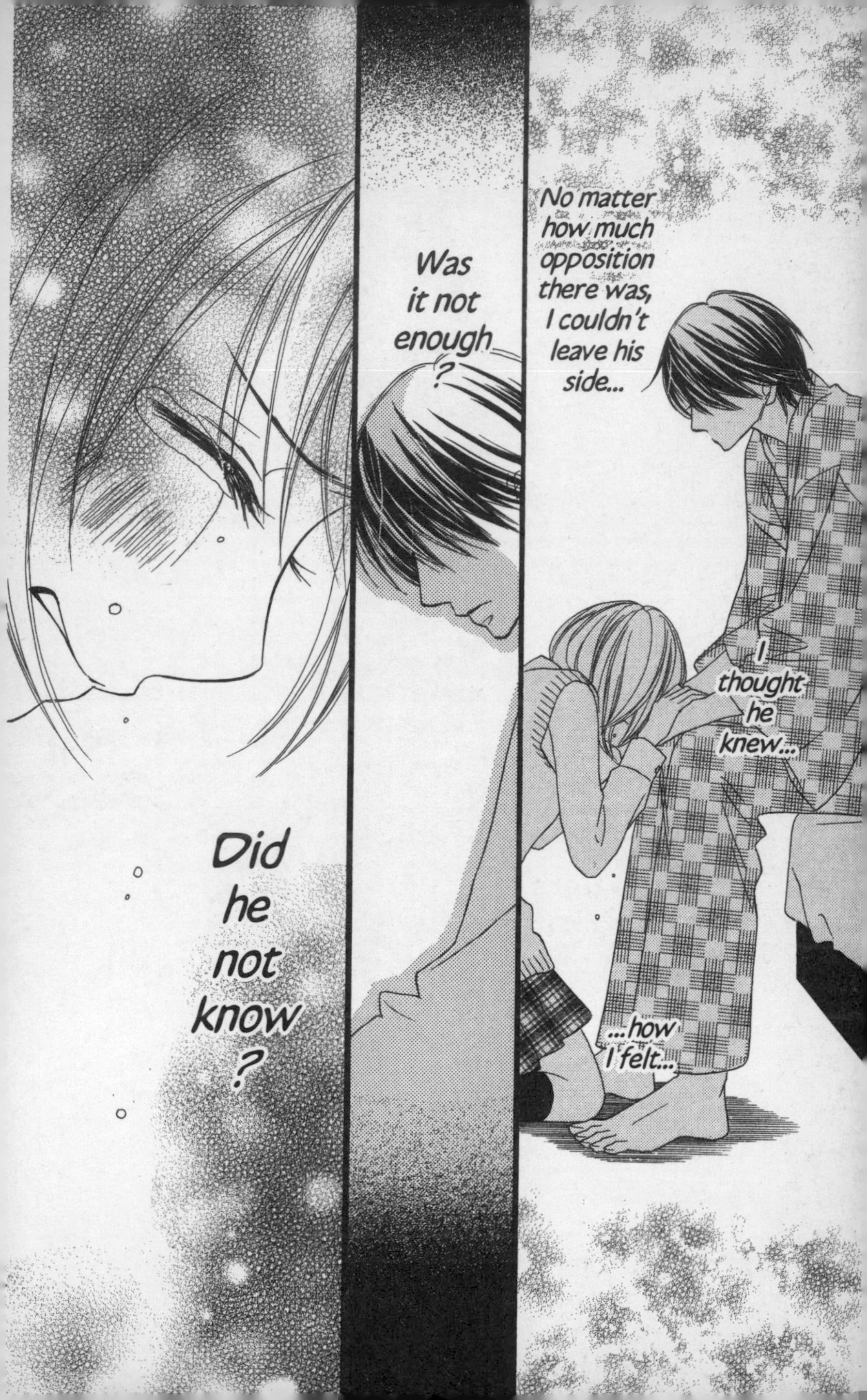
No matter how much opposition there was, I couldn't leave his side...
I thought he knew...
...how I felt...
Was it not enough?
Did he not know?

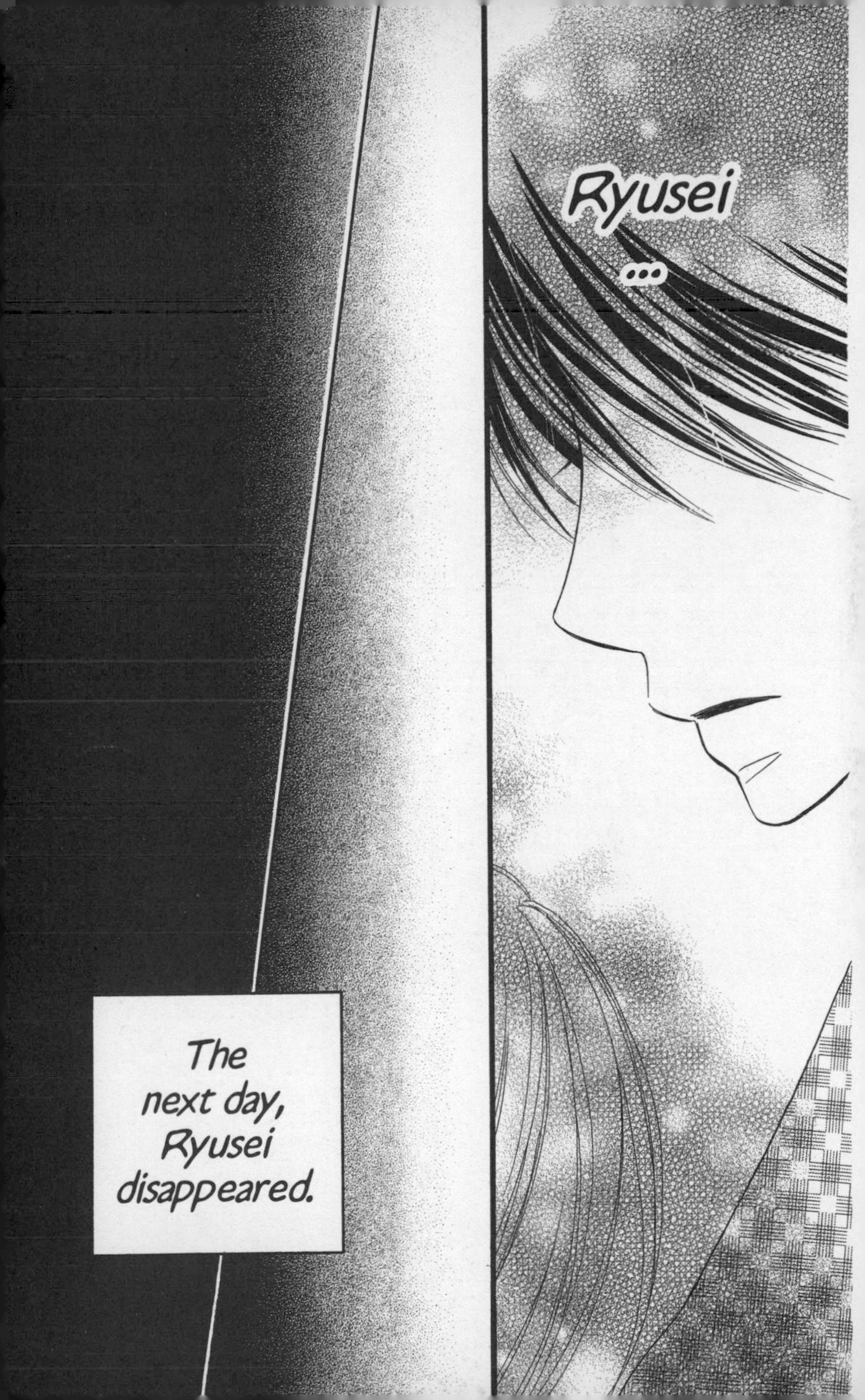
Ryusei
...
The next day, Ryusei disappeared.

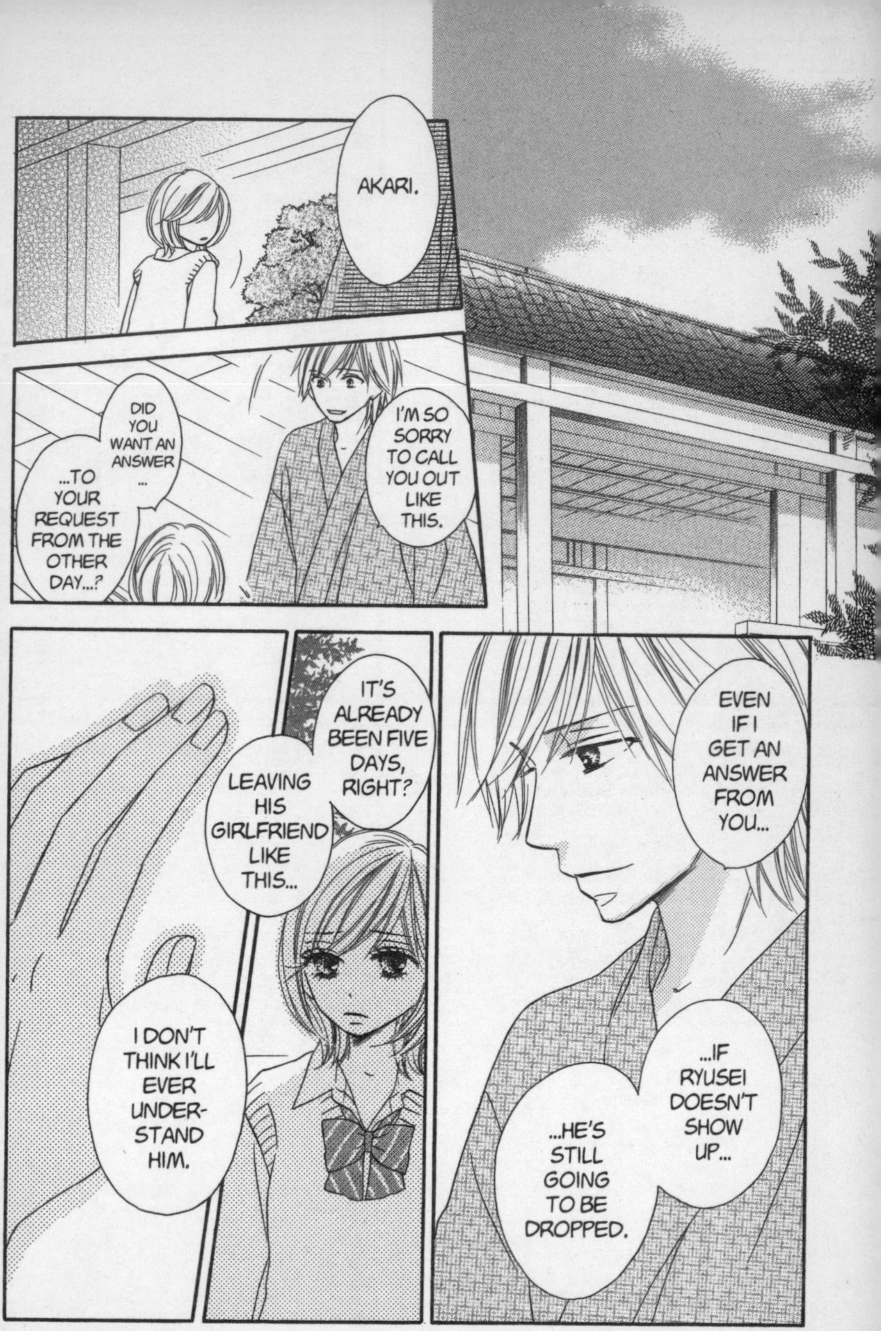
AKARI.
I'M SO SORRY TO CALL YOU OUT LIKE THIS.
DID YOU WANT AN ANSWER...
...TO YOUR REQUEST FROM THE OTHER DAY...?
EVEN IF I GET AN ANSWER FROM YOU...
...IF RYUSEI DOESN'T SHOW UP...
...HE'S STILL GOING TO BE DROPPED.
IT'S ALREADY BEEN FIVE DAYS, RIGHT?
LEAVING HIS GIRLFRIEND LIKE THIS...
I DON'T THINK I'LL EVER UNDERSTAND HIM.

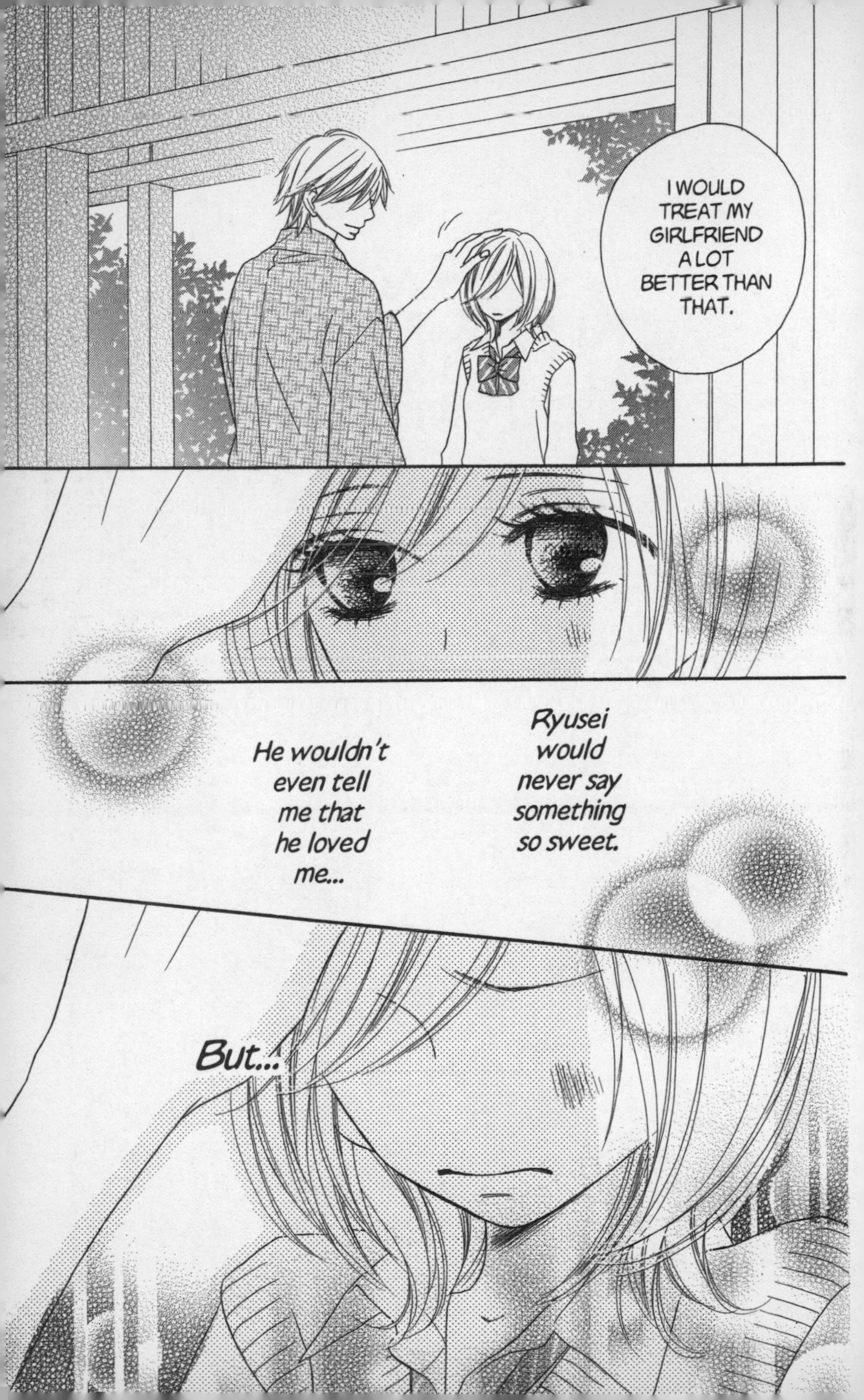
I WOULD TREAT MY GIRLFRIEND A LOT BETTER THAN THAT.
Ryusei would never say something so sweet.
He wouldn't even tell me that he loved me...
But...

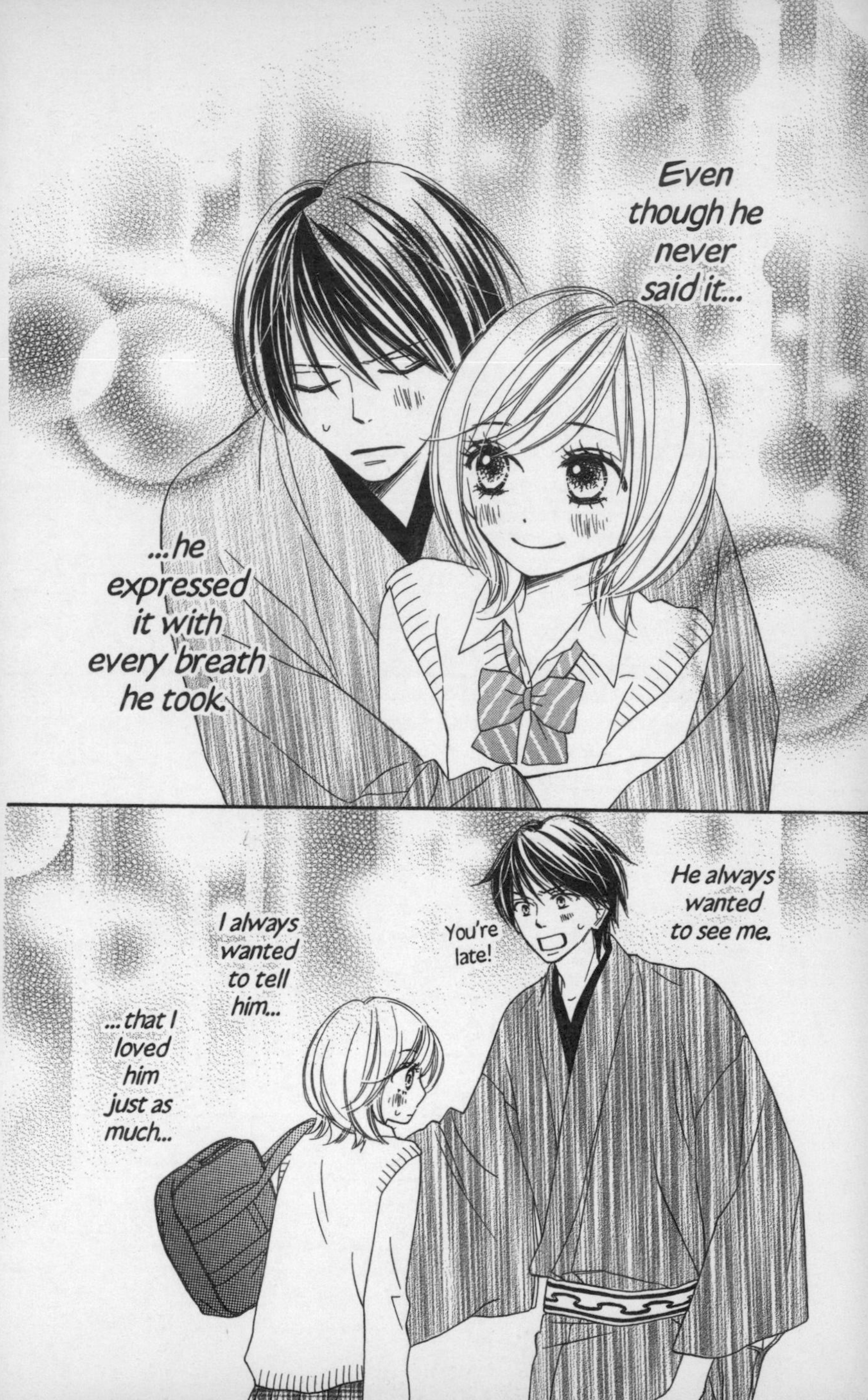
Even though he never said it...
...he expressed it with every breath he took.
He always wanted to see me.
You're late!
I always wanted to tell him...
...that I loved him just as much...

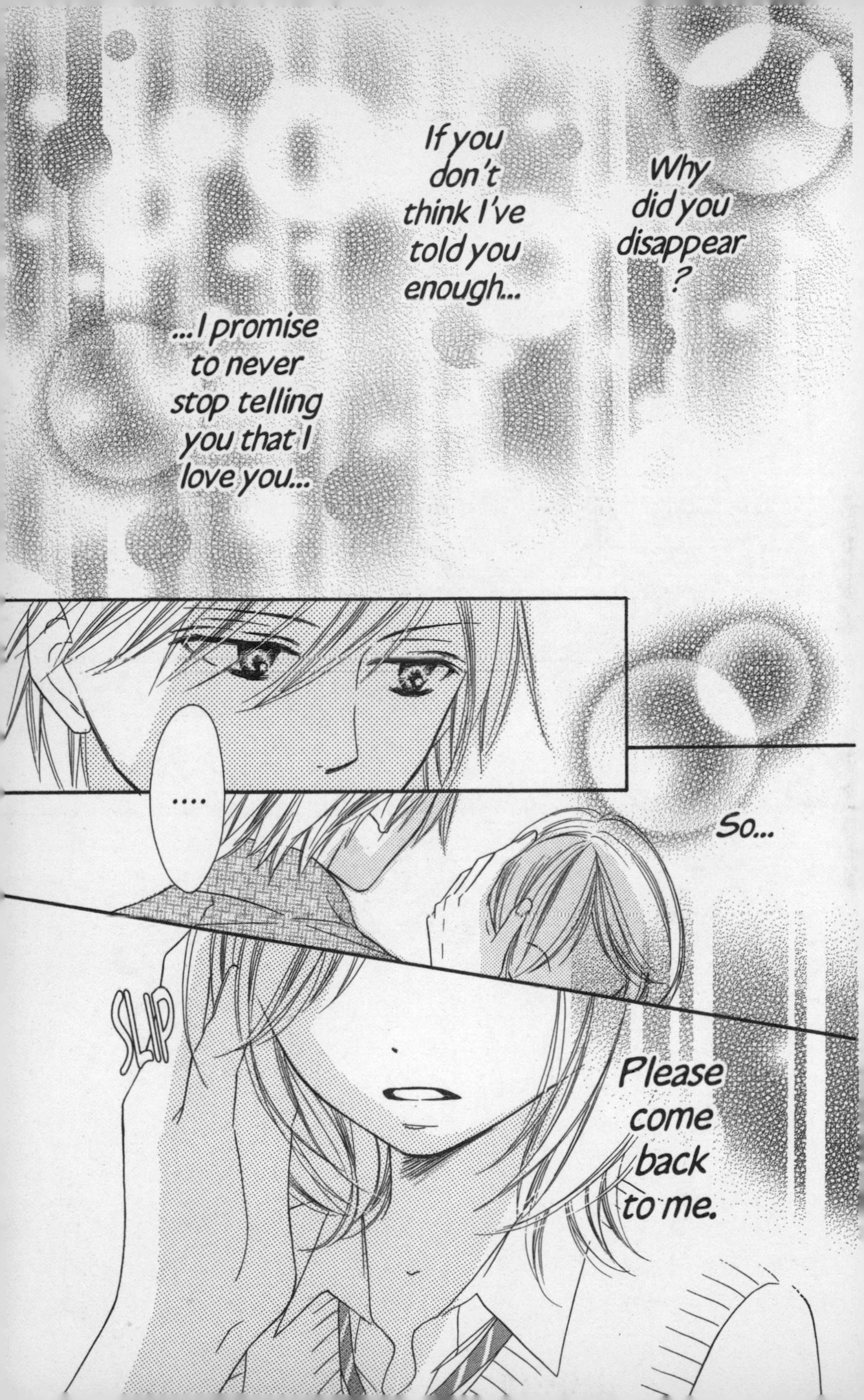
Why did you disappear?
If you don't think I've told you enough...
...I promise to never stop telling you that I love you...
....
So...
Please come back to me.
SLIP

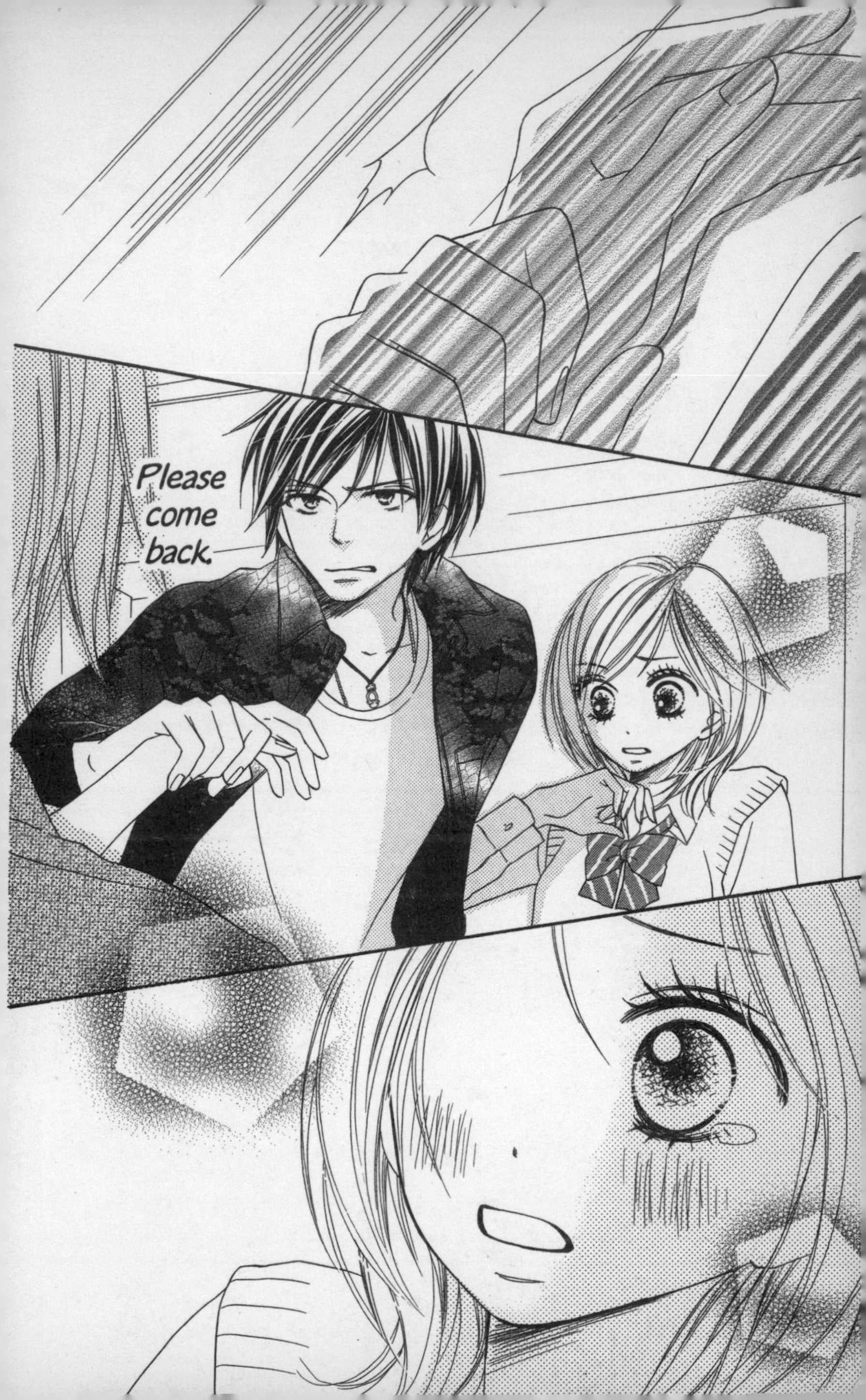
Please come back.

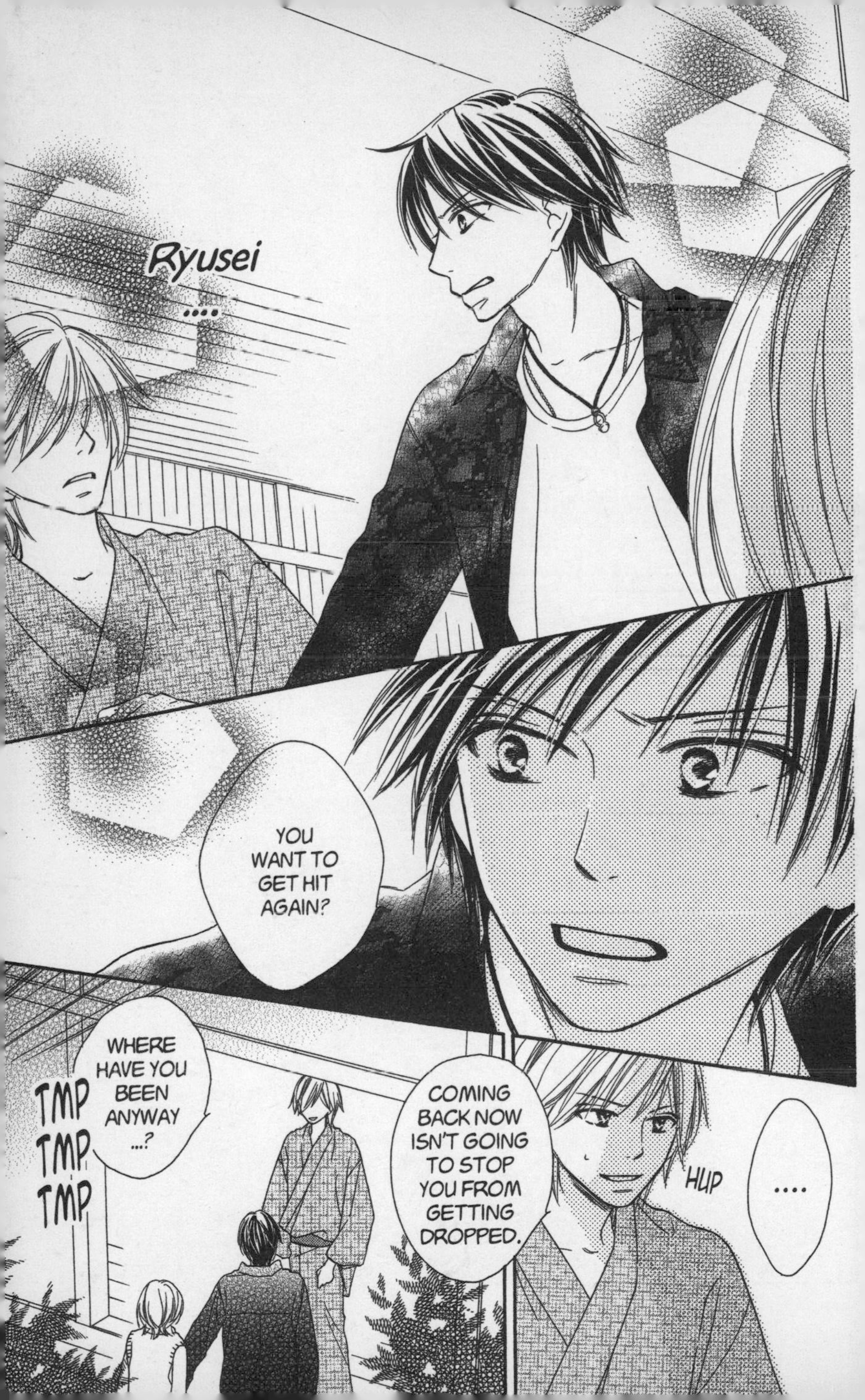
Ryusei
....
YOU WANT TO GET HIT AGAIN?
....
HUP
COMING BACK NOW ISN'T GOING TO STOP YOU FROM GETTING DROPPED.
WHERE HAVE YOU BEEN ANYWAY ...?
TMP
TMP
TMP

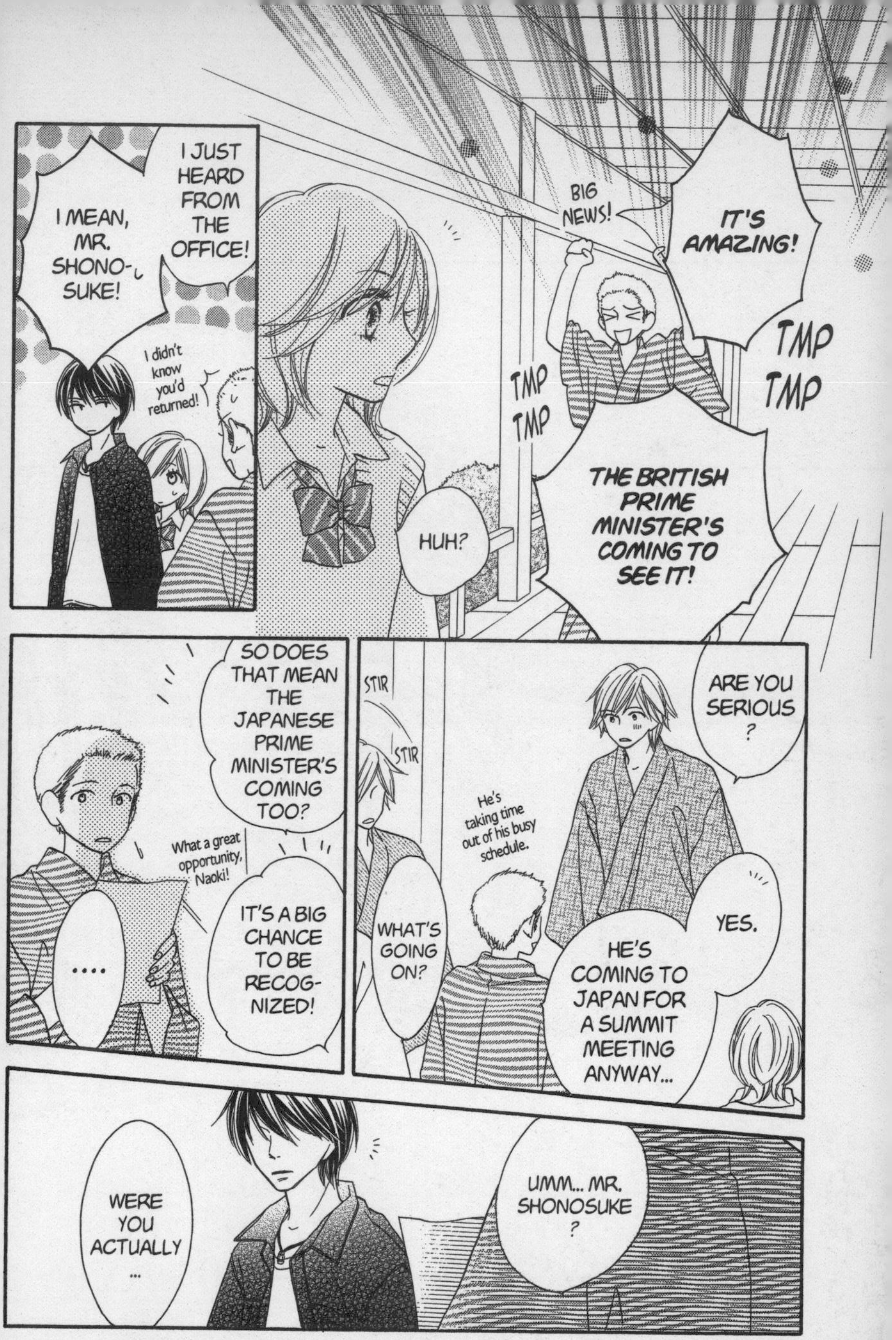
IT'S AMAZING!
BIG NEWS!
TMP TMP
TMP TMP
THE BRITISH PRIME MINISTER'S COMING TO SEE IT!
HUH?
I JUST HEARD FROM THE OFFICE!
I MEAN, MR. SHONOSUKE!
I didn't know you'd returned!
ARE YOU SERIOUS?
STIR
STIR
He's taking time out of his busy schedule.
YES.
HE'S COMING TO JAPAN FOR A SUMMIT MEETING ANYWAY...
WHAT'S GOING ON?
SO DOES THAT MEAN THE JAPANESE PRIME MINISTER'S COMING TOO?
What a great opportunity, Naoki!
IT'S A BIG CHANCE TO BE RECOGNIZED!
....
UMM... MR. SHONOSUKE?
WERE YOU ACTUALLY...

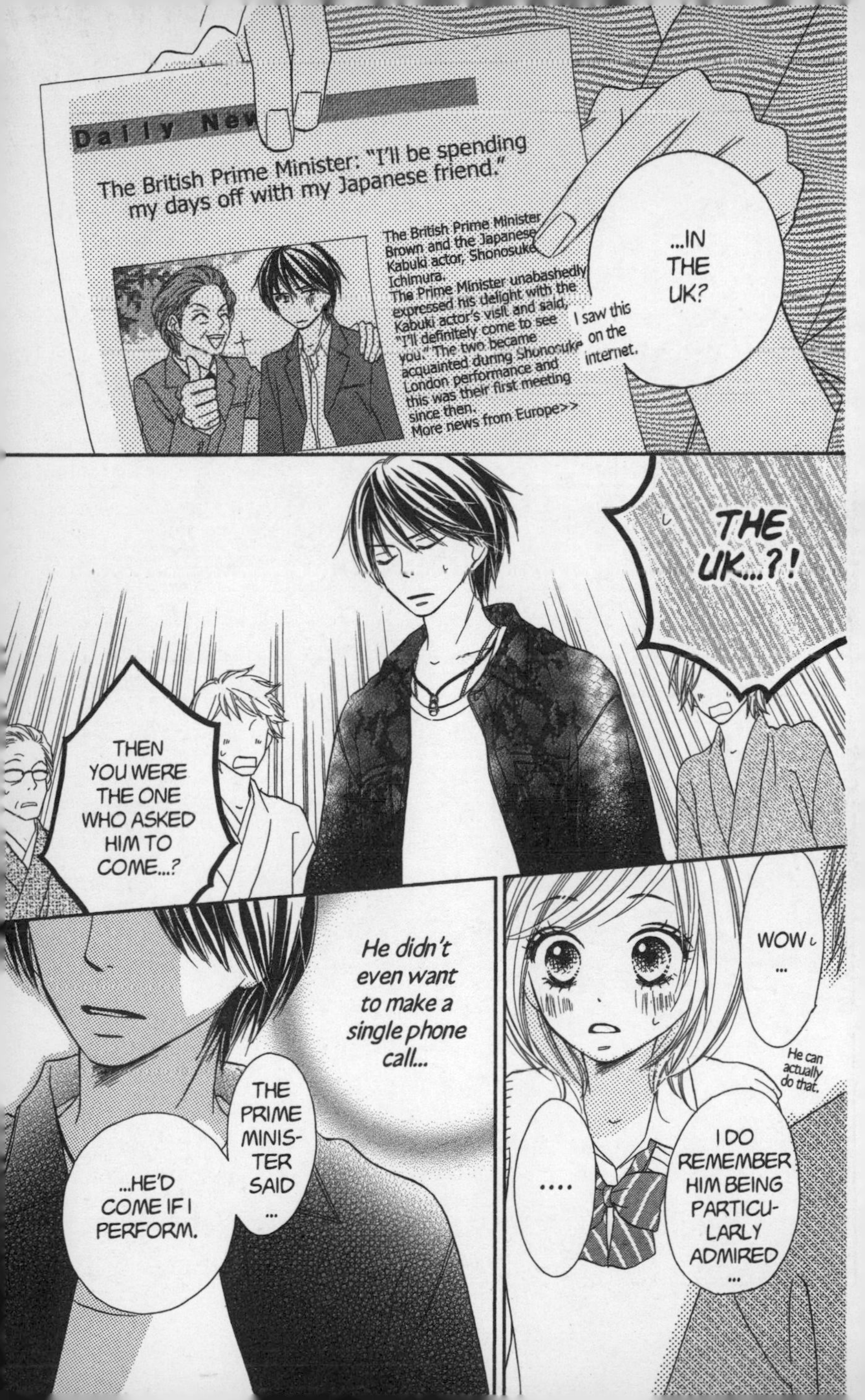
...IN THE UK?
I saw this Shonosuke on the internet.
Daily New
The British Prime Minister: "I'll be spending my days off with my Japanese friend."
The British Prime Minister Brown and the Japanese Kabuki actor, Shonosuke Ichimura.
The Prime Minister unabashedly expressed his delight with the Kabuki actor's visit and said, "I'll definitely come to see you." The two became acquainted during Shonosuke London performance and this was their first meeting since then.
More news from Europe>>
THE UK...?!
THEN YOU WERE THE ONE WHO ASKED HIM TO COME...?
WOW...
He can actually do that.
I DO REMEMBER HIM BEING PARTICULARLY ADMIRED...
....
He didn't even want to make a single phone call...
THE PRIME MINISTER SAID...
...HE'D COME IF I PERFORM.

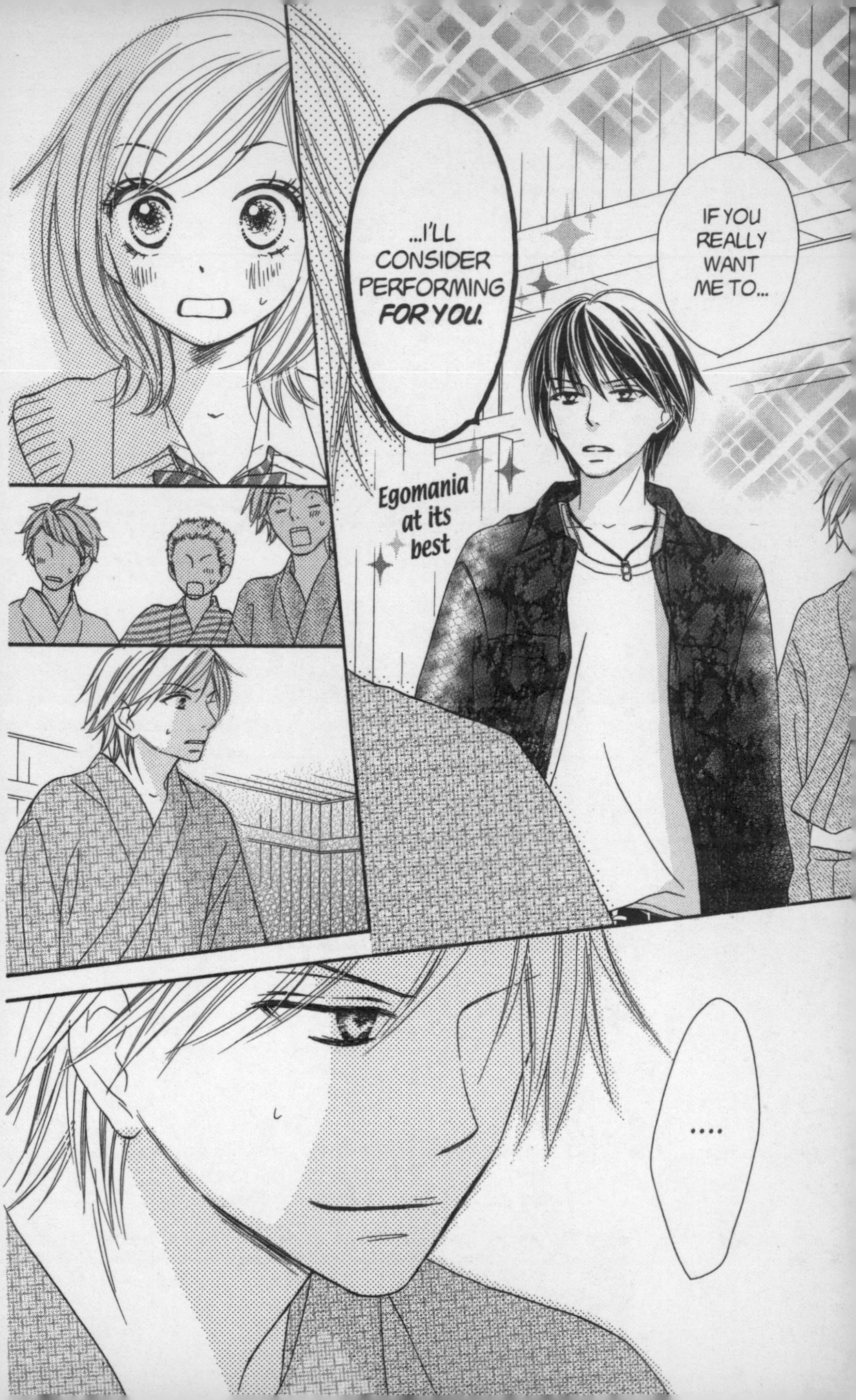
IF YOU REALLY WANT ME TO...
...I'LL CONSIDER PERFORMING FOR YOU.
Egomania at its best
....

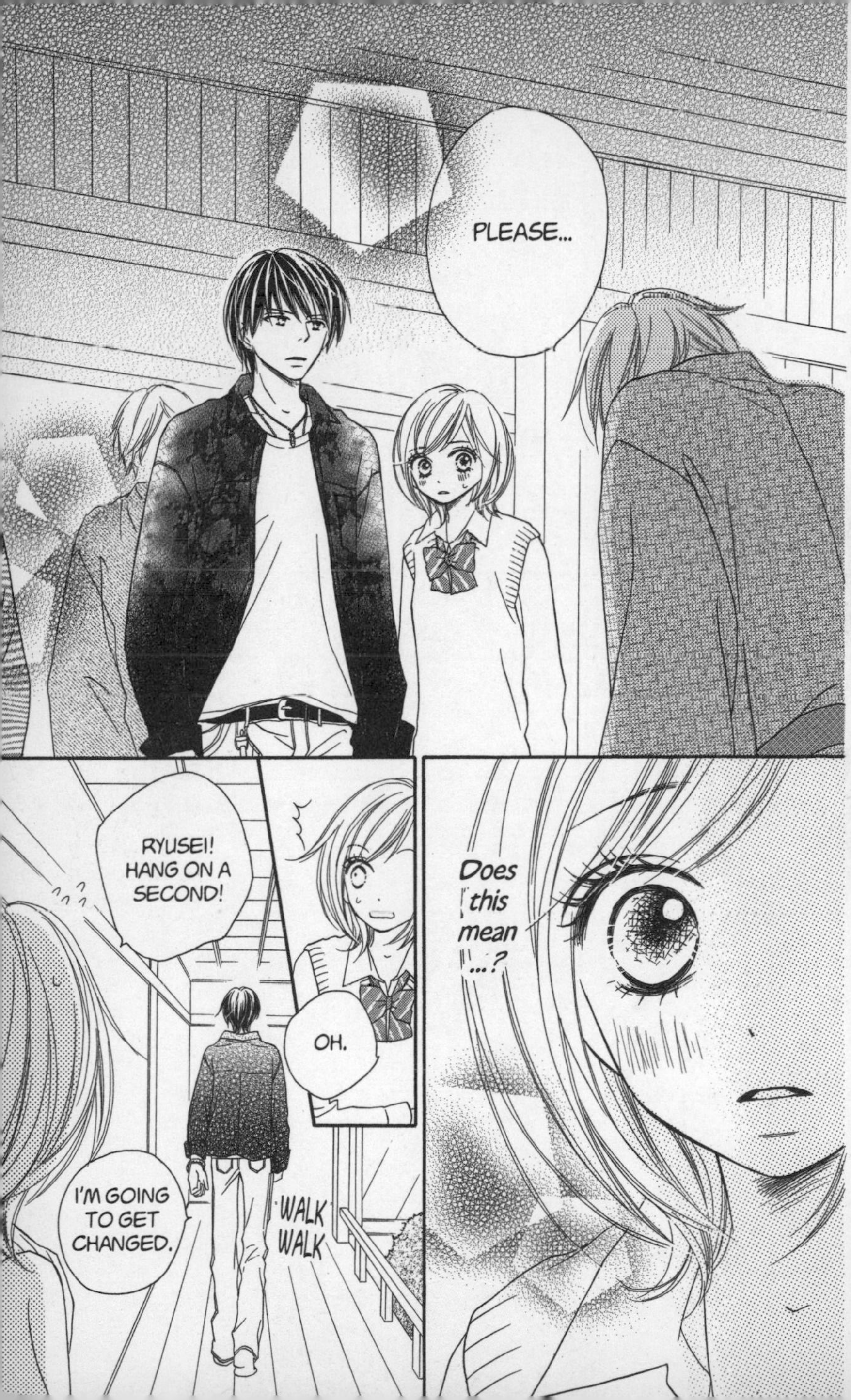
PLEASE...
Does this mean ...?
OH.
RYUSEI! HANG ON A SECOND!
I'M GOING TO GET CHANGED.
WALK WALK

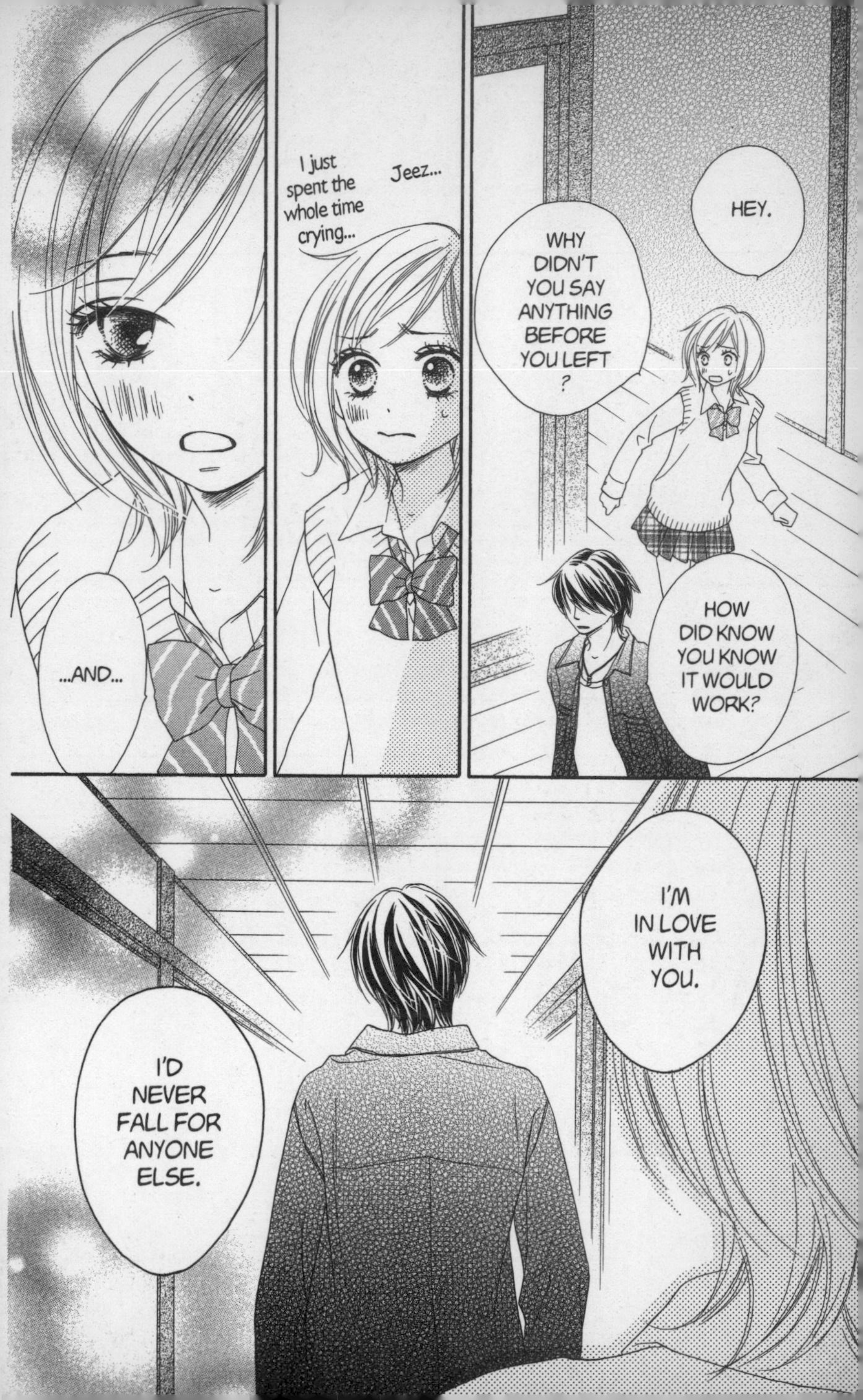
HEY.
WHY DIDN'T YOU SAY ANYTHING BEFORE YOU LEFT?
HOW DID KNOW YOU KNOW IT WOULD WORK?
Jeez...
I just spent the whole time crying...
...AND...
I'M IN LOVE WITH YOU.
I'D NEVER FALL FOR ANYONE ELSE.

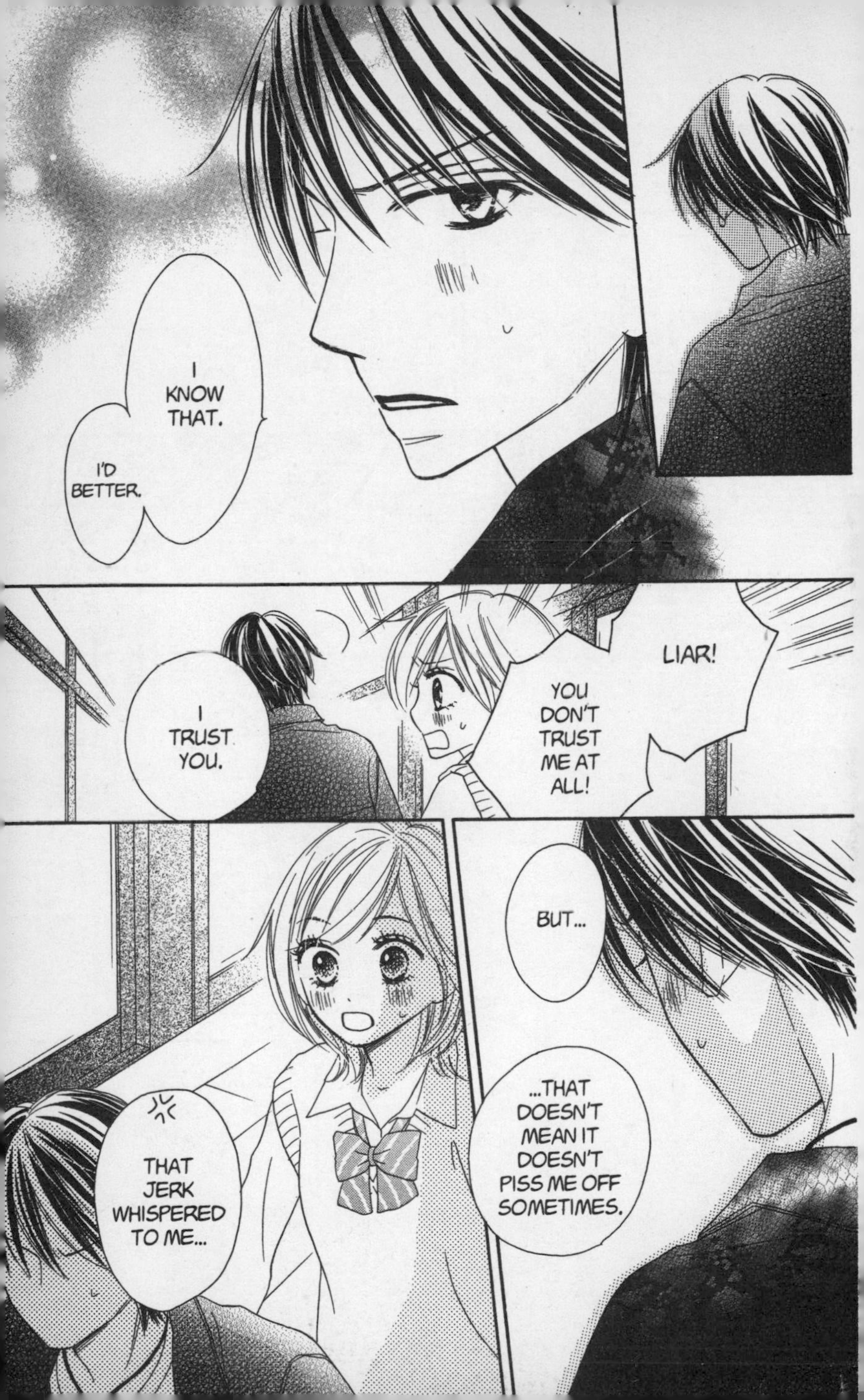
I KNOW THAT.
I'D BETTER.
LIAR!
YOU DON'T TRUST ME AT ALL!
I TRUST YOU.
BUT...
...THAT DOESN'T MEAN IT DOESN'T PISS ME OFF SOMETIMES.
THAT JERK WHISPERED TO ME...

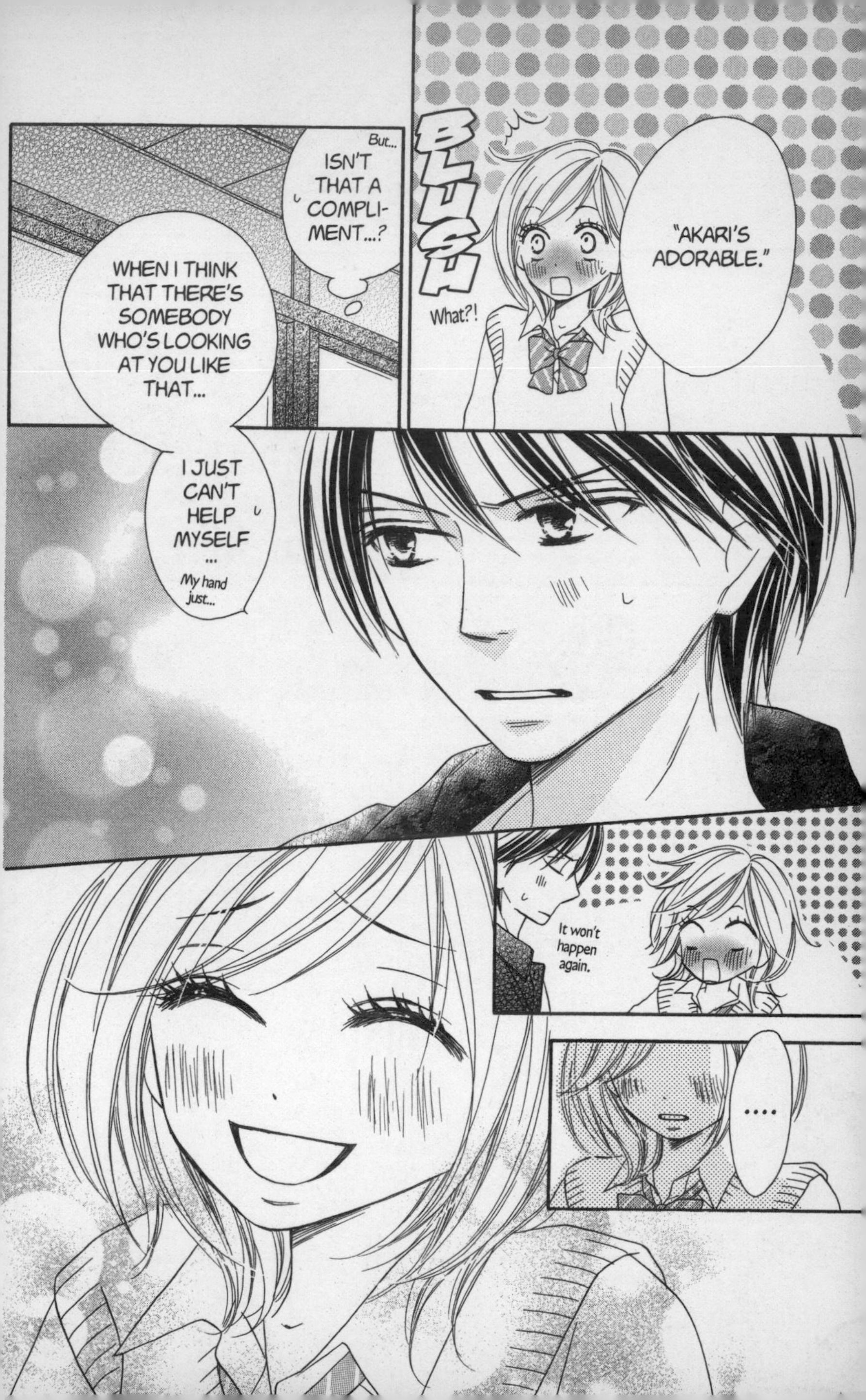
"AKARI'S ADORABLE."
BLUSH
What?!
But... ISN'T THAT A COMPLIMENT...?
WHEN I THINK THAT THERE'S SOMEBODY WHO'S LOOKING AT YOU LIKE THAT...
I JUST CAN'T HELP MYSELF...
My hand just...
It won't happen again.
....

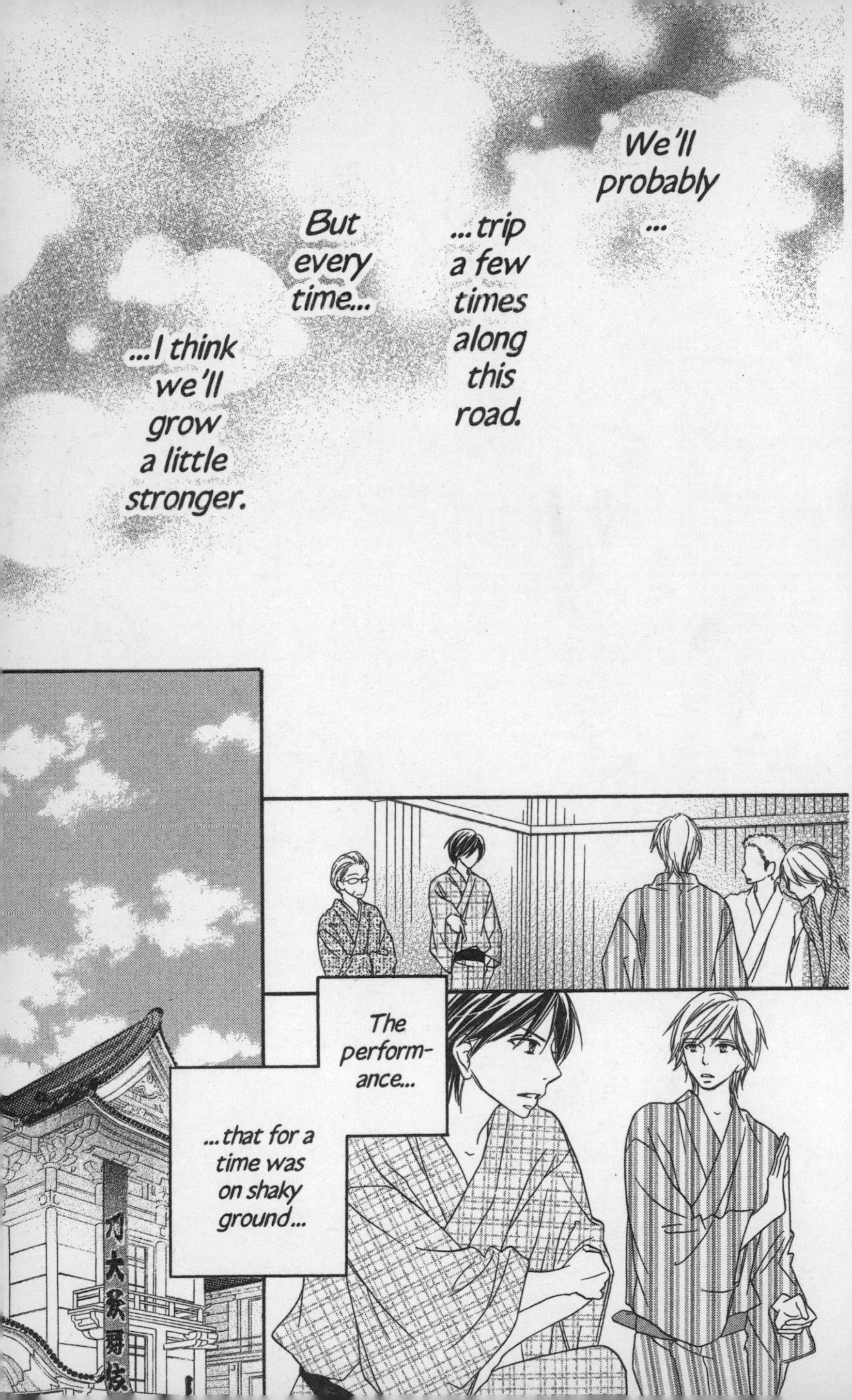
We'll probably...
...trip a few times along this road.
But every time...
...I think we'll grow a little stronger.
The perform-ance...
...that for a time was on shaky ground...

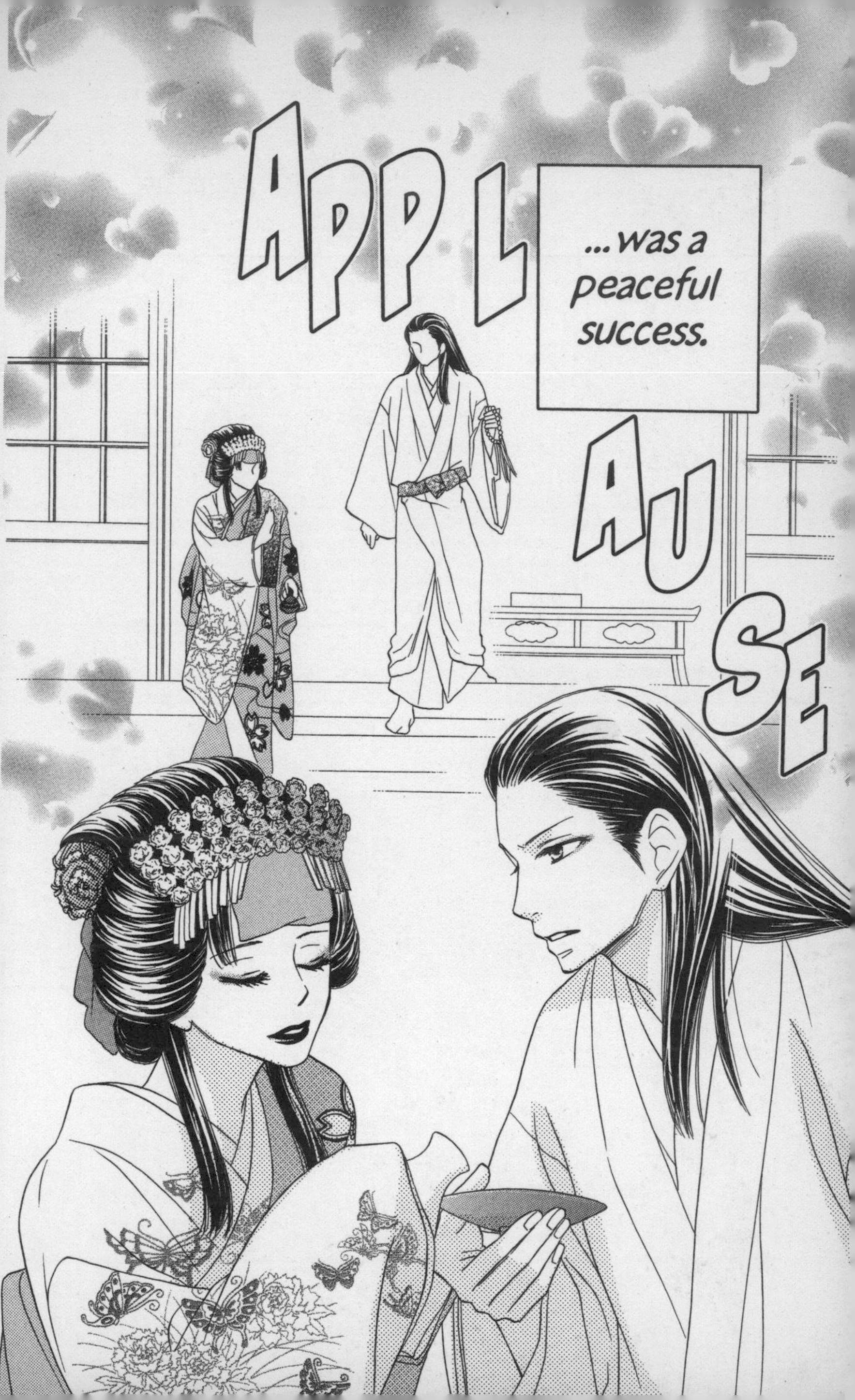
APPLAUSE
...was a peaceful success.

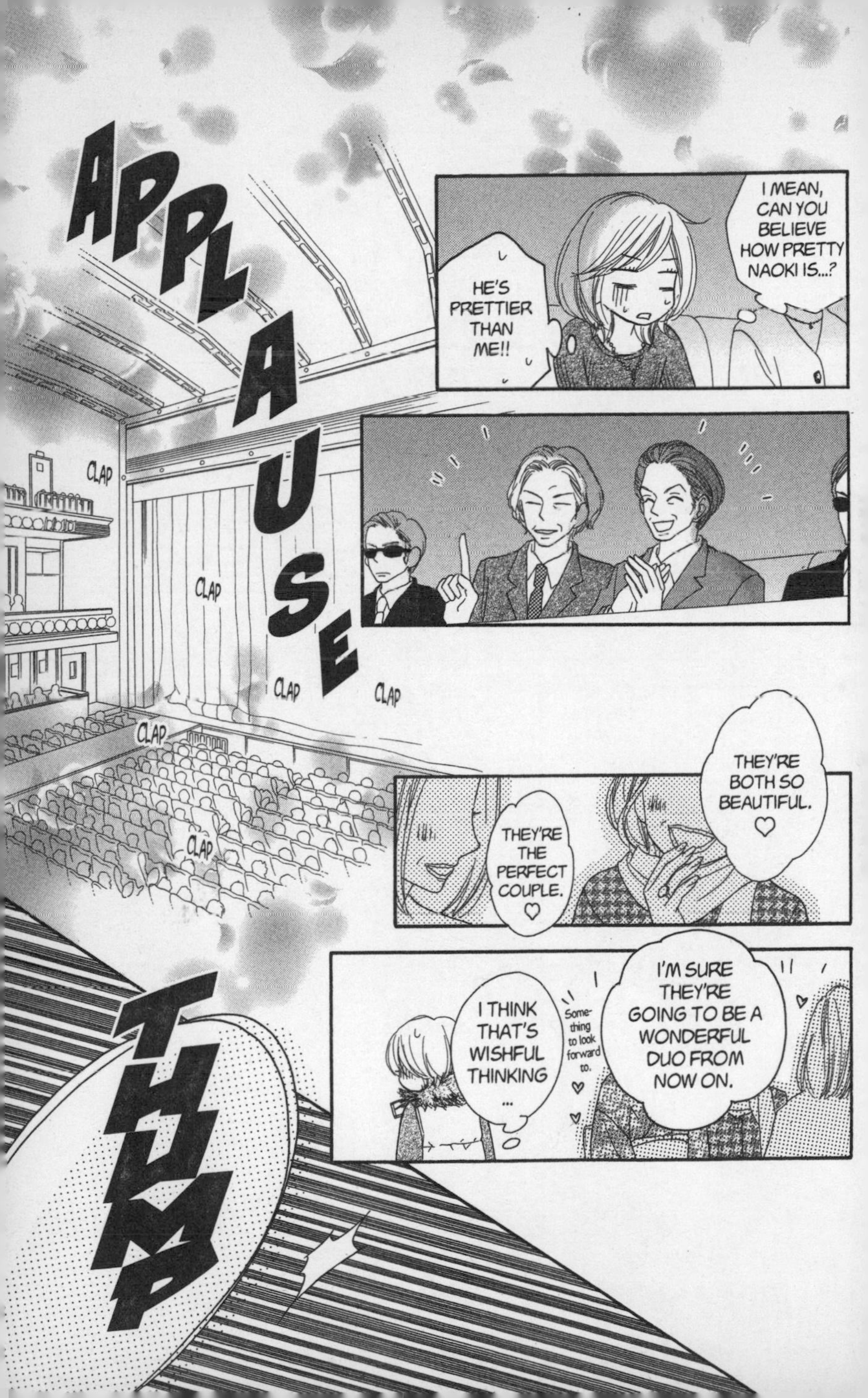
APPLAUSE
CLAP
CLAP
CLAP
CLAP
CLAP
CLAP
I MEAN, CAN YOU BELIEVE HOW PRETTY NAOKI IS...?
HE'S PRETTIER THAN ME!!
THEY'RE BOTH SO BEAUTIFUL. ♡
THEY'RE THE PERFECT COUPLE. ♡
I'M SURE THEY'RE GOING TO BE A WONDERFUL DUO FROM NOW ON.
Something to look forward to.
I THINK THAT'S WISHFUL THINKING ...
THUMP

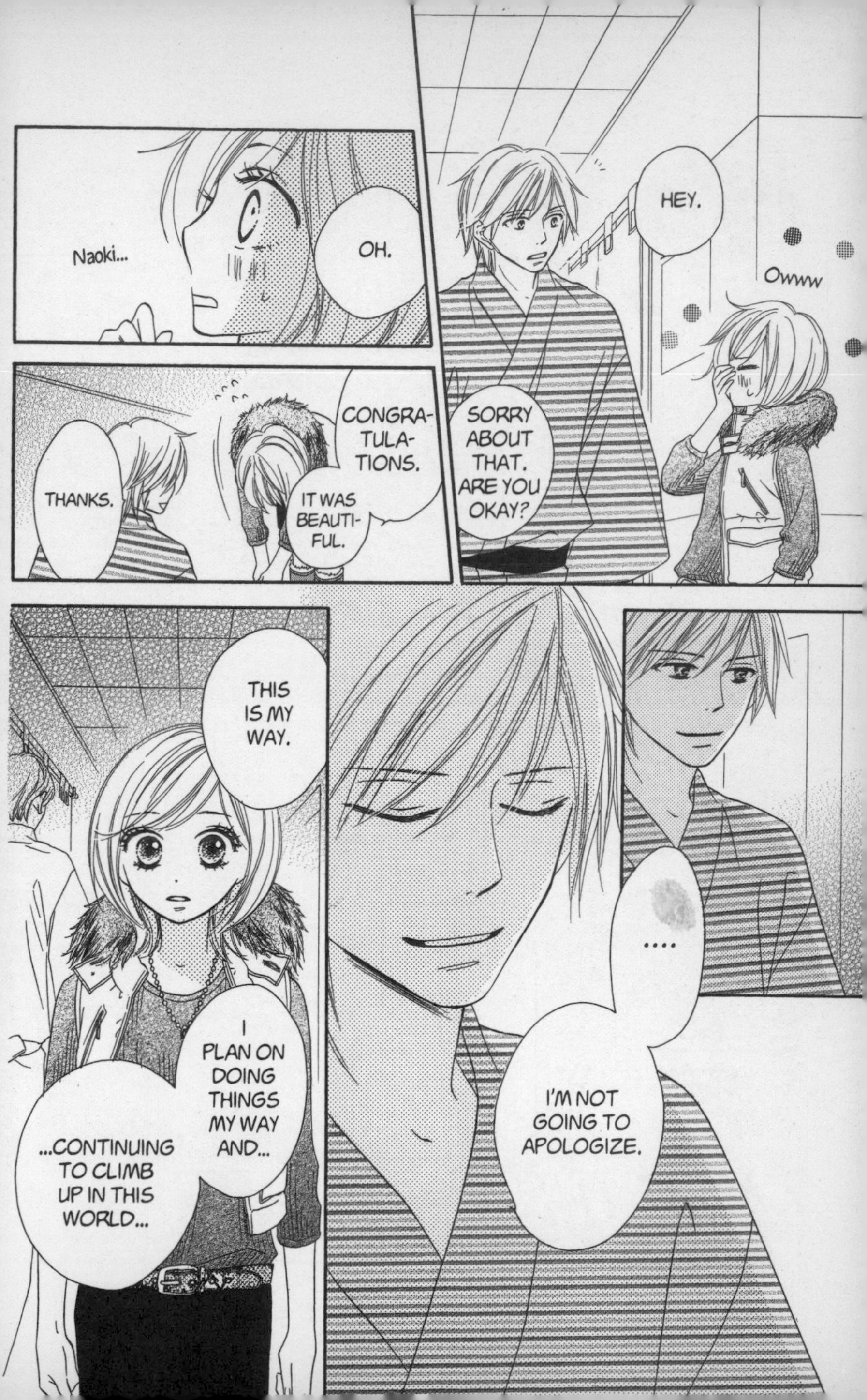
HEY.
Owww
SORRY ABOUT THAT. ARE YOU OKAY?
OH.
Naoki...
CONGRA-TULA-TIONS.
IT WAS BEAUTI-FUL.
THANKS.
....
I'M NOT GOING TO APOLOGIZE.
THIS IS MY WAY.
I PLAN ON DOING THINGS MY WAY AND...
...CONTINUING TO CLIMB UP IN THIS WORLD...

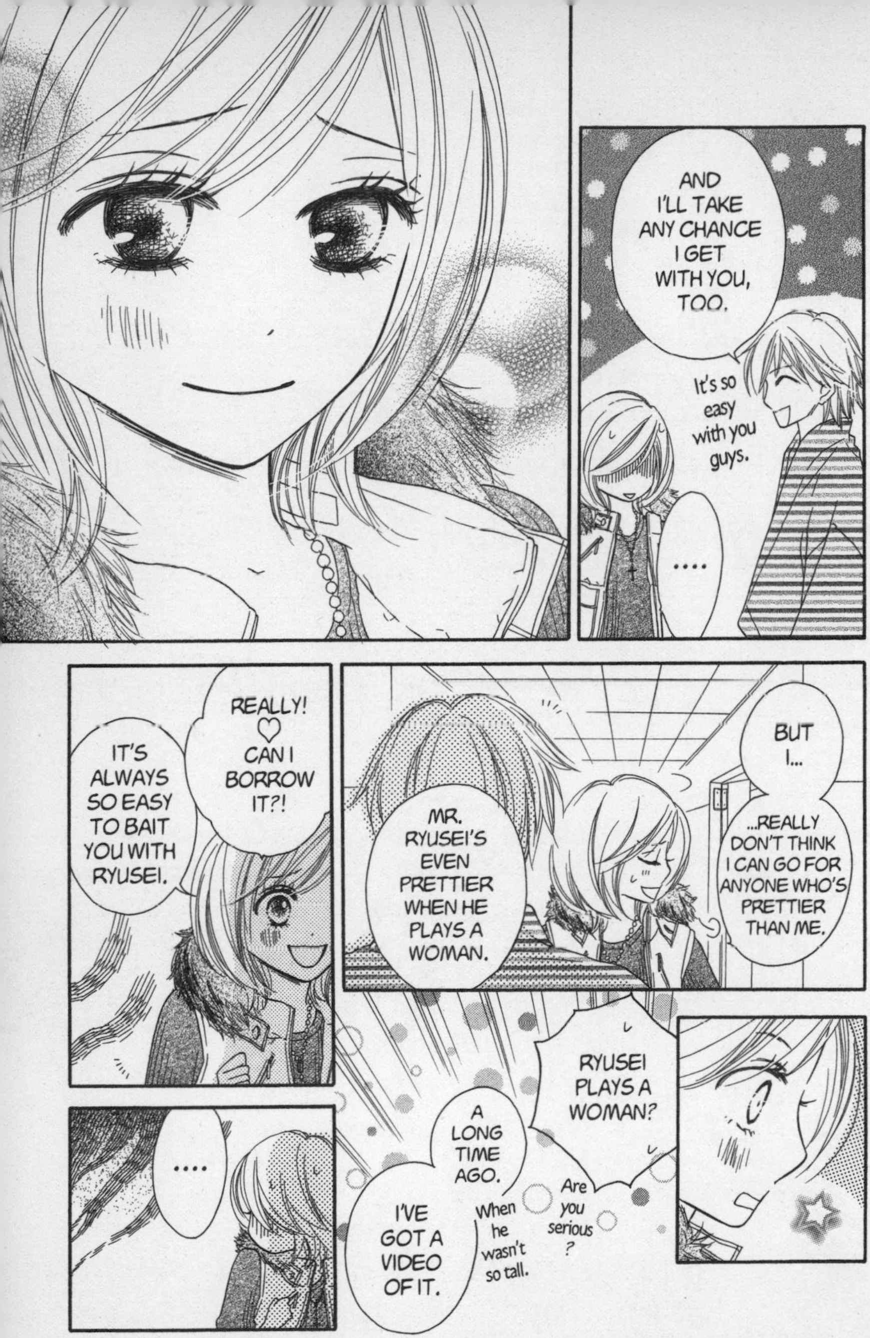
AND I'LL TAKE ANY CHANCE I GET WITH YOU, TOO.
It's so easy with you guys.
....
BUT I...
...REALLY DON'T THINK I CAN GO FOR ANYONE WHO'S PRETTIER THAN ME.
MR. RYUSEI'S EVEN PRETTIER WHEN HE PLAYS A WOMAN.
REALLY! ♡ CAN I BORROW IT?!
IT'S ALWAYS SO EASY TO BAIT YOU WITH RYUSEI.
RYUSEI PLAYS A WOMAN?
Are you serious?
A LONG TIME AGO.
When he wasn't so tall.
I'VE GOT A VIDEO OF IT.
....

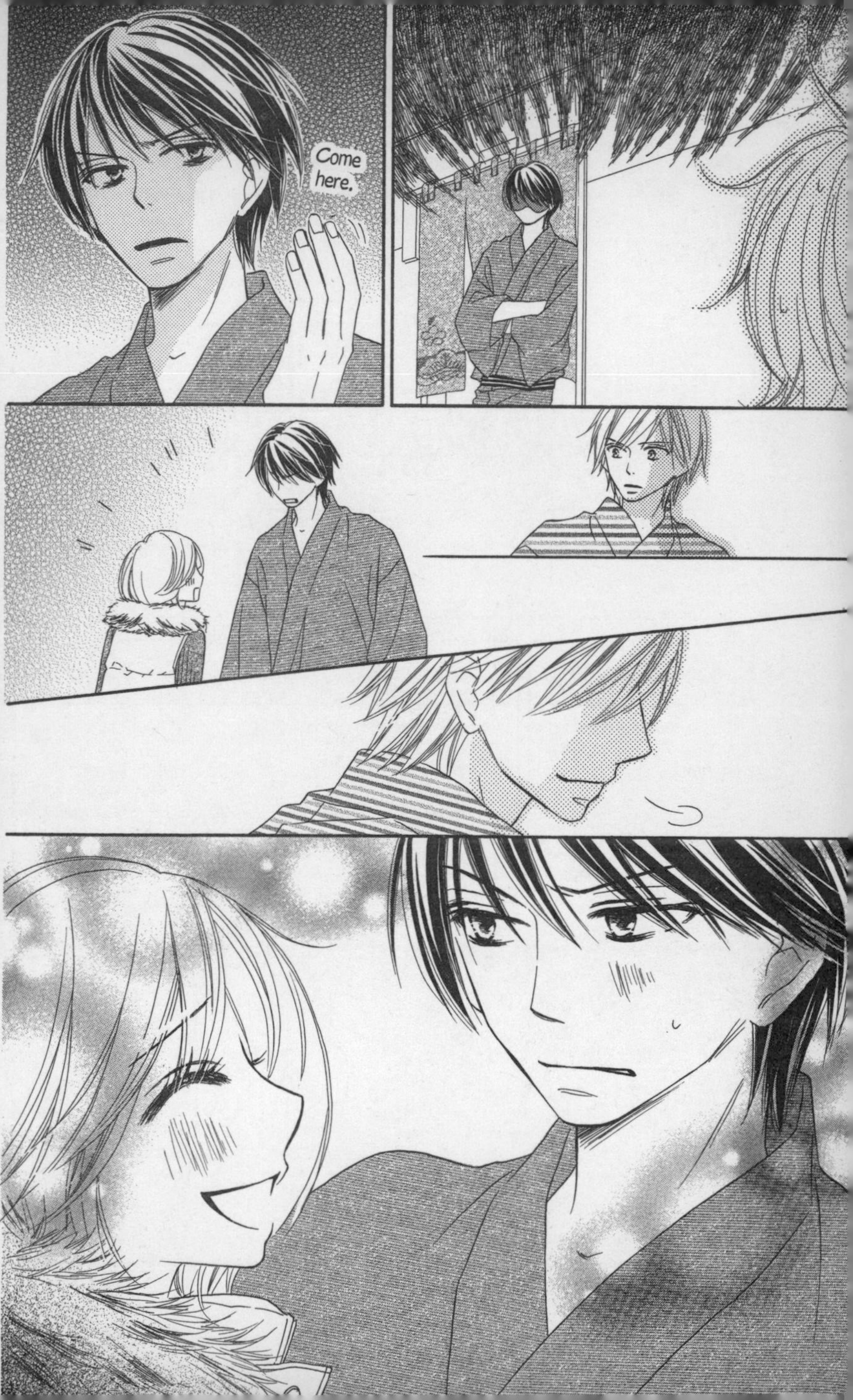
Come here.

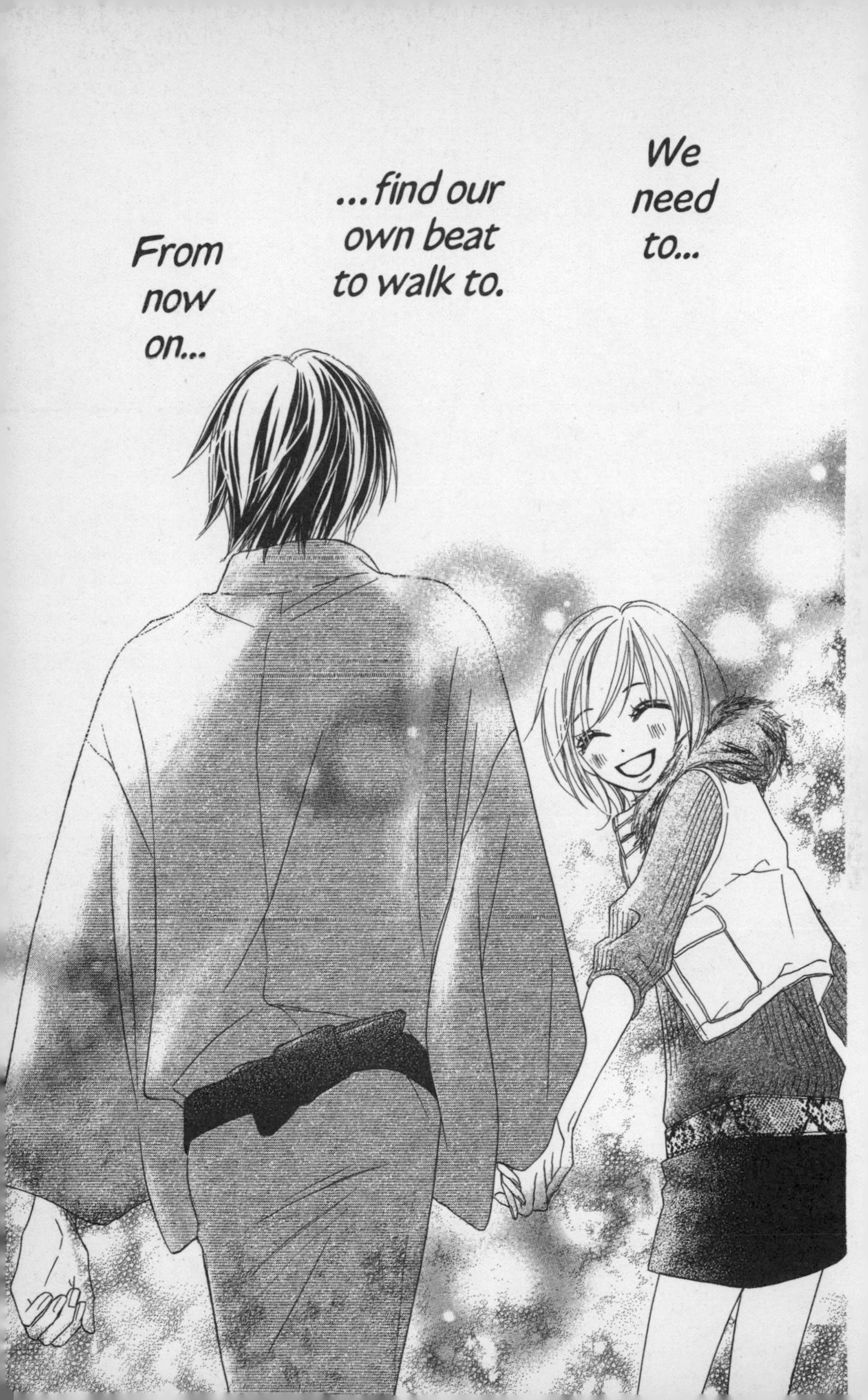
We need to...
...find our own beat to walk to.
From now on...

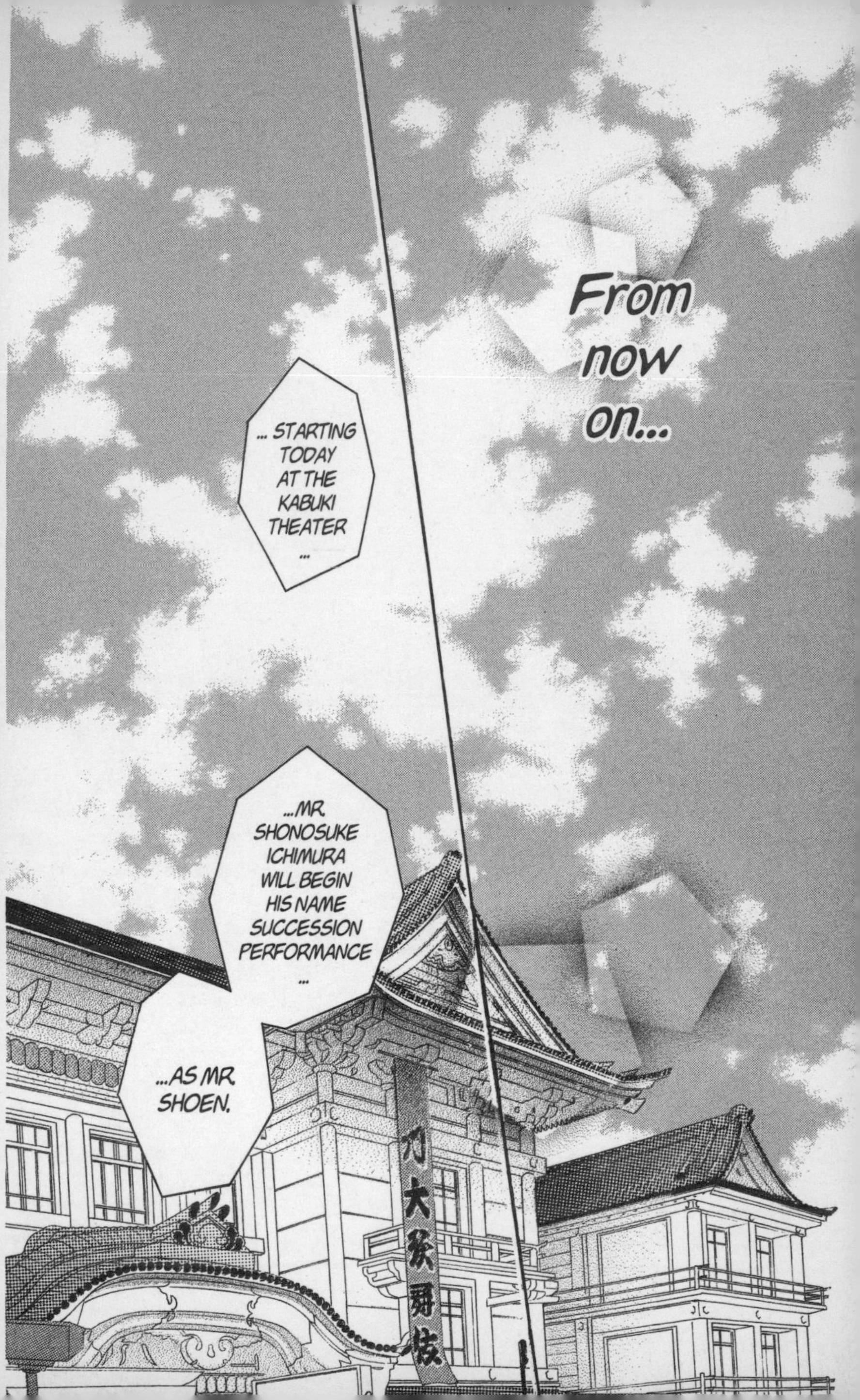
From now on...
... STARTING TODAY AT THE KABUKI THEATER ...
...MR. SHONOSUKE ICHIMURA WILL BEGIN HIS NAME SUCCESSION PERFORMANCE ...
...AS MR. SHOEN.

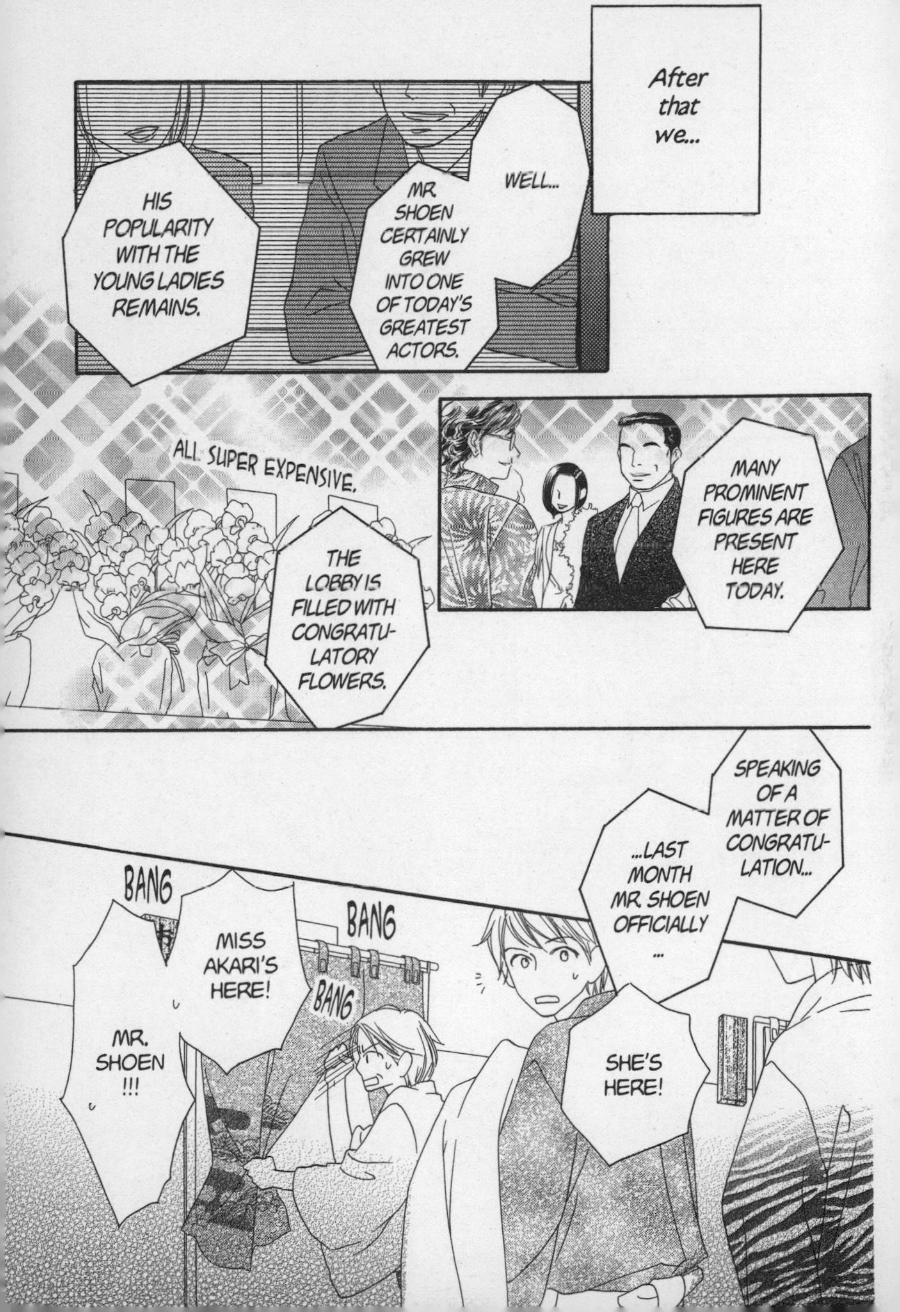
After that we...
WELL...
MR. SHOEN CERTAINLY GREW INTO ONE OF TODAY'S GREATEST ACTORS.
HIS POPULARITY WITH THE YOUNG LADIES REMAINS.
MANY PROMINENT FIGURES ARE PRESENT HERE TODAY.
THE LOBBY IS FILLED WITH CONGRATU-LATORY FLOWERS.
ALL SUPER EXPENSIVE.
SPEAKING OF A MATTER OF CONGRATU-LATION...
...LAST MONTH MR. SHOEN OFFICIALLY ...
SHE'S HERE!
BANG
BANG
MISS AKARI'S HERE!
BANG
MR. SHOEN !!!

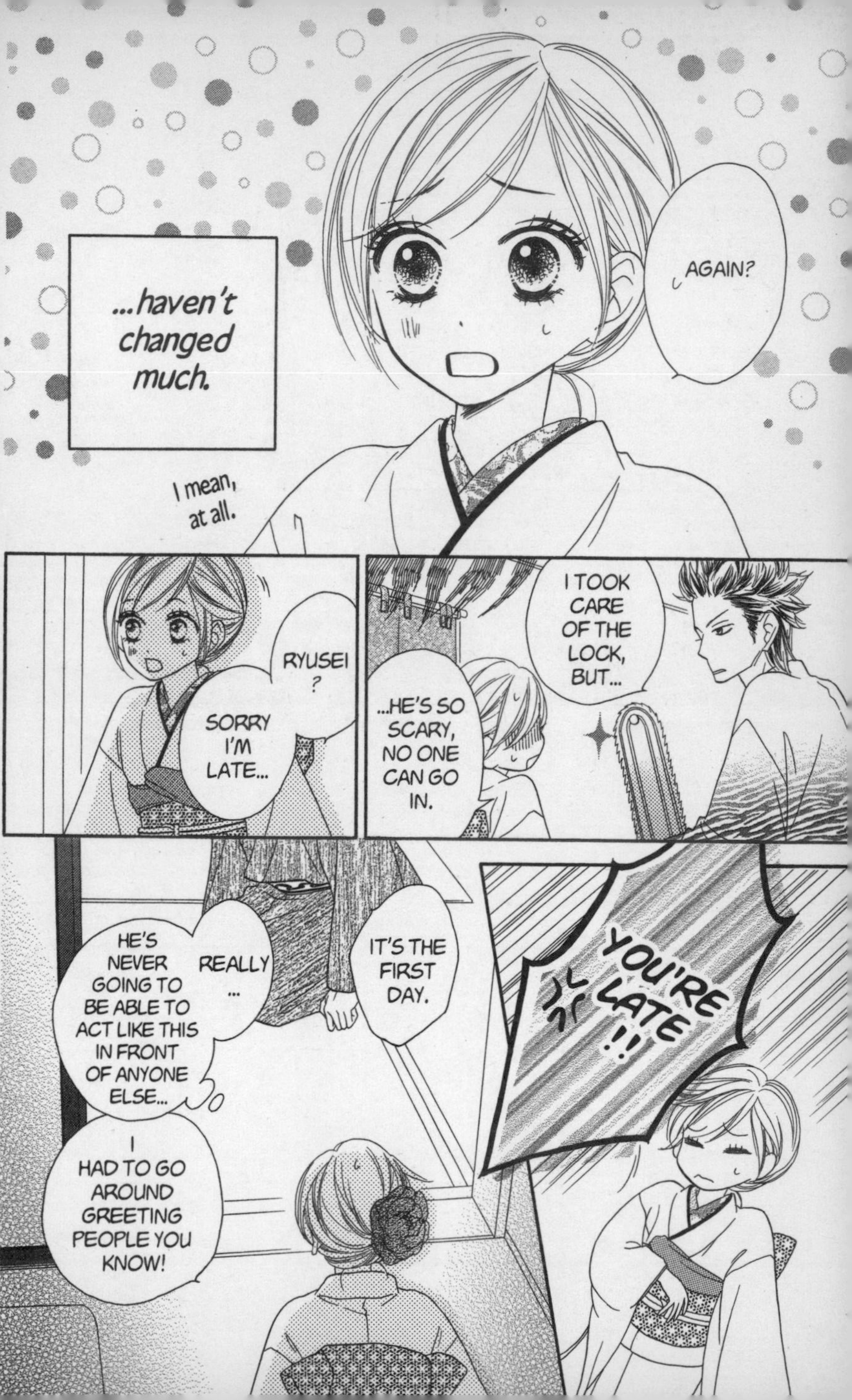
AGAIN?
...haven't changed much.
I mean, at all.
I TOOK CARE OF THE LOCK, BUT...
...HE'S SO SCARY, NO ONE CAN GO IN.
RYUSEI?
SORRY I'M LATE...
YOU'RE LATE!!
IT'S THE FIRST DAY.
REALLY...
HE'S NEVER GOING TO BE ABLE TO ACT LIKE THIS IN FRONT OF ANYONE ELSE...
I HAD TO GO AROUND GREETING PEOPLE YOU KNOW!

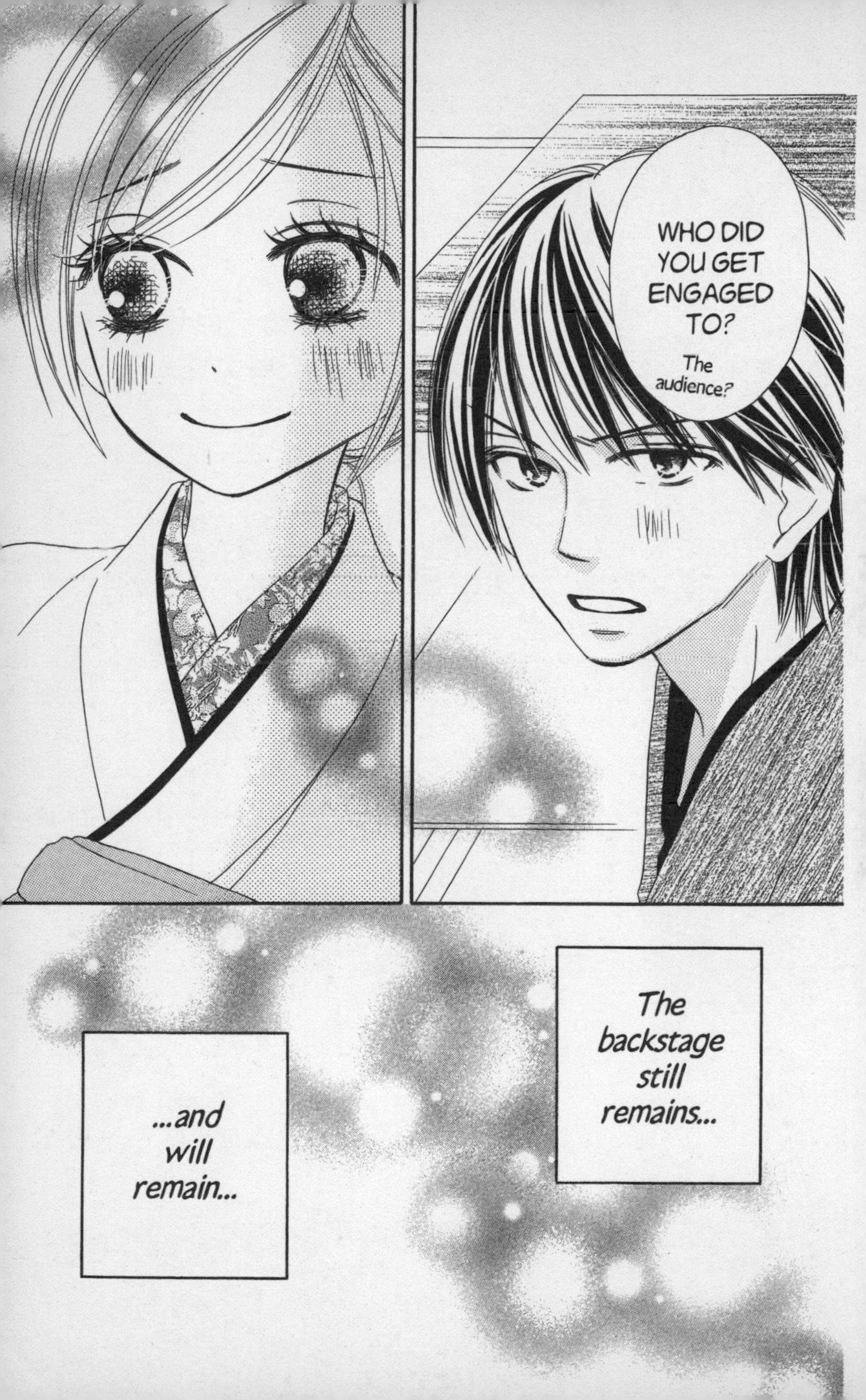
WHO DID YOU GET ENGAGED TO?
The audience?
The backstage still remains...
...and will remain...

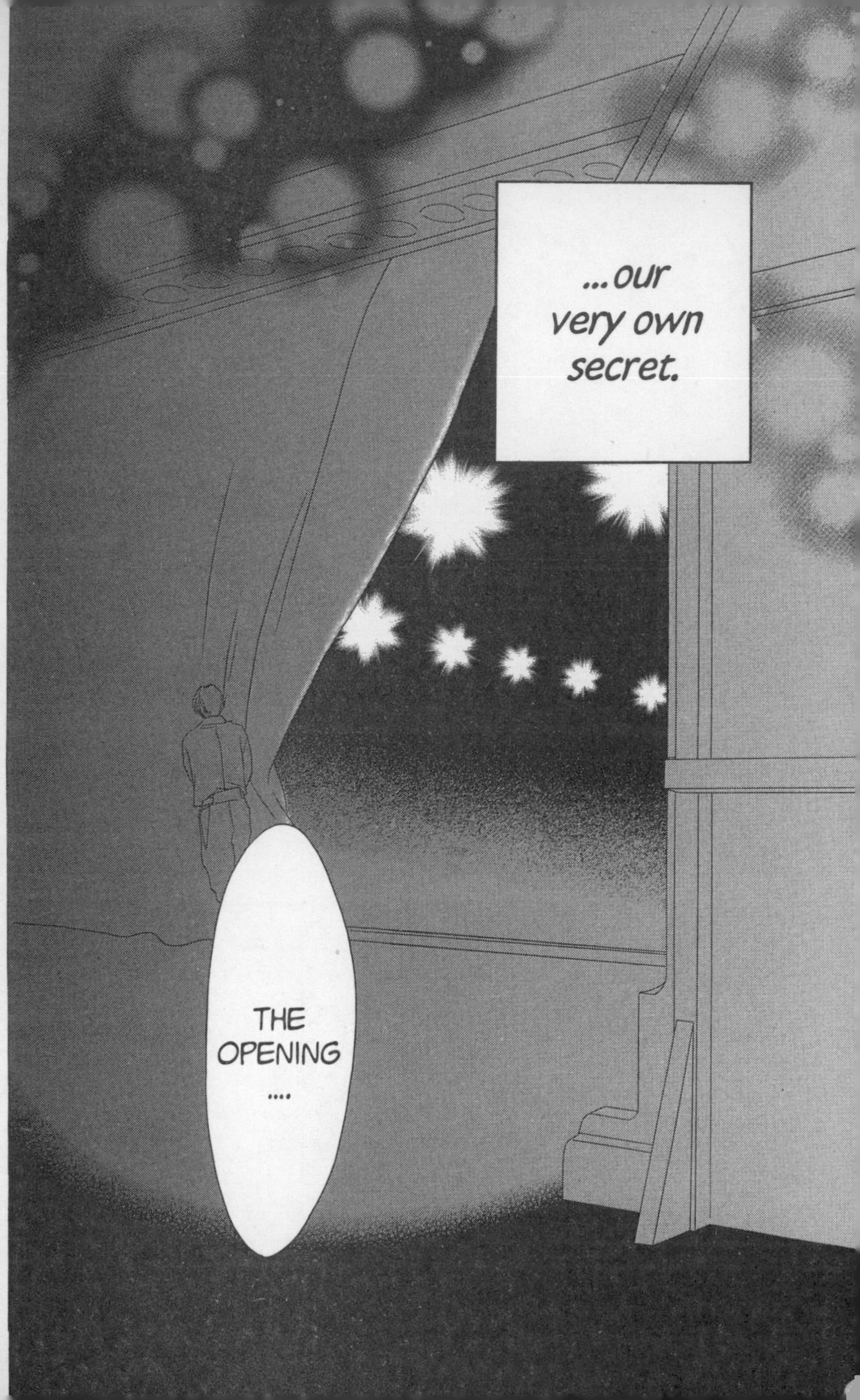
...our very own secret.
THE OPENING ....

BACKSTAGE WITH BACKSTAGE PRINCE

WE'RE HITTING UP THE BACKSTAGE ROOM OF THE SIDE CHARACTERS!

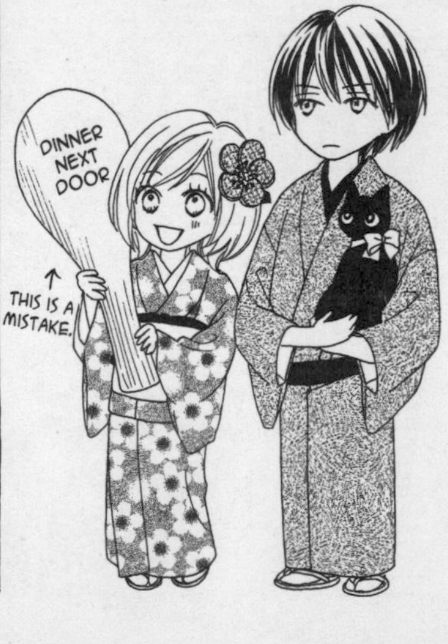
DINNER NEXT DOOR
THIS IS A MISTAKE.

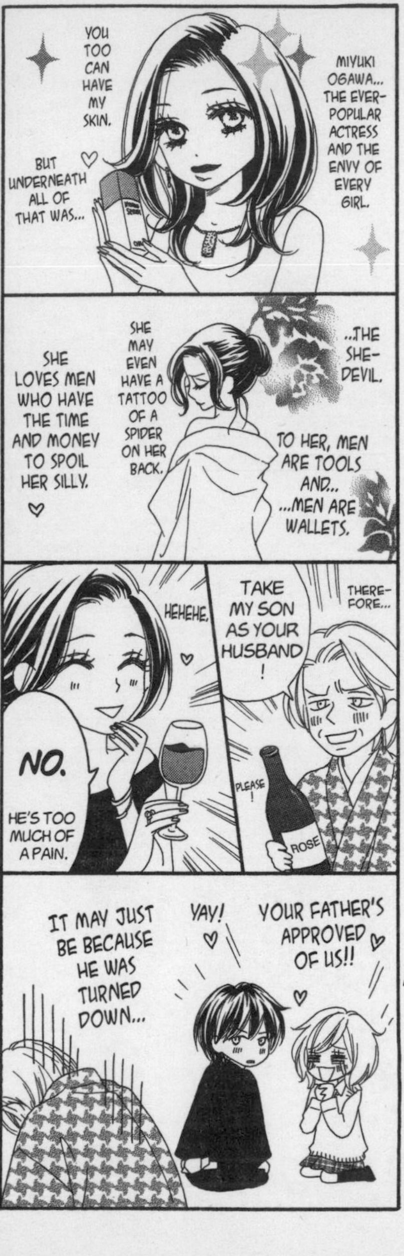
MIYUKI OGAWA... THE EVER-POPULAR ACTRESS AND THE ENVY OF EVERY GIRL.
YOU TOO CAN HAVE MY SKIN. ♡
BUT UNDERNEATH ALL OF THAT WAS...
...THE SHE-DEVIL.
SHE MAY EVEN HAVE A TATTOO OF A SPIDER ON HER BACK.
SHE LOVES MEN WHO HAVE THE TIME AND MONEY TO SPOIL HER SILLY. ♡
TO HER, MEN ARE TOOLS AND... ...MEN ARE WALLETS.
THEREFORE...
TAKE MY SON AS YOUR HUSBAND!
PLEASE!
ROSE
HEHEHE.
NO.
HE'S TOO MUCH OF A PAIN.
YOUR FATHER'S APPROVED OF US!! ♡
YAY! ♡
IT MAY JUST BE BECAUSE HE WAS TURNED DOWN...

* READ "SHISEI" BY

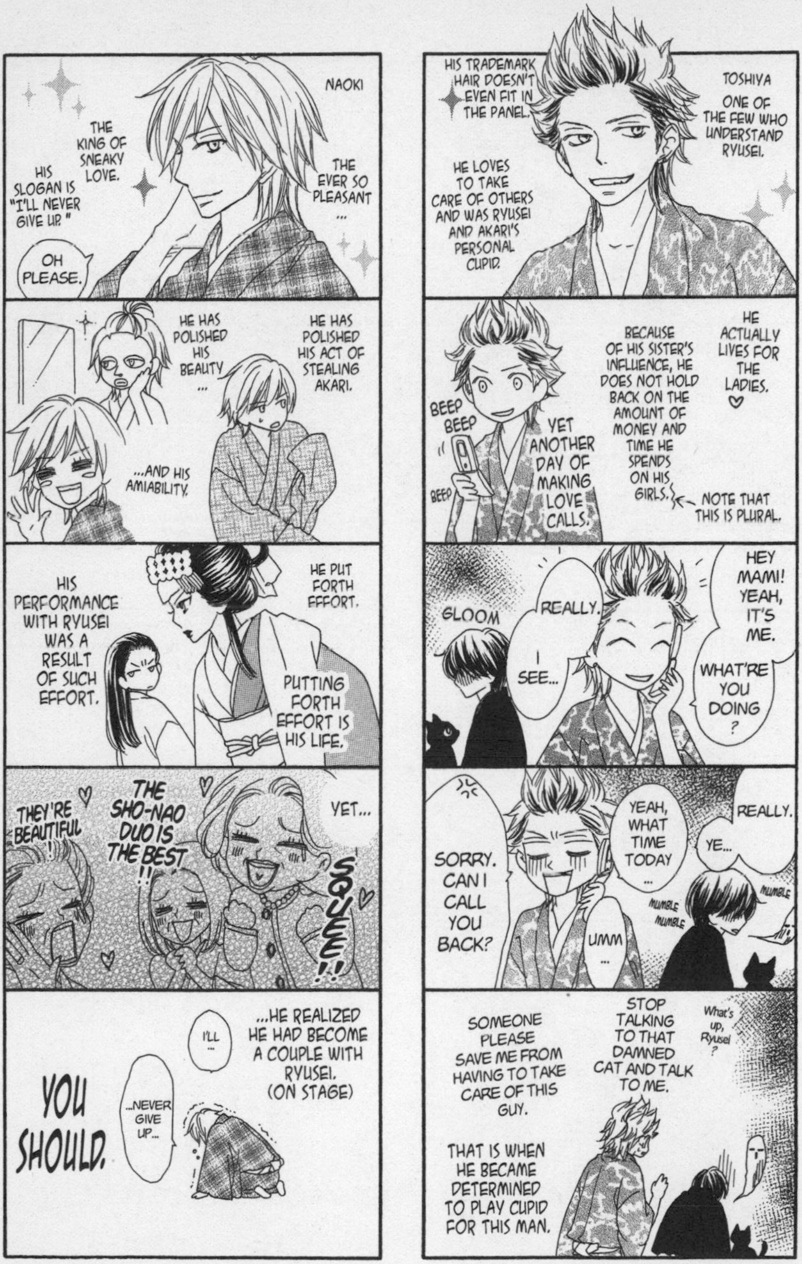
TOSHIYA
ONE OF THE FEW WHO UNDERSTAND RYUSEI.
HIS TRADEMARK HAIR DOESN'T EVEN FIT IN THE PANEL.
HE LOVES TO TAKE CARE OF OTHERS AND WAS RYUSEI AND AKARI'S PERSONAL CUPID.
HE ACTUALLY LIVES FOR THE LADIES.
BECAUSE OF HIS SISTER'S INFLUENCE, HE DOES NOT HOLD BACK ON THE AMOUNT OF MONEY AND TIME HE SPENDS ON HIS GIRLS.
NOTE THAT THIS IS PLURAL.
YET ANOTHER DAY OF MAKING LOVE CALLS.
BEEP BEEP
BEEP
HEY MAMI! YEAH, IT'S ME.
WHAT'RE YOU DOING?
REALLY.
I SEE...
GLOOM
REALLY.
YE...
YEAH, WHAT TIME TODAY...
SORRY. CAN I CALL YOU BACK?
UMM...
MUMBLE
MUMBLE
MUMBLE
What's up, Ryusei?
STOP TALKING TO THAT DAMNED CAT AND TALK TO ME.
SOMEONE PLEASE SAVE ME FROM HAVING TO TAKE CARE OF THIS GUY.
THAT IS WHEN HE BECAME DETERMINED TO PLAY CUPID FOR THIS MAN.
NAOKI
THE EVER SO PLEASANT ...
THE KING OF SNEAKY LOVE.
HIS SLOGAN IS "I'LL NEVER GIVE UP."
OH PLEASE.
HE HAS POLISHED HIS ACT OF STEALING AKARI.
HE HAS POLISHED HIS BEAUTY ...
...AND HIS AMIABILITY.
HE PUT FORTH EFFORT.
PUTTING FORTH EFFORT IS HIS LIFE.
HIS PERFORMANCE WITH RYUSEI WAS A RESULT OF SUCH EFFORT.
YET...
SQUEEE!!
THE SHO-NAO DUO IS THE BEST!!
THEY'RE BEAUTIFUL!
...HE REALIZED HE HAD BECOME A COUPLE WITH RYUSEI. (ON STAGE)
I'LL...
...NEVER GIVE UP...
YOU SHOULD.

BY THE WAY...
THE PROGRAM THAT RYUSEI AND NAOKI COSTARRED IN WAS CALLED "NARUKAMI."
THIS IS SHONIN NARUKAMI (A VIRTUOUS MAN)
HE IS A GOOD MAN...
REALLY THE PLOT WAS AS NAOKI EXPLAINED.
THE POOR UNFORTUNATE CELESTIAL BEAUTY
MY CHEST HURTS...
OH.
SHONIN ACCIDENTALLY TOUCHES HER BREAST.
WHAT WAS THAT... THAT FEELING ON MY HAND.
It was so soft...
DISCIPLE
IT'S A BOOBIE.
LET'S GET MARRIED.
I'll take responsibility.
I'M SO HAPPY. THEN LET US HAVE A CELEBRATORY DRINK.
SHONIN BECOMES A SLAVE TO ALCOHOL.
I'LL SNEAK OUT WHILE HE'S PASSED OUT...
AFTER THAT, THE ANGRY SHONIN BECOMES THE GOD OF THUNDER. KABUKI IS SO INTERESTING!!

Bye Bye

SEEING AS THIS WAS A SEQUEL VOLUME, THERE WERE A LOT OF THINGS I WANTED TO DRAW YET COULDN'T DO SO WELL. IT SERVED AS A FRESH REMINDER THAT I STILL HAVE A LOT TO LEARN, BUT IT WAS NICE TO KNOW I WAS ABLE TO GET THROUGH YET ANOTHER VOLUME. IT BECAME A VERY MEMORABLE PIECE FOR ME.

MY THANKS TO ALL WHO HAVE SUPPORTED ME THROUGH THIS JOURNEY.

A LUCKY DAY IN JANUARY, 2006

KANOKO SAKURAKOJI

PLEASE CHECK OUT MY WEBSITE IF YOU HAVE A MINUTE TO SPARE.
HTTP://SAKURAKOUJIEN.LOLIPOP.JP

BACKSTAGE PRINCE

Vol. 2

The Shojo Beat Manga Edition

This manga volume contains material that was originally published in English in *Shojo Beat* magazine, January-March 2007 issues.

STORY & ART BY
KANOKO SAKURAKOJI

Translation & Adaptation/Mai Ihara
Touch-up Art & Lettering/Rina Mapa
Additional Touch-up/Kam Li
Design/Izumi Hirayama
Editor/Pancha Diaz

Managing Editor/Megan Bates
Editorial Director/Elizabeth Kawasaki
Editor in Chief, Books/Alvin Lu
Editor in Chief, Magazines/Marc Weidenbaum
Sr. Director of Acquisitions/Rika Inouye
Sr. VP of Marketing/Liza Coppola
Exec. VP of Sales & Marketing/John Easum
Publisher/Hyoe Narita

Printed in Canada

Published by VIZ Media, LLC
P.O. Box 77064
San Francisco, CA 94107

Shojo Beat Manga Edition
10 9 8 7 6 5 4 3 2 1
First printing, June 2007

www.viz.com

store.viz.com

PARENTAL ADVISORY
BACKSTAGE PRINCE is rated T for Teen and is recommended for ages 13 and up. This volume contains suggestive themes.

Kanoko Sakurakoji's debut title, *Raibu ga Hanetara* (When the Live Jumps) was serialized in *Deluxe Betsucomi* in 2000 and won the 45th New Manga Artist Award of Shogakukan in the same year. Sakurakoji's stories often include cats—in her serialized title *Suzu-chan no Neko* (Suzu's Cat), most of the main characters are feline! *Backstage Prince* was originally serialized in Japan's *Betsucomi* anthology in 2004.

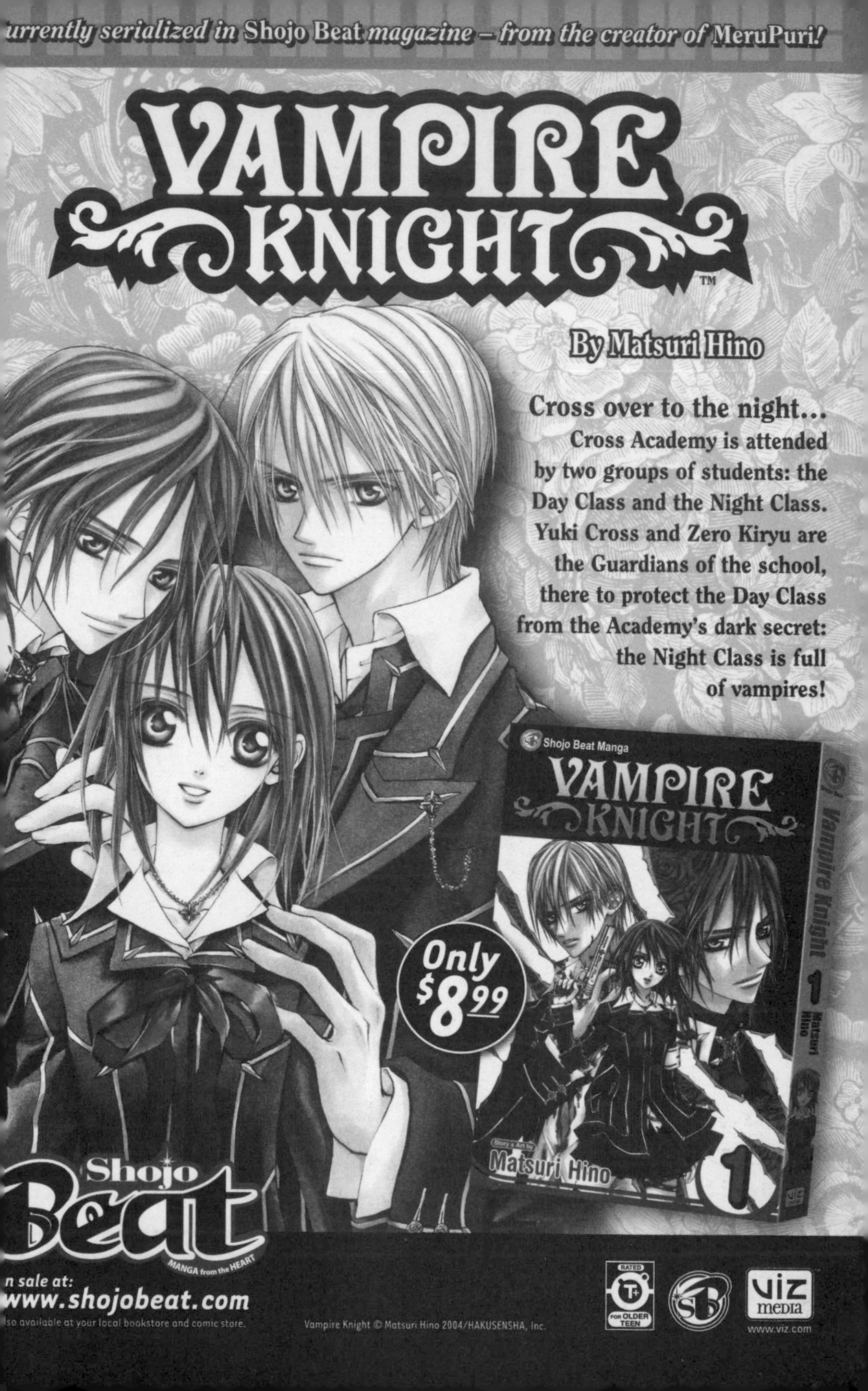
urrently serialized in Shojo Beat magazine – from the creator of MeruPuri!
VAMPIRE KNIGHT™
By Matsuri Hino
Cross over to the night...
Cross Academy is attended by two groups of students: the Day Class and the Night Class. Yuki Cross and Zero Kiryu are the Guardians of the school, there to protect the Day Class from the Academy's dark secret: the Night Class is full of vampires!
Shojo Beat Manga
VAMPIRE KNIGHT
Vampire Knight 1 Matsuri Hino
Story & Art by Matsuri Hino
1
Only $8.99
Shojo Beat MANGA from the HEART
n sale at:
www.shojobeat.com
lso available at your local bookstore and comic store.
Vampire Knight © Matsuri Hino 2004/HAKUSENSHA, Inc.
RATED T+ FOR OLDER TEEN
VIZ MEDIA
www.viz.com

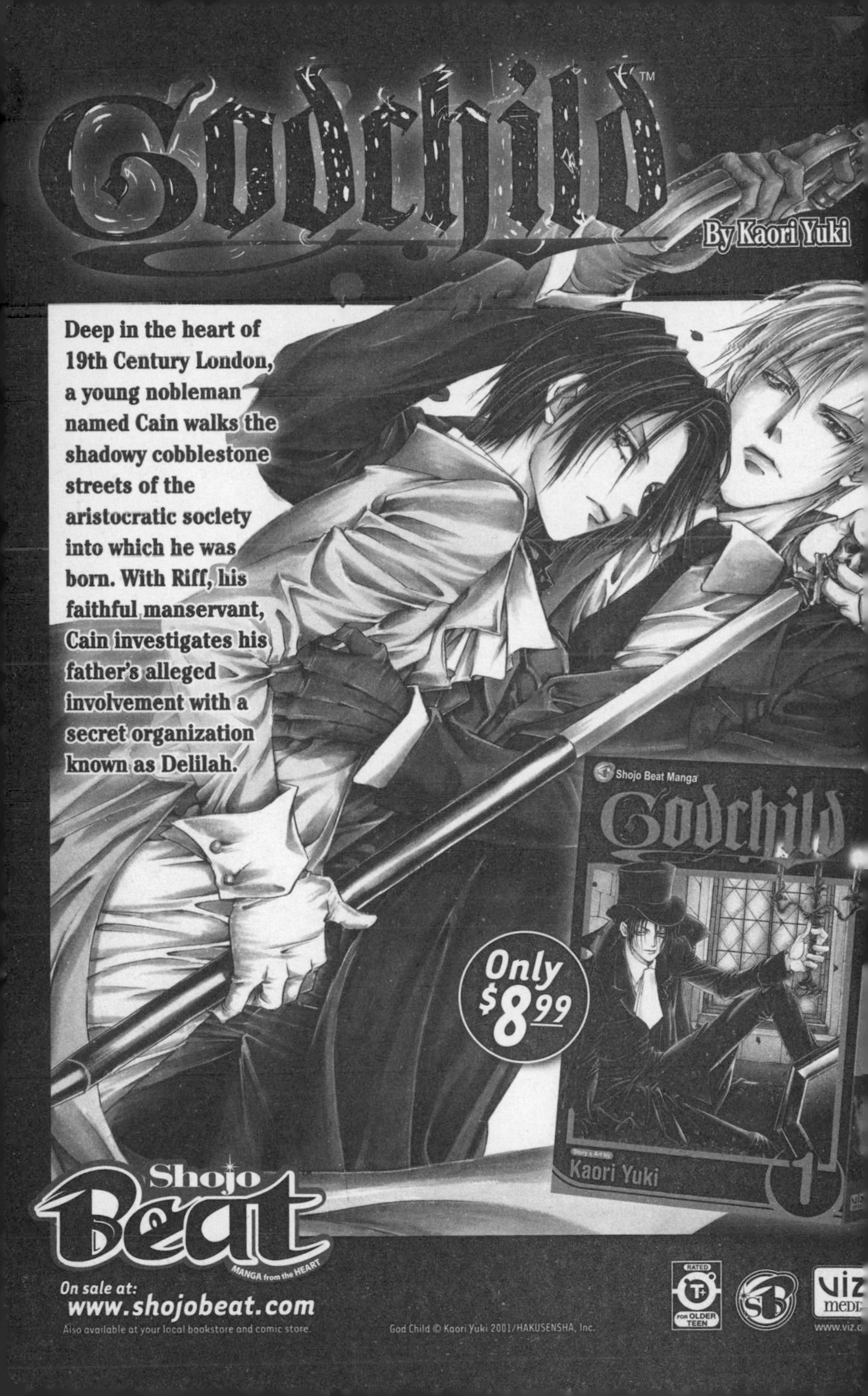
Godchild™
By Kaori Yuki
Deep in the heart of 19th Century London, a young nobleman named Cain walks the shadowy cobblestone streets of the aristocratic society into which he was born. With Riff, his faithful manservant, Cain investigates his father's alleged involvement with a secret organization known as Delilah.
Shojo Beat Manga
Godchild
Kaori Yuki
1
Only $8.99
Shojo Beat
MANGA from the HEART
On sale at:
www.shojobeat.com
Also available at your local bookstore and comic store.
God Child © Kaori Yuki 2001/HAKUSENSHA, Inc.
RATED T+ FOR OLDER TEEN
VIZ media
www.viz.c

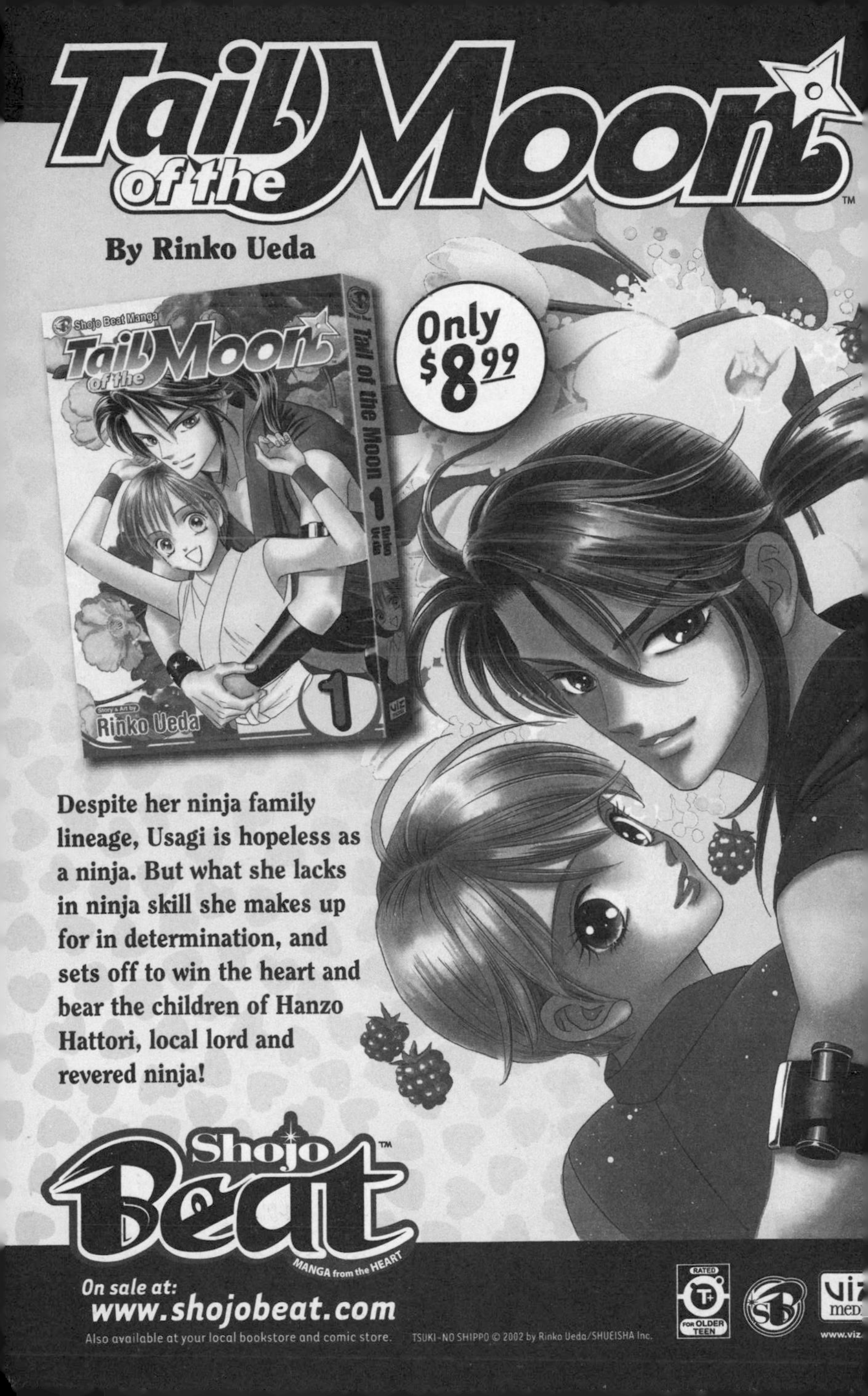
Tail of the Moon™
By Rinko Ueda
Shojo Beat Manga
Tail of the Moon
Tail of the Moon 1 Rinko Ueda
Story & Art by Rinko Ueda
1
Only $8.99
Despite her ninja family lineage, Usagi is hopeless as a ninja. But what she lacks in ninja skill she makes up for in determination, and sets off to win the heart and bear the children of Hanzo Hattori, local lord and revered ninja!
Shojo Beat™
MANGA from the HEART
On sale at:
www.shojobeat.com
Also available at your local bookstore and comic store.
TSUKI-NO SHIPPO © 2002 by Rinko Ueda/SHUEISHA Inc.
RATED T+ FOR OLDER TEEN

Tell us what you think about Shojo Beat Manga!

Our survey is now available online. Go to:

shojobeat.com/mangasurvey

Help us make our product offerings better!

VIZ media

Shojo Beat — MANGA from the HEART

THE REAL DRAMA BEGINS IN...

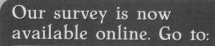